Systemic Knowledge-Based Assessment of Higher Education Programs

Edgar Oliver Cardoso Espinosa
Instituto Politécnico Nacional, Mexico

A volume in the Advances in Educational Marketing, Administration, and Leadership (AEMAL) Book Series

Information Science REFERENCE
An Imprint of IGI Global

Published in the United States of America by
Information Science Reference (an imprint of IGI Global)
701 E. Chocolate Avenue
Hershey PA, USA 17033
Tel: 717-533-8845
Fax: 717-533-8661
E-mail: cust@igi-global.com
Web site: http://www.igi-global.com

Library of Congress Cataloging-in-Publication Data

Names: Espinosa, Edgar Oliver Cardoso, 1973- editor.
Title: Systemic knowledge-based assessment of higher education programs / Edgar Oliver Cardoso Espinosa, editor.
Description: Hershey, PA : Information Science Reference, [2016] | Includes bibliographical references and index.
Identifiers: LCCN 2016011643| ISBN 9781522504573 (hardcover) | ISBN 9781522504580 (ebook)
Subjects: LCSH: Education, Higher--Evaluation. | Knowledge management. | Intellectual capital.
Classification: LCC LB2331.62 .S97 2016 | DDC 378.007--dc23 LC record available at https://lccn.loc.gov/2016011643

This book is published in the IGI Global book series Advances in Educational Marketing, Administration, and Leadership (AEMAL) (ISSN: 2326-9022; eISSN: 2326-9030)

British Cataloguing in Publication Data
A Cataloguing in Publication record for this book is available from the British Library.

Advances in Educational Marketing, Administration, and Leadership (AEMAL) Book Series

Siran Mukerji
IGNOU, India
Purnendu Tripathi
IGNOU, India

ISSN: 2326-9022
EISSN: 2326-9030

Mission

With more educational institutions entering into public, higher, and professional education, the educational environment has grown increasingly competitive. With this increase in competitiveness has come the need for a greater focus on leadership within the institutions, on administrative handling of educational matters, and on the marketing of the services offered.

The **Advances in Educational Marketing, Administration, & Leadership (AEMAL) Book Series** strives to provide publications that address all these areas and present trending, current research to assist professionals, administrators, and others involved in the education sector in making their decisions.

Coverage

- Educational Management
- Consumer Behavior
- Advertising and Promotion of Academic Programs and Institutions
- Technologies and Educational Marketing
- Faculty Administration and Management
- Educational Finance
- Educational Marketing Campaigns
- Enrollment Management
- Students as Consumers
- Direct marketing of educational programs

IGI Global is currently accepting manuscripts for publication within this series. To submit a proposal for a volume in this series, please contact our Acquisition Editors at Acquisitions@igi-global.com or visit: http://www.igi-global.com/publish/.

The Advances in Educational Marketing, Administration, and Leadership (AEMAL) Book Series (ISSN 2326-9022) is published by IGI Global, 701 E. Chocolate Avenue, Hershey, PA 17033-1240, USA, www.igi-global.com. This series is composed of titles available for purchase individually; each title is edited to be contextually exclusive from any other title within the series. For pricing and ordering information please visit http://www.igi-global.com/book-series/advances-educational-marketing-administration-leadership/73677. Postmaster: Send all address changes to above address.

Titles in this Series

For a list of additional titles in this series, please visit: www.igi-global.com

Promoting Global Peace and Civic Engagement through Education
Kshama Pandey (Dayalbagh Educational Institute, India) and Pratibha Upadhyay (University of Allahabad, India)
Information Science Reference • copyright 2016 • 464pp • H/C (ISBN: 9781522500780) • US $185.00 (our price)

Handbook of Research on Organizational Justice and Culture in Higher Education Institutions
Nwachukwu Prince Ololube (Ignatius Ajuru University of Education, Nigeria)
Information Science Reference • copyright 2016 • 571pp • H/C (ISBN: 9781466698505) • US $300.00 (our price)

Developing Effective Educational Experiences through Learning Analytics
Mark Anderson (Edge Hill University, UK) and Collette Gavan (Edge Hill University, UK)
Information Science Reference • copyright 2016 • 361pp • H/C (ISBN: 9781466699830) • US $175.00 (our price)

Handbook of Research on Quality Assurance and Value Management in Higher Education
Walter Nuninger (Université de Lille, France) and Jean-Marie Châtelet (Université de Lille, France)
Information Science Reference • copyright 2016 • 458pp • H/C (ISBN: 9781522500247) • US $295.00 (our price)

Campus Support Services, Programs, and Policies for International Students
Krishna Bista (University of Louisiana at Monroe, USA) and Charlotte Foster (Missouri Western State University, USA)
Information Science Reference • copyright 2016 • 354pp • H/C (ISBN: 9781466697522) • US $185.00 (our price)

Facilitating Higher Education Growth through Fundraising and Philanthropy
Henry C. Alphin Jr. (Drexel University, USA) Jennie Lavine (Higher Colleges of Technology, United Arab Emirates) Stormy Stark (Pennsylvania State University, USA) and Adam Hocker (Pennsylvania State University, USA)
Information Science Reference • copyright 2016 • 372pp • H/C (ISBN: 9781466696648) • US $195.00 (our price)

Developing Successful Strategies for Global Policies and Cyber Transparency in E-Learning
Gulsun Eby (Anadolu University (College of Open Education), Turkey) T. Volkan Yuzer (Anadolu University (College of Open Education), Turkey) and Simber Atay (Dokuz Eylul University (College of Art), Turkey)
Information Science Reference • copyright 2016 • 355pp • H/C (ISBN: 9781466688445) • US $195.00 (our price)

Impact of Economic Crisis on Education and the Next-Generation Workforce
Patricia Ordóñez de Pablos (University of Oviedo, Spain) and Robert D. Tennyson (University of Minnesota, USA)
Information Science Reference • copyright 2016 • 432pp • H/C (ISBN: 9781466694552) • US $195.00 (our price)

IGI GLOBAL
DISSEMINATOR OF KNOWLEDGE
www.igi-global.com

701 E. Chocolate Ave., Hershey, PA 17033
Order online at www.igi-global.com or call 717-533-8845 x100
To place a standing order for titles released in this series, contact: cust@igi-global.com
Mon-Fri 8:00 am - 5:00 pm (est) or fax 24 hours a day 717-533-8661

Table of Contents

Detailed Table of Contents

This chapter provides an overview of knowledge management from the perspective of academicians in higher education in Mexico, after considering that intellectual capital consists of human capital, structural capital and relational capital, and that is the main source of knowledge in educational institutions. It also offers four fundamental aspects proposed by knowledge economy for the production, distribution and use of knowledge in organizations. Finally, an assessment tool for knowledge management in higher education schools is proposed.

This chapter focuses on the study that will offer a systemic evaluation of the characteristics of knowledge management, from the approach of the postgraduate students in Mexico. It will consider the generation cycle – storage – distribution – utilization and generalization of knowledge. The purpose will be to design academic management strategies for the strengthening of human capital, which comprises the post-graduate students in Mexico, who are enrolled in this type of educational programmes. The proposed chapter is structured as follows: The first section centers in the description of the characteristics of knowledge management, the second one will target at the characteristics of postgraduate education in Mexico, the third section includes the study methodology, and the fourth one will be the research proposal for drawing the research conclusions.

calls for an analysis of the school and the social environment, our multiculturalism and active acceptance of that which is different from the norm and the relationship between it establishes for the formation of the common good. Therefore, we consider it necessary to address a comprehensive policy for education to eliminate exclusion factors such as: accessibility, infrastructure, equal treatment, access opportunities, gender and economic deciles access.

This chapter is an academic essay that presents six theoretical concepts about economic human development that allow the leaders and the teaching staff of the institutions of higher education to understand that the growth and integral development of a country does not only rely on the fruits of a given ideology or economic system, in a fixed time, but on the integral human development of the peoples from their culture, customs, idiosyncrasy, production means, integration with other nations, among other ways of expressing their identity and their ways of life. These concepts are: 1) economic and social growth, 2) self-sufficiency, 3) interdependence, 4) self-determination, 5) knowledge as a transformation strategy, and 6) integral human development. It is proposed the analysis of these concepts to explore utilization alternatives for the development of future research works.

This chapter deals with the evaluation and identification of professional tourism educational and training competences with the purpose of recognizing the main characteristics of labour capacity in the tourism industry. Tourism is promoted through education, as well as through the development of skills and tools that result in an optimal labour performance during the stages of school training. Moreover, it describes the relationship of knowledge management in the tourism sector that leads to quality in human capital, in addition to professional alignment, in an educational context. As this section focuses on the overview of professional tourism, the following components are considered; the preamble and classification of the tourism industry, the conceptualization of educational evaluation and competence, and concludes with the description and analysis of the works targeted at the evaluation and identification of professional competences in tourism.

Section 2
Middle School Education as Predecessor of Knowledge Management

The education enables individuals to add value to the economy, contributing to the cultural heritage, participate in society, improve health, protect the environment and increase their ability to continue to develop. Therefore it is essential that educational system promotes educational opportunities in order to be equitably distributed among all social sectors and boost that graduates and could have the opportunity to performance occupations in which they could take advantage the schooling they have acquired. So, the chapter proposal will be organized into three sections: the first related to globalization and middle education in Mexico; the second based on group interviews conducted with the technique called focus group and, third, the characteristics of the methodology-oriented design of a set of indicators that evaluate and feedback educational programs that graduates have studied, based this, they could achieve and improve educational opportunities.

In a globalized world, public policies are subject to the recommendations of international organizations that regulate and determine educational policies according to their own needs and interests. In this sense, educational skills, arising from the business world, have become the focus of curriculum design and teacher professionalism and managerial schools Basic and Secondary Education in Mexico. Specifically, the National Association of Professional Technical Education (CONALEP), has become a pillar that provides students of Media Education competent technical professional for requirements that are demanded today. Since its birth in 1978 was oriented to the formation of technical professionals, graduates of Basic Education, with the main objective job training, intersectoral linkages, community support and technological advice and assistance to businesses.

The research analyzes the problem of teachers' evaluation of Middle School Education at the Instituto Politécnico Nacional (IPN, for its acronyms in Spanish), which has been practiced using the same instrument since the assessment process started until now. From this approach, the National Education Model of high-schools, and, consequently, of the Instituto Politécnico Nacional is competency-based.

There are eight competencies assigned to teachers' development, which are included in the Comprehensive Reform of Middle School Education. The eight teaching competencies are unfolded as attributes that are displayed as performance and/or products, which make up: knowledges, skills and attitudes that are applied in the classroom in order to generate learning environments and to have students develop their own competencies to achieve the high-school degree profile. The general aim of the research is to design an evaluation instrument of middle school education at the IPN, so that students determine the teachers' development according to the model of competencies.

Currently the development of countries has acquired importance as a result of the process of economic globalization, which has established various challenges to the economic activities worldwide. So numerical, mathematical and digital competences, are very important to participating fully in the knowledge society. Thus, the chapter proposal considers Checkland's Methodology as an oriented alternative to analyze the object of study in situations with a high rate of human intervention such as education. The chapter proposal will be organized into three sections: the first one related to the factors involved in school performance, the quality of education and the impact that have the math skills at middle school; the second focused on the characteristics of the methodology of Checkland applied to mathematics, and the third, a key options proposal for designing to the students motivation for a better mathematics learning that allows assessment of the institutional management in performance in such subject and increase educational standards.

In this research several elements are exposed through a network of processes which build a quality academic system in a sequence "diagnosis-planning-management". To get the information which would generate these criteria, a Likert questionnaire for 30 students and 8 teachers was designed; also an interview for a manager based on standardized indicators by the Ministry of Education to get the self-evaluation. The gathered information generated the value judgment that when it was applied to the evaluation of the academic management, some results were highlighted. Finally, this research establishs as objective the design of a relevant proposal to ensure that the academic management achieve quality processes based on the application of knowledge management and also get the improvement of its services based on self-assessment.

Preface

For a country to be developed thoroughly, knowledge economy considers that the most valuable asset is the creation, dissemination and use of knowledge over capital goods and human capital (Sánchez & Ríos, 2011). From this economic perspective, besides human capital, knowledge management, innovation and the development of human skills are emphasized, such as sources of sustainable economic growth (CEPAL, 2008; Portnoi et. al., 2010). From here, education enables the subjects to add value to the economy, as well as to contribute to the cultural heritage, to participate in the society, to improve the health of families and communities, to preserve the environment and to increase their own capacity envisaged to continue their development (UNESCO, 2008).

On its behalf, the economic globalization has generated diverse consequences at an international level, among which we can find a society regulated by the market laws; the birth of knowledge societies, originated by the multiplication of information and communication means; the transformation of the nature of work linked with the need of more flexibility and mobility, teamwork, pro-activity of the subjects, as well as an intensive use of the new technologies.

For the educational sector, Brunner (2001) set five situations generated by the globalization: a) Knowledge stopped being slow, scarce and stable; b) the school did not stay as the only means by which the new generations may stay in touch with knowledge and information; c) the teachers' wording and the written texts were not considered as the only support for the educational communication; d) the school shall not only act to promote a receptive learning; and e) the technological change and the opening of a global knowledge-based economy. All of them have generated the redefinition of the skills that the societies must teach and learn.

In this regard, there are challenges that knowledge society must face and accomplish, such as: a quality inclusive long-life education; the fulfillment of the basic learning needs, like Reading, writing, values, cultures and moral behaviors, etc.; a preparation for staying in a society in constant change; the acquisition of new skills for living in the information and communications society; an education that promotes values and the basic ethical principles; an education that motivates the interaction and the whole personal development; an education for the active exercise of citizenship and an education that promotes the culture of peace and international solidarity (Cobo, 2005).

The overview described above has established new demands that the professional has to satisfy in a more gradually competitive market, at a national and international level; the increase in the generation of information that requires more complex techniques and methods for the analysis and systematization where the use of the Information and Communication Technologies (ICT) has constituted a main support for the attainment of these processes (Tejada & Navío, 2005).

In this line, knowledge has become a valuable resource for a country that seeks to have a competitive advantage in the world of economic globalization. So forth, the educational institutions need to assume a main role in the generation of knowledge, as well as to prepare the human capital that allows research management and innovation and, therefore, promotes an integral development.

In this regard, not only the generation of human capital, but also the management of new knowledges, the innovation in public and private organization and the development of human skills are essential as sources of sustainable economic growth.

The above has given rise to the transformation of the productive processes related to the avant-garde equipment and technologies for increasing the productivity and efficiency of the scarce resources used by the organizations, and to the new forms of management, organization, employee's training and development, which open the rational use of the resources and encourage the creative and intellectual potential of the members of the organization, in order to achieve their institutional goals and objectives (Ibarra, 2000).

Standing before this overview of knowledge society, education is the main strategy that offers the individuals a group of skills that let them add value to the economy, contribute to the cultural heritage, participate in the society, improve their health, preserve the environment and widen their own capacity for exercising their development.

Hence, the Economic Commission for Latin America and the Caribbean (CEPAL, 2010) has stated that the functions of the educational institutions must link with the social and productive sectors because they build up the guiding principles for knowledge-based development.

Consequently, it is established that the scientific and technological development of a country is possible when there is convergence between the objectives and actions among the different actors. So forth, it is essential to consider the "Triple Helix" model, which sustains the main guiding principle for development lies in the interaction of three institutional spheres: government, business/industry and education.

In this way, the educational organizations are defined as agents for the preparation of important actors in the networks of regional groups that undertake knowledge-based activities and that have the opportunity to generate innovation systems.

Even more, the UNESCO (2009) has stated that it is vital the educational institutions of the developing countries integrate new core functions, such as:

- To diminish the development gap with the developed countries by a knowledge transference to their regions;
- To search for new ways of increasing research and promoting innovation by associations with public and private sectors;
- To develop scientific and technological innovations oriented towards the solution of regional problems; and
- To generate associations with the social and entrepreneurial sectors that report mutual benefits for both of them.

To achieve this, the globalized world demands that the educational centers stop being closed systems and become open systems that observe the needs and requirements in the labor sector, so that the educational programs comply with the quality criteria: transcendence, equity, pertinence, efficacy and efficiency, as stated by knowledge management.

On the one hand, a program is transcendental when it produces long-life useful skills, prepares people capable of generating their own learning and enables knowledge transfer in the labor area. On the other hand, equity refers to the existence of different opportunities for the several circumstances reflected by the students' community that allow the conclusion of their studies and the achievement the graduate's profile.

Furthermore, the pertinence of a program focuses on the conciliation of the internal and external requirements, in order to determine the impact that it generates from the preparation and contributions made for attaining all of the society's objectives, which comprehend the social, cultural and economic environment.

Efficacy is understood as the degree to which a program achieves its objectives and goals; while efficiency is the way of attaining the purposes based on the available resources and conditions under which the program operates.

Hence, the educational organizations, besides accomplishing the main function of transmitting the universal knowledge, are imposed by the society to apply this knowledge to their environment properly and generating an impact. The quality reached by an educational program is a main factor in the life quality of the actors where the program operates.

As mentioned by Cardoso and Cerecedo (2011): educational quality is synonym of knowledge production and integral development of the students' community, so that an educational program is of quality only when do the preparation processes generate useful capacities, abilities and skills that allow the graduates design and implement intervention strategies sought to address the problem issues of the productive and services sector.

On this behalf, the objective of this book called "Handbook of Research on Systemic Knowledge-Based Assessment of Higher Education Programs" is to offer theoretical research works applied systematically to knowledge management on educational programs, at a national and international level, concerning the formulation of theoretical and methodological frameworks, as well as the dissemination of avant-garde results.

Therefore, the book is organized in three main sections: The first focuses on the studies performed in higher education; the second, in the research works, at middle school education, and the third in elementary education. These two last levels are relevant for this book because they have become the foreground of knowledge management relative to the preparation of human capital based on the development of the basic skills that every citizen that lives in the globalized world needs to use, owing to the fact that the vast amount of generated information is exhibited in different ways: writing, numeric, graphical, as well as in multiple written and technological media means.

From this perspective, the first section of this book covers seven relevant theme lines of knowledge management, which are mentioned below:

The first chapter written by Morán and Cortés focuses on the diagnosis of knowledge management from the view of the academicians. The intellectual capital is considered to be integrated by the human, structural and relational capital as a main source of knowledge in the educational organization. It also deals with the four elements proposed by knowledge economy, and that encompass: the production, distribution and use of knowledge in the institution, so that an evaluation instrument that assesses knowledge management in higher education is suggested.

The second chapter elaborated by Cortés, Morán and Vanegas covers the systemic evaluation of knowledge management, from the view of the postgraduate students in education. This chapter centers in the characteristics of knowledge management based on the cycle of generation – storage – distribution – utilization and generalization of knowledge, as stated by Nonaka and Takeuchi (1995).

The third chapter formulated by Chavarría and Cardoso is in charge of analyzing the influence of the labor sector in knowledge management, aimed at studying the importance of knowledge management and how it is related to work, in order to determine the contribution for the preparation of competitive specialists, who know the technologies and tools for a sustainable management and the protection of the environment. The end is to possibly design strategies for rising the competitive level of the organizations, through the creation of business units' value. Specifically, they cover the post-grade due to the fact that it has suffered a series of transformations because of its expansion, diversification and the demands that the knowledge society has established with the aim of improving quality and fulfilling the preparation of high-performance human capital.

The fourth chapter elaborated by Van Den Hoven and Litz work out on the evaluation of programs and their improvement in the guiding practices. This chapter centers in the use of a conceptual framework based on Morgan's (1998) organizational metaphors, relying on a qualitative study performed to the teachers for evaluating their experience in a new program for the evaluation of the processes of change that influence and institution of higher education of teachers' preparation in the United Arab Emirates. The chapter provides based on generated metaphor the general perceptions of the organizational dynamics, the management practices and the processes of change. As a consequence, the tensions surrounding the access to the communication channels and the decision in the local decision-making context are demonstrated. Besides, many metaphors are consistent with Morgan's original constructions, while a number are unique to the located context. Therefore, the organizational metaphors can be used as feedback mechanism for guiding the decision-making process related to the initiatives of systemic change in the institutions, and to encourage management research in this region and in other higher educational surroundings. The fifth chapter formulated by Skewes and Alfaro relies in the challenges posed by the public policies for an inclusive higher education. The author's center in the relevance of these policies that guarantee a quality education for all, with the aim of reaching a socially inclusive future based on knowledge management. In this line, the importance of the educational inclusion is directly associated with the task of generating different success possibilities, which require an integral educational policy that eliminate exclusion factors in such aspects as: infrastructure, gender, accessibility and access opportunities.

Furthermore, the sixth chapter elaborated by Casas, De Luna and Álvarez who directed their interest towards the alternative concepts of economic development and its implications in education. Particularly, it presents six theoretical concepts on economic human development that enable the leaders and the teachers' staff of the institutions of higher education understand that the growth and integral development of a country does not only reside in the fruits of a specific ideology or economic system, in a precise period of time, but in the integral human development of the peoples, of their culture, their customs, their idiosyncrasy, their means of production, research with other nations, among other ways of expressing their identity and their ways of life. These concepts are: 1) economic and social growth, 2) self-sufficiency, 3) interdependence, 4) self-determination, 5) knowledge as a transformation strategy, and 6) integral human development. Thus, the analysis of these concepts with the purpose of exploring alternatives of use for the development of future research works is suggested

The seventh chapter by Rivas and Cardoso focuses on the evaluation of professional skills of the graduates in the area of tourism. This chapter deals with the identification of the professional competences in tourism teaching and its relationship with knowledge management, in order to derive in the quality of human capital as well as their work performance at optimal levels. Thus, the authors emphasize that the competences required for this sector are not only individual but also social and participatory, beyond the procedural or methodological techniques.

Meanwhile, the second section of the book deals with four interesting themes and which are set out below:

The eighth chapter prepared by Briseño, Cardoso, García and Mejía, addresses the educational opportunities for the graduates of the higher education level. This chapter focuses on education as it enables individuals to add value to the economy, by contributing to the cultural heritage, to participate in the society, to improve their health, to protect the environment and to increase their ability to continue developing. Therefore, it is essential that the educational system promotes educational opportunities for distributing them proportionally among all the social sectors, and to foster that the graduates may enjoy performance occupations where they can take advantage of the education acquired.

The ninth chapter by Alfaro and Skewes relies on the assessment of leadership competences held by the directors of middle school education. This chapter focuses on the importance of the educational leader of the guided institution and the intrinsic link that it has with knowledge management. This link is generated from the need to obtain and share the intellectual property to achieve optimal results through the use, above all, of the intellectual resource to promote a more global competitive education. In this sense, we must highlight the skills that the leader must possess, develop and optimize, so that the education center, where he performs his management, fulfills the quality demands of today's society.

The tenth chapter formulated by Zepeda focuses on the evaluation of the teaching skills of middle school education. The chapter addresses from the model based on competences established by the IPN, the existence of eight teaching competences evaluated from the attributes constituted by knowledge, skills and attitudes that are applied in the classroom, in order to generate learning environments for students to develop their own competences and, thus, achieve the graduate's profile. The overall objective of the chapter was the design of an instrument of evaluation of high school, so that the students may determine the development of teaching skills.

The eleventh chapter prepared by García, Mejía and Briseño, focuses on the performance of the students in the assignment of mathematics and its influence on academic management from the perspective of soft systems. The chapter starts with the development that the countries have acquired as a result of the process of economic globalization, which has established various challenges to the economic activities in all the world. Numerical, mathematical and digital skills are very important to fully participate in the knowledge society. Also, this chapter considers the Checkland methodology as an alternative manner of analyzing the object of study in those situations where a high rate of human intervention exists, such as education. This chapter is organized into three sections: the first one is related to the factors involved in school performance, the quality of education and the impact that math skills have on high school; the second section is focused on the characteristics of the Checkland methodology applied to mathematics, and the third, is a key proposal of options for the design of the motivation of students for a better learning of mathematics that allows the evaluation of the institutional management observed in a determined subject and the improvement of the educational levels.

While the third section of the book contains two new topics: The evaluation of the academic management as a key success factor in knowledge management done by Bueno, as well as an evaluation of the curriculum program in English and the derived impact on the generation of knowledge carried out by Bricaire, Cardoso, Briseño and Garcia.

The twelfth chapter formulated by Bueno deals with several elements through a network of processes that build a quality academic system in a sequence "of planning diagnosis management." For collecting the information that would generate these criteria, the author used a Likert-type questionnaire of 30 students and 8 teachers. Also, an interview addressed to one of the managers of the indexes database standardized by the Ministry of education to obtain the self-evaluation took place. The gathered information has produced the value judgment that, when applied to the evaluation of the academic management, some of the results were highlighted. Finally, this research is aimed at the design of a proper proposal to guarantee that school management accomplishes the quality knowledge-applied management processes, and the improvement of self-evaluation services.

The thirteenth chapter elaborate by Bricaire, Cardoso, Briseño and García relies on the study of the teaching programs of foreign language, especially in the countries of Latin America, to go in line with the policies of quality demanded by agencies in the case of Mexico, where the Second Program of Study Development of Languages (English) represents a new model for the teaching of this language as a second language. The chapter seeks to provide the indicators that assess the academic management of this secondary program-level, based on the general theory of systems and, above all, in the search for considering such criteria as quality education: teachers; the processes of teaching and learning; support materials; infrastructure and training; certification; subject index accreditation; learning products; planning; students and address. The main conclusion of the study is to demonstrate the need to develop the indicators that can serve as a guide for the constant improvement of the program management and to ensure that the students learn English in a significant way.

Therefore, the impact of the book is to provide studies on systemic evaluation of knowledge management at different levels, areas and educational programs in various institutions, so that the public to whom it is directed are academicians, researchers, students in higher education, as well as administrators of universities and research centers. The reason is that this work provides up-to-date and useful information for learning about the importance of knowledge management in the field of education.

Thus, the work provides a set of contributions on knowledge management in education, such as:

- To identify the relevance of human capital for the prosperity and development of the organization.
- To generate integrated processes and teamwork in the institutions.
- To create a culture of continuous learning, both personal and organizational.
- To enable the development of not only basic skills, but also specific and transversal-type skills, which are used in the job area and personally, as well.

That means that the social function of education is recognized in the knowledge society who has established structural transformations in two ways: the first facing a paradigm shift aside from a model based on the transmission of knowledge to another based on the integral education of individuals; while the second is focused on an increase in the flexibility of the educational system where life-long learning is encouraged. Moreover, the programs must be transcendental, so that the needs of the productive and services sectors of a country are covered.

Therefore, this work aims to contribute to the generation of process-oriented educational organizations towards the formulation of a set of strategies that will enable them to promote policies and practices directed towards turning knowledge into a strategic asset that can be capable of generating a competitive advantage and a quality education by the use the technologies of information as tools for knowledge storage and dissemination.

Finally, this work by incorporating the evaluation of knowledge management in education seeks to constitute itself as a methodological tool for assessing the performance degree of the skills included in the curricula, in order to propose the respective adjustments and, thus, meet the quality criteria.

Edgar Oliver Cardoso Espinosa
Instituto Politécnico Nacional, Mexico

REFERENCES

Brunner, J. (2001). Perspectivas desde el siglo XXI. *Perspectivas*, *4*(2), 203–211.

Cardoso, E., & Cerecedo, M. (2011). Propuesta de indicadores para evaluar la calidad de un programa de posgrado en educación. *Revista Electrónica de Investigación Educativa, 13*(2), 68 – 82. Available at http://redie.uabc.mx/vol13no2/contenido-cardosocerecedo.html

CEPAL. (2008). *Espacios Iberoamericanos: La economía del conocimiento*. CEPAL. Available at http://www.cepal.org/publicaciones/xml/9/34459/EspacioIiberoIII.pdf

CEPAL. (2010). *Espacios iberoamericanos: Vínculos entre universidades y empresas para el desarrollo tecnológico*. Chile: CEPAL.

Cobo, J. (2005). *Otro mundo es posible: propuestas de una utopía para el siglo XXI*. Madrid: Biblioteca Nueva.

Ibarra, A. (2000). Formación de recursos humanos y competencia laboral. *Boletín Cinterfor*, *149*, 95–107.

Portnoi, L., Rust, V., & Bagley, S. (2010). *Higher education, policy and the global competition phenomenon*. New York: Palgrave MacMillan.

Sánchez, C., & Ríos, H. (2011). La economía del conocimiento como base del crecimiento económico en México. *Enl@ce: Revista Venezolana de Información, Tecnología y Conocimiento, 8*(2), 43 – 60. Available at http://www.redalyc.org/pdf/823/82319126004.pdf

Tejada, J., & Navío, A. (2005). El desarrollo y la gestión de competencias profesionales: una mirada desde la formación. *Revista Iberoamericana de Educación, 68*(1), 1 – 15. Available at http://www.rieoei.org/deloslectores/1089Tejada.pdf

UNESCO. (2008). *Estándares de competencia en TIC para docentes*. UNESCO. Available at http://www.oei.es/tic/UNESCOEstandaresDocentes.pdf

UNESCO. (2009). *Conferencia Mundial sobre la Educación Superior, 2009: La nueva dinámica de la educación superior y la investigación para el cambio social y el desarrollo*. París: UNESCO.

Acknowledgment

The editor would like to acknowledge the help of all the people involved in this project and, more specifically, to the authors and reviewers that took part in the review process. Without their support, this book would not have become a reality.

First, the editor would like to thank each one of the authors for their contributions. Our sincere gratitude goes to the chapter's authors who contributed their time and expertise to this book.

Second, the editor wishes to acknowledge the valuable contributions of the reviewers regarding the improvement of quality, coherence, and content presentation of chapters. Most of the authors also served as referees; we highly appreciate their double task.

Edgar Oliver Cardoso Espinosa
Instituto Politécnico Nacional, Mexico

Section 1

Knowledge Management Actors and Processes in Higher Education

Chapter 1
Diagnosis of Knowledge Management from the Perspective of Academicians at Higher-Education

Ricardo Morán Martínez
Instituto Politécnico Nacional, Mexico

Jésica Alhelí Cortés Ruíz
Instituto Politécnico Nacional, Mexico

ABSTRACT

This chapter provides an overview of knowledge management from the perspective of academicians in higher education in Mexico, after considering that intellectual capital consists of human capital, structural capital and relational capital, and that is the main source of knowledge in educational institutions. It also offers four fundamental aspects proposed by knowledge economy for the production, distribution and use of knowledge in organizations. Finally, an assessment tool for knowledge management in higher education schools is proposed.

INTRODUCTION: TECHNOLOGICAL DEVELOPMENT AND GLOBALISATION

Throughout humankind evolution, different epochs and moments are identified. They have had a significant influence on the history of this world since the beginnings of the caveman until the current or modern epoch, where the development and growth of societies or civilizations are narrowly linked with the technological advances and the present technical innovations in each one. Today we can talk of a rapid technological growth, whose origin is in the advances generates in the last two decades in the field of the technologies of information and communication (ICT). Nowadays, the ICT have shortened distance between people, reducing hold-in times and increasing the possibilities to obtain and exchange information, opening the path to a globalised world.

DOI: 10.4018/978-1-5225-0457-3.ch001

These technologies have virtually diminished the countries' borders, and, therefore, have started globalisation since the 90´s. A period of a set of changes in the economy of the countries of the world has looked forward to developing a global economy for goods and services.

Definitely, how men were used or are getting to used to proceeding, in the different human life areas, have to be modified before a prominent globalised overview, and, thus, the organizations are affected by a different performance in the economy, markets, competition, production, provision of services and different financial trends, information and communication and life in general. To sum up, it can be said that, "globalisation is the result of the integration of the economic and financial sectors at a world scale, whose arise was due to the fast and significant technological processes, especially in the area of the Technologies of Information and Communication (Cornejo, 2012).

Globalisation is a phenomenon that increases the possibilities of the development of the countries and their inhabitants, in theory it looks for homogeneous conditions for any global citizen in the world. Among its aims, poverty reduction and education access are identified. "This situation has led to make evident the need for being prepared for the future, in which the school programmes provide students and graduates with a proactive, reflective and critical attitude that addresses the inherent problems of globalisation" (Méndez & Zenteno, 2009).

GLOBALISED PERSPECTIVE ON EDUCATION

Today, more than at any other moment in the modern history of Mexico, higher education (HE) is compelled to address the multiple challenges. The rising population at age of enrolling in this educational level, the Mexican people's desire for growth, as well as Mexico's international commitments, converge and allow defining the necessary educational policies, in the last decades at a national level.

Thus, that higher education is seen as a very important and vital preparation stage for the social and economic development of the country. Higher education is also understood as that "higher education as self-learning goes beyond the notion of the students as a market consumer, it implies to invest in himself as human capital because the attributes and qualifications acquired in education change what a person can do." (Marginson, 2013). This reflection stands the relevance of HE for the transformation of people, societies and countries.

When the Sector Program of Education (SPE) 2013-2018 is revised, the worst worry, and the commitment of the Mexican state with higher-education are the coverage of education. It is also observed, that any specific aims or strategies with referred courses of action are established for the use or application of knowledge management in higher education as a key element to face the globalisation challenges.

However, in this program there can be found courses of action in which knowledge management is perceived at the bottom, with the aim to strengthen the quality and pertinence of education through the generation and dissemination of knowledge that has an impact on Mexico's development, promoting knowledge networks where the institutions of higher education can participate with the National Council for Science and Technology (CONACYT, for its acronyms in Spanish).

Equally, if an analysis is done about the courses of action of the strategies and objectives of the SEP, it is possible to detect in these the presence of activities belonging to knowledge management, without being mentioned in detail.

As follows and in regard to the observation previously made, the objectives, strategies and courses of action are identified in the SEP implicitly related to knowledge management.

- **Objective 1:** To assure the quality of learning in elementary education, and the comprehensive preparation of all the groups of the population.
- **Strategy 1.4:** To strengthen the initial preparation and the teacher's professional development focused on the school and the students.
- **Course of Action 1.4.5:** To provide schools with a set of aids so the teachers build up and develop professional learning communities.
- **Course of Action 1.4.7:** To foster the creation and strengthening of school and teachers' networks for their professional development.
- **Strategy 1.6:** To use the information drawn by the evaluations in the decision-making process to improve the quality of education and to avoid school drop outs.
- **Objective 2:** To strengthen quality and pertinence in middle and higher-education and in job training, in order to enhance Mexico's development.
- **Strategy 2.1:** To guide and assure learning quality in order to strengthen the integral preparation in middle school education.
- **Course of Action 2.1.6:** To identify the best teaching practices in middle school education and to crate socialization spaces to spread and promote their use at school.
- **Strategy 2.4:** To foster scientific and technological research, and to promote the generation and dissemination of impact knowledge for the development of the country.
- **Course of Action 2.4.5:** To promote, jointly with CONACYT, knowledge networks in which the institutions of higher-education can participate.
- **Course of Action 2.4.8:** To promote a link between researchers and universities, and middle school education programmes (SEP, 2014).

Moreover, the school enrollment of higher education in Mexico from 2012-2013 is of 3070454 students, that is distributed in Higher Technical Education with 134343, Teacher's Higher Education and University majors with 134420, and University and Technological majors with 2801691 (INEGI, 2014). The age of the students enrolled in higher education in Mexico is from 19 to 23 year old in average, according to the most up-dated information provided today by INEGI, by the year 2010 the number of people between that age range was of 9892271.

When compared the population enrolled in higher education in Mexico with the school enrollment in higher education, it is observed that Mexico faces a big problem because 6821817 students for cultural, economic or social reasons are not studying.

Nowadays, the HE coverage in Mexico is by 34.1% whereas the goal set by the Mexican government was by 40% (SEP, 2015). This coverage is and will still be insufficient to address the global needs and demands. This blurry overview compels the educational system and the society to pay more attention to the students that enroll in HE and to the quality of the educational service provided to them, so that from the innovation in strategies of academic management and school management, the results obtained are improved.

In this regard, the educational project of the higher education schools in Mexico must generally focus on the integral development of the young students, besides seeking, "that the curricular contents of every profession help the students receive a professional preparation that make them responsible people able to face, solve or address several situations that the society demands them" (Cañedo & Figueroa, 2013).

Higher education in Mexico has a high commitment with the young people that enroll, stay and leave this educational level to incorporate them to the production sector by an effective bond, from collaboration networks among the educational institution, the enterprises form the private and public sector. The knowledge networks are made up by organisations interacting in common spaces, and share, at a certain length, aims, and generate trustworthy relationships among themselves, otherwise, the achievement of common goals would be impossible, and they worry about a shared good performance and individual achievement. This means they see themselves as dependent subjects that play to win-win through the exchange of data and information, as well as explicit knowledge, that nourish reciprocally to understand their needs and goals in order to develop a process to satisfy and justify their own existence. "The perspective of networking is tuned to the systemic approach of organisation, as this conceives the system to be made up by subsystems that recognize how important interaction and interdependence are not only between each other but with the environment." (Arras, Hernández, & López, 2012).

The institutions of higher education in Mexico must assume the responsibility of achieving an overall up-date that considers knowledge management, as a necessary and unavoidable activity to obtain great advances in all areas. Moreover, knowledge management will allow the schools of HE to develop internal processes of teachers' professionalization, so that their practices are improved by increasing, consequently, the quality of the educational service.

For a long time, there has been a will to count on the experts of different fields, as teachers in higher education, in order to transmit their knowledges to the new generation of future graduates, nonetheless, the teaching task is not limited to the full command of the assignment contents, as well as labour experience. Teaching performance is a complex practice that requires specific skills for the development of the in-classroom teaching and learning process. There exists awareness of how relevant is to complete teacher's preparation, and in the last years, the Subministry of Higher Education (SHE) has expressed their worry about teacher's preparation and the improvement of in-classroom teaching performance. In this regard, the Program of Teacher's Improvement (PROMEP, for its acronyms in Spanish) was created.

Furthermore, the education received by the teachers of higher education goes from University majors up to PhDs, identifying a huge proportion of teachers holding a Master's degree, but, on the other hand, most of them do not have any pedagogical preparation. Teachers at this higher level must be capable of noticing student's learning needs over the teaching process, and that their role is as mediators or content providers, even if this situation is not completely well-accepted, who are able to design several teaching strategies that can be adapted to the student's learning style, skillful for using all the available resources enhancing student's learning, foreseer of how to plan and dosify course contents until covering aims expectancy, creative to do a dynamic and interactive job that awakens student's interest in well-designed school programs, aware of developing student's values and behave on these patterns, inside and out of school.

Counting on the school as an organization with its own vision and mission whose processes must be administered and managed in order to use all its resources optimally, and reach results efficient and effectively through planning, organization and control from evaluation. The school's rightful practice and knowledge management highly enhance it as successful in several processes and aims.

From this task of knowledge generation, the school needs to become an intelligent organization that employs human capital knowledge, structural and relational, from ICT's utilization for knowledge generation and transmission. (Minakata A., 2009).

Certainly, for both principals and teachers, today's demands of challenges and changes are high, and the expectations of excellent outcomes call for the best education graduates in all the schools, real and well-built collaboration networks to face global defying endeavors, as well as to perform an effective knowledge management.

KNOWLEDGE MANAGEMENT IN THE EDUCATIONAL FIELD

Knowledge management, from a formal viewpoint, is a relatively new activity in the organizations, and it is undeniable, that knowledge will be always be present in the economic development of the countries in the world, none the less, only until less than 30 years, the organizations have emphasized their relevance as a key aspect for their own success and related- market permanence.

Knowledge management means the necessary tasks for producing, spreading and using effectively the benefits provided by this good, "in which knowledge is conceived as a main source of richness, power and production. On behalf of knowledge management, it is understood as the development of systems and processes aimed at acquiring and sharing intellectual assets." (Romo, Villalobos, & Guadalupe, 2012). To clarify how relevant knowledge is for the people, it is compared with air, as these two resources are similar, and, thus, both are essential for human life, public and private, assessed, storable and portable, among many others, until completing an entire page, but this is not necessary, as for expressing the relevance of knowledge management can be done by only providing some examples, as an anthology. Consequently, the knowledge of the specific features of both resources will enhance its sustainable exploitation. It must be mentioned that by sustainable development we refer to the resources exploitation in order to satisfy today's generations' needs, without harming the future ones. "Sustainability is a geometrical body described by several dimension, the widest ones are social, economic and environmental. But nowadays, different authors, depending on their discipline and sector, mention other dimension, for instance: academic, spiritual, architectonic, political, landscaping, among others." (Gutiérrez & Martínez, 2009).

On this behalf, the production, distribution, and knowledge use processes must hold feasibility, viability and sustainability aspects, that guarantee knowledge's good use and prevalence, hence, this previously defined concept is wholly applicable to knowledge, as an intangible resource lying over the economic and material resources these days.

In the organizations, knowledge management establishes that intellectual capital bears a rich amount of knowledge as it is simultaneously made up by human capital, structural capital and relational capital. Through knowledge management and a cyclic conversion process, knowledge is extracted from the above mentioned triad, mainly. From human capital, knowledge derives from experiences and accrued knowledge by the organization's members; from structural capital, knowledge comes from the processes, methods and procedures for the organization's performance; and, to end up, from relational capital, knowledge gathers from the organization's relationship with the outer world, by suppliers, customers and allies.

In higher education, the personnel are a perceivable component in the three knowledge reservoirs that form intellectual capital. Here, we find experts, from different disciplines, that from the knowledge management perspective, generate explicit knowledge by every member's tacit knowledge that is directed towards the organization, through the potencialised ICT use. Therefore, it is emphasized the presence of well-qualified and trained personnel at school, because they are a key element for knowledge management, In addition to this, if is recognized that "the students show a sharp skill for the use of technological resources and that the teacher's task will preferably consist in supporting or favoring, proportionally, the acquisition of the curricular contents" (Gutiérrez & Martínez, 2009). Teacher's updating in these technologies must not stay behind, under any circumstances.

It is assumed that there are two types of knowledge in the organization: tacit knowledge and explicit knowledge. It is said that the tacit knowledge is subjective, in the deepest part of the human being, integrated by values and emotions, and difficult to transmit or communicate, formally. The explicit knowledge is codified and can be transmitted formal and systematically through documents, reports, presentation, policies and procedures. The conversion of these knowledges occurs through a spiral, in four stages. In the first stage, the person's tacit knowledge is changed into collective tacit. The second face I externalization where collective tacit knowledge turn into explicit. Then, the third one is a combination where the explicit knowledges are exchanged. Finally, the fourth stage is internalization where the explicit knowledge becomes personal tacit one. (Nonaka & Takeuchi, 1995).

In all the organizations as well as the schools, a representative concentration of knowledge can be observed. At present, it is recognized that the organizations' richness is in knowledge rather than in their material resources (Díaz, 2012), and, as a result, actions, processes, methods and procedures are essential to identify, handle, store, generate and distribute knowledge by means of knowledge management.

From this perspective, it can be observed how relevant knowledge has for the growth of the organizations and the educational institutions of HE. In fact, here, knowledge management performance must be present, from a diagnostic evaluation of this task.

Broadly speaking, evaluation means a systemic process that, with the use or application of criteria, indicators, and previously set standards, will offer value to several qualitative and quantitative variables. The aim is to gather information and/or data to develop school management strategies, and make decisions based on the real situation of the study object.

EDUCATION, CHAIN BOND OF KNOWLEDGE ECONOMY

Knowledge is an intangible propriety of all human beings, and is linked to the subject's ability to reason and learn, that is to say, intelligence by itself. Indeed, knowledge is created from a cognitive process and economic, material and technological resources. The subject's amount of knowledge relies upon the possibility and degree to which this person uses, transmits and generates knowledge himself for social development. This fact has remained identically since the first years of the *Homo sapiens* on earth, until today, and, in contrast, what differs is the amount of available resources, because they vary depending on the productions that result in the prevailing technological development. Knowledge society is the one that organizes their own resources to generate new knowledge from the existing one; without leaving behind the relevance ICTs for this society.

Human beings are social persons that organize in groups, and the organization as a social structure has always brought benefit to every member's knowledge, that for a many centuries of human history, this situation had not been either recognized or valued as it should; so, it was until time passed by and throughout different stages of social, economic and industrial evolution that was concretized. "The traditional theory of development followed the approach practiced by the theorists of growth, which consisted in underestimating the remote or bold reasons for growth in order to centre in the direct and immediate ones, as well as in capital accrual or technological change." (Rivera M., 2014).

Knowledge and technology have a proportionally close relationship as they interact simultaneously for the economic, social and cultural development of the countries in the world, when knowledge and the technological advances were scientific and professionally perceived, all the human processes experienced a notorious change, which resulted in technological revolution, that "leads to the restructuration of all the economy, starting from the modernization of the infrastructure, optimal practices, products, training profiles, localization patterns for production and intensive input use, as well. (Rivera, 2005; Acevedo, Linares, & Cachay, 2009; González, 2014).

At the arrival of the ICT stage of development, the vision of knowledge as an intangible asset of the knowledge economy is grounded, due to the fact that this knowledge is exploited from the capitalist perspective, as a resource that is over the financial and material resources of the enterprises, from the benefits gained through the use of these technologies, "knowledge is transformed into an economic good that intervenes in the design of products, processes and organizations." (Guzmán & Adriano, 2013).

Based on Rivera (2005), Acevedo, Linares, and Cachay (2009), knowledge economy is grounded in a type o technology that revolutionizes the capacity to process the information, but its economic rationality guides to a new organizational model characterizes by the capitalist use of knowledge from the information processing as main source of productivity increase. "In these days, the advanced economies have become more tributaries of knowledge, information, and high- level of human resources preparation in different ways." (Guzmán & Adriano, 2013).

The concept of knowledge economy generated by the Organization for Economic and Cooperation and Development (OECD) in 1996, sustains that knowledge is the strength of economic development of the developed countries, and that it is a key element for the production processes, as well as for capital, materials and workforce. This economy is founded in the creation, spreading and use of knowledge, for the population's integral development and, thus, knowledge economy is not the same object, because this latter lies in, instead of out or independently from this economy.

In knowledge economy, three main features can be trace: at first, it is observed as a phenomenon or intangibly global process; secondly, ICTs are necessarily used as a means for its different dynamics; and, finally, it bears a huge and rising amount of intellectual resources.

The GDP of the countries in the world depend on the level of education of their inhabitants and, straightforward, the creation, spreading and use of knowledge, that means knowledge economy (Sánchez & Ríos, 2011). For an economy to become a knowledge economy, its growth must be sustained in the technological development of knowledge derived from the knowledge contained in its human resources, according to the World Bank, quoted by Pineda (2013), Knowledge Economy (KE) uses knowledge as the key for economic growth, an economy in which knowledge is acquired, created, disseminated, and effectively used, aimed at improving the economic development. (Pineda, 2013; González, 2014).

The success of this change of economies relies on long-term investment capacity, which has four main aspects: education, infrastructure for ICTs use, innovation and policies for promoting the economic activity. These are internationally used as standards to measure the status of the countries regarding their knowledge economy and their possible adhesion to it.

On behalf of the school's education, nowadays, the subjects must develop competencies for interacting, learning and working in environments where there is more contact and access to information through the use of technology, where knowledge plays an important role for the society, and, as a result, it turns into a practically only and fundamental factor for economic development.

It is sought that ICTs suffer constant and rapid changes, transforming into powerful and essential tools for the search, analysis, evaluation and dissemination of information and the creation of knowledge in the organizations and in the knowledge society, so that a teaching-learning process is carried out in the schools of quality, where ICTs play an important for the educational process. (Sánchez & Ríos, 2011).

Teachers at the educational institutions are responsible for the educational achievement, as they in charge of generating strategies and designing activities linked with the ICTs use, so that through these ones, students build up their own competencies for developing and growing dynamically before the challenges of a globalizes world, by acquiring through knowledge production a wealth or value for the knowledge society. Education and the development of human abilities do not only enhance people to add value to the economy, but also to contribute to the cultural heritage, to participate in the society, to improve their family's and community's health, to prevail the environment and to increase their own ability to continue developing (UNESCO, 2008)

Teacher's competences for the use and handling of ICTs will increase the quality of the educational service in the classroom, by adding innovative educational processes, that is to say, that the teachers are responsible for introducing students to the use of ICTs, in order to solve everyday problems, to strengthen and assure their knowledge, as well as its own production.

Therefore, it is sought to achieve citizens able to face successfully professional challenges (Sánchez & Ríos, 2011), students that learn and share their knowledge collaboratively at school, and teachers that modify their traditional methods of teaching by using ICTs efficient and effectively.

An educational reform with policies for the economic development that will increase student's technological understanding, citizens and workforce through the integration of ICT competences in the study plans, to increase the ability of students, citizens and the workforce ability to use their knowledge in order to add value to the society and the economy, applying those knowledges to solve complex and real problems, as well as to increase the ability of students, citizens and the workforce to innovate, produce new knowledge and take advantage of it (UNESCO, 2008).

The performance of schools and teachers, in regard to the ICT use as a key element for the economic development, will pave the way to an integral growth that will boost the society to a level of economic prosperity based on the optimal and potencialised knowledge in the population by education.

An updated educational system in technological infrastructure for the ICT use, in training and professional education for the teachers in the use of these technologies for the innovation of teaching practices and the educational service, the sufficient coverage of schools proportionally relating to the number of citizens in suitable conditions for the study and the good indexes of education obtained in national and international evaluation will determine the degree of knowledge prevailing in the countries, according to the knowledge economy in the world.

In fact, it is recognized the close relationship between ICT and the identification, structuring, acquisition, creation, utilization and dissemination of knowledge, and it is determined the relevance of ICT for life world and global wide.

In knowledge economy, the educational system, the public policies for businesses and the macroeconomic balance, the innovation system for generating new knowledge, and, finally, the infrastructure for ICT access are identified as the basis on which this economy sustains, as referred by the Foundation of This country (2005).

The performance of this type of economy depends on production, distribution and the use of knowledge, its reach leaves outside the cultural and spiritual spheres, as it only involves with the social, production and information spheres.

For knowledge economy, science, technology and innovation are factors that promote the economic and social development of the countries, by improved productive processes, services, through the incorporation of new technologies that generate, at the same time, job positions where knowledge is the person's competitive advantage, obtaining, as a consequence, higher salaries, that rise people's life standards. This triad of aspects, must be nowadays fostered emphatically as the driving forces of knowledge economy, and as economic and social benefits vehicles for the modern society.

The difference of the countries, that based their economy on the use, diffusion and production of knowledge, will be in the capacity they have to incorporate science, technology and innovation advances in education, economic balance, scientific spreading and infrastructure for the use of ICT, and, thus, the countries that do not pay attention to their performance according to what is established in knowledge economy will remain excluded or left behind. (Sánchez & Ríos, 2011).

Specifically, innovation is an aspect that potencialises all the activities in the economic sectors, acquiring a vital importance for the countries seeking a huge growth.

Innovation has a transcendental role in the economic processes in the new knowledge economy, At macro level, there is evidence that the innovation is crucial for international competitiveness and, therefore, in the growth of national economies, and determines world commerce patterns. At micro level, this is inside the enterprises, as research and development (R + D) activities, that result in innovation and that are considered as a improvement factor for the capacity of an enterprise to absorb and exploit all type of new knowledge, not only technological knowledge, with the aim to optimize and maintain its competitive position (Pineda, 2013; González, 2014).

Scientific research is willing to generate new knowledge, that innovates the processes inside the organizations and that fosters it towards an integral development.

STUDY METHODOLOGY

As it has already been stated in this work, knowledge management is a relatively new activity among the members of the organization in Mexico, on the other hand, the organizations of developed countries count on more experience concerning the full command of this task, which gives them certain advantage for the use, production and distribution of knowledge over the rest of the world. This different level of approach to knowledge generation demands an accelerated pace for the achievement of significant outcomes, that avoid Mexico's economic backwardness and its organizations in the world.

The existing distance between the current moment and the beginnings of knowledge economy and management required, that in the first stage of the studio, a bibliographic research was done, and in which it was clearly described the main central study themes, that are knowledge management and HE in Mexico. The framework, as in any other research work, looks for the description for the prior knowledge of the study object, so as to understand where the element had its origin. It is highlighted the link between knowledge management with other areas, factors, aspects, specialties and activities of human live, in order to identify its origin; and, hence, it is sought that from the beginning of this work, it is defined what it will be learnt, and know what others have researched on the issue. (Hernández, Fernández, & Baptista, 2006).

The teaching personnel in the educational organizations of HE in Mexico, equal to other similar ones in different parts of the world, are essential to knowledge management, due to the fact that they are closely related to two central components for the economic developments, that is to say, the students that represent the future and the knowledge as the most valuable resource in the organizations (Díaz, 2012). The school achievement in HE schools and knowledge production as established in knowledge economy and management, relies dramatically on the presence and efficient use of ICT, (Sánchez & Ríos, 2011),, the educational research and innovation to spread new knowledge, as well as institutional programs that foster, strengthen and accomplish the school objectives based on the economy and knowledge management aims.

To evaluate knowledge management from the perspective of the academicians of HE in Mexico, is relevant to examine the aspect mentioned in the last paragraph, as sell, as the knowledge located in intellectual capital, in human, structural and relational capital.

Having as main purpose the distinction of the state of knowledge management in higher education schools, the research will be non- experimental, due to the fact that no dynamic nor strategy will be put into practice in order to inform the academicians about the basic guidelines of knowledge management, and entirely clean data will be looked for, so the study object will be observed just as it takes place in the context, without modifying or manipulating it for its evaluation and diagnosis (Hernández, Fernández, & Baptista, 2006). In this study, knowledge management represents the study object, while the context will be represented by the higher education schools.

The study will be quantitative because numerical data will be obtained by the instrument of evaluation for the diagnosis of knowledge management (Hernández, Fernández, & Baptista, 2006). These numerical outcomes will result in an analysis, through the techniques and methods for inferential statistics, in order to establish the generalities of the study object from a sample. Parallel, it will be a descriptive study, as with the results drawn from the analysis of data, it will possible to identify and describe the existence and characteristics of knowledge management in the schools of higher education, as well as how management contributes to the performance, and academic and administrative achievement of these institutions.

The design of this research will be cross-sectional provided that the evaluation instrument for this study will be applied to the teaching personnel at only once (Hernández, Fernández, & Baptista, 2006). Moreover, the survey will be of 54 items, on Likert scale, which will gather information about knowledge management in the schools of higher education.

For knowledge management, knowledge is identified, produced, distributed and used, within three main variables: human capital, all the members of the organization are considered; structural capital, the processes and uses of bibliographic and documental resources; finally, relational capita, that uses the external world and actors, either if they are clients, supplier or partners for knowledge exchange. It is through the operationalisation of the variables above mentioned that the evaluation instrument for this study is set to determine how knowledge management is present from the viewpoint of the academicians of the schools of higher education.

CONCLUSION

Undoubtedly, today knowledge has acquired a superlative value than that one from the past, but this does not mean that it was denied. Since the beginning of human history, this element was necessary for the social, technological and economic development in the world, it is known that before, and in the ancient Greece, philosophers worked with knowledge for its production and distribution, without stopping this activity until now. It would be possible to mention a number of characters who, throughout the years, have made great contributions in various fields to human development, however, the intention at this point is only to emphasize the relevance of constant use of knowledge.

With these knowledge advances, there have been changes in the various environments in which people operate; while in times, life was elementary and individuals mostly require a level of knowledge not as demanding as today, but nowadays, citizens must face environments in which many more skills are required to acquire an elementary lifestyle. In this sense, substantial changes in the needs and lifestyle of modern times, both in large cities and small communities are identified. It is paradoxical that in the past, the individual who knew something lived well, because at present, the individual must learn to live much less well.

Over the past four decades, it has been generated an exploitation of knowledge production and dissemination; today, the contents have increased and the resource flows have thickened, which cause a change in how knowledge is handled, giving rise to knowledge management. This activity, as mentioned above, is essential in any organization, whether of extraction, processing and / or services, whether private or public, that seeks to remain competitive in the world.

It is concluded that:

1. The importance of improving the quality of education in the schools, as a decisive stage in the academic training of the individual, for a meaningful participation in the economic development of Mexico is recognized.
2. Knowledge management must be a real and present activity in HE schools, to maximize the efficiency of academic and administrative results.
3. Knowledge management will lead to schools of higher education to remain with dignity in highly competitive global environments.
4. The importance of ICT teaching and management in Education, the necessary infrastructure support, the innovation generated by scientific research, and the policies that promote the intelligent use of knowledge is recognized as fundamental aspects for the economy and knowledge management.
5. Intellectual capital is formed by human, structural and relational capital, and that includes a huge content of knowledge. Thus, the schools of higher education may be able to manage this valuable resource of knowledge management.
6. By the evaluation of knowledge management from the perspective of the academicians, the state of this activity can be diagnosed in order to make decisions to develop the academic and administrative management strategies, that will result in higher outcomes until now reached at HE.
7. Knowledge management will allow the schools of HE to achieve a successful pairing, for the transfer of graduate students to the productive sector, satisfying mutually the existing needs between these two elements.
8. The existence of ICT is essential for the transmission and dissemination of knowledge from the schools of HE to the world, through its own processes of knowledge management.
9. The creation of networks of collaboration between the schools of HE and the productive sector, aimed to generate a steady flow of knowledge between both parties, allowing the design of strategies for the administrative and academic management, that improve the results of a social, technological and economic development.

REFERENCES

Acevedo, A., Linares, C., & Cachay, O. (2009). La economía y la sociedad del conocimiento. Hacia la tercera revolución: *La información*. Available at http://www.redalyc.org/articulo.oa?id=81620150002

Aguerrondo, I. (2009). La escuela inteligente en el marco de la gestión del conocimiento. *Innovación Educativa*. Available at http://www.redalyc.org/articulo.oa?id=179414895004

Alcantara, A., & Zorrilla, J. (2010). Globalización y educación media superior en México. En busca de la pertinencia curricular. *Perfiles educativos*. Available at http://www.redalyc.org/pdf/132/13211845003.pdf

Alvarez, R., & Sandoval, J. (2005). La cooperación inter-universitaria entre México y Venezuela para el estudio de la globalización, la integración y las relaciones fronterizas: un balance de 10 años. *Aldea Mundo*. Available at http://www.redalyc.org/articulo.oa?id=54301808

Amaya, K., Iriarte, M., & Perozo, D. (2006). Gestión del conocimiento como capacidad interna. *Telos*. Available at http://www.redalyc.org/articulo.oa?id=99318557007

Aparicio, P. (2009). Educación y jóvenes en contextos de desigualdad socioeconómica. *Tendencias y perspectivas en América*. Available at http://www.redalyc.org/articulo.oa?id=275019727012

Arras, A., Hernández, O., & López, J. (2012). *Redes y confianza: dimensiones del capital social en las microempresas rurales en Chihuahua, México*. Available at http://www.scielo.org.mx/scielo.php?script=sci_arttext&pid=S0185063620120002000003&lng=es&nrm=iso

Borroto, J. (2007). La gestión del conocimiento en la nueva economía. Algunos apuntes. *Ciencia en su PC*. Available at http://www.redalyc.org/articulo.oa?id=181315033004

Briceño, G. (2012). Ser estudiante en la sociedad de la información y el conocimiento: la escuela y sus actores ante el cambio cultural. *Sinéctica*. Avalilable at http://www.scielo.org.mx/scielo.php?script=sci_arttext&pid=S1665-109X2012000100004&lng=es&nrm=iso&tlng=es

Cabrera, A. (2009). América Latina y la globalización. *Opinión Jurídica*. Available at http://www.redalyc.org/articulo.oa?id=94512330003

Cañedo, T., & Figueroa, A. (2013). La práctica docente en educación superior: una mirada hacia su complejidad. *Sinéctica*. Available at http://www.scielo.org.mx/scielo.php?script=sci_arttext&pid=S1665-109X2013000200004&lng=es&nrm=iso

Chahuán, K. (2009). Evaluación cualitativa y gestión del conocimiento. *Educación y Educadores*. Available at http://www.redalyc.org/articulo.oa?id=83412235010

Cordero, G., Luna, E., & Patiño, N. (2011). La profesionalización de los maestros de educación básica. Retos para las instituciones de educación superior. *Perfiles Educativos*. Available at http://www.redalyc.org/articulo.oa?id=13221258020

Cornejo, J. (2012). Retos impuestos por la globalización a los sistemas educativos latinoamericanos. *Revista Mexicana de Incestigación educativa*. Available at http://www.scielo.org.mx/scielo.php?script=sci_arttext&pid=S1405-66662012000100002&lng=es&nrm=iso

Darceles, M. (2007). Gestión del conocimiento y creatividad. Revista *Escuela de Administración de Negocios*. Available at http://www.redalyc.org/articulo.oa?id=20611495010

Díaz, C. (2012). Tendencias y requerimientos del mercado de trabajo en la economía del conocimiento. Estudio sobre los egresados del CUCEA. *Revista de la Educación Superior*. Available at http://www.scielo.org.mx/scielo.php?script=sci_arttext&pid=S0185-27602012000100001&lng=es&nrm=iso

Domínguez, D., Sandoval, M., Cruz, F., & Pulido, A. (2013). Problemas relacionados con la eficiencia terminal desde la perspectiva de estudiantes universitarios. *Revista Iberoamericana sobre Calidad, Eficacia y Cambio en Educación*. Available at http://www.rinace.net/reice/numeros/arts/vol12num1/art2.htm

Fundación Este País. (2005). México ante el reto de la economía del conocimiento. *Este país Tendencias y Opiniones*. Available at http://archivo.estepais.com/site/category/ep/?n=174

Garbanzo, V., & Guiselle, M. (2012). Educación superior pública en américa latina: Características y desafíos. *Revista Gestão Universitária na América Latina*. Available at Obtenido de http://www.redalyc.org/articulo.oa?id=319327514012

González, P. (2014). Innovación y economía del conocimiento. ¿Qué hay que aprender para México y cuál es el papel de las élites? *Revista Enfoques: Ciencia Política y Administración Pública*. Available at http://www.redalyc.org/articulo.oa?id=96031437008

Gutiérrez, B., & Martínez, M. (2009). Dimensiones de sustentabilidad en las instituciones de educación superior. Propuesta para un centro de investigación. *Revista de la educación superior*. Available at http://www.scielo.org.mx/scielo.php?script=sci_arttext&pid=S0185-27602009000400007&lng=es&nrm=iso

Gutierrez, L. (2009). El devenir de la educación media superior. El caso del estado de México. *Tiempo de Educar*. Available at http://www.redalyc.org/articulo.oa?id=31113164007

Guzmán, R., & Adriano, A. (2013). Conocimiento, economía, desarrollo y sociedad: trazos desde la complejidad. *En-claves del pensamiento*. Available at http://www.scielo.org.mx/scielo.php?script=sci_arttext&pid=S1870-879X2013000200006&lng=es&nrm=iso

Hernández, A. (2009). Gestión de la calidad y gestión del conocimiento. *Boletín Científico Técnico INIMET*. Available at http://www.redalyc.org/articulo.oa?id=223018305004

Hernández, G., & Díaz, F. (2013). Una mirada psicoeducativa al aprendizaje: qué sabemos y hacia dónde vamos. *Sinéctica*. Available at http://www.scielo.org.mx/scielo.php?script=sci_arttext&pid=S1665-109X2013000100003&lng=es&nrm=iso

Hernández, R., Fernández, C., & Baptista, P. (2006). *Metodología de la investigación*. D.F., México: Mac Graw Hill.

Instituto Nacional de Estadística Geografía e Investigación INEGI. (2014). *Matrícula escolar en educación superior por entidad federativa según sexo, ciclo escolar 2013/2014*. Available at http://www3.inegi.org.mx/sistemas/sisept/default.aspx?t=medu42&s=est&c=21791

Jiménez, R., & Diana, M. (2012). La informalidad laboral en américa latina: ¿Explicación estructuralista o institucionalista? *Cuadernos de Economía*. Available at http://www.redalyc.org/articulo.oa?id=282125048006

Marginson, S. (2013). La Educación Superior como autoformación: el caso de estudiantes transfronterizos. *Revista de la educación superior*. Available at http://www.scielo.org.mx/pdf/resu/v43n169/v43n169a2.pdf

Mata, Y., & Pesca, C. (2011). La gestión del conocimiento en las universidades como baluarte organizacional. *InterSedes: Revista de las Sedes Regionales*. Available at http://www.redalyc.org/articulo.oa?id=66622603005

Mejía, L., Osorio, M. d., & Navarro, J. A. (2008). Impacto de la práctica docente sobre la calidad de la enseñanza en el nivel medio superior. *Espacios Públicos*. Available at http://www.redalyc.org/pdf/676/67602119.pdf

Méndez, M., & Zenteno, N. (2009). *La educación de posgrado con un enfoque humanista en un mundo globalizante: el caso del Colpos*. Available at http://www.scielo.org.mx/pdf/sine/n32/n32a5.pdf

Minakata, A. (2009). Gestión del conocimiento en educación y transformación de la escuela. Notas para un campo en construcción. *Sinéctica*. Available at http://www.scielo.org.mx/scielo.php?script=sci_arttext&pid=S1665-109X2009000100008&lng=es&nrm=iso

Ministerio del Poder Popular para la Educación. (2008). La evaluación en el sistema educativo bolivariano. *Educere*. Available at http://www.redalyc.org/pdf/356/35604024.pdf

Miranda, F. I. (2014). Educación media superior en méxico. Hacía una política de reescolarización. *Revista iberoamericana de educación*. Available at http://www.rieoei.org/deloslectores/6223Miranda.pdf

Muñoz, D., Aguado, D., & Lucía, B. (2003). El largo camino hacia la Gestión del Conocimiento. *Revista de Psicología del Trabajo y de las Organizaciones*. Available at http://www.redalyc.org/articulo.oa?id=231318052005

Nagles, D. (2007). La gestión del conocimiento como fuente de innovación. *Revista Escuela de Administración de Negocios*. Available at http://www.redalyc.org/articulo.oa?id=20611495008

Nonaka, I., & Takeuchi, H. (1995). *The knowledge-creating company: How Japanese Companies Create the Dynamics of Innovation*. New York: Oxford University Press.

Perez, D., & Dressler, M. (2007). Tecnologías de la información para la gestión del conocimiento. *Intangible Capital*. Available at http://www.redalyc.org/pdf/549/54930103.pdf

Pilar, R. (2008). Reseña de "Claves del desarrollo científico y tecnológico de América Latina" de Sebastián, J. (ed.). *Andamios. Revista de Investigación Social*. Available at http://www.redalyc.org/articulo.oa?id=62811466016

Pineda, L. (2013). Colombia frente a la economía de conocimiento, ¿un callejón sin salida? *Estudios Gerenciales*. Available at http://www.redalyc.org/articulo.oa?id=21229786006

Rivera, M. (2014). Desarrollo económico y trayectorias históricas. Una aproximación al caso de Brasil y México. *Problemas del desarrollo*. Available at http://www.scielo.org.mx/scielo.php?script=sci_arttext&pid=S0301-70362014000400002&lng=es&nrm=iso

Rivera, M. A. (2005). Cambio histórico mundial, capitalismo informático y economía del conocimiento Problemas del Desarrollo. *Revista Latinoamericana de Economía*. Available at http://www.redalyc.org/articulo.oa?id=11820075003

Rodriguez, K., & Salgado, L. (2009). Puntos críticos sobre la reforma en Educación básica y media superior en México. *Revista del Centro de Investigación*. Available at http://www.redalyc.org/articulo.oa?id=34213107009

Romo, A., Villalobos, M., & Guadalupe, L. (2012). Gestión del conocimiento: estrategia para la formación de investigadores. *Sinéctica*. Available at http://www.scielo.org.mx/scielo.php?script=sci_arttext&pid=S1665-109X2012000100007&lng=es&nrm=iso

Royero, J. (2006). Las redes de I+D como estrategia de uso de las TIC en las universidades de América Latina. *Universities and Knowledge Society Journal*. Available at http://www.redalyc.org/articulo.oa?id=78030205

Saíz, J. (2012). Ética, capital intelectual y gestión del conocimiento. *Revista Escuela de Administración de Negocios*. Available at http://www.redalyc.org/articulo.oa?id=20625032004

Salama, P. (2011). Luchas contra la pobreza en América Latina. El caso de la pobreza rural en Brasil. *Revista Latinoamericana de Economía*. Available at http://www.redalyc.org/articulo.oa?id=11819780002

Sánchez, C., & Ríos, H. (2011). La economía del conocimiento como base del crecimiento económico en México. *Revista Venezolana de Información, Tecnología y conocimiento*. Available at http://www.redalyc.org/articulo.oa?id=82319126004

Sánchez, M., & Vega, J. (2006). La gestión del conocimiento y su relación con otras gestiones. *Ciencias de la información*. Available at http://www.redalyc.org/articulo.oa?id=181418190003

Sanoja, P. (2007). ¿Globalización sin convergencia? *Revista Venezolana de Economía y Ciencias Sociales*. Available at http://www.redalyc.org/articulo.oa?id=17721562003

Santa, S., & Herrero, V. (2010). Producción científica de América Latina y el Caribe: una aproximación a través de los datos de Scopus (1996-2007). *Revista Interamericana de Bibliotecología*. Available at http://www.redalyc.org/articulo.oa?id=179015630005

Secretaría de Educación Pública. SEP. (2014). *Programa Sectorial de Educación 2013-2018*. Available at http://www.sep.gob.mx/es/sep1/programa_sectorial_de_educacion_13_18

Secretaria de Educación Pública, S. E. P. (2015). *Comunicado 014*. Available at http://www.comunicacion.sep.gob.mx/index.php/comunicados/enero-2015/876-comunicado-014-destaca-chuayffet-chemor-logros-visibles-en-educacion-superior-en-el-marco-de-la-reforma-educativa

The World Bank Group. (2014). *World Development Indicators: Science and technology*. Available at http://wdi.worldbank.org/table/5.13

Torres, S., Barona, C., & Omar, G. (2010). Infraestructura tecnológica y apropiación de las TIC en la Universidad Autónoma del Estado de Morelos. Estudio de caso. *Perfiles Educativos*. Available at http://www.scielo.org.mx/scielo.php?script=sci_arttext&pid=S0185-26982010000100006&lng=es&nrm=iso

Tovar, C., & Díaz, E. (2010). Dispersión del ingreso y demanda de educación media superior y superior en México. *Análisis Económico*. Available at http://www.redalyc.org/articulo.oa?id=41313083006

UNESCO. (2008). *Estándares de competencias en TIC para docentes*. Available at http://www.oei.es/tic/UNESCOEstandaresDocentes.pdf

Villa, L. (2007). La educación media superior ¿igualdad de oportunidades? *Revista de la Educación Superior*. Available at http://www.redalyc.org/pdf/604/60414105.pdf

Chapter 2
Systemic Evaluation of Knowledge Management:
Perspective of Graduate Students in Education in Mexico

Jésica Alhelí Cortés Ruíz
Instituto Politécnico Nacional, Mexico

Ricardo Morán Martínez
Instituto Politécnico Nacional, Mexico

Eduardo Antonio Vanegas López
Instituto Politécnico Nacional, Mexico

ABSTRACT

This chapter focuses on the study that will offer a systemic evaluation of the characteristics of knowledge management, from the approach of the postgraduate students in Mexico. It will consider the generation cycle – storage – distribution – utilization and generalization of knowledge, as stated by (Nonaka & Takeuchi, 1995). The purpose will be to design academic management strategies for the strengthening of human capital, which comprises the post-graduate students in Mexico, who are enrolled in this type of educational programmes. The proposed chapter is structured as follows: The first section centers in the description of the characteristics of knowledge management, the second one will target at the characteristics of postgraduate education in Mexico, the third section includes the study methodology, and the fourth one will be the research proposal for drawing the research conclusions.

INTRODUCTION: KNOWLEDGE MANAGEMENT AND SYSTEMIC EVALUATION

Knowledge management is a relatively new subject that aims to reach current generations interacting intellectual capital comprising human capital, structural capital and relational capital, technology and information in order to capture, produce, process, disseminate, store and use knowledge. Therefore, if

DOI: 10.4018/978-1-5225-0457-3.ch002

adopted as a tool in education, they are more likely to generate constructive changes that result in a better quality of learning. On the other hand, systemic evaluation is characterized as complex, ie, comprehensive and interrelation with which manages information with a holistic view, taking into account the components of each system, with the main objective to enrich the knowledge.

KNOWLEDGE AND TAXONOMY

Knowledge is defined as information possessed by a subject in his mind, which can be personalized and subjective, related to facts, procedures, concepts, interpretations, ideas, observations, judgments and elements that can be useful or not, precise or structural. The information turns into knowledge when processed in the mind and, then, back into information once it is articulated or communicated to other people through texts, electronic templates, oral and written communications, among others. In addition, the receiver can process and interiorize the information, and turn it back into knowledge (Alavi & Leidner, 2001).

In the same regard, (Alavi & Leidner, 2001) describe the taxonomy of knowledge barely, referring to twelve types of knowledge, as may be observed in Table 1.

TACIT AND EXPLICIT KNOWLEDGE

Nonaka & Takeuchi, (1995) mention that knowledge can be tacit or explicit. The earlier is difficult to express by formal language as it is learned from personal experience and involves intangible factors such as beliefs, viewpoints and values. The latter, can be expressed through formal language, including grammar statements, mathematical expressions, specifications, manuals and so forth, and can be

Table 1. Knowledge taxonomy

Types of Knowledge	Definitions
Tacit	Knowledge rooted in actions, experiences and particular contexts
Cognitive tacit	Mental models
Technical tacit	Know how applied to specific work
Explicit	Articulated and generalized knowledge
Individual	Knowledge created and inherent to subject
Social	Knowledge created and inherent to collectivity and to team actions
Declarative	To know about
Procedural	To know how to do
Causal	To know why
Conditional	To know when
Relational	To know how relations work
Pragmatic	Useful knowledge for an organization

Source: Self-prepared, based on (Alavi & Leidner, 2001).

easily transmitted from one subject to another. These authors argue that Japanese companies have been successful in virtue of their sills and masterising in the field of creation of organizational knowledge, which is defined as the capacity of a company to generate new knowledges, disseminate them among the members of the organization and materialize them in products, services and systems. Furthermore, it is emphasized this knowledge as the turnpoint (key) for the companies to innovate continually and the main strength of the Japanese enterprises is to manage the intangible knowledge and transform it into explicit knowledge.

So Nonaka & Takeuchi, (1995) illustrate a model of tacit – explicit knowledge in four stages, where the first one is socialization (from tacit to tacit) and starts, generally, with the creation of a field of interaction that allows the team members to share their experiences and mental models, transferring, like this, tacit knowledge from one person to another. Secondly, externalization (from tacit to explicit) starts from a dialogue or collective reflection lying on a proper metaphor or analogy allows the members express the tacit hidden knowledge, that is difficult to communicate differently. Thirdly, the combination/association (from tacit to explicit) starts with the distribution of recently-created knowledge networks and the exiting knowledge about other parts of the organization, enriching and crystallizing in new knowledge, product or service. Lastly, internalization (from explicit to tacit) that feedbacks the process again and that has its origin by learning doing it, as shown in next figure 1.

Therefore, every time this cycle completes a round, new knowledge is created, so that it increases like this, obtaining as a result a spiral that systematically expands as more and more people participate, and represents a key factor in the learning model.

Figure 1. Process of knowledge generation "spiral model"
Source: Self-prepared, based on (Nonaka & Takeuchi, 1995).

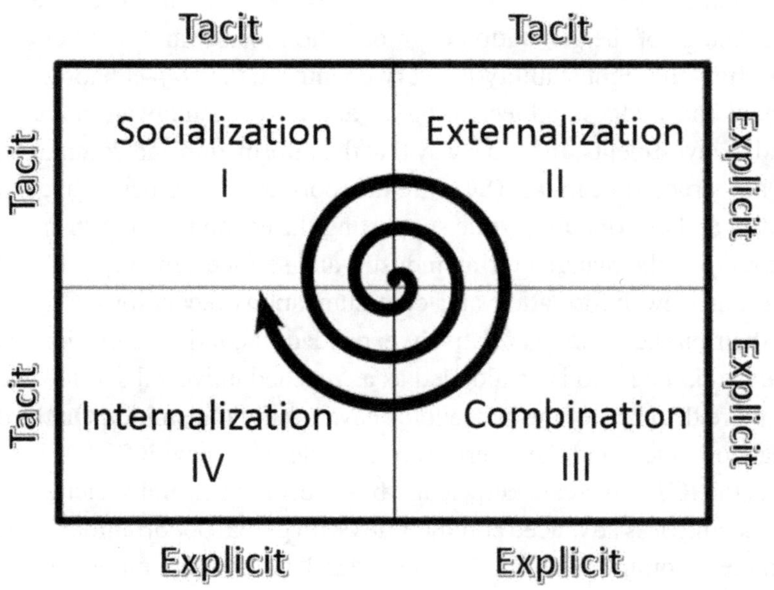

KNOWLEDGE ECONOMY

Knowledge economy is based on information and by-products, adds value to goods from advanced knowledge and technological innovation, and participates in the society of knowledge. All of them are expressions of a technological advance that has lowered transmission information costs and widened the capacity for its physical storage. But behind the futurist façade of computers, satellites and mass media, it means a type of social and economic organization relying on the right of all individuals to have access to the most suitable information for making the best decisions.

The performance of this economy is mainly sustained by production, distribution and use of knowledge and information; in contrast to a traditional economy, in a knowledge economy, information and technology are not external factors of the production process as knowledge and information have a direct influence on it. The use and creation of knowledge can increase the capacity of traditional production factors, such as work, capital and raw material, among others, and can even transform them into new products and processes (OCDE/GD, 1996).

In a conventional economy, there is a moment when the higher the investment in capital, work and raw material, the lower the profits for every new investment made. Whereas in the economies, industries and enterprises based on knowledge and information it is seen that the higher the investment in knowledge, the more profits and benefits by each new investment in knowledge use, adaptation and generation.

As the enterprises adopt knowledge input, the demand for better-qualified employees increases, new technologies are embraced, and, gradually, new knowledges are generated, which can possibly be added to the productive process. In a knowledge economy, the institutions and their links with them and with households are the core of the process of knowledge generation, adoption and dissemination. Knowledge economy and its interaction with institutions and households lies on four pillars: the educational system, the economic and institutional administration, the innovation system and the infrastructure information. The earlier provides people with the basic tools to understand information at their reach better and adapt it to generate new knowledges (OCDE/GD, 1996).

The economic administration, by their side, establishes the necessary incentives to promote innovation, and to take advantage of the generation of information locally and in other countries. Moreover, this administration offers the right stability in every country to develop economic activities, to protect the generation of new knowledges and technologies, and to foster innovation and competitiveness by opening to trade and to investments. In such a way that the information and communication technologies (ICT), also known as "structural capital" (SC), are the tools and instruments that capture, transmit and display electronic data and information, while supporting the economic growth and development of the different economic sectors, the manufacturing industry and services, mainly.

There exists old and new information and communications technology (ICT), where the earlier are developed and their public access is relatively expanded: the radio, television and fixed telephony. Particularly, on one hand, the radio is catalogued as a "reached universal service" because in most developing countries more than half of the households have a radio transmitter. On the other hand, mobile telephones, personal computers and the Internet are considered as new ICT.

At a great degree, the ICT can create knowledge-based economies and societies that foster economic development by connecting less advanced communities with global opportunities. Even though, they can raise inequalities in these communities and in knowledge-based communities (OCDE, 2002).

KNOWLEDGE SOCIETY

As defined by Anderson & Gallini, (1998), knowledge society refers to that one that uses knowledge to generate social and economic changes bringing a benefit to all the population, from their commitment with knowledge innovation, employment, protection and dissemination in order to create economic and social welfare, and to enrich people´s lives from an integral vision that includes body, mind and spirit.

In this manner, those activities that produce, distribute and use knowledge, and use the technologies of information and communication (ICT) (SC) are included. This means an influence on the productivity and competitiveness of the enterprises and on the different economic sectors. Moreover, the society of knowledge includes spiritual, social intellectual and scientific knowledge gathered in every society (Bunc, 1992).

Therefore, the influence of knowledge is spread all over the universe of knowledge creation, distribution, use and dissemination in all social spheres: economy, education, government, arts, religion, and philosophy, among others.

From this viewpoint, the information society belongs to knowledge society because information needs to be processed in order to turn into knowledge. However, this fact is relevant providing the fact that even if the technological advances have made possible to share ideas, projects and knowledge generated anywhere in the world, it seems that information is gathering faster than knowledge and the process of information transformation into knowledge is laying behind (Burkle & Robles, 2004).

MANAGEMENT KNOWLEDGE

Knowledge management comes historically to existence through the consciousness awakening of knowledge value as a resource and product of knowledge economy in the society of information. In 1970, Peter Drucker used, firstly, the term knowledge worker and started to write a letter about the persons whose experiences and knowledges are more important in an organization than their physical skills. During the eighties, in productive organizations, the programmes oriented towards productivity improvement were set to work based on initiatives for quality improvement such as: Total Quality Management, Business Process Reengineering and Six-Sigma.

In account of this, the term knowledge management starts to be known at the beginning of the nineties, although there were examples of practical development and academic contribution that could be possibly found in that field, among the first organizations that adopted the knowledge management practices and tools we find the services whose businesses are rooted in their employees' knowledges and experiences, such as Mc Kinsey & Company, Ernst & Young and Pricewaterhouse Cooper. These were followed by the corporations with needs to capture, store, systematize and distribute the employees' "gathered knowledge", like Xerox, IBM, Hewlett Packard, and so forth.

And it would be until 2006 when the publishing group Idea Group Publishers released the Encyclopedia of Knowledge Development, edited by (Schwartz, 2006); this is the first intended compiled work of Knowledge Management, in which a state of the art of the main elements that make up this field is found, characterized by the multiple approaches of themes and research questions arising, consolidating and relating to each other, as well as by the thinkers and representative groups; this consciousness awakening prefers entrepreneurial organizations (Wenger, McDermott & Synder, 2002). Also, technologies and systems to capture, store and distribute information, together with the processes of appropriation and use with it constitutes knowledge, become the cornerstones of the mobilization and management cycle in this context, the relevance acquired (sharing networks), in which access and concurrency of people who share a common purpose is a "community of practice" in real or virtual environments shared learning (Andersen, 1999).

Nevertheless, the analysis of the cycles of knowledge generation – storage – distribution – use – generalization, turn out to be the main element of the development of knowledge management, as studied by (Nonaka & Takeuchi, 1995).

To these authors, knowledge generation is carried out in four phases: socialization, which means shared personal experience and ideas that go from personal tacit to collective knowledge; externalization, that refers the step between collective tacit to explicit knowledge; combination, in which the exchange of explicit knowledges, as well as documents shared by different modalities, mainly electronic and virtual takes place; internalization or learning, where the collective explicit knowledge becomes an individual tacit one.

Three significant aspects for understanding knowledge management and development shall be mentioned:

1. It does not exist any approach to the development of knowledge management systems; it is placed in a field of multiple phases and perspectives.
2. Knowledge management is a dynamically non-stopping organizational phenomenon, constituted by diverse processes that exhibit their own characteristics and varied interest focuses.
3. Information and communication technologies (ICT) can be used for spreading knowledge management beyond the traditionally codified and systematized knowledge storage, recovery and distribution (Alavi & Leidner, 2001).

However, the main knowledge management backbone seems to be active knowledge, which can also constitute the social - productive cycle in knowledge economy.

POSTGRADUATE EDUCATIONAL PROGRAMMES REGISTERED AT 2010-2014 NATIONAL PROGRAMME OF QUALITY POSTGRADUATE STUDIES (PNPC) IN MEXICO AND ITS CONTEXT

Postgraduate education has an important role for the economic, political and social development of the country, and some of its programmes focus on the study of regional or specific educational problems. While some postgraduate programmes enable the design and implementation of solving strategies consistent to the context in which they develop, others are responsible for the preparation, training and updating of teachers in service in a specific educational field in order to strengthen the teacher's performance by providing them with fundamentals, strategies and teaching resources (Cardoso & Cerecedo, 2011).

For this reason, within the attributes and responsibilities of the National Council of Science and Technology there is the establishment of national policies on science and technology, and to achieve this end, the Council has among its substantive programmes with the National Program of Quality Postgraduate Studies (PNPC, for its acronyms in Spanish), which is administered jointly by the Ministry of Education through the Undersecretary of Higher Education and the CONACyT. The programme establishes as its mission to "promote continuous improvement and quality assurance of national graduate to give sustenance to the increase of scientific, technological, social, humanistic skills, and innovation the country." This situation of graduate education offered by both public and private institutions of higher education in Mexico and in the context of the evaluation of qualified programmes by the Federal Government, is presented in Table 2 (Registered postgraduate studies in the National Programme of Quality Postgraduate Studies (PNPC).

Based on Table 2, it is shown that, 673 out of 1,512 registered postgraduate programmes in the PNPC are from the National Postgraduate Register (PNP), and 839 from the Promotion Program Quality (PPQ), which represent 45% and 55%, respectively.

This means that less than half of the programmes that are recognized by this organization are quality either International Competition (CI) or Consolidated. Meanwhile, the remaining programmes are in a process of improving the quality of education based on the criteria established by the CONACyT, as may be observed in Table 3.

On the other hand, the total number of graduate programmes in education that have been registered in the PNPC till 2014 is 36; however, by 2010, the postgraduate programmes in education that were recorded were 39, as shown in Table 4.

Table 2. Registered postgraduate studies in the National Programme of Quality Postgraduate Studies

Stream		Doctorate	Master's Degree		Specialty	Subtotal	Total
			Professional	Research			
PNP	International Competence	61	5	86	2	154	673
	Consolidated	183	46	274	16	519	
PFC	In progress	138	151	214	19	522	839
	Recent Creation	137	68	110	2	317	
	TOTAL	519	270	684	39	1512	1512

Source: (CONACyT, 2014). National Programme of Quality Postgraduate Studies. 2014 Current Programmes. In www.conacyt.mx/index.php/becas-y-posgrados/programa-nacional-de-posgrados-decalidad/convocatorias-avisos-y-resultados/4165-listado-pnpc-2014/file, 12 de September de 2014.

Table 3. 2014 Registered Postgraduate Education Programmes in PNPC

Stream		Doctorate	Master's Degree		Specialty	Subtotal	Total
			Professional	Research			
PNP	International Competence	0	0	0	0	0	8
	Consolidated	2	0	5	1	8	
PFC	In progress	6	10	2	2	20	28
	Recent Creation	1	6	1	0	8	
	TOTAL	9	16	8	3	36	36

Source: (CONACyT, 2014). National Programme of Quality Postgraduate Studies. 2014 Current Programmes. In www.conacyt.mx/index.php/becas-y-posgrados/programa-nacional-de-posgrados-decalidad/convocatorias-avisos-y-resultados/4165-listado-pnpc-2014/file, September 12, 2014.

Table 4. 2010 Registered Postgraduate Education Programmes in PNPC

Stream		Doctorate	Master's Degree		Specialty	Subtotal	Total
			Professional	Research			
PNP	International Competence	1	0	0	0	1	18
	Consolidated	3	2	9	3	17	
PFC	In progress	2	6	5	0	13	21
	Recent Creation	0	5	2	1	8	
	TOTAL	6	13	16	4	39	39

Source: (CONACyT, 2010). National Programme of Quality Postgraduate Studies. 2010 Current Programmes. In http://www.conacyt.mx/Calidad/Listado_PNPC.pdf, February 19, 2010.

Also, the total number of programmes that have been registered in the PFCP is 443, only 12 correspond to postgraduate education (10 are located and developing and 2 and newly created) representing 3%, which is also a small proportion compared to the total registered corresponding to other areas of knowledge, such as engineering, medicine, mathematics, biotechnology, among others, meaning training of educational researchers reduced national quality, and what a strong impact programs the generation of scientific, social, humanistic and innovation for the country (Cardoso & Cerecedo, 2011) knowledge.

CURRENT STATUS OF GRADUATE EDUCATION IN MEXICO

As a matter of fact, the situation of graduate education in both the PNP and the PFCP can be explained because the CONACyT has established an evaluation criteria, that in the search for quality and efficiency, have decoupled the disciplines related to education. The parameters of the PNPC emphasize restricted notions related to the needs of the productive and technological productivity, among others, all directly linked with the natural and exact sciences and engineering. In this sense, the standards set in the programme and the assessment done by this latter are the same for both of these areas as well as for education, leaving aside the nature and orientation of each field of knowledge (Cardoso & Cerecedo, 2011).

Also, (Cardoso & Cerecedo, 2011), mention that in scientific and technological areas the culmination of graduate training (theory) is reflected in results and tangible products, such as prototyping and machinery; while for the area of education, this process is much longer, as it involves the construction of a complex argument based on the historical, economic, political and cultural background of the research object, together with a number of reasons supporting the study. Thus, there are several indicators that directly affect the graduate programmes in education, like the possibility of being accredited by the CONACyT such as terminal efficiency criteria, joint publications pupil / teacher; the realization of student-teacher and linkage to the service sector research. It is therefore necessary to establish criteria and indicators for each area of knowledge, to consider the nature and orientation of the graduate programmes, and to establish institutional arrangements in order to consolidate the postgraduate education at national level and, then, international level, from increasing their quality and relevance to the country's social and educational needs.

KNOWLEDGE MANAGEMENT IN GRADUATE EDUCATION IN MEXICO

The dynamics of the emerging knowledge society acquire a decisive role in the social and cultural systems of all nations. The educational systems, since the last century, have become one of the cornerstones of economic and social development of the nation states. Today they are immersed in the transformations of knowledge society and knowledge economy. These transformations are disrupting the nature of the schools that were organized and developed in the late nineteenth and early twentieth century in response to the then emerging modern industrial societies.

Thus, school systems are involved in two complementary dynamics that exert pressure and raise demands for radical transformation: one dynamic questions the school's historical function as a main source of knowledge production and trade in the educational and training processes. In the information society, competition from other areas, other sources and other forms of knowledge production and training are present and they are valued and socially accepted as "places of knowledge" (Castells, 2006).

The other dynamic is questioning the identity of the school as an institution responsible for transmitting and teaching new generations in a context of education decentralization and of transmission of information and knowledge for learning social skills and experiencing a productive life in a context of insecurity, uncertainty and complexity of transformation of family-school, and school-productive areas (Hargreaves, 1996) relationships.

Similarly, in knowledge society, not only learning and teaching are valued; but also the different sets of learning taking place in alternative school spaces and organizations, through the modalities and times facing the structure and the school's transmitting and forming identity, which is, which also referred to as "relational capital (RC)". Learning for social life and professional skills are no longer the almost exclusive preserve of the school's learning environment, so the schools (RC) are forced to become organizations that teach other organizations from problems and projects in the social and economic life. In this dynamic, learning, face-to-face knowledge acquired in groups in school classrooms, reach new meanings over other forms of e-learning, where the groups, sometimes formed as practicing communities, share interests visions and common problems that go beyond local areas and cultural references. Today you learn with others and others, we learn in groups of great diversity of age, gender, experience and culture, real and virtual contexts, and practicing communities (Wenger, McDermott & Synder, 2002).

Therefore, these dynamics pose a dilemma for schools (RC) or become learning organizations, open and related contexts, social and productive scenarios; or, they stagnate as obsolete and dislocated institutions from the knowledge society's dynamics. This dilemma also arises to teachers: Either to join the dynamics of change, and instead of teaching, they - become learners in the teaching process. In other words, from being individual teaching practitioners into people who teach and learn in groups and in a collaborative way; from content-centered teaching to be those who facilitate and lead the construction of situated, meaningful and reflective learning. Otherwise, they would live the effects of obsolescence and inadequacy as trainers in the knowledge society, with the consequent emptiness of professional, social and personal meaning and staff (Minakata, 2000).

In the knowledge society economy, these transformations of schools (CR), social groups and individuals and learning organizations have as a condition the incorporation of new information and communication technologies to their educational practices, and with them the ability to function as organizations of the Information Society period. None the less, this situation is not enough unless it is accompanied by adequate knowledge management, so these institutions can move from only pertaining to a modern society towards the times of knowledge society and knowledge economy.

However, schools (RC), as they currently exist in the dynamics of social change, where the generation of goods and human satisfactors depend increasingly on the capacity to generate, distribute and use the knowledge associated with the learning capabilities in a flexible, continuous and collaborative manner. In this context, learning, rather than teaching, becomes the center of gravity and the dynamic axis of the organizational development of groups and individuals.

In addition to the school's today's demands of training students for life; preparing new generations in a context of technological and economic change, with processes that extend to all stages of life, it is required to teach around the values of cooperation, solidarity, tolerance, acceptance and coexistence. Knowledge management and learning for life are two demands that the knowledge society poses to school.

As a matter of fact, it is questioned, What does this knowledge management consist of for generating the necessary changes in the educational systems and schools (RC) in order to turn them into institutions belonging to the knowledge society?, How is a school organization formed to teach in a learning organization that performs knowledge management through information and communication technologies?, Which provisions, values and skills do teachers require as a professional that learns to learn by teaching in the knowledge society by using the information and communication technologies? What functions would schools perform legitimately?, the ones which either handle or not knowledge management in the new society of knowledge and learning?

The assumption underlying these questions is that school institutions and education professionals can be transformed into their nature, functions, structure and organization to join the dynamics of the knowledge society; that knowledge management is a necessary constituent of the mobilization and revitalization of the school's organization, actors, managers, administrators, teachers, students and families for the institutional transformation. It consists mainly in the transition from an organization structured to teaching to a learning-centered one that learns by managing knowledge.

Thus, the meaning of knowledge management is studied from the school's transformation, as the assumption that knowledge management will be in the future one of the central elements of the institutional transformation of the schools (RC) constituting the school's educational system in Mexico that incorporate into the dynamics of the knowledge society. The differences among the schools (RC) of different levels, locations and socio cultural contexts, of the populations they serve and the resources at their disposal will be determinants of knowledge management as well as the dynamics of differential incorporation of these to the society knowledge, characterized by a widespread access to the information and communication technologies and by their relationship with knowledge economy.

Similarly, it is foreseen that knowledge management is a determinant to reproduce, and, maybe, to sharpen the differences and inequities among the schools (RC) and their modalities. Among those schools that whether include or not knowledge management processes and technologies. It is estimated, in this scenario, that a policy will be necessary to affect the conditions of differential access to economic, technological and human resources of the schools (RC) in areas and sectors of great social exclusion in order to lessen the effects of the "society's exclusion from the knowledge that tends to replace the own exploitation ratio of held by the industrial society" (Tedesco, 2000).

Besides knowledge management in the schools is a phenomenon that is being recently recognized, so that it cannot be spoken as a field of knowledge and practice already established. It is therefore important to examine how, in what context and for what purposes knowledge management originates, what elements are present in the process of constitution of the field and how it is incorporated into the educational environment and school organizations. This contextualization serves as a reference for identifying areas of organization and school practices which may constitute a knowledge management with the potential to transform the school into an institution of knowledge society.

VISION OF GRADUATE STUDENTS EDUCATION FOCUSED ON KNOWLEDGE MANAGEMENT

The students are a source of knowledge which in turn enables them to acquire a set of skills, including knowledge management in the educational sphere, is a relatively new subject that aims to reach the present generation, interacting with students or intellectual capital (IC), and information technology in order to capture, produce, process, disseminate, store and use knowledge. Therefore, if the students adopt it as a tool in education, they are more likely to generate constructive changes that result in a better quality of learning.

On the other hand, within the competences to be practiced, they will have the opportunity to include a systemic evaluation, which is characterized by being complex, i.e., comprehensive and interrelation with which manages information with a holistic view, taking into account components of each system, with the main aim to enrich the knowledge.

By assessing the perspective the Mexican students of postgraduates in education hold about knowledge management systemically, it will be possible to recognize and reassess the quality of teaching, as it is characterized much more than a skill or competence. In fact, it is considered as a virtue that defines a lifestyle and allows the elements to adapt to the circumstances and environmental pressure better. Thus, based on the systemic approach, the main components that the students take into account are:

- **Inputs:** Academic staff, students, curriculum, supporting infrastructure, officials and administrators, set of laws, rules and regulations, objectives and goals of the program.
- **Processes:** Teaching - learning, research and development of educational projects, operation of collegiate bodies or basic academic centers, admission, retention and student certification, acquisition, use, operation and maintenance of infrastructure.
- **Results:** Image in society, learning achieved by the students, number of graduates and academic products.

Thus, it is noteworthy that every graduate student in education has different ways of interacting with information, therefore he develops and expresses differently, and understanding turns dissimilar, as well as the results are conclusive. There will be various types of thoughts, however, each one will highlight a complex concept in common, and, thus, achieve a synergistic point, taking place as a knowledge society.

Similarly, the study will provide a systematic evaluation of the characteristics of knowledge management from the perspective of students in graduate education in Mexico, with respect to the generation cycle - storage - distribution - use and generalization of knowledge as established (Nonaka & Takeuchi, 1995), to design academic management strategies for strengthening the human capital that these educational programmes hold.

For this to take place, it is also relevant to determine the information (concepts, experiences, ideas, etc.), that cannot be stored so individualistic, however, has to be shared. The larger the opening, the better the communication, collaboration and incorporation of new data, leading to a point of enrichment and intellectual affinity among the students that make up postgraduate education in Mexico. Therefore, this research will provide academic management strategies aimed at three levels: a) Knowledge Construction; b) Knowledge Development, and c) Knowledge Consolidation.

STUDY METHODOLOGY

The methodology of this research is evaluative type, because the object of study will be evaluated based on the criteria of effectiveness, efficiency, relevance, equity and relevance (Cardoso & Cerecedo, 2011). The research is not experimental, because it does not change or manipulate the object of study, in this case, the perspective by the graduate students in education, regarding management of knowledge in postgraduate education in Mexico. It is framed as a quantitative study with an explanatory scope, as it aims to systemically assess the understanding that the graduate students in education have about knowledge management and implementation. The research design is cross-sectional, since it will only be applied at once through a research instrument (questionnaire) in order to obtain the necessary information to evaluate knowledge management systemically.

OPERATIONALIZATION OF VARIABLES

To carry out the above questionnaire, various features to be studied were identified, and referred to as a system of variables, where the term "variable" means any characteristic or quality of reality that is capable of assuming different values. In other words, that even if it can vary, for a particular object under consideration, it may have a fixed value. When variables are complex and summarise or integrate a multitude of different aspects, one must resort to subdivide or break the variable into simpler qualities and, therefore, easier to measure. These sub-qualities, which together make up the variable, are called dimensions (Sabino, 1992).

By size it is understood, a significant component of a variable that has a relative autonomy, as it is considering the variable as an aggregate complex of elements that give a unique synthetic product (Sabino, 1992). Synthetic variables, also called constructs, represent an indicator composed of a set of intermediate variables, each one of them helps explain some feature of the concept whose magnitude needs to be synthesized. To prepare the constructs, there is no specific and generic rule in the integration of the responses of intermediate variables (Silva, 1997).

However, simple indicators or true variables are the facts that correspond to the theoretical concepts of interest for the study of synthetic constructs or variables, through their concrete, practical and measurable expressions. The process of finding indicators that provide insight into the behavior of the variable is then what is called operationalization of the variable (Sabino, 1992).

In this sense, knowledge management is a multidimensional construct that manifests itself through different characteristics and organizational capabilities. Moreover, knowledge management can be considered as a model in which the dimensions, that are non-observable, represent the construct, and each dimension is represented by the construct is an abstraction from higher order size. The dimensions are themselves constructs governed as manifestations of a more general construct, so they can have sub-dimensions. As a result, the overall construct, in this case, knowledge management can be represented as an integration of dimensions, sub-dimensions and indicators (Lara, 2005). For the purpose of this research, the system of variable operationalization was designed to study the knowledge management construct and components, based on the postgraduate student's perspective.

That is why then the variable knowledge management, which is defined as a strategy that builds capacities in order to originate, store, transfer, apply and protect the organizational knowledge, with the aim to increase the intellectual capital of the production chains, within the cycle of knowledge, as well as based on projects, specific needs and an innovative environment. Likewise, the knowledge management elements are described through intellectual capital, which integrates the human, structural and relational capital, which can be defined as a support for the development of graduate educational institutions in Mexico. The dimension of this development are: the use of ICT, the improvement of internal processes, the relationships with the environment and economy. The operationalization of this variable can be seen in Table 5.

Table 5. Independent variable operationalization: Knowledge management

Variable	Dimension	Sub-Dimension
Knowledge management	Human Capital	Creation of education academies.
		Initial diagnosis of researchers of knowledge management.
		Analysis of possible research opportunities of knowledge management.
		Creation of research lines for knowledge management.
		Conferences for conceptualization of research for the knowledge management.
		Diplomate on preparation for researchers of knowledge management.
		Incentive programmes for the strengthening of researchers for the knowledge management.
	Structural capital	Aid materials for the participation in school invitations and for the elaboration of research projects.
		Procedure diagrams for the integration of files of technological projects.
		Aid manuals for the standardization of guidelines for research guidance.
		Aid congresses for the workshops and preparation for researchers.
		Design, implementation and use of multimedia materials for the integration of researchers' files.
		Design, implementation and use of web pages.
		Use of virtual libraries.
	Relational capital	Participation strategy for researchers in workshops and internal and external school invitations.
		Strategy for the dissemination of products generated from research projects by the bodies of academicians.
		Presentation of research results as congress speakers.
		Dissemination of research results generate in the institution by the establishment of internal disseminated programmes (magazines and forums).
		Participation in the national system of researchers
		Encounter of bodies of academicians and the productive sector.
		Generation of collaborative networks among bodies of academicians.

Source: Own elaboration.

PROPOSAL RESEARCH INSTRUMENT (QUESTIONNAIRE)

National Polytechnic Institute: School of Commerce and Administration, St. Tomas Campus

Section of Postgraduate Studies and Research

This questionnaire is the instrument on a draft systemic evaluation of knowledge management, referring to the prospect that students have postgraduate education in Mexico, applied to postgraduate education. Its purpose is to identify the perception of students about their responsibilities related to knowledge management. The information you provide will be anonymous and confidential.

SCHOOL/COLLEGE: ______________________________
POSTGRADUATE: ______________________________
SEMESTER: ____________

1. AGE: _______
2. Sex: Male Female

Instructions: Note with an "X" the option that you think is right based on your level of competence. The scale used is: 0 (undeveloped), 1 (sufficient), 2 (regular), 3 (good) to 4 (excellent). And accurately shown in Table 6.

CONCLUSION

Arising from economic globalization, knowledge management implemented in the postgraduate education in Mexico, through the information and communication technologies, turns out to be a strategy for educating graduate postgraduate students better. On this behalf, an institutional change may be possible, which results in innovation and continuous improvement, by making use of tangible and intangible resources, such as the cycle of knowledge generation, infrastructure, research, schools and other tools mentioned previously, in order to enrich knowledge successfully, achieving a further technological development.

The systemic evaluation of knowledge management, according to the Mexican postgraduate student's perspective, was conceptually presented by describing the general characteristics of knowledge management, as well as the status of the postgraduate educational programmes registered in the National Programme of Quality Postgraduate Studies 2010. This evaluation included a comparative study of the 2014 PNPC postgraduate educational studies 2014, resulting in a decrease in the number of registered postgraduate educational programmes by the year 2014.

Owing to the above situation, concerning the decreasing result, it is important to consider it as reference to involve knowledge management in postgraduate education in Mexico, as well as the application of a systemic evaluation for observing today's situation, from a general perception to a particular one, so that the characteristics can be integrated synergically, achieving an eclectic situation and concept.

In addition that the postgraduate students in education in Mexico are characterized by counting on a privileged space compared to any other postgraduate programmes, because they can make use of knowl-

Table 6. Proposal research instrument (questionnaire)

COMPETENCE Knowledge Management	0	1	2	3	4
1. Identify the concept of knowledge management					
2. Find information in electronic sources (magazines, articles, books, blogs, websites, virtual libraries)					
3. Find information on paper sources (books, manuals, magazines, mind maps)					
4. Share and disseminate scientific information					
5. Design strategies to improve your self-taught learning					
6. Identify knowledge management systems					
7. To involve knowledge management with your curriculum					
8. Use strategies to study before an exam					
9. Linking knowledge management with learning					
10. Having an incentive program (Grant) for your study					
11. Having support materials for participation in talks					
12. Attend national conferences at least 2 times per year					
13. Attend international conferences at least 2 times per year					
14. Employ thesis published to enrich schoolwork					
15. Communicate in writing, by the standards of science					
16. Communicate orally, by the standards of science					
17. Management of basic level office software					
18. Handling intermediate office software					
19. Management of advanced level office software					
20. Design, implementation and use of multimedia materials for presentations					
21. Management and use of hardware (lap top, PC, digital tablets, printers)					
22. Mastering the English language in writing					
23. Mastering the English language to translate text					
24. Mastering the English language orally					
25. Mastering the English language by listening to a conversation					
26. Perform teams to exchange knowledge with your school mates					
27. Having links exchange knowledge with teachers					
28. Perform linking knowledge sharing with other national schools					
29. Having knowledge exchange links with the productive sector					
30. Having knowledge exchange links with international schools					

Source: Own elaboration.

edge. On this behalf, the students remain as a key element that besides promoting their own specific knowledge-guided education, they also generate it at the same time.

Therefore, this research is a contribution focused on the academic bodies willing to consider knowledge management in the postgraduate programmes, as well as its systemic evaluation, in order to achieve higher quality learning, research projects, social and technological development, by strengthening the postgraduate programmes in education, optimizing resources, and improving results. The aim would be to locate more knowledge societies that change and adapt according to the environment.

In this regard, knowledge management is relevant for postgraduate studies in Mexico, because they constitute a substantial part of the country. This is due to the fact that education is responsible for building and teaching all the existing professional programmes in the world, counting implicitly on knowledge management.

As a result, it is important to evaluate knowledge management systemically in the postgraduate studies in Mexico, through the students' approach. Hence, this study proposes a research instrument constructed thoroughly for the collection of information about how knowledge management is systemically performed.

REFERENCES

Alavi, M., & Leidner, D. (2001). Knowledge Management and Knowledge Management Systems: Conceptual Foundations and Research Issues. *Management Information Systems Quarterly*, *25*(1), 107–136. doi:10.2307/3250961

Andersen, A. (1999). *Knowledge Management Assessment.* KMAT.

Anderson, D., & Gallini, N. (1998). *Competition policy and intellectual property rights in the knowledge based economy.* Calgary: University of Calgary Press.

Bunc, M. (1992). Global economy in the age of science-based knowledge. New York: UNITAR.

Burkle, M., & Robles, H. (2004). *Hacia la construcción de indicadores del conocimiento: Una perspectiva desde el desarrollo.* Retrieved from www.cibersociedad.net

Cardoso, E., & Cerecedo, M. (2011). Propuesta de Indicadores para Evaluar la Calidad de un Programa de Posgrado en Educación. *Revista Electrónica de Investigación Educativa*, *13*(2), 68–82.

Castells, M. (2006). The Network Society: from Knowledge to Policy. Center for Transatlantic Relations. Center for Transatlantic Relations.

CONACyT. (2014). *Programa Nacional de Posgrados de Calidad. Programas vigentes.* Retrieved 2014, from www.conacyt.mx/index.php/becas-y-posgrados/programa-nacional-de-posgrados-de-calidad/convocatorias-avisos-y-resultados/4165-listado-pnpc-2014/file

Hargreaves, A. (1996). *Profesorado, cultura y posmodernidad. Cambian los tiempos, cambia el profesorado.* Madrid, España: Morata.

Lara, P. (2005, Noviembre). Gestión de contenidos en el e-learning: acceso y uso de objetos de información como recurso estratégico. *Revista de Universidad y Sociedad del Conocimiento, 2*(2).

Minakata, A. (2000). El maestro que aprende: educación para una nueva época. *Sinéctica,* (17), 14-23.

Nonaka, I. & Takeuchi, H. (1995). *The Knowledge-Creating Company.* Oxford, UK: Oxford University Press.

OCDE. (2002). *Working Party on Indicators for the Information Society.* Estocolmo.

OCDE/GD. (1996). The knowledge based-economy. *OCDE*, *102*(96), 11.

PND. (2013-2018). *Plan Nacional de Desarrollo*. Retrieved from http://pnd.gob.mx/

Sabino, C. (1992). *El Proceso de Investigación*. Caracas, Venezuela: Panamericana.

Schwartz, D. (2006). *Encyclopedia of Knowledge Management*. Idea Group Reference. doi:10.4018/978-1-59140-573-3

SEP. (2013-2014). *DGPyEE, Formatos 911*. Retrieved 2013, from http://www.sep.gob.mx/es/sep1/programa_sectorial_de_educacion_13_18#.UzU7sPmSyz4

Silva, L. (1997). *Cultura Estadística e Investigación Científica en el Campo de la Salud: Una Mirada Crítica*. La Habana, Cuba: Díaz de Santos.

Tedesco, J. (2000). *Educar en la sociedad del conocimiento*. Buenos Aires, Argentina: FCE.

Wenger, E., McDermott, R., & Synder, W. (2002). Cultivating Communities of Practice: a Guide to Managing Knowledge. Harvard Business School Press.

KEY TERMS AND DEFINITIONS

Complexity: The state or quality of being constructed by several elements.

Distribution: The action of sharing something among a number of receivers.

Entries: The information, graduate students in education in Mexico, circumstances, academic material entering a system.

Generalization: A general declaration or concept obtained by inference from particular cases.

Generation: Knowledge production and information enrichment.

Information and Communications Technology (ICT): They are a set of services, networks, software and gadgets that aim to improve the quality of life of people in an environment, and that are integrated into a system of interconnected and complementary information.

Intellectual Capital: It includes human capital, structural capital and relational capital to form the knowledge economy.

Processes: A series of action or measurements adopted with the purpose or meeting a particular aim.

Results: Objectives achieved through research, study and investigation.

Storage: A storing action or method for the future use of information and knowledge.

System: Is the union of parts or components connected in an organized way. The meeting or set of related elements, which can be concepts, objects, subject, Therefore a system is an aggregate of living or non-living entities or both.

Thoughts: The thinking act or process; deliberation, reflection, a concept, an opinion or an idea.

Chapter 3
The Influence of the Labor Sector in Knowledge Management:
The Case of Graduate in Business Administration for Sustainability

Leticia Refugio Chavarria
Instituto Politécnico Nacional, Mexico

Edgar Oliver Cardoso Espinosa
Instituto Politécnico Nacional, Mexico

ABSTRACT

Institutions of higher education in Mexico, play a role in human development systems, since they are the generators of academic and professional knowledge and skills to meet the challenges of the country and the world. In what has reflected the state as concern through the national education system is one that relates to the training of professionals with a profile that meets the expectations of an increasingly demanding business world and global day. Postgraduate studies have undergone a series of transformations due to its expansion, diversification, and the demands that today's society presents them, and that has forced them to make a thorough review of its programs in order to improve quality and meet the formation of high level human capital. The chapter aims to: Analyze the importance of knowledge management and its relationship with labor and that this contributes to train competent specialists, who know the technologies and tools for the sustainable management and protection of the environment.

DOI: 10.4018/978-1-5225-0457-3.ch003

INTRODUCTION

This section is intended to describe how they have influenced the theories of human capital in knowledge management.

According to Suárez (1997) Theory of Human Capital takes as its basis the principles of neoclassical economic theory and functionalist sociology based on maximizing profits and benefits as well as the balancing market mechanisms. The labor market is considered as a homogeneous entity, composed of employees and employers who are facing each other for market sell buy what you need: the worker sells his labor and employer purchase. The salary that is assigned to each worker depends on productivity, directly related to their educational level. (Fernandez J., p.32, 2013).

The theory of human capital from its origins until today, remains an influential conceptual vision in the context of globalization, because it regards education as an investment that will generate profit in the future and promotes various forms of economic growth: Rate labor, technical production, research, physical mobilization and optimization of functional mobility. See Table 1: Origins and evolution of the theory of human capital.

The theory of human capital has a close relationship with the economics of education, because according Fermoso (1997), both are aimed to investigate regarding: costs, financing, planning, socio-economic growth, education and employment, among others factors.

From this perspective, education is seen as an investment, as a form of capital that integrates production which increases individual productivity and influences economic growth of society. (P.33 J. Fernandez, 2013).

Gary Becker (1964) defines human capital theory "as a set of skills that an individual acquires by accumulating general or specific knowledge of human capital theory distinguishes two ways of training:

1. The general training acquired in the education, training system. Transferability and purchase the worker explains that is underwritten by the latter, because it can enforce it on the entire labor market.
2. The specific training acquired within a unit of production or service, can develop worker productivity within the company, but nothing, or very little, beyond. In this case, the funding is secured at the same time by the company and the worker.

One can say that the history of mankind is divided into three stages or ages are chronologically: the agrarian age, the industrial and knowledge. It also indicates that knowledge becomes the economies of the late twentieth century and early twenty-first century the main source of wealth creation, and increasingly is making inroads affirming Laurence Prusak (1996).

According to Mary Parker Follett, when he defined the government as "getting results through people", the success or failure of organizations follows the commitment, skills, knowledge and contributions of its employees.

But to talk of commitment the company has to provide people with opportunities for participation, where they can contribute their creativity, their energy and their "good work", as these are the strategic resource in the company. In the care of the resource is the key to any commitment to the organization. Valencia (2005).

Table 1. Origins and evolution of the theory of human capital

Principal Author	Year	Information	Variables
Adam Smith	1776	Anticipates the definition of human capital: includes explicitly as part of the fixed capital of each nation, acquisition and maintenance of skills and knowledge that can be used to create wealth by workers.	Human Capital Growth, creation of wealth of a nation
Jacob Mincer	1958	The influence of variables such as education and experience in determining differences in income among workers.	Education and Income
Arrow	1962	The production capacity of workers improved with experience at work.	Production capacity and work experience.
Gary Becker	1964	Human capital is a decision that involves many periods: some initial periods, which is done investment spending, and a subsequent, where profits are gathered. Thus, in the case of the company, the costs (expenses) of training are opposed to the higher future labor productivity (profits).	Human capital formation, investment spending and benefits.
Theodore Shultz	1968	Production factors crucial to improving the welfare of the poor are not space, energy and the availability of arable land; the decisive factors are the improvement of the quality of the population and advances in knowledge.	Improving the quality of the population, advances in knowledge
Spence	1973	Workers invest in education to send a signal to its best potential employers. For their part, employers link their wage offers to the level of education of workers precisely because high wage offer intended to ensure that workers self-select themselves: candidates who are more productive	Level of education and wage offer.
Edward Denison	1979	He was one of the pioneers in stop considering education as a commodity and start considering it as a form of capital	Education and Capital
Mushkin	1980	Who said to understand the importance of education as a factor in capital formation is useful to think of the analogy of how natural resources of a nation, can not by themselves without improvements lead end products with a high value added.	Education and training Human Capital
Blaug	1983	Their study is done from the perspective of methodological individualism, that is, from the perspective of all social phenomena should be studied starting from its foundation in individual behavior.	Individualism and social phenomena.
Fermoso	1997	Education as an important factor in the formation of human capital, is conceived in two ways, as consumption and investment.	Human capital formation, consumption and investment
David O´connor	2002	Investment in Human Capital and economic openness associated technology. Of all the factors considered individual talent is a key element when designing educational policies, because if the differences in education levels are due to differences in the talents of individuals, there is no reason, from the perspective of efficiency, to facilitate access to education	Investment in Human Capital, economic openness and technology
Checchi	2006	Of all the factors considered individual talent is a key element when designing educational policies, because if the differences in education levels are due to differences in the talents of individuals, there is no reason, from the perspective of efficiency, to facilitate access to education	Individual talent, education policies and access to education.

Source: Prepared based on Villalobos Monroy, G. & Pedroza Flores, R. (2009)

1. KNOWLEDGE MANAGEMENT AND SKILLS DEVELOPMENT IN THE CURRICULA

Knowledge is a mix of experiences, values and information that serves as a framework for evaluation, integration and sharing them within an organization, it is essential for countries to have a competitive advantage in the globalized world resource. In this sense, institutions of higher education are configured as a structural element of the development of knowledge, since they are responsible for the formation of advanced human capital, contributing significantly to the research, development and innovation manner. Rodriguez-Ponce, (2014).

Educational reforms require guidance and implementation guidelines for teachers and accurate tracking because it implies a paradigm shift in educational practice. However, the possibility of developing skills is only possible in the activity. It is important to state that the powers exist for the need to resolve problems and situations. When a competency-based curriculum design is performed. Skills are developed through active and reflective learning that solve problems in a particular context of the profession, mobilizing diverse knowledge: learning to know, know-how and know how to be.

The paradigm of competencies poses a holistic view of education, which can integrate the education of the intellect, the will and the effectiveness and implying a personalized education to train the whole person, to undertake a profound change education that meets the current challenges facing humanity, globalization, rapid progress of ICT has generated new types of social relationships and society to be called information society where it has opened a competitive labor market It has taken us from the logic of content to the logic of action, pollution has increased in recent times forces us has to establish links between schools and society to face together and solve these problems that have generated growth the population and industry.

Indeed, the powers are justified in resolving the great problems of the profession. Move to the logic of action, this means from a problem or situation that generates the necessary context to engage in the task motivation.

This allows the activation of knowledge (both of which are owned as new), skills and attitudes and skills to intervene in the solution, which will encourage new skills and improving existing ones.

According to Lev Semenovich Vygotsky (1979) situated learning considers the social construction of reality is based on cognition and practical action that takes place in everyday life. This refers to an active learning in context and allowing linkages between the school of life, the classroom and the community through authentic educational practices to address real problems in real situations where interaction with others.

Program graduates, employers of graduates, current students and teachers who teach the program: to conduct a curriculum, following consultation of audiences is necessary.

All this is an integrated process through the following phases:

1. Determine who possess skills and profiles of graduates.
2. Establishment of a committee to design (or redesign) curriculum.
3. Consultation for the determination of the action areas of the graduate, the result of an analysis of both internal and external context.
4. Determine:
    a. General skills.
    b. disciplinary skills.

5. Construction of the graduate profile and internal and external validation.
6. Developing the skills matrix and traceability (crosses between disciplinary and generic skills.
7. Perform integration into the matrix of traceability of the subjects, units of learning modules with generic and disciplinary skills.
8. Internal and external validation of the skills matrix.
9. Determination of the expected learning outcomes.
10. Establishment of the program curriculum.
11. Structuring of each of the specific programs, taking into account at least:
    a. Generic and specific competences.
    b. Dimensions.
    c. Evidence.
    d. Criteria and indicators.
12. Development of an evaluation plan for implementation.
13. Implementation.
14. Evaluation and feedback throughout the process. (J. Pepper, 2012).

2. THE MASTERS AND THE NATIONAL DEVELOPMENT PLAN 2013-2018 IN MEXICO

This PND in the introduction to Chapter III Mexico with Quality Education says that education should foster skills and comprehensive abilities of each person, while instilling values which defends personal dignity and that of others.

To achieve quality education, it is required to study plans and programs are appropriate, making it a priority to reconcile the educational offer to social needs and requirements of the productive sector.

In addition, compared with the challenges posed by the globalization of knowledge, it is necessary to strengthen policies of internationalization of education, using an approach that considers the coherence of curricula and mobility of students and academics.

The graduate represents the top level of the education system and is the main route for the formation of highly specialized professionals requiring industry, business, science, culture, art, medicine and public service, among others. Mexico faces the challenge of boosting graduate as a factor for the development of scientific research, technological innovation and competitiveness that the country needs for efficient integration into the information society.

One of the most notable features of the Mexican case is the separation between actors related to the development of science and technology, and activities of the business sector.

34% of participants in the Citizen Consultation agreed on the importance of this idea for the development of the country. The business sector has historically contributed little to investment in research and development, contrariaa situation is observed in other OECD member countries, where this sector accounts for over 50% of the total investment in this area. This is partly a result of the lack of private sector engagement with groups and centers in the country scientific and technological research, as well as the lack of more private research centers.

While there have been significant achievements in some areas (such as biotechnology, environment, engineering, etc.), increased public and private investment must go hand in hand with strengthening communication mechanisms to translate into higher productivity. It is necessary to align the views of all stakeholders in the CTI system for enterprises to leverage existing capabilities in higher education institutions and public research centers.

Finally, to the scientific, technological development and innovation pillars for sustainable economic and social progress, a strong link between schools, universities, research centers and the private sector is required. In addition, it should increase public investment and encourage private investment in innovation and development activities. Efforts to transfer and use of knowledge will add value to Mexican products and services, and enhance the competitiveness of the national workforce.

The National Council for Science and Technology (CONACYT) is a public agency of the Mexican federal government dedicated to promote and stimulate the development of science and technology in that country. It has official responsibility for developing policies national science and technology.

Through Conacyt is possible for students to get financial support to postgraduate studies (master or doctorate) in universities with academic excellence recognized within and outside the country.

There is a CONACYT program that evaluates and accredits graduate programs offered by institutions of higher education in Mexico. Those programs that meet high quality criteria are considered as part of the National Register of Postgraduate Quality (PNPC). (Pnd.gob.mx p.65-68).

3. THE CASE OF GRADUATE IN BUSINESS ADMINISTRATION FOR SUSTAINABILITY

The National Polytechnic Institute is an innovative, flexible educational institution focused on the development of knowledge through a research model based on networks of national and international cooperation, fully linked to the production, trade and social sectors, which encourages the generation, use, circulation and protection of knowledge in strategic sectors that promote competitiveness, equity and improvement of society

For decades, postgraduate studies are a phenomenon that has marked the course of the School of Commerce and Administration, Unit St. Thomas IPN, towards the formation of human capital capable of solving problems and propose solutions to all companies so they require.

The November 14, 2014, was published in extraordinary gazette IPN, a new curriculum that aims to meet the demand that we have to address all issues related to the sustainability of the company and for this reason is born MBA Business for Sustainability, with the aim of providing a new culture in caring for the environment, is presented with the design of learning units that promote sustainable development and social responsibility.

In this sense, and in accordance with the General Rules of Graduate signed by the community of the National Polytechnic Institute, all the details of the Master are presented in Business Management for Sustainability of professionalizing orientation and specialty options. The proposal presented here has the challenge to respond to these new needs-based building management resources and protecting the environment knowledge, based on the educational model of the National Polytechnic Institute.

Another highlight of this new proposal is that this will be a unique program of its kind since the country although there are several academic institutions offering master's degrees in business administration for sustainability, there is an offer to grant master's degree specialty options with this new plan offers, besides the fact that no other offers graduate training based on business stays contrast to the theory provided in classroom practice that exists within organizations.

The overall objective of this Master is:

Train and develop professionalized teachers with the necessary skills to solve the problems of the productive and commercial sectors, for companies to participate successfully in global markets in which they operate, making rational use of natural capital, protecting the environment and corporate social responsibility.

The importance of the proposal lies in the fact that he designed a flexible graduate focused on the following:

- The comprehensive training that balances knowledge, skills, values, and provides a solid management training.
- Encourage lifelong learning and self-development of the student, ethics and social responsibility.
- Incorporate experiences of teamwork and the development of communication skills in different scenarios.
- Encourage the discovery and construction of knowledge, not only transfer.
- Involve the participant in the globalization movement with sustainable approach.

All units are learning in content mainstreaming towards sustainability and social responsibility.

Moreover, the knowledge society has given it a high priority to human capital where ideas are considered goods that have an impact on economic growth and business results of companies, therefore management is a social discipline which basic postulates invariably change. In the XXI century, the change will be the norm and the central challenge for the company will be lead change through competitiveness through people, skills and resources generated in organizations.

After analyzing the environment sought to identify national development trends in order to determine the occupational field of practice and the future labor market in professional training, in order to identify those aspects relevant to be considered as part of curriculum curriculum.

Based on the above, a program covering a niche market that gives you a competitive advantage by IPN through ESCA Santo Tomas Unit, consisting of imparting a Master of actual type with the following characteristics were designed:

1. A first group of basic materials that achieve the participant develop strategic thinking in business management for sustainability.
2. A second group of subjects, allowing professionalize the participant in one of five areas of development that presents the curriculum map.
3. At one point, the participant will have the opportunity to select a specialty designed for each development area, in original form.
4. The Grandee business will stay with three levels, where you can apply the knowledge gained in selected professionalizing areas, all with a diagnosis period, other design alternatives and finally another implementation.
5. Upon completion of the learning units, participants will have the opportunity to engage in a business simulator, whereby different companies will offer Grandee the chance to compete for international market where they apply knowledge obtained strategic thinking, with a focus on sustainability.
6. Finally, the participant will have two options for obtaining degree.

Based on the above described the curriculum map which is described below design:

- Basic training that consists of 8 learning units for the formation of human capital business.
- Area of professionalisation consists of five area specialties: Finance, Marketing, International Trade, Taxation and Sustainable Development.
- Area of specialization consists of two specialties for each area of professionalization that students may choose an option according to your interests.
- Three business units that will be mandatory in all areas of professionalization
- And finally a business simulator in which all students in all areas converge for decision-making on a specific problem in a business simulator.

Exit Profile

Students graduated from this Master program will develop the following generic competencies.

Generic Skills

- Have a strategic thinking to the management of global companies focus on corporate sustainability.
- Act with strong leadership, to achieve optimum contribution of human capital and thus teamwork decision.
- Be committed to comprehensive sustainable business development that contribute to the improvement of the economy, society and environment.
- Develop the ability to communicate effectively in different forums at national level.

Specific Skills

- Being committed to the rational use of natural capital.
- Promote competitive, interdisciplinary and collaborative work, to manage the rational use of energy.
- Develop the capacity to manage waste and emissions into the environment, in order to reduce environmental damage.
- To act with ethical reasoning, critical thinking and attitude towards sustainability.
- Thus, the Master of Business Administration for Sustainability is designed and aimed for students to understand the strategic aspects of business sustainability and propose feasible solutions in companies in which they operate and to society in general. A primary objective with companies and society is that companies can improve their environmental performance, social responsibility and ethical conduct in business.
- The program of the Master in Business Management for Sustainability responds to the needs of the productive sector and the economic reality of the country as well as the advances in knowledge management.

Finally it is to enter the quality programs CONACYT as newly created program.

REFERENCES

Fernández, J. (2013). *Formación y práctica docente Facultad de ciencias de la educación.* Ediciones D.D.S. México.

Mercado, A., Miyamoto, K., & O'connor, D. (2008). *Inversión extranjera directa: tecnología y recursos humanos en los países en Desarrollo.* El colegio de México. Available at https://books.google.com.mx/books?id=Qmj21zYfSm0C&pg=PA8&lpg=PA8&dq=Teoria+del+Capital+humano+O%C2%B4connor&source=bl&ots=tI7sbPCjE4&sig=YQeXgnkoo7wx_4QdrGCrjxNuZzc&hl=es&sa=X&ei=vW5WVe6CN4SLsAWKwICwBg&ved=0CDUQ6AEwAw#v=onepage&q=Teoria%20del%20Capital%20humano%20O%C2%B4connor&f=false

Pimienta, J. (2012). *Las competencias en la docencia universitaria.* Pearson Educación de México.

Programa Nacional de Desarrollo 2012-2018. (n.d.). Retrieved from pnd.gob.mx/wpcontent/uploads/2013/05/PND.pdfhttp://pnd.gob.mx/

Rodríguez-Ponce, E., Cohen-Hornickel, W., Pedraja-Rejas, L., Araneda-Guirriman, C., & Rodríguez-Ponce, J. (2014). La gestión del conocimiento y la calidad de la docencia de postgrado en las universidades: un estudio exploratorio. INNOVAR. *Revista de Ciencias Administrativas y Sociales, 24*(52), 59-66. Available at http://www.redalyc.org/articulo.oa?id=81830435015

Valencia Rodríguez, M. (2005). El capital humano, otro activo de su empresa. *Entramado, 1*(2), 20-33. Available at http://www.redalyc.org/articulo.oa?id=265420471004

Villalobos Monroy, G., & Pedroza Flores, R. (2009). Perspectiva de la teoría del capital humano acerca de la relación entre educación y desarrollo económico. *Tiempo de Educar, 10*(20), 273-306. Available at http://www.redalyc.org/articulo.oa?id=31112987002

Chapter 4
Organizational Metaphors and the Evaluation of Higher Education Programs, Management Practices, and Change Processes:
A UAE Case Study

Melanie Van Den Hoven
Emirates College for Advanced Education, UAE

David R. Litz
Emirates College for Advanced Education, UAE

ABSTRACT

Utilizing a conceptual framework based on Morgan's (1998) organizational metaphors, this chapter reports on a qualitative study conducted with faculty members to evaluate their experience of a new program and influence change processes in a teacher-training higher educational institution in Abu Dhabi, UAE, during a period of major educational restructuring. With respect to metaphors generated in response to overall perceptions of organizational dynamics, management practices, and change processes, the study demonstrates tensions surrounding access to channels of communication and decision making within the local educational context; however, no overt concerns on culture shock are found. Moreover, many metaphors are consistent with Morgan's original constructs, whereas a number are unique to the localized context. Organizational metaphors may thus be used as a feedback mechanism to guide systemic decision making around change initiatives within this institution, and to stimulate management research in this region and other higher educational settings.

DOI: 10.4018/978-1-5225-0457-3.ch004

INTRODUCTION

This chapter focuses on the major transformation of the K-12 and tertiary education sectors in the United Arab Emirates (UAE) by reporting on an exploratory study on an important dimension of the internationalization of higher education: the experience of foreign instructors.

Since the 1970s, the UAE has increasingly invested in English-medium federal colleges and universities, as well as international branch campuses. Consequently, the UAE has developed a great need for mobile, foreign academics (Knight, 2011, 2013, 2014). The present study targets perceptions of organizational change in a higher educational institution from the perspective of international faculty members who have sought limited-term employment in the UAE as expatriates. Previous studies have examined the individual experience of transitioning to a new academic institution in terms of culture shock (Schoepp, 2011). The current work thus addresses perceptions of managerial practices and organizational change to offer insight into a feedback mechanism relevant for leading an educated, multicultural workforce through change processes in the education sector.

Academic employment in the UAE is framed by rapid educational reform and different management practices, which shape the organizational culture of higher education (Kirk, 2010). Hired on limited-term contracts, foreign academic faculty from a range of countries are at the coalface of educational change (Knight, 2011). For academics in UAE higher educational institutions, a limited-term contract could mean making the most of a short-term commitment. Challenges include pressure to research and publish with a relative lack of academic freedom (Chapman, Austin, Farah, Wilson, & Ridge, 2014), high faculty turnover rates (Schoepp, 2011), Emiratization policies perceived as limiting promotion (Chapman et al., 2014), and students with insufficient English language proficiency (Martin, 2003). More recently, this sector faced restructuring of university programs owing to intensified accreditation processes (Smith, 2009) and threats to job security (Chapman et al., 2014). Arguably, within such a dynamic work environment, the texture of power relations amplifies the need for feedback mechanisms that can reach key decision-makers from the bottom up.

Drawing on Morgan's (1998) conceptual framework of organizational metaphors based on machines, organisms, brains, cultures, political systems, psychic prisons, flux and transformation, instruments of domination, as well as insights from change theory and the social construction of reality, this chapter examines feedback on change and decision-making processes via the metaphors generated by multicultural faculty at a teacher-training educational institution in Abu Dhabi, UAE, during a period of rapid societal transformation. This study aims to draw attention to the insights offered by one feedback mechanism that can benefit educational leaders who must not only contend with organizational change in educational institutions but also the myriad ways that academics respond to the change process.

RATIONALE

The rationale for the study is threefold. First, it targets an under-researched population. Despite the recent draw of international academics to Gulf States (i.e., Bahrain, Kuwait, Oman, Qatar, Saudi Arabia, and the UAE, all members of the Gulf Cooperation Council [GCC]), few scholarly publications in educational management have investigated expatriate academics and their experiences related to the internationalization processes of higher education organizations in the Gulf. Despite massive investments into developing this sector, research on the impacts to academics has been limited. Further, examinations of Gulf higher education institutions are often situated on the periphery of academic discourse (Burden-Leahy, 2009). Second, it targets change processes that characterize educational reforms in this emerging economy. Regional analyses of the UAE's K-12 and adult education sector (e.g., Macpherson, Kachelhoffer, & El Nemr, 2007) do not account for recent change processes, such as the recent bifurcation of the Ministry of Higher Education, development of a non-federal public higher education system in Abu Dhabi, and sudden array of choices provided by international branch campuses. Further, studies specifically targeting faculty members' perceptions of organizational change and the experience of restructuring processes in this unique context of higher education are virtually non-existent. Lastly, and most importantly, research on organizational metaphors in a higher educational context in the UAE can offer broader insights of the relevance of a feedback mechanism for academics and managers, which can enhance current understanding of shared experiences of organizational dynamics and behavior, as well as the impact of particular change initiatives. In other words, when metaphors are liberated from pedagogical purposes in classrooms and applied by academics to their workplaces, a richer and more inclusive discourse of the experience of change in educational organizations should follow.

LITERATURE REVIEW

Metaphors have long been used as linguistic tools to evoke richer understandings of social and individual realities, as well as abstract formulations (Arnold & Crawford, 2014). Regarding educational contexts today, metaphors are familiar teaching tools employed by educators, particularly those teaching literature and language (e.g., Ashton 1997; Lakoff & Johnson 1980; Littlemore 2001; Preston 1982; Shaw & Mahlios, 2013). More recently, organizational theorists have promoted metaphors for enhancing institutional awareness of different management perspectives (Morgan 1998), theories of organizational identity (e.g., Cornelissen, 2006; Jelinek, Smircich, & Hirsch, 1983), and the management of change processes (e.g., Antonacopoulou & Gabriel, 2001; Boyce, 1995; Burnes, 2014; Butcher & Atkinson 2001; Cameron & Green, 2009; Gagliardi 1986; Hall, 2013). In education, metaphors are primarily seen as linguistic concepts guiding, and guided by, thought and perception (e.g., Arnold & Crawford, 2014; Cherkowski & Walker, 2013; Lakoff &Johnson, 1980); whereas in organizational theory, metaphors target the complex meanings created when a characteristic of a concept is mapped onto another, thereby inviting new ways of seeing the strengths and weaknesses of an organization (e.g., Morgan 1998; Smircich, 1983).

To locate the interest in the use of metaphors for examining organizational change and its relevance to higher education institutions in the Gulf, this section examines the literature on language and organizational theory, metaphors of organizations, metaphors of education, and metaphors of change.

Metaphorical Language in Organizational Theory: An Overview

Interest in metaphorical language in organizational theory receives broad support from interpretative frameworks. In particular, semiotics and social constructionist views of language discuss the value of symbolic language for enabling collective sense-making (Boyce, 1995). A core principle is that everyday conversation and other "abstract imaginative structures" (Cornelissen, 2006, p. 867) play important roles in sustaining and expanding mindsets on institutional practices. According to Berger and Luckmann (1966), the construction of a shared reality is supported by daily communication. To elaborate, after primary socialization into the language and culture of the parents' world, secondary processes of socialization begin. Secondary socialization accounts for adulthood membership into other communities, such as those related to employment. During both primary and secondary socialization, language plays a critical role in maintaining a shared reality. Educational organizations, as a type of workplace environment, function as a sub-world in which positions are seen as roles that reflect the division of labor and also determine communication channels.

The recognition that "language is at once socially constructed and a framework for social construction" (Butcher & Atkinson, 2001, p. 554) has been applied to organizational study. Daily conversation and other representations of language, including stories, proverbs, metaphors, symbolic objects, and images on the shared sub-culture, ultimately convey the "experience of collective coordination and orderliness" (Smircich, 1983, p. 341). Through these communicative channels, organizational identities and realities are maintained, or changed, within a larger group or community (Denning, 2002).

Early interest in symbolic language in organizational theory was widespread in the 1980s and 1990s and reflected the importance of management procedures and hierarchal systems (Boyce 1995; Gagliardi, 1986; Keeley, 1980). Organizational metaphors were seen as useful for managers, but not in their own terms, as they require mediation. In early models, change processes are only indirectly referenced as resulting from management decisions on organizational strategies and operational practices. Moreover, the literature was dominated by the centrality of management and leadership in organizational dynamics and systems frameworks (e.g., Burns, 1978; Butcher & Atkinson 2001; Katz & Kahn, 1978). Gradually, metaphors became seen as supporting analyses of change strategies in terms of "identifying resistance to and emotions associated with change" (Butcher & Atkinson 2001, p. 556). As such, symbolic language was primarily viewed as a managerial or administrative tool in organizational development and for building cooperation toward change processes (Mitriff & Kilmann, 1975).

Although symbolic language and metaphors are seen as highly beneficial in specific bottom-up analyses of organizational structures, administrative practices, and change processes, they are not particularly prevalent in the managerial systems literature; they are virtually absent in the Gulf. One notable exception is Argyris and Schön's (1978) influential work on organizational learning, where the case is made for leaders to listen to the anecdotes and stories (i.e., generative metaphors) of other colleagues and subordinates to learn about tacit fears, taboo topics, assumptions, and information on complaints, challenges, and successes. This process could inform the tone of organizational guiding principles and provide vital insights on employees' collective attitudes, understandings, feelings, and commitments to the leadership. Likewise, Boyce's (1995) case study of members of a non-governmental organization used narratives to explore personal beliefs and commonly shared conceptualizations. Symbolic language indicates degrees of alignment to common purposes set by the manager, as opposed to critical examinations of the hierarchical or top-down organizational paradigm from the perspective of subordinates. However, a tendency to regard storytelling as a prelude to change initiatives and change processes as problems needing solutions is evidenced (Butcher & Atkinson 2001; Boyce, 1995; Mitriff & Kilmann, 1975). In other words, the pattern established is that when stories are used, they are reduced to vehicles for explaining new change initiatives.

Metaphors of Organizations

Systems theory is a fundamental component to any discussion on organizations and symbolic language. According to its proponents, human organizations should be viewed as complex, goal-oriented entities, and systems theory attempts to model these types of entities (Checkland, 1999; Katz & Kahn, 1978;

Meadows, 2008). Nevertheless, Morgan's (1998) seminal work on organizational metaphors dominates the discourse on symbolic language and organizational paradigms, partly because Morgan's framework neatly classifies the complexity of organizational worlds into typologies. Morgan indicated that "all organization and management theory is based on images, or metaphors, that lead us to understand situations in powerful yet partial ways [and] we [should] recognize that since every metaphor has limitations as well as strengths, we must always be aware of the inherent blind spots that inevitably undermine our effectiveness" (pp. 3–4). When managers verbalize their organizational metaphors, they reveal their favored ways of managing the organization as well as gaps in attention to other ways and means of managing people, resources, and change processes.

Cornelissen (2006) argued that metaphor interpretation depends on context. Metaphors "gain a certain relative stability by becoming conventionally located in a…community's network of meaning" (p. 690) where the meaning becomes conventionalized by and for the community. In this sense, metaphors "depend upon a large background of shared schemata, capacities, practices and knowledge of the community involved and the meaning generated can be considered as a genuine and meaningful description" (p. 690). Accordingly, Morgan's (1998) framework is useful for understanding bottom-up perceptions of internationalizing higher education organizations as it considers symbolic language to describe the experience of change processes and different organizational paradigms. The framework supports an investigation of how change is refracted through different orientations within the organization and embedded in daily conversations. As the framework is also conceptually clear and insightful, the core principles of popular management styles can be easily classified. Additionally, it introduces leaders and managers to less common models, which can help in re-imagining how organizations can operate from various vantage points. As such, comparing organizational metaphors generated by employees against the framework can correspondingly provide an opportunity to diagnose the work experience of individuals and evaluate its significance within the larger social structure.

According to Morgan, machines, organisms, brains, and cultures are common organizational metaphors. The most prevalent image of an organization is the machine. Machine metaphors are evident when educational organizations, such as schools, school systems, and universities, are compared to the military or vehicles. These types of metaphors can convey contested attitudes toward highly structured, mechanical, or bureaucratic operations. While machine images often convey negative orientations to a hierarchical stratification of power and dehumanization of the teaching staff, they can also carry positive associations when work conditions enhance productivity, efficiency, profit, and job security. However, in many cases, "mechanistic organizations are designed to achieve pre-determined goals [and] are not designed for innovation" (Morgan, 1998, p. 32). Thus, amid forced organizational changes, problems encountered can be ignored and institutional paralysis can ensue. Regarding management practices in higher education institutions, the strength lies in the orderliness of decision-making and goal measurement and a focus on conditions enabling goal attainment, but the weakness is the regimentation of control and a top-down movement of communication. In other words, an over-emphasis on the machine-like functioning of a work environment can impede the vital flow of feedback on change strategies from educators to administrators, who, unlike educators, are often removed from the knock-on effects for students.

Other images with more positive associations of changing educational systems are organism, brain, and culture. These images consider the impact of change in varying perspectives. In contrast to machines, organisms, brains, and cultures represent living entities that learn, adapt, and interact in dynamic environments. The operative theme is synergy, not control. For organisms, survival depends on biological interaction and adaptive responses to the external environment. Further, as open systems, organisms support and are supported by ecological diversity. They also feature self-regulation, based on the "balance or compatibility between strategy, structure, technology, the commitments and needs of people, and the external environment" (Hatch, 1997, p. 49). Organisms possess a self-corrective function that can manage change via adapting to the context at various levels of the system. This type of metaphor stresses the importance of sensitivity to changes in local and global contexts. When applied to educational organizations, images of organisms also support narratives of the birth of an institution, its growth phases and adaptive responses, and its demise (Hannan & Freeman, 1989; Hannan, Polos, & Carroll, 2007).

Brain-like images foreground the role of decentralized modes of decision making and are often supported by networked systems of communication and information technology. Current examples include "knowledge economy" (Hargreaves, 2003) and "learning organization" (Morecroft, Asay, & Sterman, 1994; Senge, 1990). In these metaphors, the operative functions are thinking and learning. The brain-like capacity of an organization supports double-loop learning, where ongoing organizational adaptations to a changing environment are required. In this orientation, educational leaders recognize the existence of different divisions within the whole, each representing different capacities. Leaders must stimulate active intelligence among the staff and faculty to enable ways of cooperating that expand the experience of the average instructor and students. Current practices should be synchronized in ways that enhance thinking, increase ambition, and lead to a shared vision based on organizational progress (Senge, 1990). Thus, when viewed as brains, organizations support members' expansive thinking by empowering employees to think and talk about change, why it is happening, and how the organization can address it. In this way, organizations support intelligent responses to change at the strategic and operational levels. However, this model clashes with traditional views of management and presents a conceptual challenge to managers of large educational organizations: how to eschew central control while balancing free-thinking forces with those resistant to dynamic change.

Organizations can also be viewed as cultures. This perspective has been popularized since the 1980s, as noted when work cultures are described in terms of the social construction of meaningful and purposeful workplace identities (Wenger 1999); the application of cultural dimensions such as beliefs, values, rituals, behaviors, and symbols to organizational entities (Blunt, 1991; Bolman & Deal, 2003; Sashkin & Walberg, 1993; Schein, 1992); and the quantification of cultural differences using national constructs as developed from studies of international employees of a multinational company (Hofstede & Hofstede, 2005; Hofstede, Hofstede, & Minkov, 2010). This orientation highlights understanding social reality via the lens of anthropological descriptions of behavior and thinking patterns. The culture metaphor identifies the vital role of shared meaning in enacting change initiatives, but managers should be aware that tacit and hidden rules are often crucial for understanding responses to change initiatives as well.

Other metaphors that represent novel and less frequent ways of seeing and managing effective organizations concern the degree and quality of orderliness. Organizational metaphors of flux and transformation and political systems highlight the status of chaos and tensions caused by competing interests. However, research using these types of metaphors to manage educational organizations is still limited. Nevertheless, Morgan argued that all of the aforementioned metaphors can be integrated into a synergistic storyline that considers the complex problems and perspectives inherent in an organization, thereby contributing to the shared construction of organizational reality.

In sum, images convey understandings of the objective nature and subjective experiences of an educational organization. The conjoining of one concept, such as higher education institution, with another concept from a different domain, such as lifeboat or sandcastle, creates a mental image in which salient features of the organization's experiences are brought to the foreground. Thus, when generated by individual employees of a university or college, metaphors can reveal lived realities of the management practices of the educational organization, as well as those hopes and ambitions that guide expectations. Daily conversations offer the platform for the expressions of organizational metaphors and lead to the social construction of reality. When contrasted with talk about the ideal workplace, these conversations then support a diagnosis and evaluation of the strengths and weaknesses of the current state of the workplace. Metaphors also promote fresh insights into management practices and expectations because they "create a shared reality in which to act and construct an identity" (Wenger, 1999, p. 178). Although feedback is ultimately valuable for leaders and managers, one clear purpose of exploring organizational metaphors among academics is that it supports reflective discussions regarding perceptions and tensions in organizational life. Face-to-face discussions across divisions and departments can reveal entrenched expectations of leadership, management, and responses to change. When rendered anonymous, the data can be further analyzed by the community in ways that acknowledge the diverse perspectives operating at various zones of the educational organization.

Metaphors of Education

In light of global economic agenda, scholarly and public commentary has addressed changes in educational systems (e.g., Hargreaves, 1994, 2006; Mansell, 2009). For instance, corporate metaphors such as "industrial age" and "assembly line structures" have been used to refer to outdated management practices of schools and universities (Schwan & McGarvey, 2011). Similarly, Archibald and Feldman (2011), Mcardale (2012), and Staton (2011) used the "higher education bubble" and "great disruption" metaphors to identify that traditional operating models of universities are becoming obsolete. However, analyses of organizational metaphors generated by teachers and academic faculty members are not widely evidenced in higher education despite the increasing necessity to commence bottom-up and participative analyses using teachers and other stakeholders (Arnold & Crawford, 2014; Cherkowski & Walker, 2013). Key literature referring to teachers' and faculty members' work and changing educational organizations is primarily limited to educational restructuring initiatives in English-speaking countries with strong expectations of civic participation.

However, a cursory investigation of responses to educational reform can help sensitize educational leaders in the Gulf region to the tensions experienced elsewhere. As evidenced by Fullan (1993) and Hargreaves (1994), educational metaphors have effectively conveyed a widespread discontent with top-down change processes in Western nations, which affected national curricula, and consequently, the communities where educators live (see also Hargreaves, 2006). For instance, Hargreaves (1994) advocated that all educators see post-modern change as an "intense compression of time and space, cultural diversity, technological complexity, national insecurity and scientific uncertainty" (p. 3). His use of metaphors of architectural collapse critiques the top-down reforms facing school communities worldwide. Morgan's (1998) framework highlights concern for top-down views of the organization, but also exposes Hargreaves' early views on change in educational organizations as theoretically weak, as teachers are regarded as passive resisters to global change. Additionally, although globalization is identified as the cause of changes, its specific effects on teaching practices are not qualified.

Metaphors showing the ideal constructions of schools and universities may also have value among educators and other stakeholders. Ritchie (2002) focused on two important metaphors that capture polarizing insights into the function of modern universities. First, "knowledge as an economic good" and "academic activity as economic activity" refer to free-market notions of productivity, profitability, and business activities, which emphasize principles guiding the commercial enterprise that universities represent. Elsewhere, the "university as community" corresponds to medieval origins and the tradition of scholarly research for knowledge acquisition and generating collective engagement for the betterment of society. Similarly, Sergiovanni (1994) argued for consciously shifting metaphors of educational organizations toward community ones. According to Sergiovanni, references, including "the team," reflect a collective sense of togetherness that can change how workers feel, reflect, imagine, and talk about work environments. In educational institutions with expatriate academics, community orientations can change how teaching faculty perceive and experience the teaching and learning that occur.

Recent examples of metaphors pertinent to UAE higher education, however, suggest tensions between community and economy. The proliferation of foreign branch campuses in the Gulf features an array of mixed metaphors where profit-making enterprises underscore the relevance of a marketplace orientation but hold a creative tension with other metaphors. The marketplace orientation is host to new vocabulary, where students are called clients, educational offerings are products, and extracurricular options are value-added incentives (Morey, 2004; Poovey, 2001; Sauntson & Morrish, 2011). Other salient metaphors for the UAE's internationalized higher education context include "cultural border crossings" (Hatherley-Greene, 2012, p.1), referring to the ways in which both students and their foreign instructors navigate cross-cultural landscapes mediated by English use and the Westernization of higher education yet are surrounded by multiple, heterogeneous borders. Thus, the formation of sub-groups and sub-worlds are instrumental in transitioning to a new country, work environment, or learning environment (Giroux, 2005).

This brief survey of metaphors in changing educational contexts demonstrates critiques of modern and machine-like orientations of schools and educational systems and forays into hybrid and localized ones. Few illuminate solutions to problematic management practices; however, when viewed in tandem with metaphors of the ideal educational organization, tensions between the real and the ideal can foster insight into the experience of change. Brain and culture-like metaphors tend to suggest a vision for responsive organizations that highlight bi-directional feedback, collaboration that is both determined and collegial, and a high regard for professional learning. Hargreaves (1994) warned that these views can be politically naïve if based on pre-modern nostalgia and ill-advised, given the rapid rate of change of post-modern conditions. For the internationalizing higher education sector in the Gulf, where hurried change characterizes the region, this warning is particularly relevant. The incredible rate of societal transformation as witnessed by the rapid pace of successive educational reforms and the steady influx of foreign instructors has led to implicit understandings of a social contract between governmental entities and their expatriate employees concerning civic, but not political, engagement (Davidson, 2009). To this end, Morgan's framework can illuminate the experience of transformation of the internationalizing context of higher education in the Gulf, but these experiences must first be contextualized by the broader context of organizational change processes.

Metaphors and Organizational Change Processes

Metaphors of organizational change are necessary to come to terms with the unpredictable and expansive rate of change. Lewin (1947) developed one of the earliest metaphors of organizational change, describing change as a symbolic three-stage process. Although deemed overly simplistic and modernistic (Fullan, 2001), this model remains relevant for higher education because it emphasizes facilitating organizational change through teams or work groups rather than individuals (Burnes, 2014). Moreover, it advises on distinct phases that sensitize leaders and managers to the nature of changing responses and how the change process can develop in various organizations and systems. The first stage, *defrosting*, involves understanding and accepting why change is necessary, and indicates the importance of a primary stage for breaking down the status quo and overcoming inertia to develop new approaches. After the uncertainty created in the *defrosting* stage, in the *change* stage, uncertainties can be resolved when people begin to look for new approaches, as they are ready to believe and act in ways that support the new direction. Meanwhile, confusion may persist as people transition to a new direction—people still do not have an entirely clear picture of the layout of various features. The third and final stage, *freezing*, occurs when a new mindset has crystallized, changes are taking shape, people's overall comfort levels have normalized, and employees have embraced new directions and ways of working.

More recently, Lewin's (1947) ideas have been merged with Rogers's (1962) diffusion of innovations theory in newer models that highlight other dimensions for leaders contending with changing educational organizations to consider. After examining and systemizing 18 models of change, Cibulskas (2006, as cited in Navickaite & Janiunaite, 2010), demonstrated that many recent depictions of organizational change processes continue to emphasize group dynamics in the ways in which people respond and adapt to change. Moreover, researchers essentially predict three main phases of organizational change: actions against change or *initiation*, *implementation* and actions after the change, and eventual *institutionalization* (see also Wallin, 2010).

The open systems approach, which views and understands the organization in its entirety, has also greatly affected the way change processes are viewed in educational institutions. Essentially, the open systems school sees organizations as being open to and interacting with their environment, as well as consisting of various sub-systems (e.g., leadership, people, structure, and technology) interacting with one another (i.e., being open internally). As such, changes to one part of the organizational system can affect other parts, both internal and external, and in turn, the organization's overall performance. From this perspective, analyses of organizational change focus on overall structural functionality, internal coordination, and interdependence, with general emphasis on goal accomplishment and synergy (Burnes, 2014; Senge, 1990).

Interestingly, Morgan's (1998) metaphors draw upon elements of the group dynamics school, as well as open systems analyses, thereby supporting interpretations of various models of change processes in organizations, which may prove insightful for the Gulf context. Cameron and Green (2009), for instance, utilized four metaphors from Morgan's framework to analyze organizational change. They suggested that the notion of organizations as machines highlights the specific roles of an organization's components toward achieving a common change-related purpose, whereas organizations as political systems highlight the different power structures and decision-making patterns of organizations, such as whether power is democratic or autocratic. Organizations as organisms reflect an organization evolving and adapting like a living organism, and acknowledge that these processes are not static, but dynamic and continuously ongoing. Consequently, organism metaphors reflect the natural change processes that typify many organizations contending with external forces. In Cameron and Green's view, organizations also function in states of flux and transformation: organizations are always operating within a complex, chaotic, and unpredictable change context.

In sum, many organizational change models provide insight for educational leaders regarding the use of metaphors in capturing the perceptions of academics in the internationalizing Gulf region higher education sector. This overview of the current literature indicates the reliance on certain metaphors to explain organizational change processes. Models of change processes, which target change on the organizational level, however, are intensely experienced by everyone within an organization. To this end, these models raise important questions as to the extent to which academics and their educational leaders in the Gulf conceptualize organizational change in educational workplaces given their undeniable role in internationalization processes in higher education.

RESEARCH CONTEXT

The organizational metaphors generated by expatriate faculty in Abu Dhabi, UAE, should first be contextualized by an overall vision of the higher educational institution and the change processes that have affected its eight-year history. This setting is profoundly shaped by rapid societal development at the national level and patterns of educational reform at the emirate level. The UAE is "a federation of seven sheikhdoms, with an Islamic constitution…formed in 1971, after the British withdrew from The Trucial Coast, an area of the Arabian Gulf they had administered since 1820" (Mercer, 2007, pp. 274–275). Subsequently, the discovery, extraction, and export of oil and gas have contributed necessary funds to modernize and internationalize the UAE educational system.

A Culture of Change: Abu Dhabi and Educational Reform

Public education in the UAE began in the 1970s with the backing of significant oil revenues. Despite the region's oil wealth, education facilities have been historically under-resourced. Al-Fahim (2006) used a rags-to-riches metaphor to characterize the changing landscape of the wider context of the institution under study. In the 1950s, education was limited to village elders teaching the Quran. Later, the first non-religious school opened in Abu Dhabi. The first school is described as basic in structure and content: a six-room building with no electricity or teaching materials. In fact, a local culture of schooling did not emerge until 1969.

The 40-year history of public education in Abu Dhabi is short but not smooth. Mass education, supported in part by the rise of Sheikh Zayed in 1971, necessitated a reliance on expatriates from the Levant and Maghreb Arab regions (Shaw, Badri, & Hukul, 1995). The development of higher education later that decade led to employment opportunities for academics within the wider Arabic-speaking region and, subsequently, from English-speaking regions. The overall process of significant growth in education has been called a "radical modernization" (Macpherson et al., 2007, p. 60). The massive influx of expatriate teachers and rapid expansion of schools and tertiary educational entities nationwide (Burden-Leahy, 2009; Nicks-McCaleb, 2005) helped fulfill the vision of education for all, but has also been popularly described as a crisis (Macpherson et al., 2007).The problems listed include the unsuitability of curricula, students' poor academic performance, untrained leadership, inadequate school buildings and facilities, shortages of Emirati teachers, low staff retention rates, and insufficient salaries (Gaad, Arif, & Fentey, 2004; Litz, 2014).These tensions are important considerations when interpreting ideal educational organizations against the present manifestations.

At the emirate level, long-standing reliance on Egyptian and other foreign models of education (Findlow, 2006), when interpreted through the academic underperformance of Emirati students, has been scrutinized by decision makers at the highest levels. One result was the development of a separate educational authority for Abu Dhabi. The bifurcation now sees a federal education authority operating from Dubai and a non-federal authority operating from Abu Dhabi governing the wider emirate. The

Abu Dhabi educational authority features far-reaching initiatives to revamp the K-12 curriculum, physical infrastructure of schools, and management of the many schools in the emirate (Badri & Al Khaili, 2014). These visions are coupled with intensifying efforts to recruit Emirati teachers.

In this regard, the context of education in this emirate paints an extraordinarily dynamic picture of change. The commitment to building an ideal educational organization to support educational reform is grounded in comparisons of the real versus ideal in everyday discourse. The presence of global educational providers and international accreditation bodies contributes to restructuring initiatives where newly created local entities take shape in an urbanizing desert landscape (Kirk, 2010). Together these influences highlight the attraction that Abu Dhabi has for expatriate academics.

If understood as an opportunity to gain insight from the tensions generated by perceptions of the experience of managing educational change of a degree program by diverse academics in a higher education setting in the Gulf, then this study on organizational metaphors can offer insights into the type of management tensions of a "home-grown" educational institution during rapid education reform and the internationalization of higher education.

A Narrative of Birth

In 2004, two unlikely partners came together to support the vision of educational reform in Abu Dhabi. The National Institute of Education (NIE), Singapore, and Abu Dhabi Educational Zones (ADEZ) conducted a feasibility study to address the chronic problems facing the education system, including low interest among UAE nationals in becoming educators and the absence of teaching qualifications of contractual public school teachers hired from Arabic-speaking countries. The study proposed a program of professional development for teachers in the emirate via a specialized teacher's college. As the emirate desperately needed thousands of locally trained national teachers taught to the highest international standard, it was proposed that the internationally accredited NIE play a founding role, and accordingly, help build the prestige of the teaching profession in the Emirates (Low & Lee, 2012). Within two years, the vision of a teacher's college was initiated in Abu Dhabi.

As the vision unfolded, a second phase of acquiring material and human resources began. A temporary location was acquired, the college was named, and then students, teachers, and administrators were recruited. The staff primarily consisted of three groups: Arab–English bilingual translators with local experience in Abu Dhabi schools, locally recruited and international instructors with post-graduate English language training and varying years of experience in the Gulf, and administrative staff consisting primarily of expatriates, not unlike patterns described elsewhere (Findlow, 2006). Increasingly, from 2009, Emiratization policies reached fuller fruition, but they were limited to management and administration at the college. The college's uniqueness and robust employment package were certainly an initial attraction of many faculty members to the college. Other distinct features included engaging with female and male Sunni Muslim students in English; teaching an education curriculum in English and Arabic-speaking context; training males to become elementary school teachers, a field traditionally-regarded as a female domain; encouraging young women to commit to a college degree amid traditional norms of marrying young and bearing children; and, relatedly, women studying in a college where men were in attendance. In sum, the college's initial structure was groundbreaking in terms of its local, regional, and international ambitions: to become a locally responsive institution in addressing problems specific to the Arabian Gulf and a regional leader in teacher education with international accreditation.

Despite the college's initial aspirations, disruption occurred in 2007–08. To the disappointment of many members, the reality of the college grounds and facilities paled in comparison to the glamorous architectural drawings of the futuristic campus used for recruitment purposes. Moreover, in the first year of operation, ADEZ was removed from the project when the newly formed Abu Dhabi Educational Council (ADEC) emerged in significance. Immediate challenges regarding limited material resources needed to run the college and house its staff threatened daily operations. Similarly, the lack of fully operational library and cafeteria areas and limited transportation services to the college suggested students' unique needs were not well considered. Further, the mismatch between the NIE curriculum and students' abilities created discourses on the low academic performance of enrolled students, the underachievement of incoming students, culturally different expectations of teaching and learning represented by the Singapore curriculum, and the overall development needs of the Emirates. Further exacerbating these issues was the greater turbulence caused by the retreat of the Singaporean management team, a temporary replacement, a successive replacement of two boards, and a frozen budget.

During the last six years, the college has relocated three times. At the time of this study, the college had newly settled into a permanent home. In many aspects, the college is blossoming, as evidenced by stronger collaborations with ADEC as well as the partnerships and memoranda of understanding established with prestigious foreign higher educational institutions. Additionally, a new budget has been approved for a dramatic increase in the number of foreign faculty members across all divisions and departments to improve the college's reputation as a center of research excellence. Course offerings were enhanced and strengthened in line with rigorous accreditation standards, and work recommenced on the creation of various graduate programs. However, several new issues have emerged from intensified accreditation pressures by the recently formed UAE Commission for Academic Accreditation (CAA) and National Qualifications Authority (NQA). Moreover, a lack of continuity among the senior administrative staff and relatively high rate of faculty turnover pose challenges for sustaining the initiatives and innovations.

In short, the college has been a site of dynamic change. Change initiatives carry the great ambitions of the college and the harsher reality of the dizzying pace of organizational transformation across successive phases of change initiatives. While each phase can be linked to outgoing and incoming leaders and managers, change has characterized this institution from its birth. At the time of the study, the tensions of visionary aspirations in the context of questions around the necessary material requirements for a viable, internationally accredited college are evident in conversations on morale and commitment caused by several cycles of flux and transformation.

Research Questions

Within this historical context, this qualitative study explored the metaphors generated by 14 expatriate academics to uncover their perception of the organizational structure and the organizational changes occurring in the college. A bottom-up research project was intended to capture empirical data on the development of organizational values and systemic processes using metaphors as perceived by both long-term employees and newer hires. The research questions were as follows:

1. What are the faculty members' metaphors for the educational organization?
2. What are the metaphors for the ideal educational organization?
3. What do the metaphors reveal about the experience of organizational change?

METHODOLOGY

The exploratory case study targeted diverse faculty perspectives on change, organizational values, and dynamics of the existing organizational culture. The study aimed to examine the practical and functional use of organizational metaphors in an internationalizing higher education context in the UAE. Metaphors are understood to offer insights on perceptions of the institution in terms of strengths and weaknesses and, consequently, offer insights to future administrative decision making, restructuring initiatives, and other transformational processes in a culturally appropriate and non-subversive way.

The research process followed two phases: in phase 1, semi-structured interviews, which incorporated guided visualization (Stiles, 2004), were conducted by two researchers. Ethics procedures were approved, and to ensure anonymity, handwritten notes were taken instead of voice recordings. The second phase consisted of compiling and analyzing the interview data. An iterative process followed thematic analysis guidelines. This process consisted of qualitatively analyzing data based on Morgan's conceptual framework. In a subsequent phase, the tensions between the metaphors generated from the current state of the educational organization against those reflecting ideal constructions were analyzed by the two researchers.

Participants

Participants were selected by purposive sampling. Expatriate faculty members were recruited from two major phases of hiring—about half were hired in 2007–08 and the other half in 2014. Fourteen male and female employees broadly reflecting the range of multicultural and multilingual diversity of the staff by nationality and mother tongue were selected, including North Africans, Arabs, Europeans, and North Americans. Half had Master's qualifications and approximately half had doctoral degrees. Participants taught various disciplines, including math, science, English and Arabic, and other education-related fields. They could be classified as "professionals who have regular and frequent contact with locals [and are] subject to the full bureaucratic pressures of the Gulf" (Williams, 1998, p. 11). All had three-year limited-term contracts and were fluent in English, but varied in terms of cultural backgrounds, area of expertise, level of relevant work experience in the Middle East, and age. The participants are distinguished from pre-existing taxonomies of academic staff in higher education in the UAE (Findlow, 2006) as there were no Emirati and no Gulf Arab academics in the sampling. This study is oriented to conceal participants by national identity and, thus, to further ensure anonymity, minimal descriptive data of the participants by age or citizenship are revealed.

FINDINGS

Metaphors for the Educational Organization

Table 1 shows the faculty's metaphors of the college categorized using Morgan's (1998) framework. Three basic patterns emerged: cultures, machines, and organic systems. For the first two categories, images included political, monarchic, and feudalistic cultures, as well as mechanistic images of machines, as noted by the cruise ship, rudderless boat, hybrid car, boat without a captain, leaking boat, and military. Together, these images convey a general critique of the hierarchical structure in which decisions are made and communicated, which could be a result of the high turnover of senior management. Further, an overall sense of a lack of direction or purpose was indicated. Tensions concerning the college's top-down and transactional management style, organizational rigidity, and lack of empowerment were revealed. This type of power structure is common for organizations in the Middle East (Hofstede et al., 2010; Kabasakal, Dastmalchian, Karacay, & Bayraktar, 2012; Litz, 2014). For foreign staff with societal inclinations favoring egalitarianism, participative management, empowerment, flexibility, and supportive work environments, this pattern can be a source of daily conflict (Hofstede et al., 2010; Litz, 2014). Accordingly, the present study suggests that, for those considering employment in the Gulf, tensions generated by expectations of egalitarian and distributed leadership and a transformational dimension of organizational governance may be a source of distress.

Additionally, there were two images of non-human organisms and two of human bodies. In one instance, a long-term employee described an inverted tree. As an organism that grows upright with roots extending into the ground, unnatural or perverted growth was highlighted, where energies are directed underground. Another long-term employee offered bees in a honeycomb to foreground purposeful movements and the focus of the worker bees ferrying resources between two zones of the playing field. This image conveys the single-minded focus of the instructors who interact with students and administrators and managers. It also conveys the regard for vital, routine, and orchestrated individual movement on behalf of the collective. A further organic metaphor was a blackened rock, which was used by one long-term employee to highlight an organic phenomenon with structural integrity, but is externally tarnished. All these entities indicate a life force and a coherent entity or ecology, yet the two metaphors illustrate two different experiences of the entity: one concerns the purposeful daily work and the other offers a snapshot of the educational institution as it matures. In comparison, there were also several striking infantile images of entities not using a brain. For instance, the metaphors offered were an orphaned toddler, a brainless body, and an unstable child. While some metaphors isolate the meaningful brokering of information from academics to students, others critique the coordinated and unintelligent movement of the educational institution. Many metaphors of this type reveal vital life energies thwarted by external forces or lack of inner coordination.

Lastly, several closed systems were generated, defying easy classification. These include a treasure hunt without a map, a rolling snowball, a size-20 boot for a size-10 shoe, and sparkling minarets. The images reveal the potency of different cultural landscapes and notions of progress and travel on meaning making. The rolling snowball conveys the building of momentum. In sharp contrast, the edifying stance indicated by the sparkling minarets suggest the enterprise reflects the timeless, devotional needs of the student and academic community and locates the institution within its own ecology, where the city's centerpiece, the Sheikh Zayed Mosque, is found. From another vantage, both the treasure hunt and the extra-large boot convey the travelers' experience of growth and discovery, which indicate readiness for foreign adventures. The metaphors also carry a reading of the need for a plan or an endpoint. These images are embedded in the overall appeal of different aspects of travel for sojourners who are relatively new to the region. While they do not reflect culture shock or problems with cultural adjustment, they remind leaders and managers that travel, growth, and discovery are vital features of the overall experience of academics seeking employment overseas.

Table 1. Metaphors of organization: Current vs. ideal

Employee	Current Organization	Image	Ideal Organization	Image
P1	Brightly painted cruise ship: heavy structure; stuck on board for a temporary journey; layers of workers, teachers in the hull, students on deck with a good view; patrons above them; a sheikh at the top with the best view.	Machine + Culture; ship's direction	Lighthouse; a community island for a small intellectual community	Culture + Organic growth
P2	Bees in a honeycomb; worker bee; keeping the system going; working for the queen bee; not standing against the grain; chained at the office for eight hours a day	Organism + Culture; natural processes / routine actions	Collective farm; a place where people with different strengths and talents design and produce. The motto is harm none and do what you will. Love all, serve all.	Culture + Organic growth
P3	An inverted tree; a top-down approach, similar to an organizational chart; I am one of the leaves or flowers fluttering; students like birds that come and go	Organism	Spider web; everything is interconnected; exchange of information that goes back and forth	Organism
P4	Body without a brain, parts do not communicate among themselves; healthy body, as in good salary; inside, nothing is connected	Brain + Organic growth	Family farm	Culture + Organic growth
P5	Size-20 shoe for a size-10 foot; mismatch of multi-talented staff; experienced academics; energy and vibrancy; aspiration of teachers lowered because students do not fit the mold; like square pegs and round holes	Closed system; lack of fit / appropriateness	Hand in glove	Closed system
P6	Infantile; baby, toddler, growing up, growing pains, like a child without parents. The focus is on survival, not strong leadership, vision is not clear; direction is not clear, no control of things, ship without a direction	Brain + Machine	Learning organization; a healthy community, a sports team; like football; support each other; people learn from one another; different strengths; encouragement, have a common goal	Organic system
P7	Military; students are the mission—we take care of them	Machine + culture	Military—an officer who respects, understands, and listens to people who know what they have to do and how to do their job	Machine + Culture
P8	Rolling snowball	Closed system + Momentum	Rolling snowball	Closed system + Momentum
P9	Treasure hunt without a map (and landmines); expectation of finding the treasure, but without enough guidance	Closed system; Purpose / direction	Mental sport such as chess; there is strategy, but fair play and rules are needed. It also requires participants to be mentally healthy; degree of unexpected issues acceptable—they are not disruptive	Closed system; Brain + Machine
P10	Two-year old, infantile; not toilet-trained, undeveloped, and dependent; issues with leadership and accreditation	Brain + Machine	The mature mind of a 30- to 40-year-old—not too young to be unwise or too old to be inflexible	Brain
P11	A blackened or darkened rock or charcoal. Ugly and dirty, but still has potential to burn brightly if a fire is lit.	Organic	Organization is a diamond, extracted from mines. Change required for organizational success just as cleaning, cutting, polishing, etc. are required for a diamond to sparkle	Organic + Flux and transformation (human-made / manufactured process)

continued on following page

Table 1. Continued

Employee	Current Organization	Image	Ideal Organization	Image
P12	Hierarchical monarchy; feudalistic system; nepotism for locals and those with the right connections. Not democratic.	Political system	Metamorphosis of caterpillar to cocoon to butterfly. Organizations need to have sustained, genuine change process – not imposed. Butterfly.	Organic + Flux and transformation (natural process)
P13	Boat without a captain or train without a conductor Who is at the top? In control? What is the plan moving toward?	Machine	A cohesive community that still requires continual back-channeling of special interest groups and lobbyists amid the undemocratic nature of UAE. There is power in people who have access.	Political system; Culture + Flux and transformation (human political process)
P14	Sparkling minarets; a structure with a bright future; image of hope/faith	Closed system	Lively ocean; dynamic; wide	Organic system

Metaphors for the Ideal Educational Organization

A variety of classifications surfaced (Table 1), including brain- and culture-based metaphors, while some appealed to several categories. Given the currency of learning communities (Morecroft, Asay, & Sterman 1994; Ritchie, 2002; Senge, 1990, 2006; Wenger, 1999), brain-like images inevitably surfaced as ideals. One noteworthy anomaly was the mental sport of chess, which features as a closed system, requiring an embodied "brain" for intelligence and tactical analysis of moves. Additionally, the "machine" metaphor was debated, as it requires systematic and rule-dependent functioning defined by structured rules. It also bends to ascription as a game culture where decisions involve fair but regulated moves. The rich overplay of each metaphor's characteristics enabled broader insights into the organization's complexity regarding the various players and key stakeholders.

In contrast to metaphors generated by the current perceived state of the organization, machine images disappeared entirely. Metaphors reflecting community-based cultures and collective desire for harmonious, cooperative, and purposeful interactions prevailed. For instance, the ideal educational organization was referred to as a lighthouse island community, collective farm, family farm, functioning military, and successful sports team. These descriptions are consistent with themes in the literature concerning educational entities as unique social organizations composed of people with a set of shared beliefs, complex rituals and relationships, and collective behaviors (Arnold & Crawford, 2014; Blunt, 1991; Bolman & Deal, 2003; Cherkowski & Walker, 2014; Deal & Kennedy, 1982; Gagliardi, 1986; Sackman, 1991; Sashkin & Walberg, 1993).

However, natural systems differently conveyed expected hierarchical demarcations of center and periphery as noted by the spider web, and to some extent, by a lively ocean. The spider web highlighted a central figure and its territorial management of the overall structure as well as multiple routes to the center. In comparison, the lively ocean reflects a fluid ecological environment that is host to many creatures. Other metaphors of the ideal organization highlight both natural and human-made processes of flux and transformation, as seen in the rolling snowball motif and the making of a diamond, which generate associations of sustained momentum and natural processes. For example, the making of a diamond is a transformational process involving sustained, intense pressure and the laborious process of expert cleaning, cutting, and polishing to acquire its sparkle, brilliance, and eventual precious status. In this case, metamorphosis conveys transformational change that is both internalized and a result of external forces. This process also resonates with the metaphor of a butterfly's emergence from its cocoon. Moreover, there were images of closed systems highlighting different processes. For instance, the motif of a gloved hand conveys mobility and a symbiotic fit between need and purpose. In comparison, the metaphor of a political system of lobbyists moving back and forth while advocating and back-channeling within a larger bureaucratic system highlights the vital role of communication in directing policy and procedure development.

In sum, the data suggested that academics consistently, but differently, prioritize various features of organizations, such as lifestyle communities, communication flows, cooperation, movement, successful and natural transformational processes, and sustained change momentum. While all of these notions are central to many of the key concepts that emerged regarding the effective functioning of educational organizations, as shown by references to learning organizations (Senge, 1990) and communities of practice (Wenger, 1999), few were reflected in the metaphors used to depict the current organization. This suggests a mismatch between expectations and reality.

Experience of Change

With respect to the experience of change, three main views emerged. One was evolutionary change evident in both real and ideal images. Evolutionary change accords with both Cameron and Green's (2009) and Morgan's (1998) perspectives of organizations evolving and adapting, much like living organisms do as they contend with natural internal and external forces. However, there were different emphases on natural processes carried by routine actions as in organic growth, which was wholesome and connected (although one reflected stunted or wayward growth) versus natural evolution and needing socialization; an ineffectual and superficial change agent operating in an organic system (i.e., non-symbiotic relationship); and an effective change agent working from within to influence the entire change process. Second, there was a contrasting view of change between real and ideal: change resulting from top-down decisions and manufactured processes versus natural, evolutionary or bottom-up-initiated transformation. While these perspectives continued to emphasize organisms and natural processes, they also reflected tensions and critiques related to different internal organizational components and patterns of hierarchal decision-making and power structures. In this way, images of machines and political systems were correspondingly emphasized. Third, stability-oriented images emerged in which change was seen as an external force, not a component of the image. This perspective likely reflected the faculty's perceptions of an organization constantly in flux, being forced to adapt and evolve owing to peripheral transformative changes being thrust upon it. It also may have reflected the staff's perception of a lack of opportunities for bottom-up change initiation, inclusiveness, or participative decision making regarding organizational innovations.

DISCUSSION

The findings provide a snapshot of faculty members' perceptions of organizational change in the internationalizing higher education sector in the UAE, as highlighted by their metaphors of real and ideal educational organizations. The study highlights areas needing attention from the organization's leaders and managers and offers generalized feedback for Emirati and international leaders in the region. In particular, the study emphasizes a shared vision for a collective community around which to orient daily practices as a guiding element for an ideal learning organization.

Relatedly, the members form a stable professional orientation at the institutional level despite their diversity. Further, there were few indications of tensions regarding the distribution of material resources across different departments. In many senses, the metaphors convey coherence around the college's mission, but tensions surrounding the communicative processes of decision-making were noted.

Surprisingly, despite focusing on expatriate faculty, culture shock was not detected as a major theme, although there were indications that cultural adjustment was needed, as seen in the treasure hunt metaphor. As noted by Knight (2011, 2013), the massive internationalization of higher education in the modern era necessitates faculty mobility and defines academic career trajectories in an increasingly globalized world.

The theme of a coherent professional community is striking because, despite individual, multicultural, or hybrid identities, the metaphors conveyed involvement with Wenger's (1999) description of brokering activities, which entails exchanging vital information about practice between diverse cultural groups in the college: students, faculty, and administrators. To an extent, however, the group also described themselves as balkanized with little or no sense of power beyond the interaction domain. This pattern is also found in research where teachers perceive their domain as being limited to teacher–student interactions in the classroom.

Although minor expressions of tensions between colleagues appeared, there were no overt contestations of the cultural differences among faculty. However, dissatisfaction with hierarchical and top-down communication was repeated, but this is not unique to Middle Eastern organizational systems. In some instances, metaphors indicated where the members located themselves as instructors in a hierarchical structure, where satisfaction with strong leadership is indicated. While awareness of the internal and external politics was evident in many metaphors, the desire for collegiality and a cooperative learning environment with stable management was highlighted. This raises the question on whether instructors in this setting are politically naïve or if the lack of top-down communication contributed to a shared sense of disempowerment.

Other related feedback concerned a central figure in charge of the organization, showing two faces of leadership and management. Problems were sometimes linked with the manager or change facilitator, as noted in the cruise ship with the upper deck stratified for the captain, a boat without a captain, and the rudderless ship with the uniformed man that looks like a captain but is not. In other cases, harmony was connected with a leader. In all images, a leader was perceived as a central figure whose identity is unknown, and to some extent, the leader was seen as the master of the ecosystem as with the spider and queen bee motif who both preside over their domain's functioning. Thus, strong leadership was assumed, but engagement with the leader was limited. Some form of clarification was expressed concerning who was actually in charge beyond the institution, such as a local Emirati or Sheikh. As such, there is an expressed need for engagement with an identifiable central leader.

Moreover, apart from two images of the sparkling minarets and the cruise ship with a Sheikh at the helm, which identifies that Abu Dhabi is a port city and a monarchy, there was little evidence of locally developed symbolism. For instance, the UAE is a desert with traditional Bedouin communities in which camels, desert sand, and nomads feature as indigenous images alongside customary pastimes of coffee drinking, pearl fishing, and date farming. Just as these traditional images were absent in the instructors' metaphors, it is noteworthy that foreign entities were featured, such as snowballs, butterflies, and lobbyists. In addition, these metaphors are accorded positive associations of change processes. However, the foreign instructor who used the metaphor of a governmental lobbyist seemed to suggest a Western political system but, in fact, described the prevalence and importance of similar people in the UAE with access to key decision-makers and the ability to influence policy and change initiatives, which is locally known as having *wasta*. In this sense, a Western conception of lobbying acknowledges Arabian practices.

Another issue may have been reflected in contrasting metaphors for the current state to the ideal. As seen in the rudderless boat, the leaking boat, an undeveloped toddler, an ill-fitting shoe, and blackened rock, there is a desire for directed coordination of the overall vision through support. There were generalized criticisms of ambiguous plans, lack of feedback opportunities, and under- engaged students. This notion of insufficient support appears to be related to internal and external politics in terms of the quest for legitimacy and accreditation, and this core issue must be resolved for the college to flourish in the coming years. Without legitimization via solidified partnerships with foreign qualification entities and higher educational institutions, "home-grown" accreditation bodies, such as the CAA and NQA, or locally sanctioned support from the rulers of the UAE, the college will remain an ambitious entity with an uncertain future.

Consequently, one takeaway for leaders and managers is that expatriate instructors desired more top-down information about the institution's overall vision. Without this, they described frustration in regard to building toward a common goal and conveyed desires to contribute toward organizational changes. While this suggests that the college has not yet completed its first phase of organizational development according to many change models (e.g., Gagliardi, 1986; Lewin, 1947; Navickaite & Janiunaite, 2010; Wallin, 2010), the lack of reference to tensions experienced by particular change initiatives, apart from accreditation, suggests that instructors in this context seem to accept the dynamic of change. In lieu of resistance to change, they find value in the adventure of the journey and reveal a commitment as manifest by daily practices with the ultimate vision of enabling young Emiratis become future teachers.

LIMITATIONS AND FUTURE RESEARCH DIRECTIONS

This study used a qualitative design, which precludes generalization to other settings. Data were collected over a short period with a purposive sample of faculty members working at a higher education institution in Abu Dhabi focusing on teacher training and other related educational fields. While this may be considered a limitation, insights from this case study should stimulate further longitudinal or large-scale studies evaluating management practices and change processes in UAE higher educational systems, as well as in other settings worldwide. This will serve to broaden the existing literature and further current understandings of expatriate academics' perspectives about changing educational environments.

Further, the subjective nature of the exploratory qualitative research should be noted. Although the researchers used semi-structured interview schedules, notes were taken in shorthand, and to preserve participants' identity, the study was conducted in private settings with no voice recordings. Thus, verbatim responses and hesitations and other aspects of speech were not recorded, suggesting that certain details may have been omitted and metaphors may have been interpreted incorrectly. Nevertheless, the interviewers read back the notes as a form of checking, which allowed the participants to clarify errors in recorded content. Additionally, the interviews were divided equally, with the first eight conducted by the female researcher, a long-standing employee herself, with other long-standing employees, and the newer employees were interviewed by the newly hired male researcher. There was little evidence that interviewer gender affected the message. However, it remains a possibility that a different dynamic would be presented if the long-standing employee had interviewed the newly hired employees and vice versa. Further studies in other types of institutions in the UAE and other contexts should be conducted to clarify issues surrounding the experience of change and expectations of change processes of expatriate and national academics. This would also make a significant and meaningful contribution to the existing literature on the use of symbolic language and metaphors among mobile academics in internationalizing higher education systems.

CONCLUSION

In conclusion, there is an abundance of literature on metaphors in organizational theory, but this study is significant as one of the first to be conducted in the UAE higher education context. More specifically, it examined expatriate faculty members' distinctive metaphors describing their reactions to continual restructuring and change processes, in addition to their perceptions of the current organizational dynamics and culture at a teacher training and educational studies institution in the Middle East. A range of positive, negative, and abstract metaphors surfaced in the interviews, and all had equal relevance and applicability to the setting. Moreover, some were consistent with Morgan's original constructs (e.g., brain, culture, organic process/organism, machine, political system, and flux and transformation) while others were unique to the venue. These metaphors can be utilized to evaluate the current program by highlighting the expressed need for improved communication channels, as well as the coherence around the professional commitments of academics despite the array of citizenships from the Arab world and far beyond. Decision-making participation should be based on these professionals. These findings are offered to guide systemic decision-making, transformation, and innovation in this institution from an exploratory, bottom-up, and non-subversive perspective. Likewise, the findings can be used as a springboard for further investigations in other higher educational environs in the UAE, as well as different countries and settings. This will serve to promote improved dialogue between various stakeholders in education. It should also assist in expanding the research, and thus the literature, on the use and function of organizational metaphors in the assessment of educational systems.

REFERENCES

Al-Fahim, M. (2006). *From rags to riches: A story of Abu Dhabi*. London: London Centre of Arab Studies.

Antonacopoulou, E. P., & Gabriel, Y. (2001). Emotion, learning and organizational change: Towards an integration of psychoanalytic and other perspectives. *Journal of Organizational Change*, *14*(5), 435–451. doi:10.1108/EUM0000000005874

Archibald, R. B., & Feldman, D. H. (2011, June 14). What bubble? *Inside Higher Ed*. Retrieved from www.insidehighered.com

Argyris, C., & Schön, D. A. (1978). *Organizational learning: A theory of action perspective*. Reading, MA: Addison-Wesley.

Arnold, N. W., & Crawford, E. R. (2014). Metaphors of leadership and spatialized practice. *International Journal of Leadership in Education: Theory and Practice*, *17*(3), 257–285. doi:10.1080/13603124.2013.835449

Ashton, E. (1997). Extending the scope of metaphor: An examination of definitions of old and new and their significance for education. *Educational Studies*, *23*(2), 195–208. doi:10.1080/0305569970230204

Badri, M., & Al Khaili, M. (2014). Migration of P–12 education from its current state to one of high quality: The aspirations of Abu Dhabi. *Policy Futures in Education*, *12*(2), 200–220. doi:10.2304/pfie.2014.12.2.200

Berger, P., & Luckmann, T. (1966). *The social construction of reality.* Penguin.

Blunt, P. (1991). Organization, culture and development. *International Journal of Human Resource Management*, *2*(1), 55–71. doi:10.1080/09585199100000051

Bolman, L. G., & Deal, T. E. (2003). *Reframing organizations – artistry, choice, and leadership* (3rd ed.). San Francisco, CA: Jossey Bass.

Boyce, M. (1995). Collective centering and collective sense-making in the stories and storytelling of one organization. *Organization Studies*, *16*(1), 107–137. doi:10.1177/017084069501600106

Burden-Leahy, S. (2009). Globalization and education in the postcolonial world: The conundrum of the higher education system of the United Arab Emirates. *Comparative Education*, *45*(4), 525–544. doi:10.1080/03050060903391578

Burnes, B. (2014). *Managing change* (6th ed.). Harlow: Pearson.

Burns, J. M. (1978). *Leadership*. New York, NY: Harper & Row.

Burrell, W. G., & Morgan, G. (1979). *Sociological paradigms and organizational analysis*. London: Heinemann.

Butcher, D., & Atkinson, S. (2001). Stealth, secrecy and subversion: The language of change management. *Journal of Organizational Change Management*, *14*(6), 554–569. doi:10.1108/EUM0000000006142

Cameron, E., & Green, M. (2009). *Making sense of change management* (2nd ed.). Philadelphia, PA: Kogan Page.

Chapman, D., Austin, A., Farah, S., Wilson, E., & Ridge, N. (2014). Academic staff in the UAE: Unsettled journey. *Higher Education Policy*, *27*(1), 131–151. doi:10.1057/hep.2013.19

Checkland, P. (1999). *Systems thinking, systems practice: Includes a 30-year retrospective*. New York, NY: John Wiley & Sons.

Cherkowski, S., & Walker, K. (2014). Flourishing communities: Re-storying educational leadership using a positive research lens. *International Journal of Leadership in Education: Theory and Practice*, *17*(2), 200–216. doi:10.1080/13603124.2013.827240

Cibulskas, G. (2006). *Švietimo subjektų pasipriešinimui edukaciniams pokyčiams įtaką darantys veiksniai: Lietuvos švietimo reformos atvejis* [Educational entities resistance to changes in factors affecting the Lithuanian education reform case] (Unpublished doctoral dissertation). Kaunas Technologijos Universitetas, Kaunas, Lithuania.

Davidson, C. R. (2009). *Abu Dhabi: Oil and beyond*. New York, NY: Columbia University Press.

Deal, T. E., & Kennedy, A. (1982). *Corporate cultures: The rites and rituals of corporate life*. Reading, MA: Addison-Wesley.

Denning, S. (2002). The narrative lens: Storytelling in 21st century organizations. *Knowledge Directions*, *3*(2), 92–101.

Findlow, S. (2006). Higher education and linguistic dualism in the Arab Gulf. *British Journal of Sociology of Education*, *27*(1), 19–36. doi:10.1080/01425690500376754

Fullan, M. (1993). *Change forces: Probing the depths of educational reform*. London: Falmer.

Fullan, M. (2001). *The new meaning of educational change* (3rd ed.). Toronto: Teachers College Press & Irwin Publishing.

Gaad, E., Arif, M., & Fentey, S. (2004). Systems analysis of the UAE education system. *International Journal of Educational Management*, *20*(4), 291–303. doi:10.1108/09513540610665405

Gagliardi, P. (1986). The creation and change of organizational cultures: A conceptual framework. *Organization Studies*, *7*(2), 117–134. doi:10.1177/017084068600700203

Giroux, H. (2005). *Border crossings: Cultural workers and the politics of education* (2nd ed.). New York, NY: Routledge.

Hall, G. E. (2013). Evaluating change processes: Assessing extent of implementation (constructs, methods and implications). *Journal of Educational Administration*, *51*(3), 264–289. doi:10.1108/09578231311311474

Hannan, M. T., & Freeman, J. (1989). *Organizational ecology*. Cambridge, MA: Harvard University Press.

Hannan, M. T., Polos, L., & Carroll, G. R. (2007). *Logics of organization theory: Audiences, code, and ecologies*. Princeton, NJ: Princeton University Press.

Hargreaves, A. (1994). *Changing teachers, changing times: Teachers' work and culture in the postmodern age*. New York, NY: Teachers College Press.

Hargreaves, A. (2003). *Teaching in the knowledge society: Education in the age of security*. New York, NY: Teachers College Press.

Hargreaves, A. (2006). Educational change over time? The sustainability and nonsustainability of three decades of secondary school change and continuity. *Educational Administration Quarterly*, *42*(3), 3–41. doi:10.1177/0013161X05277975

Hatch, M. J. (1997). *Organisational theory*. Oxford, UK: Oxford University Press.

Hatherley-Greene, P. J. (2012). *Cultural border crossings in the UAE.* Retrieved from the Sheikh Saud Bin Saqr Al Qasimi Foundation for Policy Research website: www.alqasimifoundation.com/

Hofstede, G., & Hofstede, G. J. (2005). *Cultures and organizations: Software for the mind.* New York, NY: McGraw-Hill.

Hofstede, G., Hofstede, G. J., & Minkov, M. (2010). *Cultures and organizations: Software of the mind* (3rd ed.). New York, NY: McGraw-Hill.

Jelinek, M., Smircich, L., & Hirsch, P. (1983). Introduction: A code of many colors. *Administrative Science Quarterly, 28*(3), 331–338. doi:10.2307/2392245

Kabasakal, H., Dastmalchian, A., Karacay, G., & Bayraktar, S. (2012). Leadership and culture in the MENA region: An analysis of the GLOBE project. *Journal of World Business, 47*(4), 519–529. doi:10.1016/j.jwb.2012.01.005

Katz, D., & Kahn, R. L. (1978). *The social psychology of organizations* (2nd ed.). New York, NY: John Wiley & Sons.

Keeley, M. (1980). Organizational analogy: A comparison of organismic and social contract model. *Administrative Science Quarterly, 25*(2), 337–362. doi:10.2307/2392458

Kirk, D. (2010). The development of higher education in the United Arab Emirates. *The Emirates Occasional Papers, 74*, 1-57.

Knight, J. (2011). Education hubs: A fad, a brand, an innovation. *Journal of Studies in International Education, 15*(3), 221–240. doi:10.1177/1028315311398046

Knight, J. (2013). The changing landscape of higher education internationalization – for better or worse? *Perspectives: Policy and Practice in Higher Education, 17*(3), 84–90.

Knight, J. (2014). *Professional development for faculty and staff in Ras Al Khaimah's higher education institutions.* Ras Al Khaimah: Sheikh Saud Bin Saqr Al Qasimi Foundation for Policy Research.

Lakoff, G., & Johnson, M. (1980). *Metaphors we live by.* Chicago, IL: University of Chicago Press.

Littlemore, J. (2001). Metaphoric competence: A language learning strength of students with a holistic cognitive style. *TESOL Quarterly, 35*(3), 459–491. doi:10.2307/3588031

Litz, D. (2014). *Perceptions of school leadership in the United Arab Emirates* (Unpublished doctoral dissertation). University of Calgary, Calgary, AB.

Low, E. L., & Lee, S. K. (2012). Bringing Singapore's teacher education beyond its shores. *Educational Research for Policy and Practice, 11*(1), 43–51. doi:10.1007/s10671-011-9116-7

Macpherson, R., Kachelhoffer, P., & El Nemr, M. (2007). The radical modernization of school and education system leadership in the United Arab Emirates: Towards indigenized and educative leadership. *International Studies in Educational Administration, 35*(1), 60–77.

Mansell, J. (2009, June 9). How children became customers. *The Guardian*. Retrieved from www.theguardian.com

Martin, A. (2003). An experience of teaching in the United Arab Emirates. *English Today*, *19*(2), 49–54. doi:10.1017/S0266078403002098

Mcardale, M. (2012, February 13). Envisioning a post-campus America. *The Atlantic*. Retrieved from www.theatlantic.com

Meadows, D. H. (2008). *Thinking in systems: A primer*. White River Junction, VT: Chelsea Green.

Mercer, J. (2005). Challenging appraisal orthodoxies: Teacher evaluation and professional development in the United Arab Emirates. *Journal of Personnel Evaluation in Education*, *18*(3), 273–287.

Mitriff, I., & Kilmann, R. H. (1975). Stories managers tell: A new tool for organizational problem-solving. *Management Review*, (July): 18–28.

Morecroft, J. D. W., Asay, D., & Sterman, J. D. (Eds.). (1994). *Modeling learning organizations*. Portland, OR: Productivity Press.

Morey, A. I. (2004). Globalization and the emergence of for-profit education. *Higher Education*, *48*(1), 131–150. doi:10.1023/B:HIGH.0000033768.76084.a0

Morgan, G. (1998). *Images of organization – the executive edition*. Thousand Oaks, CA: Sage.

Navickaite, J., & Janiunaite, B. (2010). Barriers of school principals' transformational leadership in implementing change: Theoretical insights. *Socialiniai Mokslai*, *4*(70), 69–81.

Nicks-McCaleb, L. (2005). The impact of state funded higher education on neighborhood and community in the United Arab Emirates. *International Education Journal*, *6*(3), 322–334.

Poovey, M. (2001). The twenty-first century university and the market: What price economic viability? *Differences: A Journal of Feminist Cultural Studies*, *12*(1), 1–16. doi:10.1215/10407391-12-1-1

Preston, W. (1982). Poetry ideas in teaching literature and writing to foreign students. *TESOL Quarterly*, *16*(4), 489–502. doi:10.2307/3586467

Rogers, E. M. (1962). *Diffusion of innovations*. Glencoe, NY: Free Press.

Sackmann, S. A. (1991). *Cultural knowledge in organizations: Exploring the collective mind*. Newbury Park, CA: Sage.

Sashkin, M. J., & Walberg, H. J. (Eds.). (1993). *Educational leadership and school culture*. Berkeley, CA: McCutchan.

Sauntson, H., & Morrish, L. (2011). Vision, values and international excellence: The 'products' that university mission statements sell to students. In M. Molesworth, R. Scullion, & E. Nixon (Eds.), *The marketization of higher education and the student as consumer* (pp. 73–85). New York, NY: Routledge.

Schein, E. H. (1992). *Organizational culture and leadership* (2nd ed.). San Francisco, CA: Jossey-Bass.

Schoepp, K. W. (2011). The path to development: Expatriate faculty retention in the UAE. *International Education*, *40*(2), 58–75.

Schwahn, C., & McGarvey, B. (2011). *Inevitable: Mass customized learning: Learning in the age of empowerment*. Lexington, KY: CreateSpace.

Senge, P. M. (1990). *The fifth discipline: The art and practice of the learning organization*. London: Century Business.

Senge, P. M. (2006). *Presence: An exploration of profound change in people, organizations, and society*. New York, NY: Currency.

Sergiovanni, T. J. (1994). Organizations or communities? Changing the metaphor changes the theory. *Educational Administration Quarterly*, *30*(2), 214–226. doi:10.1177/0013161X94030002007

Shaw, D., & Mahlios, M. (2013). Adult literacy students' metaphors of reading and writing. *International Journal of Research Studies in Education*, *3*(1), 21–34.

Shaw, K. E., Badri, A., & Hukul, A. (1995). Management concerns in the United Arab Emirates state schools. *International Journal of Educational Management*, *9*(4), 8–13. doi:10.1108/09513549510088381

Smircich, L. (1983). Concepts of culture and organizational analysis. *Administrative Science Quarterly*, *28*(3), 339–358. doi:10.2307/2392246

Smith, L. (2009). Sinking in the sand? Academic work in an offshore campus of an Australian university. *Higher Education Research & Development*, *28*(5), 467–479. doi:10.1080/07294360903154118

Staton, M. (2011, September 15). The disruption is here. *Inside Higher Ed*. Retrieved from www.insidehered.com

Stiles, D. R. (2004). Pictorial representation. In C. Cassell & G. Symon (Eds.), *Essential guide to qualitative methods in organizational research* (pp. 127–139). London: Sage. doi:10.4135/9781446280119.n11

Wallin, D. L. (2010). Looking to the future: Change leaders for tomorrow's community colleges. *New Directions for Community Colleges*, *2010*(149), 5–12. doi:10.1002/cc.390

Wenger, E. (1999). *Communities of practice: Learning, meaning, and identity*. Cambridge, UK: Cambridge University Press.

Williams, J. (1998). *Don't they know it's Friday: Cross cultural considerations for business and life in the Gulf*. Dubai, UAE: Motivate Books.

ADDITIONAL READING

Altbach, P. G., & Knight, J. (2007). The internationalization of higher education: Motivations and realities. *Journal of Studies in International Education*, *11*(3-4), 290–305. doi:10.1177/1028315307303542

Altbach, P. G., Reisberg, L., & Rumbley, L. E. (2009). *Trends in global higher education: Tracking an academic revolution*. Paris: UNESCO.

Bell, G., Warwick, J., & Galbraith, P. (Eds.). (2014). *Higher education management and operational research: Demonstrating new practices and metaphors*. Rotterdam: Sense.

Carnall, C., & Todnem, R. (2014). *Managing change in organizations* (6th ed.). Harlow: Pearson.

Donn, G., & Al Manthri, Y. (2010). Globalisation and higher education in the Arab Gulf states.Oxford: *Symposium Books Ltd.*

Duck, J. D. (1998). Managing change: The art of balancing. In *Harvard business review on change* (pp. 55–81). Boston, MA: Harvard Business School Publishing.

Edwards, R., Crosling, G., & Lim, N. C. (2014). Organizational structures for international universities: Implications for campus autonomy, academic freedom, collegiality, and conflict. *Journal of Studies in International Education*, *28*(5), 467–479.

Kapiszewski, A. (2001). *Nationals and expatriates: Population and labour dilemmas of the Gulf Cooperative Council states*. Reading: Garnet.

Romani, V. (2009). The politics of higher education in the Middle East: Problems and prospects. *Middle East Brief*, *36*, 1–8.

KEY TERMS AND DEFINITIONS

Change Processes: Refers to the way in which an organization transforms its structure(s), strategies, operations, practices, technologies, culture, etc. to affect change within the organization, as well as the effects of these changes on the organization (Burnes, 2014).

Community of Practice: Communities formed by groups of people who engage in a process of collective learning in a shared domain of human endeavor (Wenger, 1999).

Higher Education: Educational systems beyond the P-12 level.

Learning Organization: Involves the constant expansion of people's ability and capacity to create desired results, expand new creative patterns of thinking, and encourage a collective sense of ambition within an organization (Senge, 1990).

Management Practices: The various activities and processes related to the person(s) with the highest level of power and responsibility in an organization.

Metaphor: Linguistic strategies and techniques used to compare and link concepts, words or phrases in such a way that makes them appear similar (Arnold & Crawford, 2014).

Organizational Culture: The artifacts (organizational structures and processes), espoused values, and basic unconscious underlying assumptions, beliefs and perceptions within an organization (Schein, 1992).

Organizational Learning: Refers to fundamental change within systems and the continuous improvement and produced outcomes of those systems through individual and collective learning (Argyris & Schön, 1978).

Chapter 5
Challenges of Public Policies for an Inclusive Higher Education

Diana Patricia Skewes Muñoz
Instituto Politécnico Nacional, Mexico

Jesús Gerardo Alfaro Patiño
Instituto Politécnico Nacional, Mexico

ABSTRACT

This research note focuses on the major challenges of public policies emphasizing the implications guarantee quality education for all in order to contribute to achieving a socially inclusive future in a metropolis like Mexico City. The importance of inclusive education is directly linked to social, economic and sustainable development of the country, therefore, a quality education that includes everyone equally, calls for an analysis of the school and the social environment, our multiculturalism and active acceptance of that which is different from the norm and the relationship between it establishes for the formation of the common good. Therefore, we consider it necessary to address a comprehensive policy for education to eliminate exclusion factors such as: accessibility, infrastructure, equal treatment, access opportunities, gender and economic deciles access.

INTRODUCTION

This chapter is the result of a post-graduate level investigation, which represents a diagnosis about public policies in higher level education in the Federal District regarding the educational exclusion of the most disadvantaged sectors, between the 18-24 year–old group ages.

It spirit is focused on pointing out the main challenges of public policies, while producing a contribution to inclusive education in Mexico, emphasizing the implications of the challenge of ensuring quality education for all in order to help achieve an inclusively social future in a metropolis like Mexico City.

As a framework that supports this thesis is necessary to start from the idea of Abelardo Barra Ruatta in his article "Philosophy of Otherness" (2000), which states that to overcome the most pressing problems of the present and embarrassing (immoral growth poverty, preventable death of millions of children by lack of adequate, cynical and opulent appropriation medical attention from a few of the

DOI: 10.4018/978-1-5225-0457-3.ch005

cultural property, persistence of war as a means of resolving conflicts, destruction of the ecological balance of the biosphere) necessarily implies a profound modification of perceptual reality. Therefore, he considers essential to building a new formulation and relational modes of human beings to each other, human beings with other living beings and the whole of nature.

For these problems to be solved, Barra Ruatta (2000) proposes from a radically different vision in which education science should promote the exercise of plural paths that humans have to establish communication with each other and with nature, leaving aside the reductionist mechanisms of individual and social identification in force till now, since only then mankind lovingly open to that which is absolutely different, though quite valuable as them (Ruatta, 2000).

In addition, today's demands, challenges and changes claimed are very high, and excellent results are sought. This demand implies the presence of the best educational professionals in all schools, the best real collaboration networks, proper infrastructure to face global challenges, as well as an effective knowledge management.

Therefore, for the development of this article is necessary to contextualize the scenario where educational exclusion is framed, as it will answer the whys of the design and implementation of various public policies sparsely inclusive, since the issue of equity Education goes beyond a question of poverty or marginalization. It must be based on a thorough understanding of the characteristics of each community in which schools are embedded.

In this sense, the idea centers in if the school, as an organization with own vision and mission, that requires of administration and management processes to reach the results efficiently and effectively, through planning, organization, direction and control form evaluation, so, with this knowledge management, has increasing possibilities of successful achievements concerning its different processes and aims.

FRAMING

This situation is immersed in inequalities, injustices and inequities for vulnerable groups in Mexico, as well as a grotesque polarity compared with the level of development of our country, which has affected the social development towards equity, cohesion and social justice. This grim scenario is mainly framed by the global economic process in which we are immersed and knowledge management is still not a fact in our country, but surely offers a clear overview for being successfully included in the globalization.

According to Nicholas C. Burbules and Carlos Alberto Torres globalization means the emergence of supranational institutions, whose decisions determine and restrict the policy of other nations. Similarly, the term "globalization" is also seen as a phenomenon, which has tended to suffer various denotations as measures which exclude, replace, or enrich include various social sectors, impacting global economic processes, including production, consumer market, capital flows and monetary interdependence (2001, p. 12).

The truth is that "globalization" is a term that describes the current human condition exclusion, marginalization, domination and inequality, which is to generate restrictive fiscal policies reductionist monetary policy on production, income and public spending cuts, both for trade and for investment-liberalization, deregulation Limitation of legislation, except to guarantee private property and security-, and privatization as a political star with broad impact on the educational world (Vila, 2011, p. 9).

In this regard, some implications associated with the implementation of this new globally paradigm and increased the gap between rich and poor within nations are derived, resulting in increased insecurity, violence, marginalization in most damning reproduction cycle of these forms of social inequality. Some of these implications are:

- Limited management capacity of nation-states.
- Abandonment of the sectors hitherto protected by the state and instead structures that respond to the needs of supranational bodies are generated.
- Invisibility of the local usually ending in extinction.
- Concentration of industrial development with high economic, social and environmental costs.
- The State abandons basic rights such as health, education and food, and that fails to meet the costs of the total population.

Thus, in situations where social unity is lost, institutional, educational, family and work environment, and which go beyond the limitations caused by economic poverty are generated, additionally consequences for health, family, education, housing, work and accelerated the impoverishment of the majority.

Therefore, to produce, disseminate and use the benefits offered by education and knowledge efficiently, knowledge management results necessary for the development of a country, "where knowledge is conceived as main source of richness, power and production. In turn, knowledge management is understood as the development of systems and processes oriented towards acquiring and sharing intellectual assets" (Romo, Villalobos, & Guadalupe, 2012).

As is evident, these observations are calling urgently implement a set of policies that are routed to reverse this situation. Therefore, and according to Carlos Muñoz Izquierdo, it becomes necessary a global learning agent that may have attitudes, values and understandings as a multicultural democratic citizen, that emerges from an increasingly globalized world, due to the expansion of the media and technologies that produce new affiliations and identities (2003).

PUBLIC POLICIES IN MEXICO IN THE GLOBALISATION CONTEXT

For the analysis of the challenges facing public policy in the context of globalization is considered as material from the conceptualization of public policy, for which it is part of the semantic difficulty that exists in Spanish with the term policy. It should be noted at least three meanings that are linked by the same word and that the English language does distinguish. First, it conceived as the area of government of human societies, political polity in English; Second, the policy and activity of organization and struggle for control of power, politics in English; and finally, politics as designation of the purposes and programs of public authorities, policy English (Piña, 2009). Clearly, our goal has to do especially with the latter definition.

Equally, knowledge management is associated with a relatively new activity in the organizations. It is undeniable that knowledge has always been present in the economic development of the countries in the world, however, less than thirty years ago, the organizations have given enough relevance to this element, as a main aspect for their success and permanence in related markets.

Moreover, Latin American authors have defined public policy as a set of successive responses by the State (or of a specific government), in situations considered socially as problematic (Salazar, 1999, p. 50), or, as the set successive initiatives, decisions and actions of the political regime against socially problematic situations, which seek resolution from them or bring them to manageable levels (Vargas

Velasquez, 1999, p. 57). The latter definition despite being successful according to the context of Latin America, is limited itself, for primarily stating responses to external or unforeseen events.

There is a wide diversity of this term, one of the usual definitions, rather simplistic, states that public policy is what the government chooses to do or not to do (Piña, 2009).

According to the idea of Muñoz (2003), education is important and necessary for the country's development, but not enough. Therefore, public policies are those that respond to the educational and social needs, on which a shift to a paradigm framed in social justice largely depends.

A review of the text of the law shows that Mexican society an educational goal includes complexity in their basic contents and equal access to the same aims. First, it is defined that "everyone has the right to education and, therefore, all the country's inhabitants have the same opportunities of access to the national education system" (Article 7 of the Education Act). At this Mexican right, "the State is obliged to provide educational services to the entire population and take pre-school, elementary and secondary" (Article 7 bis.).

Thus, education is defined as a right, and the Mexican state assumes the obligation to ensure the conditions for this right a reality. More specifically the General Education Law, Article 4, states that everyone in the country should pursue those levels, and it is the duty of those who exercise parental rights to their children schools minors receive preschool, elementary and secondary. Thus, Mexico, like the vast majority of countries in Latin America, embodied in the General Education Act education goals proposed to be up to the demands involving the social and economic integration at international level at the beginning the new century.

As for the higher level in the legal framework also it determines public policy through the LGE, which is the state that should promote and address directly, through its decentralized bodies, through financial support or by any other means - all types and modalities of education, including higher education, necessary for the development of the nation, in the same way that support scientific and technological research, and encourage the strengthening and dissemination of national and universal culture (Art 10th).

Therefore it is necessary to clarify that the decentralized agencies and individuals with authorization or official recognition of studies, is a public service, it is made up of:

1. The students and teachers;
2. Education authorities
3. Plans, programs, methods and materials;
4. State´s Educational institutions and its decentralized agencies;
5. Authorized individual institutions or official recognition of studies, and
6. The institutions of higher education which the law grants autonomy.

It is also very important to note that the institutions of the national education system taught education so as to allow the learner to join the society and, in due course, develop a productive activity and to allow also the worker study. (Art. 10 bis) .Summed this law, Article 2 of the Education Act states that everyone has the right to education and, therefore, all the country's inhabitants have the same opportunities of access to education national, with only satisfy the requirements laid down by the general provisions applicable.

Based on this idea, in the first instance it is important to remember that public policies are the "set of decisions and actions for the target values" (Rua, 1998: 232). They are in the process of government action that requires the discussion of values, preferences, opinions and beliefs about problems or issues of a public nature. These actions produce specific effects and influence the lives of citizens. In this sense, public education policies are understood as "courses of action agreed between the various actors involved in this level of the national education system and are directed and implemented by the government in the sphere of competence" (Mendoza, 2002: 20).

EFFECTS OF GLOBALISATION ON PUBLIC POLICIES IN MEXICO

To sum up, the public policies appointed by the General Law of Education and derived from the recommendations by supranational organization, such as UNESCO with the "World Declaration on Higher Education in the XXIst century: Vision and action" or the World Bank with tests such as PISA. From this, curricular designs at all levels are obtained, leaving aside the true mission of public policies: to address the social needs by a regular communication between rulers and the ruled, which is the ideal of a democratic society.

Thus, the importance of education inclusion has as origin the idea of equity and equality in our country where all can have access to basic services, to security policies and human rights. In contrast, exclusion will only be a brake for the expansion of the domestic market and increase in productivity, as well as a reproducer of poverty, violence, social backwardness, which will bring as a consequence a hopeless youth for a common welfare.

In this way, knowledge management turns into a necessary process for a successful knowledge production, distribution and knowledge. For this, feasibility, viability and sustainability aspects are needed to guarantee its utilization and conservation as an intangible resource that is above other economic and material resources, nowadays.

In this regard, Muñoz Izquierdo's idea about making Mexico a fairer nation, since two decades ago, has been accepted. It counts on a more homogenously developed economic system, which depends on successful efforts for being more competitive, in global communication systems and networks, and using more flexible labor manners (2001), which depend on, at a great extent, educational participation, pertinence and efficiency, that is to say, knowledge management.

This can be translated into a new way of educating the generations of students and, therefore, to a renewal of the schooling system, which, nowadays, is based on an entrepreneurially competence-based approach with a degree profile relying on how to identify and address problems, as well as its adaptability to new technologies and the capacity to develop abstract tasks, autonomy and the capacity to set interpersonal relationships, according to the supranational organization.

In this regard, knowledge management in the organizations establishes that intellectual capital is made up, simultaneously, by human talent, structural capital and relational capital. By knowledge management and a cyclic process of conversion, knowledge is extracted from the three types of capital mentioned above; specifically, from human talent, knowledge from experiences and accumulated knowledges will be extracted in each one of the subjects that form the organization, from structural capital, existing knowledge in processes, methods and proceedings that the organization uses for its operation, finally from relational capital, knowledge derived from the relationships that the organization sustains with the exterior world, by suppliers, clients and allies (Buitrago, 2006).

However, as Muñoz Izquierdo (2001) explain, that for meeting these requirements and for helping Mexico take advantage of the new economic opportunities offered to grow and develop the various branches of the production, education will be essential as it must have a positive impact on the economic development, in the process of occupation assignment and the redistribution of the personnel's income. These requirements are:

1. An adequate and equitable educational offer;
2. Education to reach the quality standards required by contemporary societies;
3. Labor force with the necessary skills to face the challenges of globalization, which are also sufficient for the graduates of the school system to actively participate in the productive life opportunities.

Without these conditions is not viable the economic and social development of the country, so it is necessary to consider the need to implement parallel certain public policies that ensure a more equitable distribution of wealth, which means, among other things, to combat the technological polarity production system and the delays that have persisted in the life standards of the social sectors with lower incomes.

Although the educational policy is aimed directly at achieving quality in education, in terms of efficiency, which should be understood as the application of scarce resources, which are not necessarily for a better education and an enrollment increase. Formal education in Mexico is considered, among other things, as a channel through which they can obtain certain degrees of upward social mobility from one generation to the next and over the working life of individuals.

The school can only play this role if the policies satisfy two conditions: access to the educational system, to persevere in it and take advantage academically necessary in order to advance from one grade to the subsequent, be distributed equally among all social and regional strata of the country as one of the criteria more easily operating equity is determined by the correspondence between the share of each stratum and area and their participation in the distribution of opportunities (Izquierdo, 2003).

Identically, knowledge management works as added value for each person that is found in the organization oriented towards knowledge, and that generates and facilitates it, as well. Therefore, the key is not capital but knowledge accumulation in a world defined neither by a sustainable growth, nor by structural discontinuity, in middle of information and a *knowledge boom*. In other words, knowledge is not limited by economic condition, because each person inside the organization will enrich it academically. In fact, the resources are scarce for most organization, not only regarding capital, but also knowledge and experience. Consequently, education requires a very different organizational structure, promoted by an innovation initiative, flexibility and the ability to link with and back up the sort of knowledge created in this type of organization. (Buitrago, 2006).

In addition to knowledge management as a way of articulating and utilizing the existing knowledge, the intelligent organization needs a creative environment, a renewing attitude. W. Starbuck (1996) states that it is necessary to "stop depending on present beliefs and methods because they form perceptions that limit the people." While current beliefs and methods produce reasonable results, the people do not usually discard them. So new knowledge does not offer continuity to the existing asset (as it is not only the result of one management), but that the organization also requires ways of criticizing and overcoming what prevails now.

CHALLENGES OF CURRENT PUBLIC POLICIES IN MEXICO

According to the pressing structural changes that the contemporary society demands in the late twentieth century, some educational actions that ended up punished and public policies restricted to education, rather than benefited, were restructured. The first educational reform is evaluative. In Mexico (and the rest of Latin America), this restrictive policy begins to appear as an educational policy to help save resources, but sailing with a quality-efficiency speech on: "consequently, it is time to initiate major educational reforms, recognize the new scenario of adjustment." From mid-1980s, quality is defined in terms of greater efficiency in the application of scarce resources, which, as soon became clear, does not necessarily mean the pursuit of quality education, much less the growth in enrollment (Aboites, 2012).

This is clearly reflected in the spending on education in Mexico, which is 6.5% of GDP, although it is at the average level of OECD countries and represents a high percentage of the public budget, it is not sufficient, and spending per student remains low in absolute terms: two thousand $ 405 in Mexico, below the average of seven thousand 527 US dollars in the OECD (cronica.com.mx, 2012).

For example, according to the analysis by "Mexicanos Primero" in 2010 with respect to the ENLACE test, states such as Oaxaca, Chiapas, Guerrero and Michoacan, and even Puebla, are those with lower educational attainment, but also found, a figure that ignores this civil partnership, which are the same states that have a larger number of indigenous communities and unacceptable levels of poverty and social inequality. In contrast, with states such as Yucatan, Quintana Roo, Querétaro and Monterey, which have mostly basic services, its population tends not to be mostly occupied by indigenous peoples and by marginalized populations shows a better result in this type of testing. That is, to greater economic development, greater social welfare. Achieving quality education depends largely on the implementation of public policies for social welfare, which is a result of the efficiency of governance.

In other words, according to the data from the National Survey of Income and Expenditure Survey (ENIGH 2010) on the higher income deciles, the probability of access to higher education is very high; otherwise, the economically disadvantaged segments.

It can be seen in Table 1 how over half the public enrollment (51.6%) is concentrated in deciles VIII to X, higher income, while the top three deciles of household income (the poor) one group to 8.9 of the total public enrollment. The same applies to the following example.

Table 1. Access to higher education by income deciles undergraduate and graduate 2010

Income Deciles	IES Public	IES Private	Total
I	1.4	0.5	1.1
II	3.3	1.5	2.8
III	4.2	2.1	3.6
IV	7.9	3.7	6.6
V	7.8	4.0	6.6
VI	12.7	6.2	10.7
VII	11.1	8.1	10.2
VIII	15.0	14.7	14.9
IX	18.3	23.9	20.0
X	18.3	35.3	23.6
Total	100.0	100.0	100.0

Taken from presentation by Dr. Carlos Topete Autonomous University of Chiapas, December 2014. Source: NAFIN, 2010 National Financing Program, based on ENIGH 2010.

Table 2. Coverage by income deciles, degree and normal 2010

Income Deciles	Access	Gross Coverage
I	75,46	9.04
II	172,784	9.52
III	211,359	22.09
IV	340,113	29.95
V	356,588	33.02
VI	435,692	38.49
VII	463,727	37.34
VIII	554,763	48.08
IX	672,545	71.34
X	504,576	90.43

Taken from the presentation by Dr. Carlos Topete Autonomous University of Chiapas, December 2014: Source, SES – SEP- 2011.

UNESCO takes up the theme through his report, which states as alarming educational contrast between rich and poor is enormous, is further accentuated within the poor countries themselves, gives an example of Mexico, where 25% of young adults in the state of Chiapas receives less than four years of education, while the figure for comparatively Federal District affects only 3% of that population group (Chronic, 2012).

At present, according to INEGI data, the percentage of illiterates in the country is 6.8% of the total population; the degree of education in which the country is to 2010 is 8.6%, which means that the general population, including people who have post-graduate degrees and those who cannot read or write, is in third grade. The educational gap, i.e. people who do not obtain any study after ninth grade, for men 15 and older is from 39.91, while for women it is 41.88, -curiosa disadvantage marked by genre. Similar is the case of the Federal District, with educational backwardness 22.98 for men and 26.73 for women over 15 years of school age by 2010.

According to OECD data, the majority of Mexicans, 64%, have reached a level below the School Education (EMS), a maximum level of education, while the percentage of adults who have completed is 36%, making it one of the lowest among OECD countries, only slightly higher than those of Portugal (35%) and Turkey (32%), and considerably lower than the OECD average of 75% (Solano, 2014).

It also stresses that Mexico is the lowest between 15 to 19 year tuition fees, as four out of 10 do not attend school, despite representing the largest population in this age group in the country's history. In addition, among the young people who neither work nor study, women face the worst scenarios. In 2011, notes the report, the percentage of women who were in that situation was three times higher than for men, with 37.8 and 11 percent respectively, a condition that is accentuated with the years.

The OECD suggests that 15-29 year-old young people are at risk of spending more time unemployed and uneducated, with an average of 5.7 years, compared with their male peers, who at the same age range may take 1.7 years without work or training activities. Also, Mexico has the lowest enrollment rates in the age group 15-19, which is 56% among OECD countries, although the percentage of young people aged 15 to 19 years enrolled in education increased by 14 percentage points from 2000, still lower than the OECD average of 84% and other Latin American countries, such as Argentina (72%), Brazil (77%)

and Chile (76%), which, in more than two thirds. They have left the education system completely after compulsory education.

Analysis of the student group between 15 to 19 years, around 64% of 16 years old are enrolled in the EMS, while the figure drops significantly in higher education, according to the OECD in its Educational Panorama in Mexico only 12% of the population between 20 and 29 studies and six out of 10 young people aged 19 have dropped out of the classroom, which is less than half the average of the member countries of multinational organization (Solano, 2014).

The investment for education in Mexico in its report "Education at a Glance 2008", said that 23.4% of public expenditure from the Mexican government for education. That figure is higher than average among the 26 OECD countries. Likewise, he stressed that teacher salaries are left with the most money. Although the Mexican teachers' salaries account for little more than half the OECD average on the other hand they are among the highest in relation to GDP. (Cronica.com.mx, 2012).

Moreover, the proportion of GNP that the Mexican government dedicated to financing primary education (1.7%) is lower than that observed in five other Latin American countries; while the proportion of GNP per capita devoted by the government of this country to the same end (12%) is only lower than in two other countries in the region. However, it should be noted that this ratio represents less than half of those registered in Cuba and Costa Rica (27% and 25% respectively), both of which are in first place from the point of view of this indicator- between Latin America and the Caribbean. This means that while the effort that makes proportionally the Mexican government to secure funding for primary education is not negligible, that effort has been exceeded (in the same proportional terms) for two other nations in the region.

From the analysis, the repercussions of that growth on the structure of the pyramid during the three decades are: the percentage share of primary education fell from 81.2% to 52.3%. In contrast, pre-school education rose from 3.5% to 12.1%; the secondary school did 9.7% to 18.6%; that of the senior high school moved from 2.7% to 10.1%, and higher education grew from 2.2% to 5.7%. In short, during the three decades considered in the analysis, the enrollment growth generated the previously existing less acute pyramid (Izquierdo, 2003).

Currently, according to the level of the population pyramid, the largest deficits demand attention are concentrated in the middle and upper levels of the school system. In this analysis, the first corresponds to the educational modalities in Mexico are known as "secondary" and "upper secondary education"; so its "potential demand" is composed of all young people who are between 13 and 18 years old.

Moreover, by linking the total enrollment of the school system to the total number of individuals whose ages are between 6 and 24 years of age, corresponding calls "Gross rates of schooling" at the three levels of the system they are obtained education together, from this point of view, Mexico occupies tenth place among the countries of the region. It is, however, of particular interest to note that over the corresponding rate for the male population, our country occupies ninth place; while, over the corresponding female population, Mexico is in the eleventh place.

Specifically, in this study, the 19-23 group coverage is defined from the conditions of access and permanence in the upper level and expresses the degree of social inclusion achieved by the system at a point of time, as shown in Table 3. Thus, the percentage represented by the normal school students enrolled in university degree programs and technology, and education, in relation to the population between 19 and 23 years of age corresponds to the gross enrollment rate in Mexico (Mendoza, 2014).

Table 3. Mexico: Enrollment growth in the national educational system, 1970-1999 (thousands of students)

Educational Levels	Year				Annual Increase Rate		
	1970	1980	1990	1999	70-80	80-90	90-100
Pre-school	400.1	1071.6	2734.1	3408.9	16.8	15.5	2.7
Elementary	9 248.2	14 666.3	14 401.6	14 766.2	5.9	-0.2	0.3
High school	1 102.2	3 033.9	4 190.2	5 264.1	17.5	3.8	2.8
Middle school	312.9	1 180.1	2 100.5	2 860.5	27.7	7.8	4.0
Normal	75.0	332.5	109.0	201.5	34.3	-6.7	9.4
Higher*	252.2	811.3	1 097.1	1 620.6	22.2	3.5	5.3
Post-graduate**	-	42.5	45.9	118.2	-	0.8	17.5
Total	11 390.6	21 138.2	24 678.4	28 240.0	8.6	1.7	1.6

*For the period 1970-1971, post-graduate enrollment is included.

**For the post-graduate, data correspond to the 1985-1986 year term; not any disaggregated data for that level is found in earlier dates. Data is only included for a comparative reference.

Taken from Muñoz Izquierdo (2001): SEP, "Informes de labores", varios años y Poder Ejecutivo Federal, Anexos estadísticos de informes de gobierno, varios años.

Figure 1. Coverage of higher education in Mexico

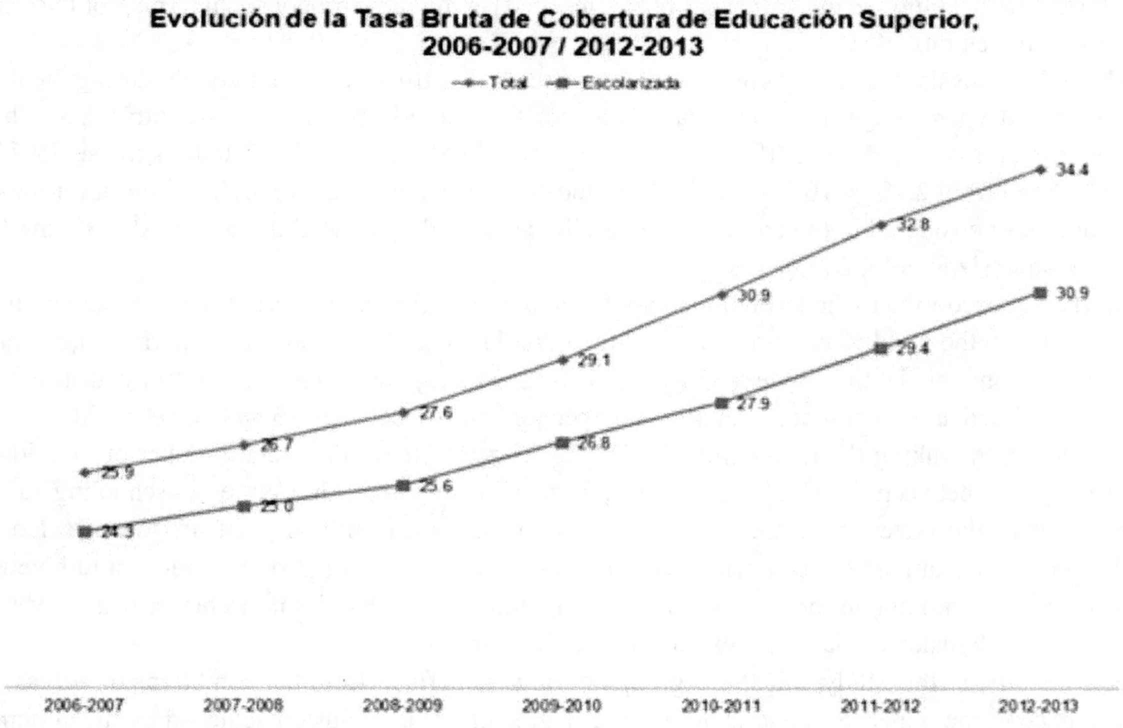

Thus, the evolution of the coverage in Mexico is transcribed, according to Table 5, significant changes in 10 at about five years, thereby opening gaps for the most abysmal inclusion, resulting in projections by at least seven decades to achieve significant changes in the educational reality in Mexico, taking into account that this dynamic was maintained.

As a result of this modus operandi of school systems, and public policies that regulate the distribution of social wealth, they have persisted in the region various problems, such as illiteracy and poor schooling of adults; persistent poverty; concentration of income, and gaps in the quality of life of the population.

Among the most serious consequences of exclusion from school is adult illiteracy. In our country, the rate of literacy of the population belonging to demographic cohorts aged beyond 14 years of age is 84.8%, which considerably slows the economic and sustainable development; only adults 25-59 years of age, living in urban areas have an average schooling of 8.6 degrees.

Moreover, the situation of women is somewhat different, despite laws governing their inclusion, promote growth in the education and workplace and is more level playing field, it is still subject to old canons of "regulation "as moral norms that impede their professional development and notes that the rate of literacy of them is below average.

On the other hand, it remembers that when analyzing the corresponding relationship between public spending on education and GDP data, it was observed that, from that standpoint, Mexico occupies the fifth place in Latin America. Since then, it is likely that this asymmetry is due to the contributions of the private sector to education which are relatively lower than those observed in other Latin American countries, Mexico; or, due to the demographic structure of our population (and the dispersion thereof) our country has to make greater financial efforts to meet their educational demands. However, it is also likely that this observation can be attributed to our country for not leveraging its financial resources efficiently.

Unfortunately, there is quite scarce and scattered information available about the quality of education provided in the school system of the country (and, in general, in the other countries of the region). However, we can say that at least the studies published in Mexico over the past decade (although all vary in scope and are based on different methodologies) - indicate, first, that quality is far from achieving the one required by the supranational organizations, secondly, that quality education is concentrated on the more developed regions of the country, and more specifically in public and private schools attended by students from the socially disadvantaged strata (Rama, 2006).

Table 4. Coverage of higher education in Mexico: Trends, challenges and prospects

Year	Enrollment	Population	Coverage
1970	271,275	4,032,341	6.7
1980	935,789	6,580,325	14.2
1990	1,206,128	7,829,163	15.4
1995	1,455,082	9,397,424	15.5
2000	1,918,948	9,951,709	19.3
2005	2,292,819	10,226,380	22.4
2010	2,981,300	10,293,156	29.0
2012	3,161,200	10,558,683	29.9

Taken from: Manuel Gil-Antón, Javier Mendoza-Rojas, Roberto Rodríguez-Gómez and María Jesús Pérez-García. Cobertura de la Educación Superior en México. Tendencias, retos y perspectivas. México: ANUIES, 2009.

This statement is even of worse consequences, the educational outcomes of the of the educational system about the youth who managed to complete the Higher Education, the OECD warns that, despite having one of the best educational levels, these students are more vulnerable to unemployment, as at least 7.2 percent of those who have college degrees and are in an age range of 25-34 years are unemployed, and just 3.4 percent of adults aged between 35-44 years are in this situation (La Jornada, 2014).

There are many increasingly limitations that prevent Mexico from developing a fair, equitable and egalitarian society. In education, the challenges the country must face and that have a direct impact on education in the last two decades are summarized in five areas:

- The socioeconomic status they belong to.
- The level of education and occupation that has the tutors of the students in the 18-25 years-old group.
- The distribution of opportunities in underserved communities.
- Educational supplies: school infrastructure and education and teacher experience.
- The genius belonging to students in higher education for supremacy.

Added to that, the top-level education coverage is about 20% and ranks last in the group of OECD (Universal, *ibid*). Despite the low completion rate in higher education, more than 60% cannot find work for the specialty in which they were trained.

From here the importance of knowledge management, because these days there exists a transformation in the concept of knowledge, which has passed from an applicable *to be* to an applicable *to do* situation, in other words, from a situation related to intellectual development of a person to one as a production factor. Taking knowledge management use as a basis, according to 60% reported by OECD of unemployed university graduates in Mexico, knowledge must turn into an instrument or means to obtain results, in which *neither is been*, nor *is done*.

According to the figures, the results of knowledge utilization are not optimistic. As a result, attention needs to be paid to two relevant management aspects, on one side, the idea of management shows, somehow, the organization, planning, direction and control of the processes for setting or holding certain aims. Nonetheless, this process has failures, due to the fact that it leaves present knowledge aside, whose normativity is obsolete for education. On the other side, when talking about knowledge, it is declared that an organization, as any human being, is submitted to a dynamics by which from inside and outside it perceives, recognizes, organizes, stores and analyses, evaluates information, and responds outside based on this information and immerse in all the stored information aiming a result (Buitrago, 2006). That is to say, an ideal scenario consists in a knowledge management system that allows the reutilization of information stored in the organization and its incorporation in the working and operating processes integrating the existing information systems and enhancing the information and knowledge durability.

There is still not an agreement on the concept of knowledge management; however, the theme is every time more share at management level, recognizing that knowledge in the minds of the organization members is the biggest value among the organizational resources. This richness in knowledge is called in different forms: knowledge capital, knowledge resources, knowledge intangible resources, intellectual capital, among others,

Knowledge management focuses on "doing things well" instead of "correcting things already done." From this conception, knowledge management is a frame in which the organization sees all its processes as knowledge processes. In this regard, all commercial processes include knowledge creation, dissemination, renovation and application towards the organization sustainment and survival. In this way, the prosperous organizations will see a revolution in the era of knowledge, and not a passing fashion for defining success once more. So forth, knowledge revolution will also be part of democracy, a movement characterized by power dispersion and by the managers that empower their lowest-rank employees towards knowledge, in order to contribute and make decisions (Buitrago, 2006).

Added to that, the factor of educational backwardness is not just of poverty, but of other factors, as described above, which inhibit the distribution of educational opportunities at all levels of education involved.

INCLUSION: THEIR IMPORTANCE AND THEIR MEANINGS

The reality of exclusion -the-related absences intercultural otherness of presence implies to respond, three processes in constant interaction a synthesis: inequality, since no redistribution; the difference, understood from the non-recognition; disconnection, as denial of access to communication networks and possibilities of coexistence Boaventura de Sousa Santos

Achieving successful educational practices, that is, where most are educated and have access to the benefits of a developed country, requires the development of institutional and educational strategies designed from a deep understanding of the characteristics of each community in which schools are embedded, the territory in which education and create an educational policy based on otherness practices are inscribed. Quality education calls for an analysis of the school and the social environment of our multiculturalism and active acceptance of what is different from us and the relationship between them is established for the creation of the common good.

Thus, inclusion is the framework that provides viability and support to achieve what Fernando Solana considered a knowledge society in which the majority of adults who compose it are healthy, productive, informed, free, respectful of the rights, beliefs and opinions of others, and have acquired the ability to enjoy, live and learn throughout life, then we can say that they enjoy a decent life and quality (2005).

The inclusion movement has emerged strongly in recent years to address the high levels of exclusion and discrimination and educational inequalities in most educational systems in the world. The prospect of demand inclusion moves towards a single educational system that is more diversified to meet adequately the needs of different groups and individuals, in order to achieve, by different routes equivalent in quality, comparable learning for the entire population. This means overcoming the current separation between education for all and education for those who for various reasons are considered "different".

The difference in itself holds more wealth than those who are perceived simplistically. According to the thesis of Abelardo Barra Ruatta in his article "Philosophy of Otherness", which states that to overcome troublesome situations it is necessarily implied a profound modification of perceptual reality. Therefore, it is considered essential to build a new formulation and relational modes of human beings to each other, human beings with other living beings and the whole of nature, as discussed earlier in this article.

All this is only possible if one starts from a radically different vision. The science of education which constitutes around this new paradigm should promote the exercise of plural paths that humans have to establish communication with each other and with nature. That is, an education that appeals to the anthropological value of emotion, emotion or fantasy (as well as the value of intellect) to form knowledge, skills and attitudes that make life more pleasant for everyone, by leaving aside the present reductionist mechanisms of individual and social identification till now. It means to open lovingly to the other different person, to the other person that expresses his subjectivity by an absolutely different ethos from mine, but valuable as mine. (Ruatta, 2000).

The diversity of existing human requires a predisposition to accept differences. Such predisposition is not only an epistemological expression of openness, but also an ethical and political one. This be willing to live with difference is prefigured in the *misanthropic centralization* that imposes the linking with the other living orders. The recognition of the inherent or intrinsic value possessed by non-rational forms of life is a valuable cosmological background for the enunciation of this ontology of difference (Singer, 1997).

So, as simple as it may seem, it is relevant that knowledge, as well as data and information are not exchangeable concepts. Frequently, the success of failure of and organization can obey to which of them we need, which we have, and what is possible to do or not to do with each one. This knowledge management is vital for the acknowledgement and inclusion of diversity as a way of enriching our own knowledge, environment, present and construction of a better future in which we stay all included.

Thus, inclusion is the framework that enables mobility, innovation, ideas, sustainability, ethics and morality from a more realistic perspective for all sectors, as it has been enriched with the peculiarities of each and has been fed with millions of ideas that depart from all; not the imposition by a few, but of love and wealth for all, taking into account the human, social, environmental and educational development of each.

CONCLUSION

The new global system is based on the capacity to generate knowledge and efficient information processing, which depends, in turn, on the cultural and technological capacities of individuals, businesses and territories. In the information economy, education and innovation constitute straightforward productive forces.

To achieve a real and favorable change for the development for of a country, which is focused on the course of the characteristics of the overall system described above and can compete fairly and effectively, a change of the educational paradigm through knowledge management. Paulo Freire states that education is necessary but not sufficient (2000), which is unavoidable for analyzing and designing intervention opportunities to build and serve the educational management opportunities for the design of the policies that prioritize inclusion.

At this point, it must be highlighted that knowledge management is the ideal strategy for educational organization due to its capacity of learning or generating new knowledge or improving the current one. It is the basis for the generation of intellectual talent, organizational capacities, new information and communication technologies, as well as strategic resources for innovation, productivity, and permanence of the organizations. Therefore, knowledge management must be immediately established in the organization of higher education and in each of its management, intellectual, capital and structural processes, as well. (Buitrago, 2006).

It should be noted that the political dimension of education in Mexico is for the educational reforms that have been made at various levels, whereas the technical dimension of policies concerns to the education policies aimed specifically at resolving undesirable situations related to factors associated with educational attainment, but both contribute to understanding and explaining the change, continuity and results of the educational policies (Castillo-German, 2011).

Therefore, it can be interpreted that if followed by implementing educational and similar economic development policies that have been in place so far, restrictive, evaluative and punishing, the country will not be oriented towards a more just and sustainable social situation, because it will not count on either a fair, efficient and effective education system or a sufficiently inclusive and competitive production system that grants enough access opportunities to the sector. Among these opportunities, we can mention some ones interrelated with quality:

- **Accessibility:** Transport costs, accommodation, food and staying in much closer to the lower income deciles, with special attention to the first school groups lag.
- **Proximity:** More number of universities / offices / powers to regions / disadvantaged areas that are linked to their production methods and help the students to be used later in a formal sector.
- **Infrastructure:** Access to the education system alternate routes: distance learning via the Internet to access a certain number of hours / class that do not need to be face or, disseminate degrees who already have a remote curriculum for students who find it difficult it transported to universities, either for lack of financial resources, shortage of time, lack of access roads, barriers to physical presence at universities and so on. In this sense, the distribution of computer equipment suitable for the race, and the network will be required to do so, the state will be the distributor and regulator of such infrastructure.
- **Equal Treatment:** "Giving more to those who have less" was a speech that has remained just that, in speech, but in the field of higher education, scholarships may be granted according to serious social studies, in this case You can help support expenses such as transportation, copying, printing, access to libraries (virtual and 24 hrs.), which are often cause for desertion.
- **Access Opportunities:** Design programs that allow access and guidance to the vocation of the students and not exclusion through a single examination for all, as well as a preparatory course for the race leveling according to which the student must access.

Thus, the information contained herein has been analyzed and indicates the need to review the policies that have governed the development of our school system, thoroughly, as well as all the policies that together with the education ones, have taken part in the guidance of Mexico's economic and social development.

Added to that, you cannot dismiss the likelihood of inefficient use of financial resources has prevented improving coefficients satisfying the demand for education in the middle and upper levels, raising the quality of education and reduce inequality in the distribution school opportunities.

It is also likely that insufficient demand satisfaction, poor quality of basic education, and unequal distribution of educational opportunities have affected the educational inclusion, first, on the accessibility of universities; secondly, the capacity to stay and exit from different areas of knowledge and finally, those problems could prevent an improvement in the education of the productive adult population, which could also have been reflected in an unsatisfactory relationship between schooling and income developers perceive economic activities as well in an infinite vicious circle.

Finally, all this could have prevented from reducing poverty, improving the income distribution and reducing the deficits that are still observed in the population's life standards.

However, the above mediations refer to, on the one hand, the influence of the own social inequality on the distribution of educational opportunities; however, it must be emphasized that the educational policies (especially the policies relating to the unfair distribution of financial resources amongst the schools, the poor quality of educational expenses that receive the most vulnerable social sectors, and the inflexibility of a school system that was not designed to suit the various conditions of the students who had late access to the school system) also reinforce, by themselves, the unequal distribution of educational opportunities.

Moreover, among these mediations, there is also the strategy of economic development that has been in vigor in the region since the eighties. As it is known, this strategy prevented to expand the social opportunities at a pace that would have been necessary for the graduates of the school system (and those who leave prematurely) to perform, in the productive system, complex tasks proportional to the different levels of education studied.

Therefore, returning to the initial idea of this article, within the framework of inclusion as a way to open ourselves lovingly to other people, education can help support the construction of our *self*, in a more general level and the constitution of identities within globalization:

Reducing education to the fields of capital, efficiency, competitiveness and academic success is to deprive this process from its skin and bones, to turn its vital organs into dysfunctional elements that barely allow education vehicular its corporeality and distort it until being unrecognizable and, ultimately, provokes that education holds an imposed mask, diluting its identity, making it shipwreck (Santos, 2009).

Thus, we conclude that nowadays a global student is required, who can display attitudes, values and understandings as a multicultural democratic citizen, who sets off this increasingly globalized world, due to the expansion of the media and technologies producing new affiliations and identities.

The role of a modern state is essential to lessen the severity of the impacts at all levels. To conciliate the interests not only the interest amongst the economic system, the environment, science and technology and social interests, but to also perform actively the role of main character and responsible and responsible for promoting the production of social and economic satisfiers that the population of a country demand, such as employment, social spending, economic and social stability in a sustainable environment and a fair and equitable distribution of wealth. Therefore, one must analyze the contradictions that the system produces to fight them through a change of the social paradigm and an unwavering pro-choice in favour of the most disadvantaged people and groups, where the inclusive intercultural approach grasps sense and sustainability.

REFERENCES

Aboites, H. (2012). *La medida de una nación. Los primeros años de la evaluación en México.* México: UAM, CLACSO, ITACA.

Buitrago, D. Y. (2006). *Repository. UdeRosario.* Obtenido de La gestión del conocimiento. Documento No. 29. Available at http://repository.urosario.edu.co/bitstream/handle/10336/1207/BI%2029.pdf?sequence=1

Castillo-Alemán, G. (2011). Las políticas educativas en México desde una perspectiva de política pública: gobernabilidad y gobernanza. *Magis*, (9), 639-652. Available at http://cippec.org/mapeal/wp-content/uploads/2014/05/CASTILLO-ALEMAN-Las-pol-ed-en-M%C3%A9xico-dde-una-persp-de-pol-p%C3%BAb.pdf

Izquierdo, C. M. (2003). *Origen y consecuencias de las desigualdades educativas. Investigaciones realizadas en América Latina sobre el problema.* México: Fondo de Cultura Económica.

Mendoza, J. (2014). *Cobertura de la educación superior en México. Tendencias, retos y perspectivas.* México: ANUIES.

Piña, A. D. (2009). *Las políticas públicas en materia educativa.* México: SEP.

Romo, A., Villalobos, M., & Guadalupe, L. (2012). *Gestión del conocimiento: estrategia para la formación de investigadores.* Available at http://www.scielo.org.mx/scielo.php?script=sci_arttext&pid=S1665-109X2012000100007&lng=es&nrm=iso

Ruatta, A. B. (2000). *Filosofía de la Otredad.* Recuperado el 12 de enero de 2015, de "La enseñanza de los derechos humanos en la universidad": Available at https://www.unrc.edu.ar/publicar/cde/Barra%20 Ruatta.htm

Santos, B. D. (2009). *Una epistemología del Sur.* México: FLACSO.

KEY TERMS AND DEFINITIONS

Education: Is the mental process of transferring knowledge, skills and values from one person to many others.

Effectiveness: Criteria focuses on determining the scope of objectives and goals of a program.

Efficiency: Criteria focused on determining the distribution of resources to operate a program.

Intellectual Capital: It includes human capital, structural capital and relational capital to form the knowledge economy.

Results: Objectives achieved through research, study and investigation.

Chapter 6
Alternative Concepts of Economic Development and Their Implications for Higher Education

Isaías Álvarez García
Instituto Politécnico Nacional, Mexico

Juan de Luna Flores
Instituto Politécnico Nacional, Mexico

Maribel del Carmen Casas Haro
Instituto Politécnico Nacional & Instituto Superior de Intérpretes y Traductores, Mexico

ABSTRACT

This chapter is an academic essay that presents six theoretical concepts about economic human development that allow the leaders and the teaching staff of the institutions of higher education to understand that the growth and integral development of a country does not only rely on the fruits of a given ideology or economic system, in a fixed time, but on the integral human development of the peoples from their culture, customs, idiosyncrasy, production means, integration with other nations, among other ways of expressing their identity and their ways of life. These concepts are: 1) economic and social growth, 2) self-sufficiency, 3) interdependence, 4) self-determination, 5) knowledge as a transformation strategy, and 6) integral human development. It is proposed the analysis of these concepts to explore utilization alternatives for the development of future research works.

INTRODUCTION

The aim of this work is to present brief comments on the main theoretical contributions and experiences in the economic development of the Latin American and the Caribbean countries, and the recently independent nations in Africa and other nations of the so called Third World. This topic has been of

DOI: 10.4018/978-1-5225-0457-3.ch006

special interest for economists, sociologists and politicians, and higher education leaders from amidst the last century. Some theories and models that have been offered rely on past ideological systems, such as neoliberalism, neomarxism, structuralism, and the theory of dependence and Keynesianism, among others. This chapter offers some alternative concepts that reflect more the ways of thinking and dealing whit development rather than pure theoretical systems. There are conceptualizations that have led to the practical application and others that express desires and aspirations of the people, of the inhabitants of these nations, who must be subjects and objects of all idealization about economic development

All of these concepts, from an educational approach, pose challenges for the development and goal achievement of the institutions of higher education in the context of paradigms shift in the society of knowledge nowadays.

1. CONCEPT OF ECONOMIC AND SOCIAL HUMAN GROWTH

The origin of this concept lies on the economic factors that contribute to the production of goods and services necessary to the welfare of the peoples, and promote a sustained growth of this production.

An idealized definition of this concept that includes the comprehensive human development shall be understood as *a balanced and sustainable growth of the production of goods and services that goes beyond the average population growth, but that, in turn, guarantees a fair and equal distribution of the goods and services, without damaging the ecological environment, as well.* (Escribano, G.2005).

The indicators to be considered are, among others: the *per capita* product, which results from the average rate between the *gross domestic product* (GDP) and the *average population growth.*

The very concept of economic growth implies tight bonds with the *modernization processes* of the so called *modern economies.* But in practice, these economies have not either guaranteed the fair distribution of goods and services or the issue of environmental balance. (The economic crisis in the United States, in 2009, and in China, recently).

Modernization can be defined from two viewpoints: the man's overall control of the inanimate or material energy forces; or the man's control of the social organization. To overcome the big economic and social issues, an alternative ideal concept of *integral human development* has taken place. (Reyes, G. 2009).

As for the strategic processes of the modernization of countries *concerns*, it could be understood from two main alternatives: a) the *socialist model* and b) the *capitalist model.* Even though, both models have collapsed. The former, between 1989 and 1990, as a consequence of the social its systems fall in the former Soviet Union (Perestroika); and the latter, due to the European Union crisis, since the years 2009 till now.

Schumpeter has offered an explanation about the economic development that matches with the law of decreasing yield rates with the facts observed in reality. The waves of findings and inventions (technology revolution) cause sudden capital rate increase the *cost benefit* of capital investment. But while the new knowledges start spreading and the new technologies are imitated, the benefits start diminishing, and the cost benefit to the capital, as well; until a new wave of finding show up. (Schumpeter, 1963).

The higher education institutions (HEI) live overwhelmed by the pressures of *meeting the coverage demand or* the claim for rationalizing models guided by the motto *"doing more with less",* which constitutes a misconceived sophism.

From the last quarter of the twentieth century, the (HEI) were dominated by the trends of quantitative growth model of students' enrollment; with no consideration of the resources of institutional infrastructure and services, and the staff availability for teaching at higher education. These trends of growth did not guarantee quality, relevance and competiveness of their educational services.

In the case of the university technical and engineering programmes, the educational supply of these studies did increase but not guarantee competitive quality levels and commitment to the social issues; under conditions of fewer employment opportunities in the industry, and the technological development centers.

In addition to the quality level requirements, the society of the developing countries requires a great commitment of higher education to the role of social service to the society and to the environmental balance issues, as well.

2. CONCEPT OF SELF-SUFFICIENCY IN DEVELOPMENT PLANNING

In some countries the economic development has been seen as their capacity conditions that the human groups or peoples have built in order to be able of addressing their social, economic and cultural development problems with their own resources.

But historically, neither self-sufficient human groups, nor countries have been found; although, in some small towns or countries, there appear some events that could support this concept. Therefore, welfare or progress, as well as a better standard of life for the people are pursued. (Chaparro, F. 2006).

From the *self-sufficiency development viewpoint*, the higher education institutions that have achieved a greater academic progress in the world haven't been absorbed by the self-sufficiency criteria; but, deliberately, seek to build up alliances with other academic and social institutions because they consider inter-institutional action as a key strategy for higher education development. The academic inter-institutional exchange and shared work is taken as an advantage.

By the end of 1960, Tanzania was one of the poorest countries of the world. As many other nations it suffered from a heavy external indebtment, a weak foreign aid and a fall in the prices of basic goods. The project country development proposal made by President Julius Neyrere was the collectivization of agriculture and nationalization at a great scale. The vision was established in the Arusha Declaration from 1967.

In the Tanzania educational context, Neyrere considered education system mission as a mean of *restoring self-reliance* to the African man, because the colonial educational system had broken with the African man.

For this reason, the first priority of educational policy was adult education, before any other type of instruction.

The leaders of (HEI) tend to achieve this model of self-sufficiency that is both, unviable and undesirable for the higher education development (academic endogamy).

3. CONCEPT OF INTERDEPENDENCE STRATEGY

Since the concept of self-sufficiency results unviable and undesirable, the interdependence strategy for the goal achievement of economic and human development arose.

According to Prebish and the CEPAL, Interdependence is a generic term that is used for describing the complex and multiple economic relationships that the modern nations have established among themselves. If in a past period a small group of industrialized nations exchanged their manufactured products for raw material and food sold by less developed countries, today, in virtue of the technological advances and an increasing trade, there is a less restricted and unilateral exchange, because even many productive processes are carried out nowadays crossing the national borders several times.

The idea of interdependence, on the other hand, reflects the lack of possibility of thinking in an unsustainable growth, and within the limited borders of no national economy, no mattering if they are very large or powerful. This concept also expresses how relevant the agreements of economic integration which have been developed lately are. (Eumed, 1991).

Therefore, it is considered necessary that the human groups and peoples communicate and interact with each other in order to address their economic, social, cultural and educational problems, without falling in the exploitation, control or colonialism phenomena.

The complex processes of *globalization*, *regionalization* and *industrial labor international organization* have received mutual benefits from this very model.

Furthermore, the necessary condition for this development model assumes this criterion that self-reliance of people and countries is always necessary for profiting from the exchange relationships with other countries. Also, it is vital to include the change of relationships between the State Government institutions and the State Civil Society in the integral concept of *state*. This model comprises the models of sensitivity and vulnerability.

As for the interdependence *process concerns*, it tries to gather not only inter-states relationships, but also the social and institutional groups with the state government

The traditional concepts of *national security* coined in by the military force shall be self-restrained. A great contribution to strengthen the processes of interdependence has been offered by the revolution of information and communication; as well as a good labor organization among countries, institutions and enterprises.

4. CONCEPT OF SELF-DETERMINATION AS DEVELOPMENT STRATEGY OF A COUNTRY

The Charter of the United Nations (San Francisco, 1945) has granted the self-government right to the peoples to celebrate international pacts and agreements among countries. Furthermore, the principles and criteria based on the International Public Law have been set out, on the one hand, as the peoples' inalienable right but, on the other hand, as a right that also places mutual liabilities and demands the respect of individual human rights

The concept of self-determination has a great force and a polemic character, especially the Committee on Human Rights has manifested its essential nature by pointing that self-determination is necessary for plain effectiveness of individual human rights. But when this concept is mentioned in today's political speeches, it can raise destabilizing fears, violent, inclusively. It also has been associated with extreme political positions.

This array of meanings derives from the fact that self-determination is linked with other "peoples," which, in turn, is troublesome and does not offer any meaning. On the contrary, doctrine and the States or other international agents have tried to make their conceptualizations valid. From 1960, the definition of colonial peoples as subjects of free determination supposed an essential motivation for decolonization and collaborated in an authentic universalization of the international society.

Culture is a group of beliefs, values, customs and traditions that form the identity of a people, includes arts, work and science.

From the seventies, some social researchers and academic leaders have dealt with the concept of *alternative development.*

The concept of *self-determination* refers to equal and mutual respect relationships among the peoples and nations, either large or small. (Jiménez B. Y, 2011).

This concept assumes that a mid-human group or developing country is not willing to make an holocaust of their own culture or their rights when they intend to address their economic, social, political and educational problems or when they accept some advice or suggestions from more powerful countries or groups.

This concept of *self-determination* comprises two aspects:

The *external aspect* deals with the States' sovereignty to freely choose their government and social systems, according to their culture, individual human rights and the right of the minority groups.

The *internal aspect* is seen as the right to decide and define the political organization and look for the people´s cultural, social and economic development. For this purpose, the cultural identity shall be strengthened without any race, creed, color or any other type of distinction or discrimination. It is relevant to respect and value the demands for social participation in education.

The interpretation and practical experience of the self-ruled institutions of higher education and the acknowledgement of self-ruling for the school centers constitute an important element to favor the criteria of transparency and accountability concerning the fulfillment of their own mission.

The institutions of higher education that belong to the public sector are not enough themselves, so they need other types of economic funding for their academic aims, as well as the private institution do depend only on their own revenues, so they look for other financing sources.

The concept of self-determination implies that not any other powerful group can impose their ideology or policies over other more vulnerable groups.

5. KNOWLEDGE AS A PRODUCTIVE TRANSFORMATION STRATEGY FOR DEVELOPMENT WITH EQUITY AND SUSTAINABILITY

The factors that generate the development of a country are very diverse, but, nowadays, among them, *knowledge is emphasized.* The capacity of a population to learn is a factor that can foster the economic and social development issues. In this globalized world, the fact of owning a literate population capable of understanding the new technologies is gaining more relevance every time. But elementary education (basic education) is a starting condition for development; it is also necessary a scientific community at the country's service and that responds to the needs of the population. (Reyes, G. 2001).

Surely, the development is not merely an economic matter, as other factors like the social, political and cultural ones, among others, can be also considered as measurement indicators of growth and development; however, the relationship economy-development is a research area that has been more developed and studied. Independently, the theories of development face complexities today, as from origin they integrate social, cultural and political approximations in the economic analysis. Any explanations of underdevelopment that exclude this integration are condemned to wreck.

The situation described above has recently changed as a result of the development of technologies, communication, and the globalization of the economy and the internationalization of enterprises. *Knowledge* has become to be a production factor that traces development differences, which means that in the countries with a greater development expectation comprise a better literate and basic education, who can learn technologies and innovate.

An educated population is essential for the enterprises of a country to be more highly competitive, and for the promotion of foreign investment. On the one hand, the educational policies have become to be a State's issue with an economic impact. On the other hand, the education indexes explain certain patterns of the economic sectors where the countries perform more. While the countries with high indexes of illiteracy are dedicated to agrarian activities and basic industry, the highly literate countries are focused on the services sector and research.

The sectors linked with services generate a higher income to the countries due to the fact that the high pricing for these services rely on the strong use of knowledge. Poor countries suffer more from offering services in the international market.

According to the Organization of Iberoamerican States (OIS), in the program, "Science, technology and innovation for the development and social cohesion, scientific and technological knowledge is one of the main richnesses of today's societies and a necessary element to foster economic and social development. Science, technology and innovation have turned to be essential tools to transform the production structures, the rational exploitation of natural resources, healthcare, education and other social demands.

The 21st century is characterized by the arise of the so called Knowledge Society or Knowledge Economy, that relies on the intensive use of information and knowledge as production factors and defined by a rapid scientific and technological progress generating an unprecedented volume of industrial innovations, and that has transformed the world context.

We are experiencing the birth of an economy based on the capacity to generate and use knowledge, on the quality of human resources, and on high demands for entrepreneurial capacity. (Krüger, Karsten. 2006).

This concept was proposed by Fernando Fanjzilber in the *Regional Office of Education for Latin America and the Caribbean's media*, at the UNESCO, since 1991. (Fanjzilber, 1991). (See Figure 1).

Figure 1 chose is an *alternative transformation strategy* for the achievement of the integral human development that has as basis:

1. *Education* and *training* to which we consider necessary to add the concept of culture;
2. *Culture* arises as result of the interaction of the man with the nature and other human beings, in the peculiar way in which a human group thinks about itself, about its relationships with other human groups, as well as its particular way of seeing and understanding the life, the world and the universe. The *culture* also constitutes an integral expression of the human being and the activities of the persons, the human groups and the social institutions, which understand: their origin and history, a system of values that bring them identity and distinguish them from other human groups or institutions. (Alvarez, 2014).
3. *Scientific and technological infrastructure*, represented by the development of the systems of information and communication (certainly including the ICTs in the society of knowledge);
4. *Entrepreneurial leadership capacity* to face the risks and uncertainty and the rising of new economic and social development problems.

Figure 1. Knowledge as a strategy for productive transformation with equity and sustainable relations of causality

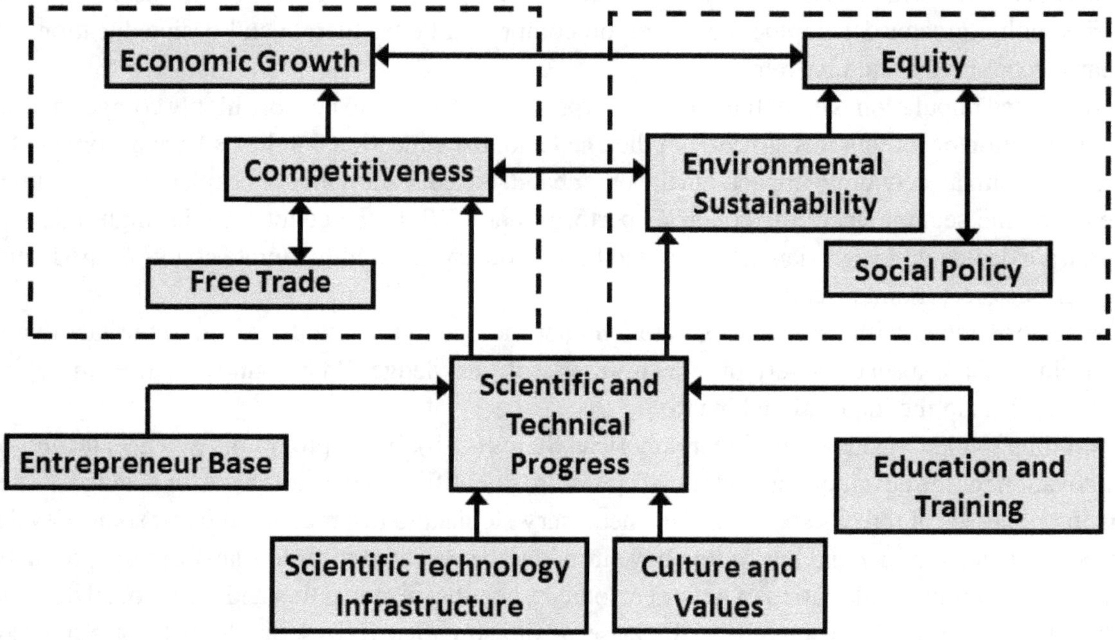

Reference: Fajnzylber, Fernando (1991) Educación y Conocimiento: Eje de la transformación productiva con equidad, Santiago (Chile) CEPAL/UNESCO.

These aspects are focused on the material, scientific and cultural progress of the countries that have complied with the integral human development of the social groups and subjects.

In the model of knowledge strategy, it is searched an *equity and sustainably economic growth*, in a context of *competitiveness and free market*, which is defined from the criteria and interests of the most powerful countries.

Two other important conditions for the knowledge strategy are the equity and fair distribution of growth benefits for people and the environmental balance as well.

Social politics or *democracy* is a key element of the knowledge strategy, in which democracy is not an optional assignment in the international context, because all the countries need to be or, at least, seem to be as democracies (China).

It is vital to know how far this knowledge strategy can get for the achievement of the integral human development.

One of the theorists of the analysis of the "Strategy of Development based on Knowledge," is Francisco Javier Carrillo, researcher at the *Tecnológico de Monterrey, Monterrey Campus,* who states that Knowledge-based Development (DBC) is a theoretical and practical field that derives from the convergence between a discipline and a movement. The origin discipline comes from the traditionally known economic science known as Development Theory (DT), which focuses on the understanding of the socioeconomic principles that guide the production growth worldwide. (Carillo, J. 2004).

The origin movement is *Knowledge Management* (KM), which emerges, firstly, in businesses as a response to the need of identifying, assessing and capitalizing the factors of value creation and, broadly, of individual, organizational and social knowledge-based development.

Knowledge Management is a movement at the end of the century born after the Second World War, emphasizing, for the first time, the production factors based on knowledge, in an increasing number of industries and regions. In the nineties, Knowledge Management strengthens in virtue of three huge economic vectors:

1. Insufficiency of business industrial models to capitalize Information and Communication Technologies (ICT), known as "Productivity Paradox;"
2. Increasing acceleration of the obsolescence rate of productive competences;
3. Pressure on identifying, measuring, understanding and capitalizing intangible assets (or knowledge) in the generation of richness and, more widely, in social development.

Knowledge-based development is the explicative and administrative efforts that respond to the emergence of knowledge societies.

The analyses by Gary Becker and Richard Solow offer an empirical grounding to Human Capital and Technology in the economic growth. They were distinguished with *laureate* Nobel prizes. The approaches of the great international development agencies that were transformed, as the century finishes, from investment in civil works towards knowledge-based programmes. Knowledge Management passed from being a business consultancy branch to become the dominating approach of public policies on development in the main Asian and European countries.

Three Levels of Knowledge-Based Development

Knowledge-based development programmes can be distinguished from the focus of their development actions or how they understand knowledge, which can be understood as:

1. An object or content (mostly).
2. Capacity transfer (increasingly).
3. Significant or valuable context.

Carrillo explains the three levels of (DBC) in the article previously quoted:

DBC Level I: Infrastructure of social knowledge

Most DBC programmes start focusing on the most immediate impact area: the instrumental basis that empowers the capacities of the productive agents, mainly, information communication technologies, which, in general, the social infrastructure of knowledge (universities, research and development centers, technological parks, etc.) constitute a necessary, but not enough, condition, to foster development.

DBC Level II: Human Capital development

DBC policies leaning towards human capital development are favored by the New Theory of Development. Learning self-management, the incorporation to virtuous circles of self-esteem and *entrepreneurship*, the articulation of practical communities, the integration of talent platforms, the establishment of knowledge clusters, the construction of social networks and innovation regional systems, build up some of the most frequent representations. The issue of knowledge meaning or value is appointed as fundamental. DBC is revealed as a qualitative instead of a quantitative matter, as a social transformation issue, rather than of industrial growth.

DBC Level III: Development of the Social System of Capitals

The avant-garde DBC thinking goes beyond the multiplication of knowledge objects and the flows between knowledge agents, focusing on *knowledge value-based systems*. These systems are defined as human groups that deliberately pursue a sustainable integral development with a special emphasis on tangible or knowledge goods. These goods include, to start with, all the significant dimensions of human experience and, hence, all possibilities of human realization. From this approach, while a better human condition (value dimension) recovers its purpose, the goods or human talent sets the instrumental character as their main goal. Moreover, this DBC, level III, reaches a strategic sense, because the system of capitals constitute the very ideal expression of identity and the purpose of a community, as well as of human competences and the means for reaching them.

The main tasks given from this approach are:

- The social capitals conjunct in a complete, consistent and homogeneous system.
- The operationalization and measurement of themselves.
- The strategic breach determination.
- The initiatives starting to resolve such breaches.
- The feedback and adjustment of the started initiatives.

The conditions for cities, regions and countries to become Knowledge-Based Development entities are as follows:

1. Overall compromised leadership, with the integral development of his community.
2. Critical mass of change agents having enough understanding of the KBD qualitative differences.
3. Exact and transparent diagnosis of the knowledge-based social capital state.
4. A series of strategic initiatives to get an optimal equilibrium of the capitals that feeds with the best global practices.
5. An international relationships network with the leading entities in knowledge-based innovation.

Another important contribution related to knowledge as a strategic production factor was the classical works of the economist Robert Solow, performed in the sixties about the factors that are linked with economic growth and general development. He found 70% of the growth in the United States and developed countries cannot be explained by the increase in traditional production factors (capital, land, work). This led him to formulate his well-known "Theory of Residual Factor," to refer to this great component of economic dynamism that cannot be explained by the "traditional production factors." (Solow, R. 1963)

The first identified aspects were a) the instruction of human resources (education) and b) the scientific and technological development as they are (technology). Education quality and human resources are performed, on one hand, and technology, on the other hand, both of which contribute to generate a capacity of economic growth and, therefore, of social welfare. (Chaparro, F. 2006).

Another important thinker in this context of search of a new meaning of knowledge in the modern society is the Danish economist Bengt-Äke Lundvall, professor of the Department of Economic Studies at the University of Aalborg, Denmark and of Political Sciences in Paris, who sustains that knowledge has become the main resource of the globalized economy of the XXIst century. He is author of the concepts of "learning economy" and of "innovation system". Moreover, he proposes that the capacity of managing and interpreting information for the people's welfare, changing it to knowledge through learning, is the capacity of excellence to obtain a sustainable development that can satisfy the basic needs of the population.

This characteristic of the new environment is what leads to the concept of Knowledge Society or Knowledge Economy and to the concept of Knowledge-based development strategies. Knowledge Society visualizes a social and economic development based on the processes for sharing knowledge with people in order to create value and innovations (learning processes), that can be translated to products and services and, finally, in welfare for the citizens.

One of the main objectives of the proposed analysis by the Theories on Knowledge Society and Knowledge Organizations is to understand how innovation takes place and how it can promote creativity in enterprises, universities, in production chains or in territory spaces (regions).

It is important to mention that in the context of Knowledge Economy, that characterizes the 21st century, innovation does not limit to changes in products and production processes. Innovation basis are found in processes related to knowledge creation and application and, therefore, with Knowledge Management processes in corporative contexts.

Knowledge management has acquired a significant importance as a change and development factor in all the tasks of the society; so that the main mission is to create an environment where available knowledge and information in an organization are accessible and can be used to promote innovation, provoke decision making improvements and produce new knowledges. The key is to create a culture where information and knowledge are valued, shared, managed and effectively and efficiently used.

The progressive changes generated by the so called technological revolution, whose main vectors were innovation in all science fields and, particularly, in the Information and Communication Technologies (ICT), have not only determined multi-dimensional changes, but have also given origin to a new social paradigm and a new culture.

In this context, the terms "Information Society" and "knowledge Society" are born. The first one is understood as the group of social relationships of any kind that are established using as ICT, mainly telematics networks, as a communication means and support. The second one is a broader concept that refers to the increasing importance that science and technology have for the creation of richness and economic development. In this area, knowledge has become relevant by changing to a strategic factor that responds to multi-causal stimulus in a dynamic scenario, in permanent change. (Carrillo, 2004).

Knowledge Management is all the group of activities performed with the aim of using, sharing and developing knowledges of an organization and of the members working in it, leading them to achieve their aims better.

It can also be understood as a specific systemic and organizational process for the acquisition, organization and communication of knowledge to employees, in such a way that they can make use of it for being more effective and productive at work. (Alavi. M. 2001).

Also, knowledge management resolves the problem about how to manage the intangible goods of an organization, so as to increase the accrued value and competitiveness by innovation and continuous perfection. By intangible goods, we can find: a) Human Talent. Staff capacities, limitation and attitudes. b) Organizational capital. Technology, strategies, culture, structures, proceedings. c) Relational Capital. Integrated by the group of relationships of the organization with clients, suppliers, distributors, and partners.

Finally, ICT are an important key, but do not represent the main component of knowledge management, because the people perform this main role. The purpose of ICT is to facilitate knowledge conservation and storage, organization and categorization, as well as to offer the possibilities of sharing it and to increase the knowledge transfer rate.

Some suggested criteria for the selection of academic staff are:

6. CONCEPT OF INTEGRAL HUMAN DEVELOPMENT

According to this position, it is also called humanism, the main mistake of other theories that focus on the method that forget the objective, and that is not necessarily, the economic development. This approach

Table 1. Criteria for human resources selection

Actual Society **Offer Spaces and Opportunities with** *Excluding Criteria*	**The Society We Need to Live** **Offers Spaces and Opportunities with** *Including Criteria*
1. Recommended persons.	1. Competent personnel and commitment with the institutional and mission.
2. High level preparation and education in the same institution.	2. Looks for diversified education training to organize interdisciplinary teams and a learning attitude.
3. Companions of the self-group or party are preferred.	3. Brings opportunities to independent people and from other parties.
4. They look for obedient and disciplined people who sustain the worship and respect to the chief.	4. Leadership - ability and attitudes favorable to team work.
5. Centralized management or bureaucratic management without delegation authority.	5. Decentralized management (local institutional and regional). Respects to the management freedom of school centers.
6. Able to sustain the control for the control.	6. People with work habits and service to give accountability and transparence.
7. Considers education as source so power in the government hands.	7. Considers education as the state policy to guarantee the natural right of the education for all.
8. Search the *education reform* to get nothing change.	8. Search the education reform to achieve structural and qualitative changes.

Source: Álvarez, Isaías. 2015.

is very critical about capitalism, as it sustain that radical changes must be done to the economic system in order to guarantee a better welfare for the people. It also states that the economic development is not enough, because what really matters in the different countries where capitalism reigns is a social and human improvement. (Reyes, G. 2009).

The criteria of the paradigm of the United Nations that lies as a basis for the elaboration of the Report on World Human Development are as follows:

the term development is understood as the social condition in a country, in which the real needs of a population are satisfied with the rational and sustainable use of natural resources and systems, based on a technology that respects cultural aspects and human rights. It includes a specification about that the social groups have access to basic organizations and services, such as education, living, health and nutrition. There exist employment opportunities, a positive rate of distribution and redistribution, of increasing capacities in the country. In political terms, the government system has legal and concrete legitimacy, which is an important characteristic for social inclusion. (UNO, 1945).

Changes must lead to progress, humanization of development concept, which is in conflict with the production increases theme. According with this development focus, it is negative to follow the same way than reach countries do, because it is a highly ecological and social price. So they consider that traditional development based on industrialization and production is the wrong way, and substitute it with a model in human development, it means: the increase of socio-economic opportunities and human abilities following development, regarding the next minimum requirements.

1. Products' availability and a better increase in life's level.
2. Better hopeful life, as an indicator of welfare and health.
3. Access to education, as a criterion of culture and information.

The basis that found this thought surge from these sources:

1. **Social:** An increasing production by traditional way that requires the exploitation and repression of the poor.
2. **Ecology:** Traditional industrialization implicating a non-repairable damage to the environment, without regarding future consequences. The planet would not resist that the countries traditionally developed.
3. **Feminism:** Very male thoughts about growth put women in disadvantage and exclude them from the world population, and leaves them vulnerable in front of economic crisis.

For this human development defenders, it is clear that better production of goods and services *(knowledge)* increases opportunities, capabilities and election possibilities (*freedom*) and economic growth, and the economic growth and a greater freedom contribute significantly to human development.

But economic growth is valued in measure that it contributes to human development. However, as the rent of a country is higher, it seems that the additional economic growth increases less than human development.

For that, it is necessary to adopt political decisions that sustain a favorable growth for human development. It is urgent to favor an economic growth based on an intensive employment of work, to proceed to redistribution of generated rents, and to center the economic growth in human capital education.

In addition, the economists call a virtuous circle in which growth and human development are backed up mutually. Also, they say that investing in people will result economically rentable and, besides all, ethically desirable. A healthy worker, well-nourished and with a high qualification, results more productive and contributes to growth, greatly. A person with those characteristics enjoys a more satisfactory life and contributes to a better human development of the society in where he participates: pays more taxes for improving the social services provided by the State, has more tools for educating his children, can help improve the situation in which the community lives.

This concept understands as development the life's condition of a society where the authentic needs of the population are satisfied by the rational and sustainable utilization of natural resources and systems. For this, technologies that are not contradictory to the related cultural groups will be used. (Reyes, Giovanni. 2002).

This concept integrates economic, technological and conservation elements, and has an ecological utilization, as well as a social and political ones. This power sphere, within the social context, is necessary as an organizational form and of legitimate, legal and functional cohesion inside social groups and as an instance for decision making among the persons. Thus the development would be characterized by condition in which the goods and services are increasing at the reach of the social groups of the country. This would imply a better social and economic integration in the societies and, consequently, the number of marginal group would be diminished.

Human development establishes Access to social services and an active social participation. In the first case, it is referred to the education systems and to the satisfaction of survival needs in terms of food, housing, dressing, health and security. In the second case, it refers to the capacity of the people and of the social institutions to guarantee that the groups in power are intermediary instances between subjects and actors in the decision making process.

The process of economic development, so that the "developing countries" become "developed countries," supposes legal and institutional adjustments in public policies, that are fact for granting incentives and promoting innovations and investments aimed at creating an efficient system of production and a system of distribution for goods and services.

In the nineties when a new concept of development is consolidated, that is called "sustainable human development," that means equal growth and in harmony with nature.

Sustainable development occurs when the economic development goes with the human, social and environmental developments (prevalence of natural and cultural resources), and with the display of control actions of the negative impacts of human activities. We cannot refer to development if the natural and cultural resources are considerably affected or worsen, or certain deplorable conditions, such as poverty, inequality or unemployment, not mattering if the income per capita increases.

CONCLUSION

The authors have considered that the conclusions of this work should be better presented in terms of *working hypotheses* for the future policies of development in higher education:

1. The concept of *growth* of the development and third world countries have already had enough experiences on the growing student enrollment figures which show no balance with the academic and management personnel (professors, researchers and school management staff) for higher education. These figures are too big to guarantee the fulfillment of the quality goal issues with reasonable levels of efficiency, quality relevance for social service commitment, and to face the challenges of education, innovation and the construction of a more just, social, democratic and inclusive society.
2. The *self-sufficiency* concept by no means is pertinent for the sustainable development of higher education institutions. Furthermore, the governmental financing is not enough for the state higher education institutions; as the student fees are not enough to guarantee the development of private higher education institutions; all of them badly need alternative funding sources.
3. The concept of *interdependence* seems to be more suitable for supporting inter-institutional academic exchange and educational innovation issues, such as students and professors mobility, new education models required by the future general policies of higher education. But this concept supposes the *self-reliance* for higher education communities themselves, in order to be capable of building reliance and common academic work with other higher education and social institutions. They have to move away from highly-rigid centralized and bureaucratic management processes, so that they can give more protagonism to the academic bodies and teacher and researcher teams, saving for themselves more strategic functions for the benefit of the higher education institutions.
4. The concept of *self-determination* contributes for the nations and the higher education institutions development; because they may govern by themselves in accordance with the great institutional mission and the academic research freedom in order to build a more just, equal, fair and inclusive society. But they do not have to be seen as an island in the very local, state and international community.
5. The concept of *knowledge as a productive transformation strategy* for the general economic and competitive issues in the context of social development and the care of environmental balance and sustainability of the more just, social and democratic policies. Besides that, the system of information and communication technologies has increased the demands for a change of paradigms in the curricula learning programmes, and of educational, curricula and teaching models in higher education.
6. The concept of *integral human development* represents a big challenge in the context of new higher education paradigms demands. Education is considered a key strategy element for reaching the goals of integral human development at the level of local, state and international community. The access of majorities to the different levels of education is a necessary condition for a sustained and an authentic integral human development process in all the higher education institutions.

The higher education institutions play an important role in the economic and human development of the peoples and the countries for rising their educational expectations, as well as their economic, political, social, cultural and environmental development in the context of knowledge society and the demand of a more just and inclusive society.

REFERENCES

Gonzalez & Saxe-Fernandez. (2002). Globalidad, neoliberalismo y democracia. In *El mundo actual: situación y alternativas*. Mexico: Siglo XXI editores.

Álvarez, I., & Romay, M. (2015). *Cultura de evaluación y desafíos para el desarrollo de las instituciones educativas*. México: Limusa.

Alvavi, M. (2001). Review: Knowledge management and knowledge management systems: conceptual foundations and research issues. *MIS Journal Quarterly, 38*(3).

Barrera, J. Y. (2011). Teorías del Desarrollo Económico. In Contribuciones a la Economía, Noviembre 2011. Universidad de Pinar del Río. Cuba.

Biografias. (n.d.). Available at www.biografiasyvida.com/biografia/n/nyerere.htm

Carrillo, J. (2004). Desarrollo basado en el Conocimiento. In *Transferencia. Año. 17. Núm. 65. Enero 2004*. Mexico: Instituto Tecnológico de Monterrey.

Chaparro, F. (2006). *Una estrategia de Desarrollo basado en el Conocimiento para el Eje Cafetero. Reflexiones sobre su potencialidad y cómo medirlo*. Pereira: Universidad del Rosario.

Escribano, G. (2005). Teorías del Desarrollo Económico. Universidad Nacional de Educación a Distancia. Madrid.

Eumed. (1991). Available at www.eumed.net/cursecon/dic/l.htm#interdependencia

Fajnzylber, F. (1991). *Boletín del Proyecto Principal de Educación, UNESCO/OREALC, No. 26*. Santiago de Chile.

Giovanni, R. (2001). *E. Principales Teorías sobre el Desarrollo Económico y social. Nómadas No. 4. Revista crítica de Ciencias Sociales y Jurídicas*. Universidad Complutense de Madrid. España.

Krüger, K. (2006). El concepto de sociedad de conocimiento. Universidad de Barcelona.

Reyes, G. (2002). *E. Comercio y Desarrollo: Bases conceptuales y enfoque para América Latina y el Caribe*. Zona Económica.

Reyes, G. E. (2009). Teorías de Desarrollo Económico y Social: Articulación con el planteamiento de Desarrollo Humano. Revista Tendencias. Revista de la Facultad de Ciencias Económicas y Administrativas, 10(1).

Schumpeter, J. (1963). *Teoría del Desenvolvimiento Económico*. Mexico: Fondo de Cultura Económica.

Solow, R. (1963). *Capital Theory and Rate of Return*. Amsterdam: North-Holland Publishing Company.

United Nations Organization. (1945). *Charter of the United Nations*. San Francisco: Author.

KEY TERMS AND DEFINITIONS

Economic Growth: An idealized definition of this concept that includes the comprehensive human development shall be understood as a balanced and sustainable growth of the production of goods and services that goes beyond the average population growth, but that, in turn, guarantees a fair and equal distribution of the goods and services, without damaging the ecological environment, as well.

Integral Human Development: It is understood as the social condition in a country, in which the real needs of a population are satisfied with the rational and sustainable use of natural resources and systems, based on a technology that respects cultural aspects and human rights.

Interdependence: It is a generic term that is used for describing the complex and multiple economic relationships that the modern nations have established among themselves.

Knowledge as a Transformation Strategy: A strategy where Knowledge-based Development (DBC) is a theoretical and practical field that derives from the convergence between a discipline and a movement.

Knowledge Management: It emerges, firstly, in businesses as a response to the need of identifying, assessing and capitalizing the factors of value creation and, broadly, of individual, organizational and social knowledge-based development.

Knowledge Society: Knowledge Society or Knowledge Economy, that relies on the intensive use of information and knowledge as production factors and defined by a rapid scientific and technological progress.

Self-Determination: The concept of self-determination refers to equal and mutual respect relationships among the peoples and nations, either large or small.

Self-Sufficiency: Intention of some countries to sustain themselves with their natural, economic and social resources.

Chapter 7
Evaluation and Identification of Professional Tourism Educational and Training Competences

Rosa María Rivas García
Instituto Politécnico Nacional, Mexico

Edgar Oliver Cardoso Espinosa
Instituto Politécnico Nacional, Mexico

ABSTRACT

This chapter deals with the evaluation and identification of professional tourism educational and training competences with the purpose of recognizing the main characteristics of labour capacity in the tourism industry. Tourism is promoted through education, as well as through the development of skills and tools that result in an optimal labour performance during the stages of school training. Moreover, it describes the relationship of knowledge management in the tourism sector that leads to quality in human capital, in addition to professional alignment, in an educational context. As this section focuses on the overview of professional tourism, the following components are considered; the preamble and classification of the tourism industry, the conceptualization of educational evaluation and competence, and concludes with the description and analysis of the works targeted at the evaluation and identification of professional competences in tourism.

INTRODUCTION

First of all, it is vital to determine the main basis of this chapter, tourism. In virtue of being the object of this section, tourism can be studied from several approaches and disciplines in regard to the complexity of relationships among the elements of this area of study.

DOI: 10.4018/978-1-5225-0457-3.ch007

Tourism as a subject of university research becomes to be a matter of interest during the period between the two world wars of this century (1919-1938). Authors and organizations, like Hunziker and Krapf (1942), and Medlik Burkart (1981), Mathieson and Wall (1982) UNWTO (1994-2014) have studied and described the term tourism, which has observed changes, modifications, adaptations over time, by virtue of their social characteristics.

According to the UNWTO (2014), tourism is a social, cultural and economic phenomenon related to the movement of people to the places that are outside their usual location of residence for personal or business / professional reasons. While these people are called visitors (which may be tourists or excursionists; residents or non-residents), tourism is associated with the people's activities and, therefore, implies tourism expenditure.

Also, another element that needs to be explained is Knowledge Management, which is treated in two parameters, first as knowledge and then as management.

Knowledge can be defined in different ways. Firstly, for philosophers, it means intelligence, understanding, and reason; and secondly, it is studied from diverse disciplines, such as psychology, philosophy, and informatics. According to Muñante (2004), knowledge means to embrace the properties and relationships of objects, and understand what they represent or not. The Philosophical Dictionary of Rosental and ludin (1973), based on dialectical materialism, defines knowledge as a process by which the reality is reflected and reproduced in human thinking. This process is subjected to the laws of social development and is closely linked with practical activity

On the other hand, knowledge management, according to Cortes and Pineda (2006), is intimately related to the subject's education, obliged to live in a changing and accelerated environment, in a globalized society that requires a high degree of competitiveness. Hence, the person must and will be willing to learn and re-learn throughout his life.

Instead of remaining only in the mind or in the subject's thinking, knowledge must transcend, transform, share and renew. Therefore, we refer to incorporate and combine it with the individual and collective experience, with the different everyday applications people have had with knowledge.

Knowledge management must be understood as the intended development of one of the people's and organization's competences, as an innovation supported by an interactive learning process, where the members involved rise their competence and take care of innovation (Minakata, 2009).

Prior to what has been mentioned above, it is convenient to analyze the evaluation and identification of the professional tourism competences in order to strengthen the human capital capacities in the tourism industry. This will be the beginning of educational management in the educational context. Nowadays worldwide societies tend to face frequent changes, mainly in the economic structure and, therefore, in the labour markets, which have an impact on tourism education and training. When knowledge is performed, it is not perceived as static because it responds to the needs of immediate application. As a result, the professional competences that meet the industries' demands must be valued, exprofeso in tourism activities.

PREAMBLE TO THE TOURISM INDUSTRY

In recent decades, activity in the tourism industry has witnessed a rapid development; the panorama of international tourism of UNWTO (2013) states a growing number of destinations have opened up to tourism and have invested in this sector, making it a key factor of socio-economic progress by obtaining export earnings, job creation and business and implementing infrastructure. Tourism has experienced continued expansion and diversification, becoming one of the economic sectors larger and growing in the world, he has experienced continuous growth and a deep diversification to become one of the economic sectors that are growing faster. Global tourism is closely linked to development and a growing number of new destinations are part of it. This dynamic has turned tourism into a key driver of socioeconomic progress.

Tourism generates directly and indirectly an increase in economic activity in the visited (and beyond them) places, mainly due to the demand for goods and services to be produced and provided. In the economic analysis of tourism, one must distinguish between the 'financial contribution' tourism refers to the direct effect of tourism that can be measured by the TSA (Tourism Satellite Account), and the 'economic impact' of tourism It is a much broader concept that encapsulates the direct, indirect and induced effects of tourism and should be estimated by applying models. The purpose of the study is to estimate the economic impact the economic benefits, namely, the net increase in the wealth of residents arising from tourism, measured in monetary terms, in relation to levels that would prevail in the absence of this activity. So it is necessary to narrow the current developments and forecasts of tourism UNWTO (2015) in global terms in order to identify the economic and social importance of the activity;

- The international tourist arrivals worldwide grew by 4.3% in 2014 to reach 1,133 million;
- International tourism in 2014 generated USD 1.5 billion US in export earnings;
- UNWTO forecasts a growth in international tourist arrivals of between 3% and 4% in 2015.

Additionally, the following figures confirm the socioeconomic value of world tourism;

- Generates 10% of GDP (direct, indirect and induced).
- Stir in 1 of every 11 jobs (direct, indirect and induced).
- It is 6% of International Trade.
- It represents 30% of exports of services.
- In the United States it generated USD 1.5 billion in exports.

For decades, tourism has experienced a non-stopping growth and a deep diversification until becoming one of the economic sectors that are growing faster in the globe. World tourism is closely linked to development and a growing number of new destinations are part of it. This dynamic has turned tourism into a key driver of socioeconomic progress.

According to the UNWTO, the demand exceeds expectations for the year 2013 due to the fact that international tourist arrivals (overnight visitors) increased 5% at that year, reaching the record figure of 1,087 million arrivals worldwide, compared with 1.035 million in 2012, when for the first time the milestone of one billion was exceeded. Although the global economy moves at a slow pace, the demand for international tourism in 2013 exceeded expectations, with over 52 million international tourists traveling the world. Europe led the growth in absolute terms, having received more than 29 million international tourists in 2013, reaching a total of 563 million.

Growth (+ 5%) was twice the average for the region for the period 2005-2012 (+ 2.5% annually). Asia and the Pacific recorded the fastest growth of all UNWTO's regions, exhibiting a 6% increase in international arrivals, or 14 million more than in 2012. Africa recorded a growth by 5%, equivalent to 3 more million tourists and a total of 56 million. In the Americas, international arrivals grew 3%, up to

168 million, equivalent to an increase of 5 million. The Middle East (0%) has not yet managed to grow back again, although some destinations had a pretty good behaviour and others recorded a moderate recovery. Growth is expected to continue in 2014 at a steady pace between 4.0% and 4.5% worldwide rate. By WTO regions, the best prospects for 2014 correspond to Asia and the Pacific regions (between + 5% and + 6%), followed by Europe and the Americas (both between + 3% and + 4%). Middle East (from 0% to + 5%), the outlook is positive but uncertain.

Today, the business volume of tourism equals or even surpasses that of oil exports, food products or automobiles. Tourism has become one of the major players in the international commerce, and represents a major source of income for many developing countries. This growth goes hand-in-hand with an increased diversification and the competition among the different destinations.

Based on data from the World Tourism Organization (2011), the general expansion of tourism in industrialized and developing countries has been beneficial in terms of economy and employment, for many related sectors, from construction to agriculture or telecommunications. It is important to define the term tourism industries, according to the activities concerned, companies, providers, actors, etc. which mainly generate typical tourism products, and cover one or both of the following criteria, as well:

1. Tourism expenditure on the product should represent a significant part of total tourism expenditure (ratio corresponding expenditure / demand).
2. Tourism expenditure on the product should represent an important share of the product supply in the economy (condition of the proportion corresponding to the supply). This criterion implies that the supply of a typical tourism product would be considerably reduced if there were no visitors.

Based on the methodological notes of the UNWTO's database on tourism statistics (2012); the term tourism industries includes the factory complexes that regularly produce tourism products; and is one of the most colloquial terms used in the tourism sector. The following the lists exhibits these specified industries:

1. Accommodation for visitors.
2. Activities of provision of food and beverages.
3. Passenger transport by railway.
4. Passenger transport by road.
5. Passenger transport by water.
6. Passenger Air Transport.
7. Rental of transport equipment.
8. Activities of travel agencies and other reservation services.
9. Cultural Activities.
10. Sports and recreational activities.
11. Retail commerce of typical tourism goods.
12. Other features of tourism activities, specific of each country.

Having described the activities, businesses, providers, stakeholders of the tourism industry is timely perform stress that described in advance are the activities in which tourism professionals carry out their work activity; so it is vital knowledge of the skills required for the human capital of tourism companies in an effort to increase productivity and competitiveness of the sector through knowledge management to use the academic preparation to benefit tourism.

Derived from the importance of the tourism industry in the world as a key factor for the socio-economic progress, we find export revenues, the creation of jobs and enterprises and the implementation of infrastructure. (UNWTO, 2014); It is necessary to raise the issue of identification and evaluation of educational skills in tourism educational and training by focusing the analysis on the educational processes, the environment and adaptation to current and future needs of the tourism sector. Moreover, based on the criteria established by the UNWTO, a tourism educational system must ensure its competitiveness while observing the following principles:

- To adapt the skills offered during the educational process to the real needs and expectations of demand (external and internal customers).
- To provide the tourism training system just in time, at the right time: an early or late training can have equally negative results.
- To ensure individual and collective efficacy, through the convergence of the educational objectives of the sector.
- To introduce the expected results to the demand of the educational systems, without raising false expectations that will be difficult to meet.
- To ensure a maximum efficiency through optimization of resources. Conducting regular quality audits to rectify the deviations and permanently update the educational content.

EVALUATION

In making the evaluation and identification of the educational tourism skills, the concepts of evaluation and educational competence must be made clear. Firstly, the theme of evaluation will be studied.

Evaluation is conceived as an indispensable and previous activity conducive to raising the quality of education action; besides being identified with the last stage of the natural process of knowledge which concludes with the issuance of informed judgments; a process leading to decisions and human action. In its simplest form, the evaluation leads to a judgment on the value of something and is expressed by the view that something is significant. This judgment is generated by describing the meeting of a set of standards or criteria against which the subject or object of study is compared. (De la Garza, 2004).

The evaluation and assessment of the competences needs the use of strategies that as teachers we must have; and according to Tobon (2005), these competences seek the meaningful learning of contents during the development of thinking skills, so that the students become self-sufficient learners. The basic principles of competency-based assessment are: validity, reliability, flexibility and fairness. At present the educational model based on developing skills and assess their development has the following features; cannot be observed directly and is based on evidence of acquired learning, are not absolute judgments so there are three basic principles.

1. Integrated competence; It includes knowledge, understanding, problem solving, technical skills, attitudes and ethics.

2. Direct and relevant methods; ensure that the efforts of student learning are properly addressed; and ensure that the criteria to be used for trial evaluation are clear to students. (Contexts and specific strategies)
3. Use broad base of evidence for evaluating competence; it involves mixing methods to provide sufficient evidence that emphasizes performance.

Pérez Juste (2006) defines that the qualitative leap of evaluation is produced when the evaluation is recognized with an improvement function, fully consistent with the essence of the educational events; not forgetting that education is an intentional and systemic activity for people's improvement or refinement. The improvement function, characterized by in school learning evaluation, represents the expansion of the objects evaluated, passing to incorporate not only teaching alongside with learning, but the whole set of elements that contribute to learning: tools, contexts and educators, and the primary means together with the provided scheduled activities.

Ruiz (2004) suggests that the evaluation is a process of structured and thoughtful analysis, for understanding the nature of the subject matter and make value judgments on it, providing information to help improve and adjust educational activities. Understanding as "structured analysis process" that which is based on the prior planning of what will be evaluated, the development implemented data collection and subsequent rigorous analysis of the information obtained.

Worthen, Sanders and Fitzpatrick (1996) in the book of Educational evaluation: analysis of their practices Rueda (2013); describe the evaluation conducted in an ethical and professional manner allows to know the strengths and areas of opportunity for different systems, institutions, programs, products or actors, in order that the information generated guide decisions at different levels; from the political to the operational and also promote the establishment of a culture of evaluation.

In the field of educational assessment according to the Ministry of Public Education of Mexico (2012) assessment is a comprehensive and systematic process through which it is collected the information in a methodical and rigorous manner, to understand, analyze and judge the value a certain learning object of learning of students, teacher performance, the degree of mastery of the curriculum and its characteristics, the educational programs of the state and federal level, the management of institutions based on defined guidelines underlying making aimed at helping improve educational activities and adjust decisions.

The evaluation involves an assessment refers to quality. The rating allows quantification refers to the amount. The value should be taken into account several subjective elements, such as: opinions, feelings, perceptions. It refers only measuring elements observed and quantified. So you can evaluate and accredit without any qualifications involved. (UAM, s.f.).

Once an overview of the evaluation and its importance in the educational process took place, it is concluded that the assessment and evaluation are important and fundamental to the learning process, since they realize the developed competencies in addition to investigate what you can change during the course development, endeavoring to achieve the goals. Also in assessing the professional skills in education and tourism training it is necessary to validate the learning process with greater feasibility possible as should be demonstrated skills acquired in the educational process in a workplace through knowledge management in companies and specific tourism activities.

EDUCATIONAL COMPETENCE

Another issue of vital importance for the development of this section is the subject of educational competence, which are addressed some conceptualizations about it.

Competence defined from the labour environment is conceived as a capacity that can only be deployed in a work situation. This deployment has its rules, procedures, tools and consequences. The concept of competence that is defined from the world of education, schools and universities seems to answer the same basic idea, but its demonstration is developed in in situations of educational evaluation. By questioning the role of universities in the society, the European Space of Higher Education was created; in which the need for universities to be responsible for the training of citizens was raised, in order to cope with the changes arising from globalization and technological development. That is, the university was requested to undertake the necessary reforms to develop citizens able to contribute to the society, to adapt and anticipate to new requirements, that is to say, to continue with their life-long learning.

In response to this, the process of European Convergence incorporated the suggestions of Tuning project (González & Wagenaar, 2003) posed a university education based on skills and making explicit reference to training in general skills to ensure employability of the new professional. The definition of employability do Hager, Holland and Beckett (2002) is the ability and security in retaining employment, to increase productivity, be competitive and able to decide within the various occupational choices that may arise in their environment labour. It depends on the ability of "learning to learn" to adapt to changes and new opportunities in a changing environment.

In the academic context, the Tuning project identifies specific skills as those that are related to each subject area. These skills are crucial to any situation because they are specifically related to the concrete knowledge of a subject area. The Tuning project named the shared attributes that may arise in any situation and are considered important by graduates and employers as general skills.

Mertens (1997) White Fernandez (2009) describes as generic and specific skills; the former are related to behaviors and attitudes own work different areas of production; for example, the capacity for teamwork, negotiation skills, planning, etc. The latter-specific- comprise the technical aspects covering the occupation and are not easily transferable to other work settings (operation of specialized machinery, development of infrastructure projects, etc.).

The European Commission (2004) describes the term "competence" as a combination of skills, knowledge, skills and attitudes, and the inclusion of eagerness to learn, besides the *know-how* acquisition. Key competences represent a transferable, multi-functional package of knowledge, skills and attitudes that all the individuals need for their personal fulfillment and development, inclusion and employment.

As Tobon argues (2007), the educational competences are described as complex processes of performance with expertise in certain contexts, integrating different knowledge *(knowing how to be*, *knowing how, knowing to know* and *knowing how to live with*), in order to perform activities and / or solve problems with a sense of challenge, motivation, flexibility, creativity, understanding and endeavor, within a perspective of meta-cognitive processing, continuous improvement and ethical commitment. The goal would be to contribute to enhancing personal development, the construction and strengthening of the social fabric, the continuous pursuit of a sustainable economic and entrepreneurial development, and the care and protection of the environment and living species, as well.

Zabala and Arnau (2007) suggest that effective intervention powers consist in different areas of life through the actions in which they mobilize, at the same time and interrelated, the attitudinal, procedural and conceptual components. These authors comment that the definition means the implementation of effective actions to various different situations and problems, which require the use of available resources. The attitude attribute associated with the term competence refers to the willingness to solve the problem situation with a definite intention, without ignoring the domain of procedures, abilities and skills, as the field of performance and reference objects knowledge (facts, concepts and conceptual systems). As Arnau Zabala explains it, the execution of a competent action works from the problem situations that are considered as unique and complex: unique, because the circumstances and criteria can change; and complex depending on the number of variables involved and the relationships already established.

A competence for the Organization for Economic Cooperation and Development (2013) is more than knowledge and skills. It involves the ability to meet complex demands, using and mobilizing psychosocial resources (including skills and attitudes) in a particular context.

Through conceptualizations described in advance it has been identified that educational schemes worldwide have aligned, adopted and adapted the term "competition", first emerged in the workplace ; the competency-based approach is an attempt to equal opportunities with educational tool. The review of the thematic -educational competence- is for the purpose of meeting the educational and training demands in tourism education, in response to cultural changes which places the school and education in context considering the transformations among them They can be highlighted ; increasing the level of requirements to join the knowledge society, increase the general level of training, continuing training content crisis that soon become obsolete, changing the educational paradigm and not focused on teacher and school, but the individual learner.

PROFESSIONAL COMPETENCE

The issue of professional competence emerged as controversial in industrialized countries about the need to improve the relationship of the educational system with the production in the eighties, in order to promote adequate training of the workforce. Through the development of the concept it took shape new models in the understanding of educational training for the workplace. The dynamics of professional competence has been incorporated into the emerging and developing countries, particularly Latin America, resulting from global economic environment, which has led to the need to incorporate different schemes of education and training related to professional competence that consolidate a new how to address the relationship between training and employment.

Professional competence is defined as the individual's behavior in the execution of professional practice and is closely linked with the social role of the professional.

Kane (1992) defines professional competence as "the utilization of knowledge, skills and judgment associated with the profession, in all situations that may confront in the course of professional practice".

Professional competence is the ability of performance, which depends on three components: the professional profile determined by the skills and personality traits, knowledge, skills and attitudes acquired in training and developed in professional practice. This involves knowledge and actions linked to personal attitudes and values.

Productive capacity of an individual is defined and measured in terms of performance in a certain labor context, not only of knowledge, skills and attitudes; these are necessary but not sufficient by themselves to effective performance. (CONOCER, 1997).

From the educational context, the focus of professional competence reinforces an option to promote education and training in a way that match the needs of people, businesses and society in general; translating a scheme close relationship of the educational and productive scenarios that provide results in terms of competitiveness, job quality and knowledge management by incorporating human capital possessing skills in line with labor needs

PROFESSIONAL TOURISM EDUCATIONAL AND TRAINING COMPETENCES

Derived from the importance of the tourism industry in the world to be a key factor for socio-economic progress by earning export revenues, the creation of jobs and enterprises, implementation of infrastructure. (UNWTO, 2014).

Tourism is closely linked to certain elements that constitute it as a functional system, because each has a specific function and significantly contributes to the activity occurs; so to bring the element of human capital in the tourist industry combined with the particularities of tourism, is inescapable training of competent personnel to generate effective solutions to the needs posed by tourism, so it is relevant to analyze the tourism education and training; It is necessary to raise the issue of identification and evaluation of educational skills in education and training in tourism; focusing the analysis to the educational processes, the environment and adapt current and future needs of the tourism sector; based on criteria established by some research of professional training in tourism entity in the global parameter in the position of educational skills and approaches.

With the firm purpose of framing the professional competences in tourism educational and training, the theme will be based on previous inquiries that have been identified. So forth, three approaches will be discussed; firstly, the methodology of the World Tourism Organization - TEDQUAL (Tourism Education Quality - Quality in Tourism Education). This is an evaluation and quality assurance-oriented tool and quality assurance in tourism education and training. The second work is called University's Degree in Tourism of the National Agency for Quality Assessment and Accreditation, from the University of Girona, within the European Convergence Program, which performs a thorough analysis of tourism studies in the Spanish University to create a proposal for adapting these studies to the parameters that mark convergence towards this new European Higher Education system, by defining the statements of the Sorbonne (1998) and Bologna (1999), and the Prague *Communiqué* (2001). Then, the third revised research derives from SECTUR, CONACYT, CESTUR, and La Salle University, Cancun campus in Mexico (2012), and is called Alignment of the study programs of tourism education to the workplace needs.

TEDQUAL (Tourism Education Quality: Quality in Tourism Education)

Under the specialized tourism agency it has Plan on Tourism Education and defines its mission as "achieving quality in tourism education and training, responding to the needs of future professionals, of employers in the tourism industry and the Member States ". The ultimate objectives of that plan are:

- Permanent detection of the employers' human capital needs in the tourism industry, within the Member States (observatory of human resources in tourism, cooperation offices, etc.).
- Definition of quality standards in tourism education and training, applicable globally and in world tourism regions (TEDQUAL, GTAT, etc.).
- Strengthening of national tourism administrations regarding their own human capital needs and those of the tourism industries who manage (tourist education systems, scholarships, internships, etc.).
- Definition of tourism training programs that comply with the quality standards and meet the needs of future professionals of tourism employers of each country and of the Member States (tourism education systems, new technologies in education and tourism training, teaching materials, strategic actions, etc.).

Detecting needs of tourism education and schooling is the basic point of any education system that seeks to provide quality and gain success by meeting one of the conditions for achieving competitiveness. So quality is to meet customer needs and exceed the expectations they have placed on the product or service. (Mayor, 2009).

According to the UNE-EN ISO 9000 (2005), the term quality is understood as the degree to which a set of characteristics (distinguishing features) meet certain requirements (needs or expectations set). The requirements must meet customer expectations.

Quality defined as optimizing customer's satisfaction acquires paramount importance in generating competitive advantages, both for the results in customer's loyalty and the improvement in profitability, and for reducing the social impact. (Nightgown, Fabra & Monfort, 2011)

The basic notion on which Total Quality rests is the possibility of avoiding the gaps before they occur, with an emphasis on prevention and the establishment of systems that eliminate the possibility of error: the concept *right first time*. This is essential to meet the expectations / needs and critical factors that influence the final perception of quality and, thus, a group of regular and systematic research must be done. These studies must gather firsthand information from interested users, in this case, the employers immersed in the tourism industry.

Through a focus on Total Quality, TEDQUAL aims to contribute to the definition of training needs in tourism, starting from the basic premise that the quality of tourism products and services in subjective terms of consumer satisfaction is equal to development human resources which in turn is equivalent to the training role of employers and employees.

Even if anything prevents from applying the TEDQUAL methodology to the detection of the tourism schooling gaps, from the perspective of teachers or students, it is from the perceptions of the ultimate consumer (tourist employer), where it is collected the most relevant information regarding the training needs of the tourism labour market and, therefore, of the most important shortcomings of the current education supply. In this context, there will be quality in the schooling system when the skills and knowledge of the employees respond to previous expectations of the employers.

Otherwise, a training gap will occur. On the other hand, it is necessary to refer the quality gaps to specific schooling areas, for adapting, later on, the schooling supply to educational contents and specific curricula.

Degree in Tourism ANCEA European Convergence Program

According to research Degree in Tourism ANCEA to assess the impact of transversal or generic competencies in the case of tourism studies the specificity of these studies lies in its multidisciplinary nature (economics, geography, law, history, political science, languages, computer science, business, communication ...), multidisciplinary and trans disciplinary forcing cope with knowledge of various sciences, while the proper exercise of the profession is determined by the need to face the problems of managing people, companies and institutions. The evaluated transversal competences are grouped into three categories: instrumental, personal and systemic, all refer to the formation of a university in a generic sense. They explain the reasons noted above that the valuation of all the competences has given very high results, concluding that tourism training is to ensure coverage of a wide range of generic skills marked in the project proposal.

To delimit the different contents that should configure the curriculum for the Degree in Tourism, it was considered to study the various proposals for the description of possible contents that should be associated with the selected specific skills. In that sense, the universities were commissioned to undertaken the following reflections; which are the contents that lead us to acquire a specific skill set? They can be defined as the set of knowledge and scientific, technical and cultural resources required. In order to select the contents of a competence, it is interesting to keep in mind the different types of knowledge that can work: a) acquiring knowledge: knowledge based on facts, rules, concepts, theories, that is to say, necessary information to know the reality and move in it. b) Learning to do: knowledge related to a set of steps, rules and actions to get a result, "*know how.*" c) Learn to develop attitudes: knowledge related to attitudes and reflected in the array of "transferable skills."

To facilitate the selection of content, you can help to respond to a series of questions concerning the competence in question;

1. What information is necessary to transmit?
2. What content does the student need in order to achieve the competence?
3. Why is this content important?
4. What degree of correspondence does the selected content have with the tourism graduate's profile?

From here, the following steps to identify the needed content are: To write freely everything related to the content of competence; to check if there is any repetition of topics; to establish logical relationships between needed items; to simplify the descriptor of powers limiting it to 3O four sentences for each. With all this, it is possible to segment the information under the following headings: DISCIPLINARY KNOWLEDGE (*know how*), a list of the main knowledge of the different competence-based disciplines; and PROFESSIONAL KNOWLEDGE (skills), a list of the major professional competence-based knowledge. After receiving the considerations of each university about the assigned competences, different options were adapted to generate a homogeneous development of competences.

The next step to consider is the fusion of the information gathered from the generic transversal skills jointly with specific educational and professional skills in order to set the final framework, which works as the basis of the degree's curriculum. When making this merge. It is evident that some of the generic skills correspond exactly to some skills that the working group foresaw as specific competences for tourism graduates. All this means that our proposal considers that the generic skills are and must be present in the educational processes of each and every one of the specific competencies. The nature of both categories of competences (generic and specific) and their role in building a teaching structure allows that, by coexisting both of them, the presence of the teaching guides of these competences is guaranteed. As an example, if one of the specific skills that a tourism student must have is to know the operating procedure in the field of housing, the teaching development of this skill will involve taking into account the generic skills of problem solving, critical thinking or motivation for quality. From a closer analysis of this process, we can establish the following correspondences between the definition of generic skills and specific skills for the degree in tourism.

Once discussed the professional competences that the graduates must hold, it was necessary to compare through different routes the proposal of the Working Group made up by the representatives of the sector. It would not make sense to design a curriculum without considering the needs that are daily detected by professionals. The survey work directed to the sector concerning to the specific competences had a table as a support, in which a list of competences was provided for being assessed by using a scaled with the following criteria:

1. This competence is not necessary to develop the tasks of this profile, therefore, any level of learning is required.
2. This competence is hardly necessary to develop the characteristics of this profile tasks; As a result, a basic level of training is required.
3. This competence is quite necessary to develop the tasks of this profile, therefore, a sufficient level of learning required.
4. This competence is very necessary to develop the tasks of this profile, so a full level of learning is required.

Several expert meetings with professionals coming from the following areas were performed: Subsector brokerage hosting of Professional Representatives (bearing in mind that, given the dislocation in the industry, you cannot meet with a single professional association bringing together the different profiles that we have taken into consideration). Representatives of associations and Representatives of the public sector (both central administration and the autonomous administration and other institutions).

Once the sector has been consulted on the work being done, we proceeded to contrast the graduates' project, regarding their experience as students, as well as the perspective gained of having completed their studies. These viewpoints turn their opinions into invaluable elements when dealing with the new definition of a proposal for education.

Aligning the Curricula of Tourism Education to the Needs of the Workplace: SECTUR, CONACYT, CESTUR

The research assumes that the curricula of the majors in tourism are not aligned to the needs of the labour market and that do not meet the requirements of the tourism facilities. For this aim, 799 university degree study plans (graduate, post-graduate and technical) were reviewed. At the same time, Mexico's tourism supply was verified through the division of the territory in 6 regions. Furthermore, students, graduates, school authorities and employers were interviewed to find the gaps and today's schooling status.

Ordinarily, under the competence-based approach, the graduate profile is understood as an articulated set of skills that presumably will allow students to exercise a (relevant, effective and efficient) successful performance when addressing and resolving the most common problems in the field of their profession. From this perspective, competences are demonstrated in action or execution. Competences are, in brief, the expert's know-how under different scenarios and circumstances.

Applied research, descriptive, transversal and mixed to make an interpretation of facts and realities.

Methodological Steps

1. Identification of study areas
    a. To group by geographical curricula in order to relate, in the first instance, with the regional supply, and a second term with the national. States are grouped into six areas, number of recognized schools by the SEP and similarity in travel.
    b. To determine, in the official records of the state ministries of tourism, chambers of commerce, the Mexican Association of Hotels and Motels and other agencies, the number of tourist establishments and tourism-oriented by region and the number of rooms per category, number of chairs for food and beverage centre and additional services.
    c. To make an inventory of the educational institutions (IE) offering tourism, from technical level programs recognized by the SEP.
    d. To get the academic plans of the programs offered, developing a matrix that contains general programs, with specialization, number of theoretical hours - practices, percentage of participation in the sector, among others.
2. Analysis of the gap and elements of coincidence and differences between curricula and labour supply.
    a. To determine the job profiles where graduates working in tourism.
    b. To identify the set of competences according to job profiles, based on the work of CENEVAL, CONAET and the White Paper.
    c. To feedback from students, alumni, coordinators and employers, by applying a questionnaire on certain skills according to job profile.
    d. To feedback from graduates and trainers (coordinators), by applying a survey on the strengths and weaknesses of the curriculum, (1200 800 educational and business sectors). To know the opinion of employers by in-depth interviews (5 per turn, by region) and area coordinators or directors (100) in order to detect the gaps among the programs of established practices, the graduates' educational needs when being hired, and the labour competences that should be based on the survey results.
    e. To develop two focus groups in each of the main tourist areas, with graduates of tourism schools (8-12 per focus group) to know the process of integration into the labour market, the profits of their programs of professional practices, the highlights in their education and their shortcomings.
3. To determine the strengths and weaknesses of the programs of study under analysis levels, in relation to knowledge and skills, attitudes and other (language, teamwork).
4. To prepare a report that includes the findings and the best practices programs.

5. To prepare strategies to align the curricula to the labour skills required.
6. To develop teaching material for the workshops for entrepreneurs, coordinators and tourism principals, as well as for government representatives about the results, proposals and suggested implementation strategies.
7. To develop 12 workshops, two for each particular geographical area at stage 1.

The research universe arises in two ways: educational institutions and employers (tourist facilities in the country). Also, the educational institutions that offer courses in tourism, and that are registered at the Ministry of Tourism.

The objects under study are:

1. Students.
2. Graduates.
3. Teachers.
4. Coordinators and School principals.

The country's tourism platform. The information supplying entities are:

1. School principals.
2. Operating managers.
3. Human resources managers.

In the alignment project of the study plans with the labour market, the following aims are pursued:

- To define the graduate's profile by the educational institutions (technical and higher levels) and enterprises dedicated to training (enterprises, organisms, associations and schools).
- To identify the competences required by the productive sector, aimed at defining an employer's profile of competitiveness and excellence.
- To percentually dimension the coefficient of existent differentiation between the supply and demand needs.

The methodology includes the segmentation of the national territory in 6 regions that share common tourism product features. The regions are characterized obeying to the available labour supply in every region, and considering the natural attractions as well as the tourism enterprises (lodging, foods and beverages; air and land transport; travel agencies; entertainment; government). The characteristics of this supply are gathered from the database provided by the Ministries of Tourism, at federal and state levels, the chambers and associations, through phone calls, personal assistance and internet searches. It was obtained the total number of hotel rooms, food and beverages establishments, certified tourist guides, car leasers, and convention centers and naval posts. Moreover, the tourism platform of the country was identified, as well as the main attractions of every state were defined for establishing the geographic zones of analysis.

CONCLUSION

Based on the investigations, and proposed definitions described earlier in this chapter for the evaluation and identification of skills in the tourism education and training; they can be recognized the following skills and characteristics under the three explorations focused on the theme of tourism education and training in information coincide. So the following skills are described and analyzed in the work of the World Tourism Organization - TEDQUAL (Tourism Education Quality - Quality in Tourism Education); Degree in Tourism of the National Agency for Quality Assessment and Accreditation of the University of Girona European Convergence program; SECTUR research, CONACYT, CESTUR, and La Salle University Cancun from Mexico (2012) Aligning the curricula of tourism education to the needs of the workplace.

The concurrent jurisdiction in the investigations focused on tourism education and training above are defined in the following sets; Basic training, technical knowledge and personal skills; when human capital the main asset of the organizations that in turn make industries and in this chapter relates particularly to the tourism industry are identified intangible assets (intellectual and relational) to develop professional skills in tourism education and training to manage the knowledge to be transferred the experiences, skills, abilities within the tourism industry and are identified coincidentally competencies that must be managed systematically on knowledge. As for the basic training; communication skills, business skills, marketing, administrative, legal knowledge related to tourism, trends and knowledge of the tourism industry, strategic planning. Technical formation; computer and language. Personal skills; work in multinational environments, motivation and initiative, teamwork, loyalty, courtesy, problem solving, personal ethics, flexibility, decision making.

REFERENCES

Camisón, C., Fabra, M., & Monfort, V. (2011). *La fidelidad del turista al destino en el caso español.* Spain: Estudios turísticos.

Comisión Europea. (2004). Competencias clave para un aprendizaje a lo largo de la vida. Un marco de referencia europeo. Puesta en práctica del programa de trabajo Educación y Formación 2010. Grupo de trabajo B. Competencias clave. *Comisión Europea. Dirección General de Educación y Cultura.* Available at http://www.educastur.princast.es/info/calidad/indicadores/doc/comision_europea.pdf

CONOCER. (1997). *La normalización y certificación de Competencia Profesional: Medio para incrementar la productividad de las empresas.* Mexico: CONOCER.

Cortes C. & Pineda J. (2006). Aproximación a la gestión del conocimiento. *Revista ventana informática, 15,* 170.

Díaz, J. (2004). *Modelo de gestión del conocimiento (GC) aplicado a la universidad pública en el Perú.* Available at http://sisbib.unmsm.edu.pe/Bibvirtual/monografias/Principal.asp

González, J., & Wagenaar, R. (2003). *Tuning Educational Structures in Europe.* Spain: Universidad de Deusto.

Hager, P., Holland, S., & Becket, D. (2002). *Enhancing the learning and employability of graduates: The role of generic skills*. Australia: Business/Higher Education Round Table.

Hunziker, W., & Krapf, K. (1942). *Outline of the general theory of tourism*. Zurich: Polygraphischer Verlag AG.

Kane, M. (1992). The assessment of professional competence. *Education and the Health Professions*, *15*(2), 163–182. doi:10.1177/016327879201500203 PMID:10119160

Mertens, L. (1997). *Competencia laboral: sistemas, surgimiento y modelos*. Mexico: OIT.

Minakata Arceo, A. (2009). Gestión del conocimiento en educación y transformación de la escuela: Notas para un campo en construcción. *Sinéctica,* (32), 17-19.

Norma Internacional ISO 9000. (2005). *Sistemas de gestión de la calidad - Fundamentos y vocabulario*. Switzerland.: ISO 2005.

OECD. (2013). *Panorama de la educación 2013 Indicadores de la OCDE*. Spain: Santillana.

OMT. (2015). *¿Porque el turismo?* Available at http://www2.unwto.org/es/content/por-que-el-turismo

Rosental, M., & Iudin, P. (1973). *Diccionario Filosófico*. La Habana: Editora Política.

Rueda, M. (2013). *La evaluación educativa: un análisis de sus prácticas*. Mexico: UNAM.

Ruiz, J. (2004). *Como hacer una evaluación de centros educativos 3ª*. Madrid: Narcea Ediciones.

Secretaria de Educación Pública, (2012). *El enfoque formativo de la evaluación*. Mexico: SEP

SECTUR. CESTUR, CONACYT. (2012). *Alineación de los programas de estudio de educación turística a las necesidades del campo laboral.* Mexico: Universidad La Salle Cancún. Available at http://ictur.sectur.gob.mx/pdf/estudioseinvestigacion/sintesisprincipalesestudios/PROYECTO_FINAL_ALINEACION_Final_10L.pdf

Tobón, S. (2007). *Gestión curricular y ciclos propedéuticos*. Bogotá: ECOE.

Worthen, Sanders, & Fitzpatrick. (1996). *Program evaluation. Alternative approaches and practical guidelines*. New York: Adison – Wiley Longman.

WTO. (2003). Introducción a TedQual. Una Metodología para la Calidad en Educación y Formación Turística. Spain: World Tourism Organization (WTO-UNWTO).

WTO. (2014). Panorama OMT del turismo internacional. Spain: World Tourism Organization (WTO-UNWTO).

Zabala, A. y Arnau, L. (2007). La enseñanza de las competencias. *Aula de Innovación Educativa, 161.*

KEY TERMS AND DEFINITIONS

Educational Competence: Complex development processes which are suitable in set contexts, by integrating different knowledge (knowing how to be, knowing how to do, knowing to know, knowing to live with), in order to do activities and/or solve problems with a sense of challenge, motivation, flexibility, creativity, understanding and undertaking, within an approach of meta-cognitive thinking, ongoing improvement and ethical commitment, which are aimed at contributing to personal development, the construction and strengthening of the social networking, the continuous search of a sustainable economic and business development, and the care and protection of the environment and the living organisms.

Evaluation: An indispensable and previous activity conducive to raising the degree; besides being identified with the last stage of the natural process of knowledge which concludes with the issuance of informed judgments; a process leading to decisions and human action.

Knowledge Management: Intended development of one of the people's and organization's competences, as an innovation supported by an interactive learning process, where the members involved rise their competence and take care of innovation.

Professional Competence: The degree of utilization of knowledge, skills and the good judgment related to the people's profession, and in correspondence with all the situations that can be lived in the exercise of professional practice.

Tourism: A social, cultural and economic phenomenon related to the movement of people to the places that are outside their usual location of residence for personal or business / professional reasons. While these people are called visitors (which may be tourists or excursionists; residents or non-residents), tourism is associated with the people's activities and, therefore, implies tourism expenditure.

Tourism Industry: The term tourism industries includes the factory complexes that regularly produce tourism products; and is one of the most colloquial terms used in the tourism sector.

UNWTO: The World Tourism Organization (UNWTO) is the United Nations agency responsible for the promotion of responsible, sustainable and universally accessible tourism.

Section 2

Middle School Education as Predecessor of Knowledge Management

Chapter 8
Evaluation of the Educational Opportunities of Middle High School Graduates

Fernando Briseño Hurtado
Instituto Politécnico Nacional, Mexico

Edgar Oliver Cardoso Espinosa
Instituto Politécnico Nacional, Mexico

Joel García Mendoza
Instituto Politécnico Nacional, Mexico

Jorge Mejía Bricaire
Instituto Politécnico Nacional, Mexico

ABSTRACT

The education enables individuals to add value to the economy, contributing to the cultural heritage, participate in society, improve health, protect the environment and increase their ability to continue to develop. Therefore it is essential that educational system promotes educational opportunities in order to be equitably distributed among all social sectors and boost that graduates and could have the opportunity to performance occupations in which they could take advantage the schooling they have acquired. So, the chapter proposal will be organized into three sections: the first related to globalization and middle education in Mexico; the second based on group interviews conducted with the technique called focus group and, third, the characteristics of the methodology-oriented design of a set of indicators that evaluate and feedback educational programs that graduates have studied, based this, they could achieve and improve educational opportunities.

INTRODUCTION

Currently, the process of globalization that have experienced all the Nations has manifested itself in different ways in most of countries, both in cultural, social, economic ones. This has established new economic activities that affect the forms of labour and human capital formation. For this reason, it is essential that individuals of Nations insert in the best way in this dynamic world to deal with such demands.

In this sense, education enables individuals to add value to the economy, contributing to the cultural heritage, participate in society, improve health, protect the environment and increase their ability to continue to develop. Therefore it is essential that educational system promotes educational opportunities

DOI: 10.4018/978-1-5225-0457-3.ch008

in order to be equitably distributed among all social sectors and boost that graduates and could have the opportunity to performance occupations in which they could take advantage the schooling they have acquired.

This leads to enormous implications for the future shape of a quality education, directed to the consolidation of a professional academic profile that provides students' knowledge, skills and core competencies to access upper level studies or to the labour market, which undergo transformations in contexts of information, knowledge, labor, technological and cultural meanings of teaching-learning processes faced by globalization effects.

In relation to ideas above, this work fits as a project of diagnosis, which the electronic directory of students of middle education at each institution; graduates monitoring program and as a tasks support that secondary education institutions must carry out to inquire about the different paths that students have followed after completing their high school studies.

This project has been considered suitable performing a qualitative analysis based on statistical information collected through surveys on the topics of working conditions related to the continuity in higher education, the insertion in the labour field and the satisfaction level of training received for the evaluation purposes and feedback educational programs that students have been coursed.

Therefore the chapter proposal considers a methodology based on group interviews, which is conducted by the technique called "focus group", known in Spanish as "Grupos Focales" It is a qualitative technique of data collection, originally proposed by the sociologist Robert K. Merton in order to obtain and analyze groups' responses of different subjects.

In this sense, it was proposed, in a path, showing from the collection, systematization and analysis of statistical information the familiar, economic, organizational, occupational, educational and social conditions which are or could be associated to educational opportunities that have made graduates at middle school; and, on the other hand, designing a set of indicators that could help to follow up on the results of the efforts of schools to achieve better opportunities for its graduates in a systematic way.

So, the chapter proposal will be organized into three sections: the first related to globalization and middle education in Mexico; the second based on group interviews conducted with the technique called focus group and, third, the characteristics of the methodology-oriented design of a set of indicators that evaluate and feedback educational programs that graduates have studied, based this, they could achieve and improve educational opportunities.

GLOBALIZATION AND HIGH SCHOOL EDUCATION

This chapter is carried out a general sketch on the challenges that globalization imposes to education, in particular to the Middle High Education (MHE) and Higher Education (HE), which require a reconceptualization of the deep of his work, since the phenomenon of globalization is gradually becoming a daily reference, in an important element of our vital stage, and extends its incidence to different fields such as economic, cultural, social, among which the world of education is also, increasingly a prominent place.

In relation to above, a cornerstone for this work is that the concept of globalization was coined in 1992 by Ronald Robertson, of the University of Pittsburgh, to refer the intensification of the consciousness of the world as a whole, its social process by which verifies an inhibition of geographical determinations about cultural and social practices.

In this sense it is important to consider what is mentioned by Castells, (1999) which defines globalization as an increasing integration of national economies; at its core, the global economy would include the globalization of financial markets, "whose behavior determines the movements of capital, currencies, credit and therefore the economies of all countries", similarly, Ordorika, (2002) mentions that globalization is the concept that we design to complex arrangements of contemporary society and the current stage of development of capitalism.

On the other hand, Romero, (2002) explains that "from the ideological point of view, globalization, is the neo-liberal argument that tries to justify the inevitability of the development of development countries the management of the market under the assumption of equal opportunities for all".

Against this background, education is bound to suffer serious transformations, both in its most immediate, didactic, micro-systemic, elements such as the processes of teaching and learning, to the more complex, structural components and macro - systemic, as the Organization of the educational system.

The impact of globalization on the MHSE educational Mexican system can be seen in several elements: standardized tests (such as the International Programme for the Assessment of Students, IPAS) guidelines from the World Bank, the technologies of information and communication technology (ICT), the signing of economic agreements (e.g. the Treaty of the North American free trade, NAFTA), etc.

Government agencies and international organizations such as the World Bank, cited by ECLAC (2000), for example, have studied education and its relationship with social conditions, is considered essential to the association between socio-economic conditions and different educational outcomes and the field of research in which higher education is included.

While, education is considered as important in the socio-economic conditions overcoming, in recent years, is seen as the only way to take advantage of these conditions; There are other associated factors, which are related to socio-economic policies of world order. Not enough, for example, have a college degree to get a good job nowadays (Cañedo, 2008).

In the field of higher education, the term globalization has been used in many and varied forms. Highlights for example its usage to denote the role of the University in the production of symbolic analysts for a global economy based on knowledge (Altbach, 2003; Morrow & Torres, 1995 cited by Ordorika 2006).

Therefore, Latin American educational systems (LA) they are confronted to a deep and rapid transformation of these contexts, at least in the dimensions of access to information, management of knowledge, relationship with the labour market, employment of technologies and socialization in the culture of the time, i.e., such changes will force systems to transform themselves to be able to adapt to the new scenario. In other words, the future of education in LA, will be configured for the trajectory of these adaptations, the greater or lesser success in carrying them out, faced with two enormous challenges currently faced.

In this context, universities, especially in the last two decades, are facing new challenges, that they have put at risk the quality of vocational training. Stand as current problems of higher education, the permanence of students from low socio-economic levels, as government policies have tended to move away from a welfare approach, to make way for the liberation of the economy (ECLAC, 2000).

On the other hand, the universities in the 21st century are in a correlation of dependence on economic growth, social equity and cultural integration, adapting to their structures, processes, results and educational policies to transformations undergoing due to globalization of information, knowledge, labor, technological and contexts of cultural meanings in which they operate the processes of teaching and learning.

Therefore, the institutions of MHE and also HE is found in a process of transformation in order to guarantee coverage; to incorporate indigenous peoples into the school system; improve the quality and results of the teaching of basic skills, particularly among the poorest sectors of the youth and adult population; modernizing technical education of middle and upper level; massively tertiary-level education.

For this reason, it is important to analyze that globalization incites to re-think the education system, i.e. induced to carry out a re-engineering of the University, since the comparative advantages of countries depends on human resources development and the capacity to generate and apply knowledge, both in production and in the solution of social problems for this reason, the development of human resources, improving the quality of education, research and extension, require also rethink the relationship of the institutions of higher level with the State, society and the productive sector.

In this way, Tunnerman (undated) mentions that "the higher education institutions (HEI) have rule with complete independence and full responsibility on the ethical and social problems, as a kind of intellectual power that society needs will help her to reflect, understand and act", since the contemporary world demands today an education with quality and equity, taking into account human development, the relationship of man with the society and nature, the relationship with labour world.

I.e. on the horizon where the society demands a quality education, equity, pertinence and internationalization, higher education institutions require flexible and modern curricula, develop science, enhancing its research capacity, generate research programs and consolidate them through work to contribute to the solution of social problems and the satisfaction of human needs.

Accordingly, an education that provides educational opportunities involves extending their coverage, i.e., democratize it, to reduce the thousands of young people from marginalized sectors that are today excluded from public higher education, what higher education institutions have to reflect on this issue, in this context, the relevance of education in this globalized world will depend on the response that this offer with respect to human problems as those of population, environment, peace, international understanding, democracy, identity, culture, human rights, etc.

Various forms of globalization are all deeply affected by the dynamics of international relations in the last few years, and by implication, influence the role that higher education through educational reforms that play a strategic and key role in the improvement of the lives of the people and societies where they are.

CHALLENGES OF KNOWLEDGE MANAGEMENT IN EDUCATION

In the last decade of the 20th century and the first decade of the 21st century, knowledge management has become a specific field of conceptual development and practical application in the field of Administrative Sciences and the organizations.

In this sense, the new economy, globalization and new technologies are some of the elements that made that knowledge management acquires more and more importance. Knowledge, it is understood today, as a resource that not only allows us to interpret our surroundings, it also gives us the ability to act.

Therefore, a knowledge-based economy assumes a major qualitative change in the nature of growth, due to the concurrence between a repeated tendency to the growth of the part of the intangible capital (education, training and technology) with the spectacular spread of information and communication technologies.

In this way, knowledge acquires a strategic importance in the competition by the markets, i.e., that knowledge that reaches an added value because of its ability to offer solutions to problems in specific application contexts.

In this context, knowledge society transforms the spaces of social coexistence, as well as the forms of thinking, living, education and work. These modifications are also expressed in the political, scientific and socio-cultural fields in such way that they have driven the development of a knowledge society, thereby expanding the horizons of the knowledge management in educational institutions and on the conditions in which they can carry out effective management of your intellectual capital and generate institutional competencies to better serve its social commitment and inserted in a positive manner in the new realities of the of the knowledge society.

I.e., the knowledge management condescending optimization of the necessary conditions so that knowledge flows are moving better. What we actually manage, is not the knowledge itself, but the conditions, the environment and all that is possible and promotes two fundamental processes: the creation and transmission of knowledge within, specifically educational institutions.

Against this background, it is essential to be clear that the challenges of knowledge management in the institutions of higher education must consider different aspects to carry out effective processes of creation and transmission of knowledge, therefore, the analysis of the academic bodies as forms of collaborative work, the curriculum through information and communication technologies the formation of knowledge workers in the institutions of higher education, the institutional linkage with the labor sector, theory with practice, the classroom community, and student's teacher, will be important pieces that will have to be taken into account to promote the creation of knowledge and, also, to improve or promote its transmission within an educational institution.

So, knowledge management will have to be a systemic process that allows to detect, select, organize, present and disseminate the information cooperatively by the participants of an institution (Moral, et. al. 2007: 15), to transform information into knowledge and development skills to improve human capital (graduates of MHE) required to enter the top level or inserted into the workforce, these knowledge and skills will enable the graduate to act in a context of specific work, combining knowledge, know how to use valuable information, make complex decisions or mobilize external resources, among others.

For this reason, it is necessary to develop mechanisms that enable all people having all the potential of knowledge that is dispersed in the institution. This involves creating and deploying a strategy of knowledge management that integrates five key actions: understand needs and opportunities of knowledge; build relevant knowledge to students; organize and distribute knowledge of the institution; create conditions for the application of knowledge in the field and exploit knowledge.

Finally, from the conception of the design of new processes (innovation), knowledge management, and management systems is the way to make visible the process of exploitation of the knowledge, the resources and capacities of institutions; It is also a tangible way to show the degree of development and the effectiveness of the strategy of knowledge management that benefits for the society." (Ortiz & Nagles, 2007: 73).

SOCIOECONOMIC STATUS AND EDUCATIONAL OPPORTUNITIES IN THE MIDDLE HIGH EDUCATION AND HIGHER EDUCATION

It is clear that education is therefore intimately connected with used cutting socio-economic variables, in MHE and the HE, has been considered the work of the student, the educational level of the parents and the economic level as crucial factors in the opportunities that students will have during and at the conclusion of his studies in these educational levels. In this regard, Armenta, Pacheco and Pineda (2008) considered that a higher economic level, it is better academic performance and therefore, better educational opportunities, provide specifically; in the sense that when the pre-college and college student works, their academic performance low and their opportunities are limited.

Meanwhile, Plasencia, Vizcondet, Ruiz, Araujo and Salazar (2008), to develop the topic about the influence of socioeconomic factors in University student performance, consider that influence between socioeconomic factors and educational opportunities, there is as in socioeconomically disadvantaged students academic performance is low, which in some cases cause the abandonment of studies.

I.e. the low level of education tends to be associated with socioeconomic and cultural low levels, these levels people pooled with the category of poor and, in this regard, poor households-school age population reproduced similar socio-economic conditions in which living parents.

Households with low educational attainment are the main sources of poor future generation; people whose homes are characterized with low socio-economic levels. The phenomenon of educational backwardness is not exclusive to a particular type of home, since also the homes of high socioeconomic levels could be generating, also, future poor, by also having percentages, although minor, children with low educational attainment (Ramos, 2000).

In this context, based on the contributions of De Ibarrola (2009), Gutierrez (2009), Muñoz (2001) and Villa (2007), analysed the educational opportunities that are taking the students, culminating in his studies of secondary education in our country.

According to Muñoz (2001) one of the essential formal purpose is to provide pupils and students the knowledge and skills suitable to participate in the labour world. To this purpose is fulfilled, the school system contributes to combating poverty and the concentration of national income in a few hands.

Which, it is necessary to satisfy two conditions. The first relates to that educational opportunities are distributed equitably among all sectors of society; the second, to which all graduates and graduates of the system have the opportunity to play occupations in which to fully leverage the schooling they have acquired.

According to Villa (2007):

For the structure and operation of the MHE subsystem promote [equality of opportunities] most decidedly it is necessary:

1. *To open more educational level spaces, so that there is no income restriction due to lack of space, likewise, [it should] ensure that schooling does not depend on just the economic level to which they belongs,*
2. *To promote an education that outweigh the disadvantages socio-cultural and educational achievement, both from academic measures that reinforce learning, and those oriented to people who require supports... the most vulnerable people.*

3. *Implement teaching strategies that take into account the levels of backlog of students in various contexts, in order to raise the learning to acceptable standards. (p 109)*

According to this:

The education quality of is much lower for students from low-income families, most of them are attended in public schools and cannot access a better quality higher education. In short, education is deeply stratified in Latin America, situation that perpetuated the inequalities of income. (Beverley, 2002, p. 124)

On the other hand, according to Gutierrez (2009, p. 173), the classrooms of public school in general in our country show "inequality and inequity among the students: wealth and poverty;" knowledge and ignorance; authoritarianism and authority; power and social status. In the end, subordination, margination and exclusion".

Many of students at MHE students are composed of students, between 15 and 18 years of age, they live in poverty, marginalization and, therefore exclusion. Those guys and those girls have the same opportunities as other students to access global information to manage and domain new information and communication technologies, to develop at the pace of a globalized and accelerated world.

According to De Ibarrola (2009, p. 5):

Accepts the general distinction of heterogeneity between formal and informal sectors, and the five occupational sectors: informal two (workers for self-employment and micro-enterprises of less than five workers), and three formal (public sector, large companies of the industrial sector and large companies in the services sector) ", [by giving] national statistical data on the way in to the growth of the schooling of the EAP [(Economically Active Population)] in Mexico" between 1992 and 2004, distributed among various occupational sectors defined according to its formality or informality, and on the differences causing reached schooling and the labour sector's inclusion in income based on table 1.

Likewise, De Ibarrola (2009, p. 9) mentions "that average incomes increase steadily based on the increase in schooling; the difference between those who have higher schooling and those not concluded

Table 1. EAP Distribution of formal and informal sectors 1992-2004

Laboural Sector	1992	2004	Difference
Informal Sector	33.1%	34.6%	-1.5
Own Count	06.5%	08.8%	-2.3
Owners, employers and companies	26.6%	25.8%	-0.8
Formal Sector	66.9%	65.4%	-1.5
Public Sector	04.6%	06%.0	-1.4
Secondary sector large companies	22.4%	21%.0	-1.4
Tertiary sector large companies	40.0%	38.4%	-1.5

Note: System of information and educational trends in Latin America (SIETLA) (s.f.), cited by De Ibarrola, M. (2009, p. 12).

elementary school is very high in the two designated years, 4.5 times in 1992, although for 2004 dropped to 3.9."

In this context, it is relevant to know that MHE is coordinated by the General direction of the Middle High School this is located in the introductory option and is offered in three modalities (school, school, and mixed); Likewise, it assumes the purpose of generating in learners the development of a first personal and social synthesis allowing access to higher education, and to give you an understanding of his society and his time and prepare for possible incorporation to productive work.

Their functions are as follows:

- **Formative:** This provides the student a well-rounded education that includes the most important elements of the culture of his time: scientific, technical and humanistic, expertise allowing it to assimilate and participate in the constant changes in society...
- **Propaedeutic:** It prepares the student for the continuation in higher education, through the knowledge of different disciplines...
- **Preparation for the Job:** This offers to the learner training enough that allows you to engage in various aspects of the work environment, fostering a positive attitude toward work and, where appropriate, their integration into the productive sector (Secretariat of Public Education [SEP], 2013, "functions", pa. 1-3).

In this sense, one of the purposes of the educational system in Mexico, is currently providing students and the students competences (knowledge, abilities, skills, and attitudes), enabling them to continue with their studies or join the workforce. To this regard, Briseño, Cardoso, and Mejia (2014), consider that it is an essential part of MHE to analyze educational opportunities that its graduates are reaching to the end of baccalaureate studies.

It is important to note that studies of graduates play a very important role to examine these opportunities, generally seek to describe features on the inclusion in the labour market, its continuity at the top level and ask his opinion on the training received, for the purposes of evaluating and feedback programs education who have studied.

METHODOLOGICAL CONSIDERATIONS OF THE STUDY

This study applied techniques of collection and qualitative analysis, Focus Group technique from an interview related to educational opportunities which have had graduates who have completed their high school studies, whereas four categories: socio-economic level, continuity in higher education, insertion into the workforce and the degree of satisfaction of the training received

Focus Group

The Focus Group is a technique that focuses on the plurality of responses obtained from a group of people, and is defined as a technique of qualitative research whose objective is to obtain data through perception, feelings, attitudes and opinions of groups of people.

Matus and Molina (2005) point out that this qualitative technique intended to apprehend the meanings that subjects share and that are expressed through language.

On the other hand, Romo and Castle (2007) point out that the target group has predominantly a practical purpose that seeks to collect as much information as possible on a defined topic.

Criteria to Select the Study Population

For this study, the population consisted of MHE graduates from generations 2005-2008 and 2008 - 2011 in the State of Mexico, which gives a total of 462 persons (see table 2). While the sample was stratified-type and is expected to be of at least of 20% in accordance with the following information:

The implementation of this technique part to establish the objective of the research:

To determine the educational opportunities that have had graduates and graduates of the MHES in the State of Mexico.

Once defined the objective, it was prepared the script with open questions in general and also specific type so the interviewee can answer either so general or deeply, and obtain the necessary information for our research whereas the following categories: socio-economic profile of graduates and graduates, employability, the continuity in the higher education and satisfaction of the quality of the service provided by upper secondary education.

The number of people who complete the focal group was 7 students that culminated his high school (graduated generations 2005-2008 and 2008-2011), since they will provide the required information; Some authors like Young and Harmony (1998) point out that the participants can be between 7-10 people. Matus and Molina (2006), on the other hand, mentioned among 5 to 10 members; most agree in pointing out that more than 10 people can hinder the focal group.

The interview was carried out in a classroom of Union high schools in the State of Mexico and it was conducted by a moderator whose function was to provide a brief introduction on what to discuss, mention the objectives of the study and directed the series of questions; and an observer who had the Mission of taking note of the responses of those interviewed.

Once the number of questions were finished the moderator terminated the session and thanked the participation and attendance of members, noting the importance of their valuable comments and replies to them.

Finally, information was collected and processed, also results were analysed and a final report on the study was held. The report record how the research was carried out, who were participants, and what were the results, conclusions and recommendations of the research.

Table 2. General sample of graduate students by generation

Generation	Graduates	Sample
2005- 2008	209	19
2008- 2011	253	46

Note: Own processing from statistics of the institution

Figure 1. Outline of the steps to perform an investigation through the focal group technique (Cortés, 2005, p. 68)

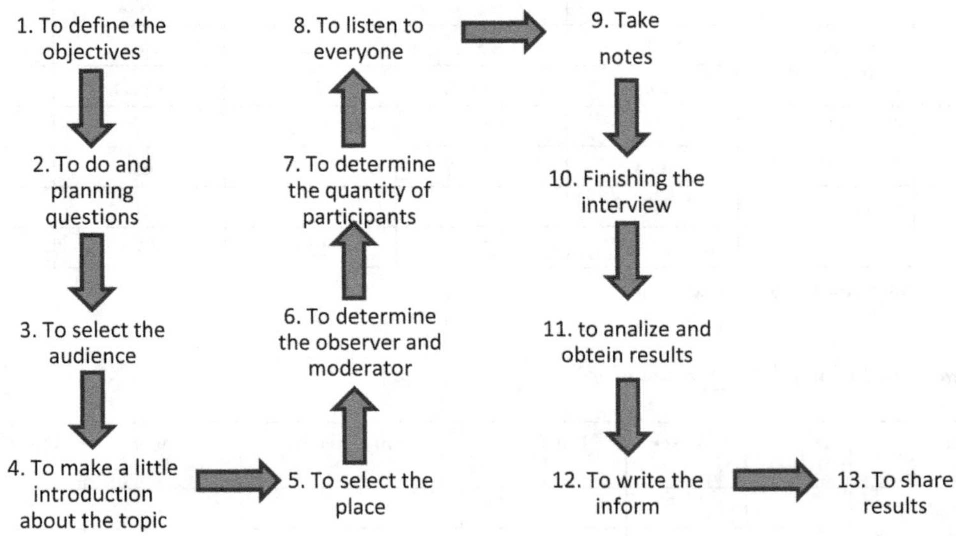

ANALYSIS AND RESULTS

Based on the information that is thrown by the interviews carried out 65 graduates (36) and graduates (29) of the generations 2005-2008 and 2008-2011 of the MHE of the State of Mexico, there were gotten important data that allowed to observe and analyze educational opportunities concerning socio-economic profile, job placement, continuity in higher education and the level of satisfaction of baccalaureate studies.

With regard to the type of housing you can see that in general terms the 72.3% of graduates live in own home, 15.4% rent and 12.3% live in borrowed houses. These data suggest that one-third of the families of the graduates and graduates do not have a heritage to their children (see Table 3).

In Table 4 is observed that 84.6% of the sample have monthly family income ranging from $4000 to $6999 (Mexican pesos) and only 15.4% have incomes greater than $7000.

Table 5 shows in general terms than the 36.9% of the graduates and graduates of the study sample play a post employee, 13.8% are workmen, 12.3% are traders, 9.2% other and 20% does not work.

Table 3. What kind of house do you live in?

Generation		Own	Rented	Borrowed	Total
2008	Count of	12	4	3	19
	% total	18.59	6.2	4.6	29.2
2011	Count of	35	6	5	46
	% total	53.8	9.2	7.7	70.8
Total	Count of	47	10	8	65
	% total	72.3	15.4	12.3	100

Note: Own preparation based on SPSS V.20 results

Table 4. What is the (approximate) monthly income amount of your family?

Generation		$4000-4999	$5000-5999	$6000-6999	More than $7000	Total
2008	Count of	9	3	1	6	19
	% total	13.8	4.6	1.5	9.2	29.2
2011	Count of	25	10	7	4	46
	% total	38.5	15.4	10.8	6.2	70.8
Total	Count of	34	13	8	10	65
	% total	52.3	20.0	12.3	15.4	100

Note: Own preparation based on SPSS V.20 results

Table 5. What kind of work do you develop?

Generation		Do Not Work	Worker	Employee	Administrative	Trader	Othet	Total
2008	Count of	3	1	6	4	3	2	19
	% total	4.6	1.5	9.2	6.2	4.6	3.1	29.2
2011	Count of	10	8	18	1	5	4	46
	% total	15.4	12.3	27.7	1.5	7.7	6.2	70.8
Total	Count of	13	9	24	5	8	6	65
	% total	20.0	13.8	36.9	7.7	12.3	9.2	100

Note: Own preparation based on SPSS V.20 results

Finally, based on the diagnostic study in high schools of the MHE of the State of Mexico with regard to educational opportunities for its graduates and graduates, the following was found:

Parents of graduates and graduates do not have sufficient economic resources, since they work in jobs mainly for workers and employees, obtaining on average as family income twice the minimum wage, so it was corroborated that mentioned by Gutierrez (2009, p. 173): "much of [the students and the students] of public schools high school composed of young men and girls, between fifteen and eighteen years of age, living in poverty, of marginalization and therefore exclusion... "."

Likewise, it was found that approximately one-third of graduates and graduates they don't have their own home and nearly half of the graduates has no internet service in your home, which is confirmed by Gutierrez (2009): "these young people don't have the same opportunities as other students to access global information to manage and master new information and communication technologies, and to develop at the pace of a world globalized, accelerated".

In regards to the employability, it was found that about half of graduates and graduates up to 15 employees joined the work in the informal sector (micro enterprises). This reaffirms what is mentioned by De Ibarrola (2009):

Accepts the general distinction of heterogeneity between formal and informal sectors, and the five occupational sectors: two informals (workers for self-employment and micro-enterprises of fewer than five employees), and three formal (public sector, large companies of the industrial sector and large companies in the services sector).

In relation to the upper level, it was found that approximately one-third of the total number of graduates and graduates managed to enter to study a degree in public school, likewise, a similar proportion had no access to that level, which is described by Beverley (2002, p. 124): "the quality of education is much lower than for students from low-income families ", most of whom attend public schools and cannot access a better quality higher education".

With respect to the position in which they operate the graduates of both generations, it was found that it is intimately related to their level of education, since in our days the minimum grade level required to enter to work at levels lower than a company or institution (in Mexico) is the baccalaureate, which evidence that incomes who receive two-thirds of these graduates and graduates ranges between one and two minimum wages, confirming by De Ibarrola (2009, p. 9): "average incomes increase steadily based on the increase in schooling".

In this context, it is important to consider a proposal of indicators to evaluate the educational opportunities at the upper level, for which contributions of authors concerning the topic of opportunities were considered, it should be noted that human beings are different in many respects, that is why you can search for equality in some of them, but not all at the same time. Cited by (EGREES, 2003), Amaritya poses that we always answer the question equal what? Since it designates, must choose between if we give priority to income equality (accepting that there is a certain degree of inequality in terms of social welfare) or, on the contrary, we seek that some homogeneity existed in the standard of living (accepting that there was inequality level income (Sen, 1987).

For this reason, although it is complex to aspire to a completely egalitarian society, that you can search for an equitable society, which promotes equality in an aspect deemed essential to build a just society.

In this regard set out five principles of equality proposed by Grisay cited by European Group of Research on Equity of de Educational Systems (EGREES, 2003):

1. **"Natural" or "Libertarian" Position:** It is considered the birth, power or membership of a particular social group to determine rights. Any redistribution is an "artificial" measure affecting the freedom and therefore is harmful, so it supports the reproduction and the maintenance of the "natural" order and differences based on an acquisition just, based only on the full exercise of freedom.
2. **Equality of Access and Opportunities:** For this concept, the important thing is equality of access to opportunities of study for children who have the same capacity, regardless of the socio-economic or cultural context that come. Schools should offer a variety of educational options adapted to the skills of students and especially help talented students coming from unfavourable contexts, for example through the granting of scholarships.
3. **Equality of Treatment:** He admits the existence of talents or natural ability that can cause uneven results, provided that students have been able to benefit from similar quality learning environments. What is inadmissible are unequal outcomes arising from receiving education of different quality, such as when there are schools for elites and ghettos. Ideally, all to achieve at least one certain level of education.
4. **Equality of Success or Achievement:** It is considered that individual characteristics such as cognitive ability can be modified so that people accessing learning. Although it admits that there may be different results, criticises the ideology of the talents and negative discrimination that occurs

in situations where the uneven quality of teaching wide initial inequalities. For this design you should achieve equality of outcomes in the essential skills and positive discrimination, formative assessment, and any other arrangements that are necessary to reduce the initial inequalities should be promoted.

5. **Equality in the Development of Capabilities:** Although it admits that there are cultural or motivational differences between individuals, is not considered that there is a hierarchy between them, therefore criticizes the idea of a single standard of excellence or that there is a cultural elite or a subculture and advocates for individualized instruction.

Similarly, Demeuse cited by López (2005) proposes four principles of educational equality:

1. **Equality of Access:** This is the way in which is expressed the principle of equal opportunities in the field of education: an educational system is equitable if all people have equal opportunities to access it. If this principle is true, are considered legitimate inequalities that may arise in school, paths or educational achievements from social and cultural differences of the students.
2. **Equality in the Conditions or Means of Learning:** It puts the emphasis on the teaching strategies and institutional proposals from which dealt with educational practices and accept the differences in outcomes that result from diversity in students. It does not propose to serve that diversity, as it is not considered that students have different resources to participate in the proposed educational practices.
3. **Equality in the Achievements or Results:** All persons, regardless of their social or cultural origin, should have equal access to knowledge. Education systems should recognize the initial differences and take action to remediate them and ensure that everyone has access to a similar level of educational achievement.
4. **Equality in the Social Realization of Educational Attainment:** An educational system is fair if the social impact of education is the same in each of the social settings in which it is deployed.

Likewise Muñoz (2003:8), mentioned that education meets the criteria of equity, if all members of the society sectors rolling equal opportunities to play certain occupations, participate in the economically active population, the desired income and promote intergenerationally in the system of social stratification.

It is clear that in certain contexts educational opportunities can be improved, however, holding social problems inequalities continue to manifest in society, as happens when young people who conclude their baccalaureate or professional studies fail to insert into well-paying jobs. However, it is important to study the correlation between certain scheme of access to educational opportunities and the economic, social and cultural consequences that access to such opportunities or failure of these have had on the lives of the people.

In our country, the existing educational legislation is based on the idea that all individuals, irrespective of their socio-cultural origin, demand equal access to knowledge, since it is considered that the educational system requires to recognize these initial differences and authorizes it to take measures to counter them, so the current regulatory framework based on the principle of equality of results.

Therefore, in connection with the foregoing, and with reference to the contributions of the principles of equality proposed by Grisay cited by (EGREES, 2003), Demeuse cited by López (2005) and that proposed by Muñoz (2003), it is proposed a system of indicators to learn about educational opportunities that arise in the socio-economic context in which they graduated from upper secondary education. Which, it was considered a dimension identifies four variables, which are measured by means of a set of indicators which can be processed to identify educational opportunities that may exist to graduating from Middle High Education.

Table 6. Three proposal of indicators on educational opportunities in the MHE

Dimension	Variable	Indicator
MHE graduated educational opportunities	Socioeconomic status of graduates	AGE
		Gender
		Status
		Monthly incomes
		Parents Occupation
		Number of people who live at home
		Number of people who integrates the family
		Father, tutor degrees
		Home services
	Degree satisfaction level of the training received	Assistance percentage
		Student scholarship percentage
		Usefulness of the contents offered by the institution
		Useful skills for development in other fields
		Percentage of educational achievement
		Percentage of compliance of the student concerning the training received
		Percentage of attendance of teachers
	Higher education access	Percentage of students receiving vocational guidance to access the Higher education
		Percentage of graduates who were able to enter the Higher education in their first choice
		Percentage of graduates who entered to s public schools
		Percentage of graduates who entered to s private schools
		Percentage of the training areas where manage to enter the students that complete a Bachelor's degree.
	Sign in laboral field	Skills that are useful in functions that plays in their work
		Percentage of links between the school and the industry
		Position at work after completing his Bachelor's degree.
		Percentage of graduates who work amounted to completing their Bachelor's degree
		Ability to work in team

CONCLUSION

in our country where much of young people attending a MHE and HE level live in conditions of poverty, schooling remains the mode so that society, and not just the subjects, to develop and to overcome obstacles that represent the social class and the modes of stratified and differential access to opportunities, this congruent, as described by Muñoz (2001), to combat poverty and the concentration of national income in few hands:

It is necessary to satisfy two conditions. The first concerns that educational opportunities are distributed equitably among all sectors of society and, second, to all the graduates of the system have the opportunity to carry out occupations in which to fully leverage the schooling they have acquired.

As a recommendation, it is necessary to conduct a study of employers to expand and detail the requirements of the employer in the work concerning: knowledge, ability to package management Informatics, skill demanding workplaces, so that from these decisions and feedback plans and programs of study with a look to get better job opportunities graduates, etc., as well as a study in greater depth the reasons for which graduates and graduates have failed to enter the top level, since these are two key aspects to offer development opportunities to prospective students that completed its MHE in our country.

REFERENCES

Armenta, N. G., Pacheco, C. C., & Pineda, E. D. (2008). Factores económicos que intervienen en el desempeño académico de los estudiantes universitarios de la Facultad de Ciencias Humanas de la Universidad autónoma de Baja California. *Revista IIPSI, 11*(1), 153-165. Recuperado de http://sisbib.unmsm.edu.pe/bvrevistas/investigacion_psicologia/v11_ n1/pdf/a10.pdf

Berverley, C. (agosto, 2002). Educación y mercado del trabajo en América Latina, frente a la globalización. *Revista de la CEPAL,* 77, 123-141. Recuperado de http://www.eclac.org/ publicaciones/xml/9/19289/lcg2180e_Carlson.pdf

Briseño, F., Cardoso, E. O. & Mejía, J. (2014). Diagnóstico de oportunidades escolares de egresados y egresadas del nivel medio superior del municipio de Tlalnepantla del estado de México. *Revista Electrónica Educare, 18*(2), 141-157. Recuperado de10.15359/ree.18-2.7

Cañedo, R. (2008). *Educación superior y mercado de trabajo: El caso de los egresados de la Universidad Autónoma de Guerrero. (Tesis doctoral inédita).* San José, Costa Rica: Universidad de Costa Rica.

CEPAL. (2000). *Universidad y desarrollo. Proyecto latinoamericano*. México: Autor.

De Ibarrola, M. (2009). El incremento de la escolaridad de la PEA en México y los efectos sobre su situación laboral y sus ingresos, 1992-2004 *REDIE. Revista Electrónica de Investigación Educativa, 11*(2), 1-19. Recuperado de http://www.redalyc.org/articulo.oa?id=15512151002

DEL MORAL. (2007). *Anselmo, PAZOS, Juan, RODRIGUEZ, Esteban, RODRÍGUEZ-PATÓN, Alfonso y SUÁREZ, Sonia; Gestión del conocimiento*. Madrid: International Thomson Editores.

EGREES, European Group of Research on Equity of the Educational Systems. (2003). *Equity of the European Educational System. A set of indicators.* Department of Theoretical and Experimental education University of Liège: European Commsissión, Directorate General of Education and Culture Project Socrates SO2-61OBGE. Bruselas, Recuperado de: http://ec.europa.eu/education/programmes/socrates/observation/equality_en.pdf

Gutiérrez, L. (enero-junio, 2009). El devenir de la educación media superior. El caso del estado de México. *Tiempo de Educar, 10*(19), 171-204. Recuperado de http://www.redalyc.org/articulo.oa?id=31113164007

López, N. (2005). Equidad educativa y desigualdad social. Desafíos de la educación en el nuevo escenario latinoamericano. Buenos Aires: Instituto Internacional de Planteamiento de la Educación, UNESCO.

Matus, G., & Molina, F. (2006). *Metodología cualitativa: un aporte de la Sociología para investigar Bibliotecología*. Valparaíso: Universidad de Playa Ancha.

Muñoz, C. (2001). *Implicaciones de la escolaridad en la calidad del empleo. In Los jóvenes y el trabajo: La educación frente a la exclusión social* (pp. 155–200). D.F., México: Universidad Iberoamericana. Recuperado de; http://www.oei.es/etp/jovenes_trabajo.pdf

Muñoz, C. (2003). *Desarrollo de una propuesta para la construcción de indicadores de impacto social de la educación en América Latina y el Caribe.* Recuperado de: http://www.prie.oas.org/espanol/documentos/Indicadores_impacto_social_sp.PDF

Ordorika, I. (2006). Educación superior y globalización: las universidades públicas frente a una nueva hegemonía. *Revista Electrónica Scielo, 3*(5), 31-47. Recuperado de http://www.scielo.org.mx/pdf/anda/v3n5/v3n5a3.pdf

Ortiz Pabón. (2007). *Efraín, NAGLES GARCÍA, Nofal; Gestión de tecnología e innovación. Teoría, proceso y práctica*. Bogotá: Universidad EAN.

Plasencia, S. R., Vizconde, L. E., Ruiz, I. R., Araujo, M. E., & Salazar, P. (2008). Estudio: Factores socioeconómicos y su relación con el rendimiento académico en estudiantes de la Universidad Nacional de Cajamarca. Recuperado de http://nuevo.unc.edu.pe/paginas/educacion/IIEDUCA/Archivos/Articulo%20Cientifico%20-%20PLASENCIA%20CARRERA.pdf

Ramos, V. (2000). *La educación y la circularidad de la pobreza: Resultados de la encueta nacional de hogares 1997-1998*. Perú: Instituto Nacional de Estadística e Informática.

Secretaría de Educación Pública (SEP). (2013). *Bachillerato general.* Recuperado de http://www. dgb.sep.gob.mx/02-m1/01-dgb/bachillerato_general.php

Sen, A. (1987). Equality of What? In *En: liberty, equality and law. Selected Tanner lectures on moral philosophy*. Salt Lake City, UT: University of Utah Press.

Villa, L. (enero-marzo, 2007). La educación media superior: ¿Igualdad de oportunidades? *Revista de la Educación Superior, 36*(1), 93-110. Recuperado de http://www.redalyc.org/articulo.oa?id=60414105

Young, R. & Harmony, S. (1998). *Working with faculty to design undergraduate information literacy programs: a how–to–do–it manual for librarians*. London: Neal-Achuman Publishers.

Chapter 9
Evaluation of Institutional Management Based on Leadership Competencies in Middle School Education

Jesus Gerardo Alfaro Patiño
Instituto Politécnico Nacional, Mexico

Diana Patricia Skewes Muñoz
Instituto Politécnico Nacional, Mexico

ABSTRACT

In a globalized world, public policies are subject to the recommendations of international organizations that regulate and determine educational policies according to their own needs and interests. In this sense, educational skills, arising from the business world, have become the focus of curriculum design and teacher professionalism and managerial schools Basic and Secondary Education in Mexico. Specifically, the National Association of Professional Technical Education (CONALEP), has become a pillar that provides students of Media Education competent technical professional for requirements that are demanded today. Since its birth in 1978 was oriented to the formation of technical professionals, graduates of Basic Education, with the main objective job training, intersectoral linkages, community support and technological advice and assistance to businesses.

INTRODUCTION

Neither doubt nor change, how important education is in the world. No mattering what latitude, moment or culture, education lies as a basis for offering cohesion, guidance and strength to the society, and its only main purpose is the integral preparation of human beings towards a common welfare. In addition, nowadays, education does not only represent a right, but also a liability, and in parenthesis a condition for the economic, political and social development of a country, as well as for the nation's permanent sovereignty.

DOI: 10.4018/978-1-5225-0457-3.ch009

It is unquestionable that Middle Education is significant because the quality observed at this level of studies enhances the preparation of the young generations that shall enroll in the workforce or shall continue their education as professionals. Moreover, it is transcendentally emphasised that, at this preparation stage, the people's essential traces must be developed, so that their life's project is defined.

Traditionally, the level of middle school studies has been considered as a preparation stage to enter at the university's level and study a major programme. So much so that by this association, as the pre-exhibition room of higher education, there are still high-schools relying on universities, straightforwardly. But as time passes by, a technically terminal education or bivalent education, which trains for work and prepares for higher education, has been added to the conception of middle school studies.

In a globalized world, public policies are subordinated to the recommendations made by the International Organisations that regulate and set educational policies according to their own needs and interests. In this sense, educational competences, born in a business environment, have become the principle of curricular designs and the professionalisation of the body of teachers and principals in Elementary and Middle Schools.

Equally, knowledge management is immersed in today's competitive environment, the organisations are facing great challenges, such as: globalisation, technological advances, economic agreements, the steady demographic growth, by only mentioning some of them. Therefore, we need to effectively and efficiently adapt to these challenges, as well as their tendencies, in order to survive to the globalisation.

In this context, the National College of Professional Technical Education (*CONALEP, for its acronyms in Spanish*) has become a milestone that offers Middle School students a competitively technical professionalisation in order to meet today's requirements. From its origin, in 1978, this College has geared towards the preparation of technical professionals, who finished their elementary education, and has had as main aims: labor training, a school-industry-government *liaison*, communitary aid, and enterprise-oriented technological consultancy and support. Later on, in 1994, the CONALEP, adopted a Competence-based Education (CBE) framework, –starting the reform of the College's educational model. Moreover, in 1999, students are granted the opportunity to continue their studies and to professionalize in some branches of higher education.

Nonetheless, and not mattering the multiple benefits, the CONALEP has been losing its institutional vision, and, so forth, the value and significance of this College for the country and the youth that are enrolled at this stage are being looked down. This vision is very often unaccredited by the CONALEP students and external observers due to the fact that mainly most students enrolling into this College show very low averages or an acceptance exam with negative results.

These observations must be studied from the educational and political conditions under which the College has been lying and that, finally, have labeled it as negative, and not as a choice for the personal development of the students who cannot step on higher-degree studies, or as a platform that encourages the students to reach higher goals by employing the tools acquired in the CONALEP. However, this is not the focus of this study, but one of its reasons.

Another worse problem is the absence of leadership within the College's schools, which has damaged it up to its dismemberment, to a lack of unity and to little clarity of the institution's vision and mission that generate much worse trouble situations. Among which, we can find weak infrastructure, non- professional teachers with work field experience, but that do not count on the necessary teaching practice to help students develop their competences, as well as the harsh contexts where these schools are located.

These are some of the unfavorable conditions under which the CONALEP works with their students day after day. Besides the significance of every aspect mentioned above, the guiding principle of this analysis comes from the idea of a lack of leadership by the principals that govern this College and its impact on the CONALEP schools located in Mexico City.

In this regard, this study focuses on how important the principal's management role is, as well as the leadership competences that he needs to own, develop and optimize, so that the educational center under his responsibility reaches today's desired quality, leaving behind any backwardness, rejection, and inefficiency. Therefore, this study is aimed at promoting the principal's leadership, with its pertaining competences, within the CONALEP schools, in order to reach the educational quality that can act as reference for the technological education, which positively impacts the welfare of students, their families, the school, the teachers and the own context.

1. BACKGROUND

From the seventies, in the context of labour, there is a new way of understanding and interpreting human skills seen from their performance and the degree of success attained by a subject before his labor conditions: "competence." Chronologically, this new vision would rise into a whole approach that in the future would restructure all labor policies inside the enterprises, and that would be appointed as competence-based approach. The origin of this term comes from the sixties, with Noam Chomsky (1965), however, the psychologist David McClellan (1973) is the scientist who formally opens this approach.

It must be appointed that the attempt to decipher and define the concept of 'competences' can be done according to several authors who belong to three different theoretical trends: functionalist, behaviorist and constructivist.

More precisely, the functionalist trend is characterized by focusing on the task rather than the process. Competences as "groups of attributes that people must reflect in order to accomplish the goals of labour-professional processes, framed in well-based functions" (Tobón 2006) defined the main criticism to the term, where the competence acquisition can be verified, but without knowing how it was learnt. From a pedagogical viewpoint, it is an approach from which we cannot link a labour competence with training because, by the approach's own nature, the aim is not to develop the competence.

The behaviourist approach is born in the United States and directs its attention towards the managerial positions. It identifies people's skills that are not so visible, that is to say, the skills that people hold and that come to light when non-planned situations start arising, such as when decision-making takes place, organizing skills and taking action before emergency situations. Therefore, this type of actions is the result of a great analysis skill that can be associated to the higher-positions in an enterprise.

The constructivist approach has a French origin, and its premise is: "to assume competences as: abilities, knowledges and skills to address difficulties in labour-professional processes, from the organisational framework," therefore, in this trend we can see the competences that are learnt in a formal educational institution and are, so forth, reinforced at the workplace. It can be assumed that the attention of this approach is in the competence-based preparation process, so that, when entering to the labour market, the person is capable of performing well.

Once the enterprises established the model of labour flexibility and engaged in the personnel's training to increase their productivity and, therefore, their competitiveness, the people in charge of human resources set to the task of analyzing the personnel's flaws in terms of qualifications and, as Preciado (2006) mentions it, "they paid special attention to the analysis of the training methods, and the way to teach the knowledges to the newly-hired as well as to the senior employees, but responsible for new activities." This is the exact moment when the enterprises turn their sight to the institution where their employees come from and question about the preparation they received in these places, but they do not only see this aspect, they go further and turn their sight to their life-learning skills and labour-learning skills. This is the reason why the theme of preparation of human resources is linked with the institutions of higher-education. At a first glance, it turned out to be and emerging theme that agreed and redefined the educational curricula that could meet the market needs.

In this regard, the enterprises worry about their workers' preparation, resulting positively as it can be translated as how much they are preoccupied with the workers' long-life's schooling, where the person is the most important being because when his preparation, qualifications and competences are strengthened, the possibility of attaining a higher position is greater, and, in turn, the workers' self-esteem is increased, as well as their personal prestige and human nature. All these aspects make the enterprise more competitive and have a better market position. On this behalf, the educational institutions acquire, from that moment, a main role in the context of globalisation because they are seen as responsible for forging the human being with competences.

Before the inclusion of job competences, several international organisations, such as the World Bank, the United Nations Educational, Scientific and Cultural Organisation (UNESCO), the International Labour Organisation (OLI), and the Organisation for Economic Cooperation and Development (OECD), just by mentioning some of them, promote the educational competence-based approach as a factor of economic development and, thus, the social development of all the nations.

In the Tuning Project, the competence-based education of the European Union remotes to the first years of this century, exactly after the nineties, when the projects of curricular reform came to scene at a great scale, in other words, the reforms to the curricula, so that the programmes agreed with the competence-based approach, which were exhibited as an alternative option for improvement, even from the behaviourist trend or the constructivist approach (Victorino & Medina, 2008). While for behaviourism, the competence-based approach represents a good selection because it offers an observable and provable criteria that reflects the way in which these competences are being acquired, constructivism embraces the competence-based education by assuring that school learning must be significant for students, as well as useful and applicable to real life scenarios and with a future perspective, —not only an accumulation of knowledge.

On one hand, in 1988 a gathering is celebrated with educational representatives from the European Union at Sorbone University, where the necessary educational changes for future labour events were analyzed. In this perspective, they foresaw the necessity to offer students the correct tools to stand out. They created the conditions that opened the enrollment of students to the academic world at any moment of their lives, such as facilities for students' mobility, cooperation among educational institutions, and credit validation, considered as good alternatives. From this reunion, the "Declaration of Sorbone" arose, that was held on May 25th, 1998 in Paris, France. Here, the participating ministers invited and exhorted other countries of the European Union to join this initiative in order to harmonize the European System of Higher-education, and with the aim of strengthening it by an up-dated continuous education. From then, the main purpose is to illustrate the fact that the universities instead of being looking for a harmonization of their degree programmes or mandatory study plans, they are willing to set up a reference, converging and shared understanding framework. In this regard, the Tuning project comes from the English word "you tune" that means to tune in musical terms *this with hi;* and the word is used as a gerund because it is an ongoing construction process, that never stops (Victorino & Medina, 2008).

On the other hand, the Organisation for Economic Cooperation and Development (OECD) started in 1997 a project called Definition and Selection of Competencies (DESECO), which was aimed at defining a set of competences that were fundamental for life, as well as necessary for the people's social and economic welfare. This programme is justified, among others, by the declaration of the Ministers of Education wherein it is mentioned that "sustainable development and social cohesion depend critically on the competences of all our people, with competences that cover knowledge, skills, attitudes and values" (OECD, 2005). Therefore, the competences are seen as a factor for a good society's performance because through them, and, particularly, the sum of the subject's individual competences contribute to reach the society's shared goals, a source of social cohesion.

Competences

Accordingly, even if the word competence is more common than some years ago, the term competences is still confusing for the term ambiguity itself, so in order to clarify the concept of this word, it is necessary to start from the meaning. Thus, the word competence has many definitions according to the Dictionary of the Royal Spanish Academy (RAE, 2008), the first of them defines it as a "skill, aptitude, suitability for doing something or to intervene in a particular issue," similarly, in the same dictionary forwards, competence means "a dispute or an argument between two or more people about something", and a third meaning that is a synonym of jurisdiction, "liability or responsible for something."

Levy-Leboyer (Preciado, 2006), mentions that "competences are repertoires of behaviours that some people control better than others, which makes them efficient at a particular situation. These behaviours are observable in every work day as well as in *test* situations. Moreover, aptitudes, personality traces and acquired knowledges are put altogether into practice."

For Vargas (2004), the term competence is defined by the Labour International Organisation (LIO), which states that this term is "the effective capacity to take up a wholly-identified labour activity. Labour competence is not a probability of success in job performance, but a real and expressed capacity." On the other side, Spencer (Preciado, 2006) mentions that "is an underlying characteristic of an individual, that is cause-related to an effective or higher performance in a particular job situation, defined in terms of a criteria." Furthermore, (Preciado, 2006) mentions that "is the real skill to achieve an objective or a result in a particular context." From these four viewpoints on what competences imply, it may be possible to identify them as the person's skill to be successful in a well-determined labour and/or occupational context. This success obeys to the subject's skills and abilities, such as knowledges, aptitudes, skills and attitudes, according to Preciado (2006): "in summary, a competence is a personal characteristic related to a successful labour performance at an appointed position (role or profile in a particular organisation. Competences define, concretely, the difference between an excellent performance and just a good or proper one."

Educational Management Competences

In the educational institutions, different acting and proceeding roles, for their nature and characteristics, assumed by the members of these institutions are identified. These members have to work towards the good performance of the institutions and the accomplishment of the set goals for which they were created.

In this regard, knowledge management is highly significant in the institutions of higher education, and if it is properly done by a leader, it is possible to:

- Align the individual objectives, offer equally effective communication channels to all the parties.
- Identify where the knowledge source is centred and how to change and distribute it for the generation of intellectual capital.
- Carry out research and the development of activities that offer the meaning of permanent innovation and improvement of all the processes that are executed.
- Establish follow-up mechanisms that measure the results of the knowledge that is generated.
- Do the decision making processes and their execution more efficient and assertive, utilising all the resources at hand, so that the processes' performance and their response capacity are optimised.
- Multiply knowledge, by taking it from an individual approach to a collective one.
- Create a competitive advantage through the generation of organisational knowledge-based strategies (Castrillón, 2006).
- Therefore, an organisation needs to recognise the intellectual, financial, tangible and administrative resources which it relies on. It is also endeavoured to synthesise this knowledge and incorporate it to the key organizational tasks, in order to promote an ongoing innovation process in the institution where they perform as educational leaders.

The people who use their ability to influence on people's way of doing work done perform leadership functions. The ability or power is conferred by the status they have in the organisation, for their hierarchical position. Some others are recognized for their charisma, their leadership ability or because they have been acknowledged.

In this regard, being a principal can be translated into the institution's school management, considering the abilities that he needs to lead the organisation's destiny successfully. To lead means "the action of influencing other's behaviours in order to meet all the student`s proper needs, by assuming the responsibility of their actions" (Serafín, 1998). Antúñez identifies 127 typical principal's assignments that are grouped in the following 16 roles:

1. Self-guidance.
2. Visible head.
3. Leader.
4. Formal bond.
5. Negotiator or Middle-man.
6. Information management expert.
7. Technician in organization.
8. Curriculum manager.
9. Professor.
10. Evaluator.
11. Manager of material resources.
12. Manager of economic resources.
13. Promotor of change.
14. Promotor of culture.
15. Management of faults and/unforeseen aspects.
16. Employee and manager.

To direct an educational institution, the role of the authority must possess certain competences for facing the everyday challenges that arise in a social and cultural context. The competences contain or integrate professionally-developed resources (knowledges, abilities and attitudes). Elena Cano mentions that these competences can be subdivided in:

- **Basic or Cross-Sectional:** They are essential for the individual's vital development, and these are divided according to the following areas:
    - **Intellectual-Cognitive:** Related to reasoning and a critical sense.
    - **Interpersonal:** Refers to the capacity of team working and leadership performance.
    - Identification and communication of information.
    - **Management:** Means planning, decision-making and responsibility.
    - **Ethical-Professional Values:** Seek respect to the environment and confidentiality.
- **Specific:** They derive from the demands of a context or particular work. They can be divided according to the following areas:
    - **Knowledges:** Relative to the acquisition of techniques and theories.
    - **Professional:** Includes communication and inquiry skills.
    - **Academic:** Related to the areas of communication and research.

In addition to these leadership competences, the educational organisation is strengthened through dynamic action spaces, where a major innovation is observed and, so forth, the democratisation of knowledge. This assures the circulation of knowledge among the different areas and the demands that each person has concerning this (knowledge) resource.

Definitely Knowledge Management (KM) refers to the capacity of learning and generating new knowledge or to improve the existing one. On this behalf, knowledge management can be defined as an enhancing system of search, codification, systematisation and diffusion of the individual and collective experiences of human talent in the organization. These experiences can be transformed into globalised knowledge, of mutual understanding and useful for performing the inherent tasks, which allows the generation of sustainable and competitive advantages in a dynamic environment (Castrillón, 2006).

Evaluation

It was in the entrepreneurial sector where the production results started being measured, and, afterwards, in the educational sector, regarding every student's progress, —all quantitatively speaking.

Until this moment the term can only be referred to as measurement, nor as evaluation; even when at the beginning, evaluation was understood as an inherent activity to all intentional and systemic human activity, aimed at setting the value of something (Popham, 1980).

Subsequently, the concept of evaluation continues changing and separating from the concept of measurement and, at that moment, is when evaluation is seen as a process that goes beyond a simple assignment of values.

Evaluation assumes a specific way of knowing and getting along with reality, so that optimized changes occur. It is a transforming praxis that needs, for a deep impact, to activate the most relevant cultural, social and political springs in the context where it acts.

By the end of the XXth century and the beginnings of this one, evaluation has gained interest in academic and research activities, favouring the creation of communities, institutions, publications and governmental initiatives, which have allowed the setting of the principles and methods adopted by the educational evaluation. In this field, several disciplines, such as psychology, pedagogy, statistics and informatics merge together, characterizing evaluation as a dynamic area, in constant change and development, where different instances and actors reunite.

The definition of educational evaluation has changed throughout time, giving rise to a wide and diverse conceptual framework. Nonetheless, the most relevant proposed definitions can be grouped or classified by standing out four of their elements, and are those that:

- Contrast results vs. objectives.
- Identify and apply criteria to determine the value or merit of an object.
- Include the emission of valued judgments on the object.
- Address the needs of the audiences, considering the value of all involved agents. (Tyler, 1977).

As a matter of fact, several concepts of evaluation can be placed from the approach of different authors, such as:

- Evaluation as a systemic judgment of the value of an object, highlighting that all processes must be useful, exact, feasible and ethically guided. It is systemic because it must be followed and carried out in a particular context and in accordance with a model or a defined methodology. (Committee, 1981).
- On an educational basis, it is defined as the process of structured and reflective analysis that allows the understanding of the nature of the studied object and the emission of value judgments on the same object, which provides information for adjusting and improving the study process. (Ruíz, 1998).
- A programmed on action reflecting activity, based on systemic procedures of information gathering, analysis and interpretation, that is aimed at making grounded and communicative valid judgments on the activities, results and impact of every project or programme, and which may make suggestions for the decision-making process guided towards the adjustment of today's action for a better outcome in the future. (Nirenberg, *et al*, 2000).

A definition that encompasses clearly these elements is proposed by Stufflebeam (1987), who defines evaluation as a systemic research on the value of a programme or an object through the process of outlining, attaining, disseminating and using descriptive and judgment information about the merit, value and distinctive qualities of an object in order to lead the decision-making process, to aid effective practices and to increase the understanding of the involved phenomenon. ANUIES defines evaluation as "a continuous, holistic and participative process that identifies, analyzes and explains a problem by the use of significant information that draws up the necessary valid judgments that, consequently, hold decision making. (2000).

On this basis, the definition by Sánchez Guerrero that includes almost all the aspects more operatively: "It is an inquiry process, by which, in a system oriented towards the accomplishment of certain results, several significant aspects are compared (of the suprasystem, input, process, results, path, impacts) of the system against the aims (ideals, objectives, goals) of the system and suprasystem, and a pattern (criteria, attributes, rules), established plurally and participatively, attaining a (qualitative and/or quantitative) value measurement through a preferential order, adapting to a specific role (context influence, interests, necessities, ideology), and producing recommendations for the system (aims, structure-functions, process and actors) to reach the foreseen objectives." (Sánchez, 2000).

Carmen Carrión includes a new element concerning the opinions of participants about the school relationships at all levels: "to evaluate means to question about the institution's direction, meaning and purpose. True and legitimate evaluation encourages to reflect about the educational mission of the institution and for the participants of the school relationships to recognize their opinions and values at the account of facts and conclusions." (Carrión, 2001). And adds, "We will conventionally call evaluation to the communication process of a school community aimed at identifying the attributes of the institutional system of education, that integrate the essence, nature and structure of a particular institution, in order to qualify these attributes and determine their virtues and faults. Its last main goal is the improvement of the subject's education."

What stands out from all these definitions and must not stay out of sight is the axiological character of evaluation, which requires the acceptance, acknowledgement and responsibility of the judgments made. Thus, the persons that emit valued judgments have an unavoidable social commitment that cannot stand at a superficial neutrality or at the other extreme, to be influenced by a merely quantitative criteria or political interests.

In addition to the proposed definitions, it would be convenient to offer a brief view of the different generations of evaluation.

At first, there it is a huge tendency to use and to develop instruments where the terms evaluation and measurements are indistinctively employed. The aim of these tests is to detect and to establish individual non similarities through differential performance punctuations. In this phase, defined as the first generation or the generation of measurement or tests, the evaluator tends to generate measurement instruments that guarantee the validity and objectivity of the collected information. (Fernández, 2008).

Secondly, formal evaluation can be traced from Tyler's reform, who coins in the term educational evaluation and points out to the use of the systemic method of educational evaluation to determine at what extent the set objectives have been addressed in the curriculum as well as how the activities to achieve these objectives were valued. At this moment, the evaluation turns from a measurement process to the incorporation of value judgments that seek to identify the student's change. (Escudero, 2003).

In the sixties, the third generation is conceived, where the intrinsic value of evaluation is considered as an improvement element. This new process goes beyond the programmes, and forms part of the programs and educational practice by incorporating judgment to the associated criterion. In theoretically methodological terms, some models impacting the decision-making process arise, which can be considered as an improvement ground (Fernández, 2008).

The fourth generation is framed as evaluation research and enables a deeper study of theoretical-practical grounds, where Guba and Lincoln, at the end of the eighties, define it as constructivist when Stake's model and the epistemology of constructivism were integrated. For its development, the transit through different phases is proposed, such as: the establishment of a contract, organisation and process planning, identification of audiences, implementation, gathering and contrast of information, responses to people`s demands, information gathering, generation of proper reports for the audiences and metaevaluation (Escudero, 2003).

Stufflebeam points out that all evaluation must be: useful, proper, adequate, legitimate, liable and accurate whereas Scriven emphasizes that the significance of evaluation is in the decision-making process. This is inherent to the evaluation culture—authorities, entities, professors, students, plans and programmes—shown at the end of the XXth century, as well as at the reach of all the involved agents in the educational sector. (Fernández, 2008).

Structure and Evaluation Characteristics

From the conceptualizations of educational evaluation, a structure can be identified, where evaluation is considered as a dynamic, open and contextualized process that develops in a period of time and that covers three main characteristics (Castillo, 2002):

1. To obtain information systematically by applying valid and reliable instruments.
2. To formulate judgments on gathered data that lies as a basis for the analysis and assessment of facts.
3. To make adequate decisions from the assessments on available information.

Moreover, many characteristics of the concept can be identified, as mentioned below:

1. It is a systemic and methodic process that for its execution, a series of ordered and established steps related to each other is required.
2. Guided towards achievements, as the level of achievement of the proposed educational aims must be known. Focusing on a better understanding of what occurs and as a basis for the decision-making process.
3. It is interpretative, descriptive and assessing because it studies in detail the activities to be evaluated as well as the link between theory and practice. Thus, concepts and theoretical principles are used to explain real events, and to make judgments where the applied rules and criterion are not universal, as they arise from the peculiarities of the studied situation (Rosales, 1990).
4. Based on aims as all evaluation processes comprise a programmatic element that identifies the target at which the resources must be canalized and the efforts to address the pre-set aims by answering the questions "what" and "what for," of the evaluation (Ruíz, 1996).
5. It is done in an internal and external environment. Whereas in the internal evaluation, every participant evaluates the way of performing his or her own educational task; the external evaluation occurs at all levels (Rosales, 1990).
6. Criterion or reference points. There must exist organisms, that is to say, institutions that can act as reference elements to know the reality of the studied object according to the study programmes and the education offered, and can assess how far quality has been reached. (Ramos M. J., 2011).
7. It is useful to provide information about the virtues and faults, and their possible solutions.
8. It must be accurate when describing the object in evolution and in context, when exhibiting the virtues and faults, when being free of influences and when drawing conclusions and possible solutions to the prior knowledge phenomenon that will be evaluated and assessed. Therefore, it must be aware of the entire student's process, the professors, the place, the plan or situation that will be evaluated in order to set the goals or the areas of action and improvement.

Each of these characteristics includes all the aspects that every evaluation process must have, where all and each one of these aspects interact constantly and continually, with a specific and wholly-integrated systemic goal for its own success.

To sum up, evaluation is considered as a systemic process that allows the integration of qualitative and quantitative information for setting the object value or merit. From the collected information, judgments can be made in order to guide the decision making process that is aimed at better results.

2. RESEARCH

Relevance for Middle School Education

Article 17 of the General Law of Education states that in the Mexican Educational System, three types of education exist: Basic, including pre-school, elementary, and junior high-school; Middle School Education (all modalities); and higher education, considering post-graduate studies (LGE, 2013).

Middle School education in Mexico is a complex group made up by federal, state, autonomous and private managed schools, whose responsibility goes beyond the Ministry of Education, due to the fact that other ministries also offer middle school studies, but without any unified purposes.

Middle school education in Mexico, with an enrollment of 4 million students, merely attends 43% of the 15 -17 year population; the average terminal efficiency accounts for 60.61%, compared with 2005 and 20013 (main figures of the System of National Education 2012 -2013).

It is unquestionable that Middle Education is significant because the quality observed at this level of studies enhances the preparation of the young generations that shall enroll in the workforce or shall continue their education as professionals. Moreover, it is transcendentally emphasised that, at this preparation stage, the people's essential traces must be developed, so that their life's project is defined.

For the optimal development of the educational organization and the achievement of its mission and vision, the processes of knowledge management must be followed, where six stages are set out:

1. **Initial Diagnosis of Knowledge Management:** It is foreseen to determine the real situation of the organisation in terms of knowledge, that is to say, the identification of what the organisation either knows or not about itself.
2. **Definition of Objectives:** It accounts for all the purposes and strategies oriented towards the accomplishment of strategies.
3. **Production of Organisational Knowledge:** It is based on the capacity of organisational learning.
4. **Storage and Up-Date:** The knowledge is codified, classified and up-dated in easy access real-time databases for all users.
5. **Knowledges Circulation and Utilisation:** The creation of conversation spaces and exchange of experiences and knowledges, inside the organisation.
6. **Performance Measurement:** It determines the knowledge management cycles and the indicators that measure it's impact on the desired results (Buitrago, 2006).

From this task of knowledge generation, the school needs to transform into an intelligent organization, that utilizes the knowledge that is found in the human, structural and relational capital, form the use of the ICT, for knowledge generation and transmission (Minakata A., 2009).

In a globalised world, public policies are subordinated to the recommendations made by the International Organisations that regulate and determine the educational policies according to their needs and interests. Therefore, the educational competences, born in the entrepreneurial sector, have become guidance for the design of curricula and the professionalisation of teachers and principals of elementary and middle school education in Mexico

In this context, the National College of Technical and Professional Education (CONALEP) has become a pillar that offers middle school students a competent technical professionalisation for meeting today's needs. From its origin, in 1978, this College was aimed at the preparation of technical professionals, that finished their elementary education, having as main objectives: labor training, the school-industry-government liaison, community aid, and technological consultancy and support to enterprises. Later on, in 1994, the CONALEP adopted the scheme of competence-based education (CBE) that led to the reform of the educational model based on this approach. Then, in 1999, in addition to this educational framework, the students had the choice to continue their studies and professionalise in one of the higher education trends.

Nonetheless, and despite all the CONALEP multiple benefits, this College's institutional vision has been fading, and, thus, the value and significance that it has for the country and the youngsters that are studying this level are gradually looked down. Most times this College looks repulsive for the own students and many external observers, also.

That means the CONALEP is considered as a school without educational quality, where only the low-average students or the students that took an entrance exam and their results were negative are enrolled. These observations deserve a formal study about the educational and political conditions under which this College has been working and that, as a result, have labeled it as negative, and not as a good choice for the personal development of the students that cannot or do not want to follow their professional studies or as a platform to boost them to reach higher goals employing the tools provided at school. However, even if this is not the reason of this study, it is surely one of its purposes.

Another main problem is the absence of leadership within the College's schools, which has brought the College to be dismembered, as well as the lack of unity and a narrow clarity of the institutional vision and mission that derive in worse problems. Among these, there are infrastructure deficiencies and a teacher's lack of professionalisation; even if most teachers are professionals in their labour sector, they do not count on the necessary didactics to help students develop their competences. Moreover, the harsh contexts in which these schools are located.

Additionally, knowledge management faces a series of difficulties arising in the same environment, specially, regarding cultural factors, individual positions, the lack of knowledge-based culture, the isolation from the environment and its members, as well from the short-term perspectives, and so on.

These are some of the unfavourable conditions under which the CONALEP works with the students every day. Despite the fact of how important these points are, the guiding principle of this analysis comes from the idea of a lack of principal's leadership and its impact on the CONALEP schools in Mexico City.

In relation to knowledge management, the undertaking of any projects needs to foresee a series of variables that can be considered influencing or determinant in the results. The absence of these variables can lead any action to the failure of the implementation of the knowledge-based management system. These variables have already been defined in this research.

This Project named "Evaluation of institutional management based on leadership competences in middle school education", emerges with the aim to do a research that undertakes the systematization of experiences by the principals of middle schools before their management, and take advantage of the good practices carried out directly help to accomplish the mission and to near to the institutional vision.

To meet the objective set in this research, a cross methodology was chosen. At the beginning the study function was qualitative in order to describe the qualities and characteristic of a phenomenon, as well as to describe the qualities of the study object. This methodology was essential because it was set as a first priority to understand the nature of its discoveries, instead of the measurement and certainty without being proper for its approaches. The interpretative analysis and contextual method was used.

Jointly with a qualitative methodology, the quantitative one was used, characterized by the "use of measurement and comparison instruments that offer data whose study requires the use of mathematical models and statistics" (Hurtado & Toro, 2001). The purpose is to control variables and other studied situations, as making up alone the study group(s), and establishing the magnitude or frequency at which an event or phenomenon occurs in a studied subject (community), and, lastly, defines how values, numbers or frequencies of one or more study variables are distributed. Therefore, some other part that contributed to the study analysis was the use of cloze questionnaires, which served for enriching the vision on principal's managements and leadership in the schools.

It is a non-experimental research where not any situation is built, but only observed, and are not either intentionally provoked or their variables manipulated. That is to say, it is research where the independent variables are not deliberately changed. In contrast, phenomena are observed just as they are in their natural context so then they can be analyzed. As stated by Kerlinger (1979), "Non-experimental *expost-facto* research is any one where the variables cannot be manipulated or be randomly appointed to subjects or conditions." So that there are no conditions or stimuli to which the study subjects are exposed –they are observed in their natural environment, in their reality. As it is quantitative, data can be explored scientifically using mainly numbers with the aid of tools in the statistics field.

The population of the study includes 27 principals located in each one of the school in Mexico City, their closest collaborators and teachers. While the earlier are the people who interact with principals every day, and account for 25 subjects sorted out in every administrative area, the latter are the teachers in charge or teaching the school's students, whose number is variable in every school. Regarding the research characteristics, the sample selection was non probabilistic or also called directed sampled, and the type of sampling used was of "theory-guide sample," also known as "criteria sample."

For the optimal development of the present study the questionnaires for teachers were applied as instruments, and from which several results were obtained, which can be interpreted from different approaches, however, for the aims of this research, the approach will be towards the leadership and communication competencies that the CONALEP's principals must have and develop.

The schools of Gustavo A. Madero I (GAMI), Gustavo A. Madero II (GAMII), Azcapotzalco (AZCA), Álvaro Obregón (Alv-Ob), Aeropuerto (Aero), Coyoacán (Coyo), Aragón (Arag) and Iztapalapa (Izta) were visited, and in virtue of the support provided by the Only Worker's Union of CONALEP (SUTCONALEP, for its acronyms in Spanish), the professors accepted to respond, however, in the last school, the teachers denied to answer the instrument by orders of the school's Principal.

No mattering this incident, the study was concreted and the results and their analysis is presented. Every graphic was developed in regard to the variation of results, and the answers that did not show a great discrepancy between each one of the frequency ranges was analyzed differently.

A leader must be a communicator by excellence as he is the one who will transmit the vision to his coworkers and will encourage them to defeat any obstacles. Thus, he must have a full control of the oral and written communication techniques, as well as to use several ways of expression.

Figure 1. Competence: Communication

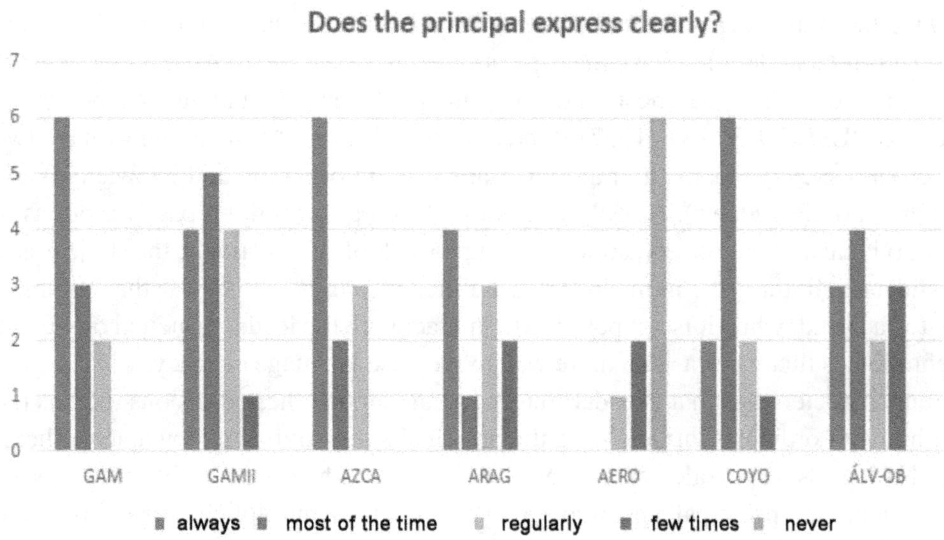

The skill to communicate effectively by the use of words and writing is absolutely one of the most valuable leader's features, because communication is the means to unite and lead a group. Therefore, the results gathered by this competency are grouped accordingly, GAM I, GAM II and Azcapotzalco showed a higher index on behalf of the principal's communication towards the teachers. Whereas, in the Airport school, followed by Alvaro Obregon and Aragon Schools, the teachers assure that the principal never expresses clearly. Coyoacan school considers that the principal generally expresses clearly, although he does not reach excellence.

Figure 2. Competence: Communication

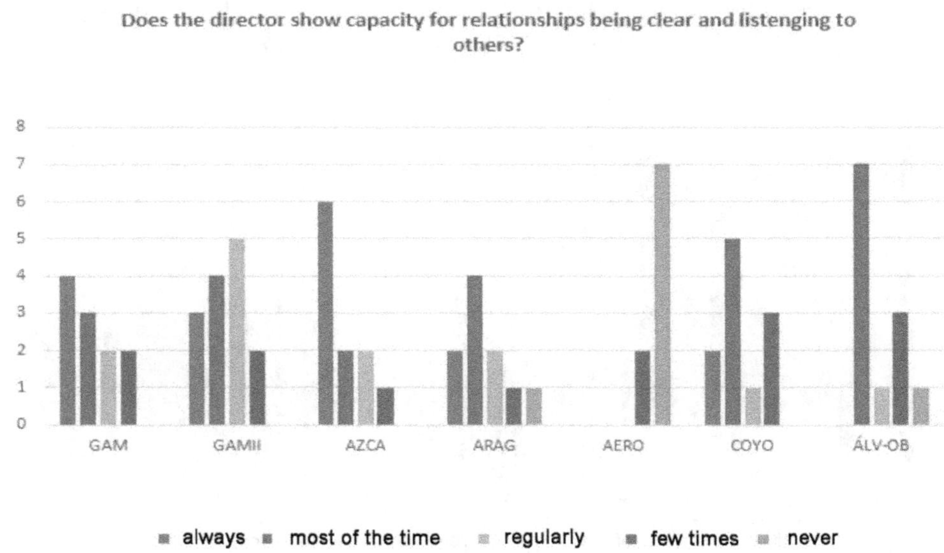

For this second question, the CONALEP Azcapotzalco has very positive results, from 10 interviewed, six consider that the director has capacity to listen to and understand the teachers, followed by GAMI y GAM II. Once more the Airport school presents negative results due to the fact that seven teachers consider that the principal does not have the capacity to understand them. Álvaro Obregón is located at the mid-point again, on behalf that most times the principal listened to and understands them,

Therefore, the DESECO Project (1997) stands out the idea that "human beings have two types of tolls to interact with society: socio cultural tools (language, information and knowledge) and physical tools (computers, mobile gadgets). A tool must not be taken as something passive, but as a mediator between the individual and the society, so when using these tools interactively, the subject-environment relationship widens and, thus, the number of possibilities increases." It is clear that communication is not only face-to-face and, when it is not possible to interact with the leader principal or vice versa, there exist new technologies that work as one more way to increase language efficacy.

The different characteristics that a leader must have and among these divisions there is the capacity to interact with his subordinates, highlighting the principal's sensitivity and touch (Sverdick, 1991). In this sense, CONALEP Azcapotzalco and GAM I are located with very favorable results, six out of ten interviewed consider their principal empathic, which turns out to a multiplicity of positive results. While Coyoacán and GAM II believe that most time their principal is empathic, Aragón and Álvaro Obregón draw regular results. Airport shows negative results again, four out of ten consider that their principal is never empathic and the rest only considers him with this competence, rarely.

For the growth and development in every school towards an education of quality, it is necessary that every member of his community participates in issues related to their area, and that the principal must foster this task through an effective communication.

The school that meets this function adequately is Azcapotzalco, where four out of ten consider that they are always informed about the activities; very similar to GAM I, where most times this communi-

Figure 3. Competence: Communication

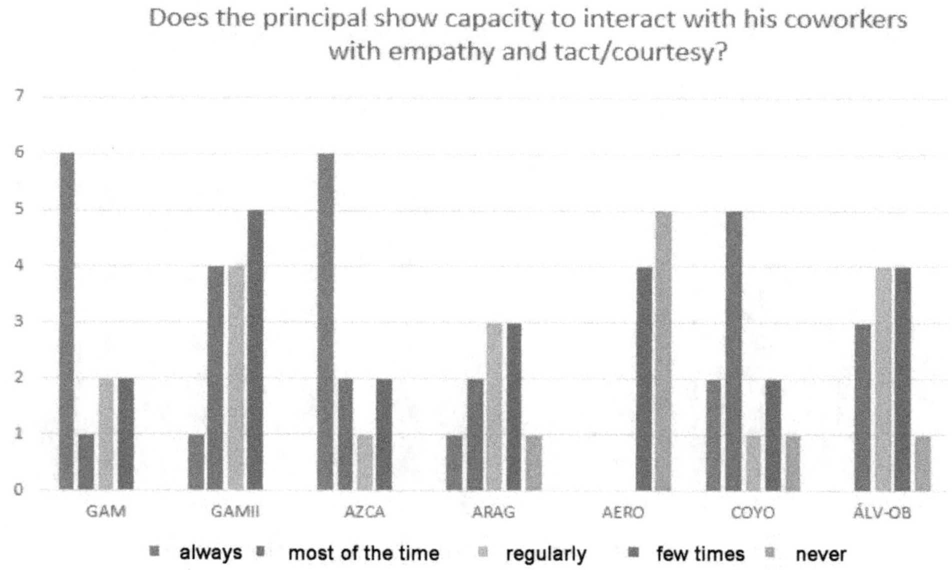

Figure 4. Competence: Communication

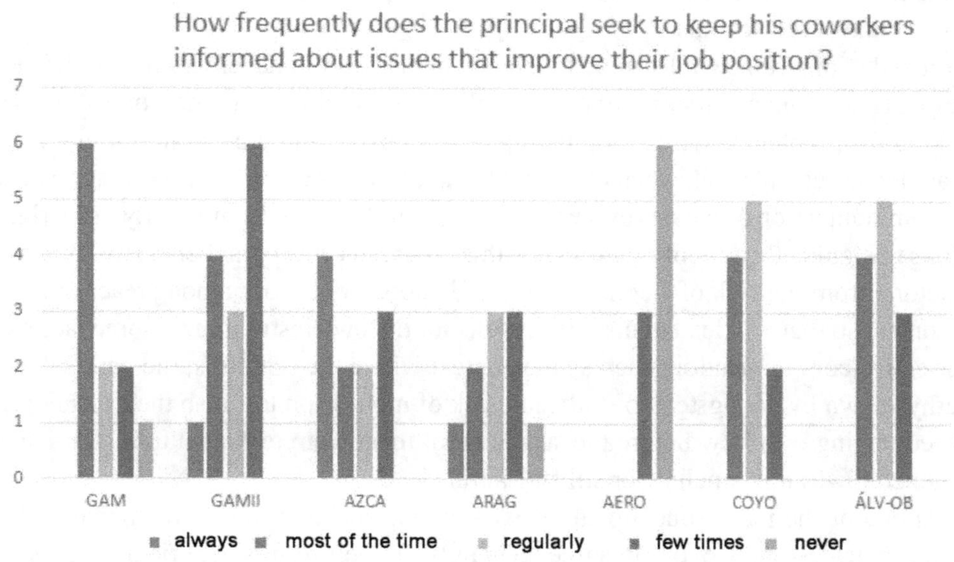

cation is done; in this order, GAM II and Álvaro Obregón consider they are informed regularly, while Aragon has regular results, and Airport school has negative results again.

This is one of less favoured items in spite of how important is to regulate human relationships through norms, rules and laws, which is translated as one of the main education pillars: "to learn to interact." CONALEP Coyoacan is one of the schools that considers that the norms and procedures are disseminated, five out of then interviewed; GAM I follows in this line of positive answers, as four out of ten

Figure 5. Competence: Communication

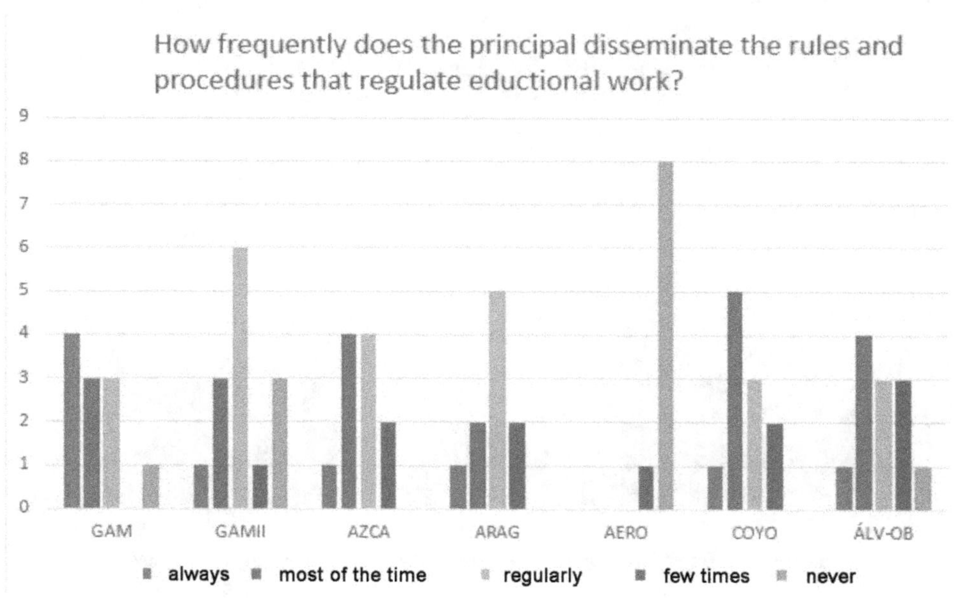

realise that the norms are disseminated and that they do not exceed the negative results to this answer. GAM I considers this dissemination as regular, equal to Aragón and Airport schools, which continue to figure the most unfavoured schools.

In addition to the importance of learning to interact in the educational environment, the development of the educational management process is the principal's responsibility. Planning, control, aims definition, decision making for problem solving, propitiating an effective communication, training personnel are actions that are left at second hand, when they forget that the norms are the ones regulating these actions.

Effective communication orientates every member of the educational community to the right development of actions that guide the school to success. If this communication is not effective there is an impact on several factors, from the lack of a collaborative and cooperative work among teachers, students and school's personnel, so that will lead to negative results for the own institution. If some factors are added to the low-effective communication, such as the context where the school is, the parents' absence, the sense of apathy shown by youngsters to study and lack of motivation to finish their technological studies, and a discouraging overview before the scarce enrollment from technical to higher education, the students, in general, will not conclude or sill stay at this level

Empathy is one of the main educational leader's competencies. It must be emphasized that GAM I, GAM II, Azcapotzalco and Coyoacán agree, generally, in their results. Confidence, cooperation and support among coworkers are elements of a collaborative work, thus, these schools keep a sufficient level for the full development towards the school's quality. Oppostie to Airport school, where its personnel assures that the principal never motivate group work.

In this respect, Lussier assures that the leader is the person who not only communicates his ideas, but that convinces his followers and they accept his ideas and feel motivated to back them up and make the change through their influence (Lussier, *et al*, 2002). Based on this idea, it must be practically impossible to make a change in the CONALEP schools in order to achieve success if the leader does not communicate his ideas and, thus, does not have an influence on their followers.

Figure 6. . Competence: Leadership

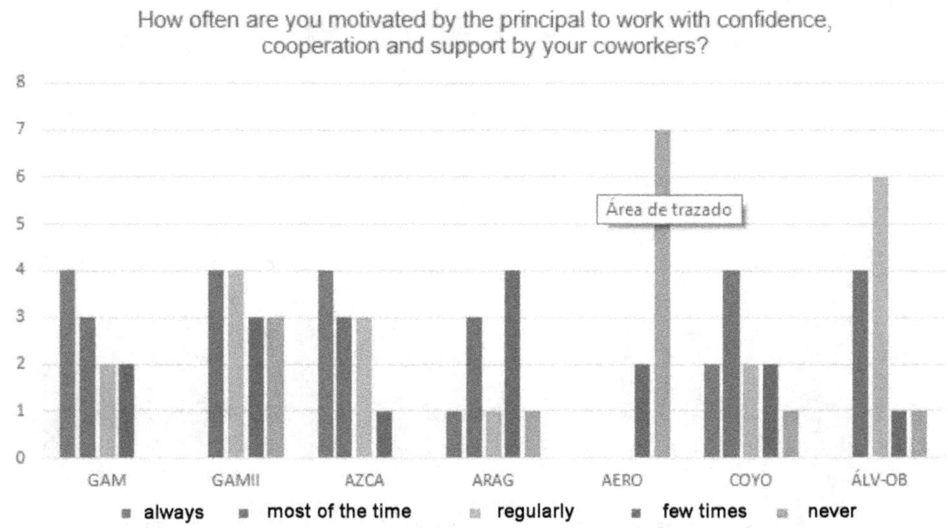

Figure 7. Competence: Leadership

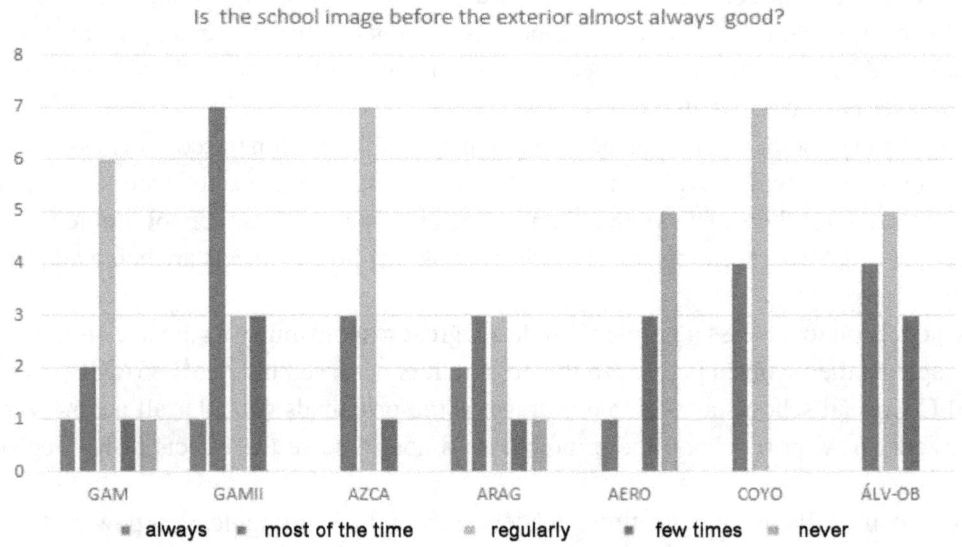

Based on theory, a good school leadership consists in transforming feelings, attitudes and opinions, as well as practices, with the aim to improve school culture.

Thus, this is one of the items in which most schools agree, except for GAM II that considers having a good image of their community. The other schools realise that they keep a positive image in their context very often.

Figure 8. Competence: Leadership

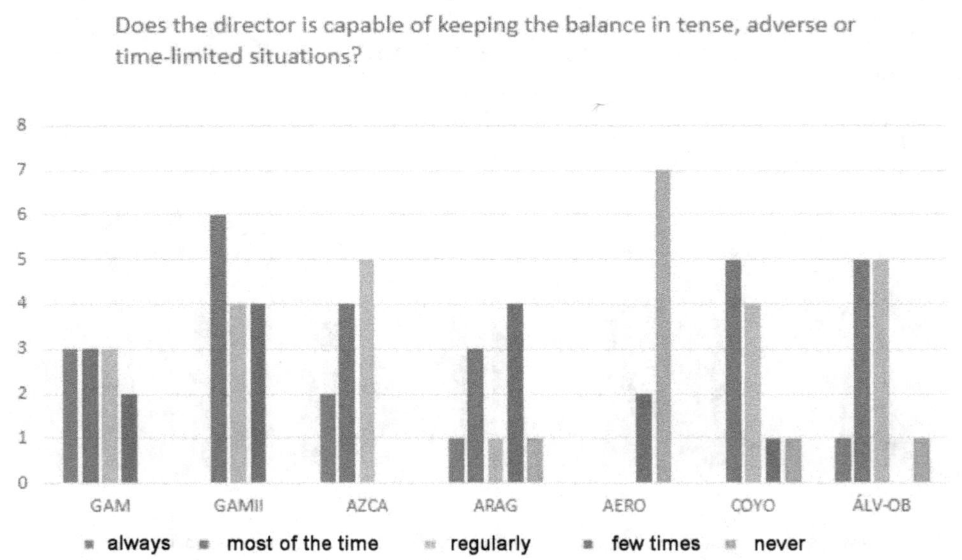

This competence on negotiation and conflict solving in time and form does not reflect satisfactory results. Only in GAMII, six out of then interviewed admit that in most tense situation, the director keeps balance, followed by Coyoacan and Airport schools, five out of ten. In a descending scale, Azcapotazalco is located, after GAM I and Aragon, respectively, to conclude with Airport school, which assumes that conflicts are never balancedly-addressed.

According to the principal 's competencies previously studied, within the cognitive skills, we find the right skill for problem solving, and for this item, the results drawn in Azcapotzalco, GAM I and Álvaro Obregón schools, the teachers observe that the way the principals address school problems is assertive, while in GAM II and Airport schools, most teachers think that how conflicts are being addressed do not generate a positive result.

Making a decision to address a problem implies a great responsibility as the decision impact can be in favour or against the involved people. In this regard, it is observed in GAMI, GAMII, Azcapotzalco, Aragón and Coyoacán schools a favorable average as the principals consider all actors when making a decision, while in Airport school, the principal does not perceive the effects of his decision on his personnel.

One of the main skills by an educational leader relies on his communication power, due to the fact that through this skill he will achieve the delegation of responsibilities, the course or direction of the own school, as well as the right or (wrong) course of the school actions and the effective relationship with the school community, including, firstly, students, teacher, parents and the space where the school is located.

In GAMI, GAMII, Azcapotzalco, Coyoacán and Álvaro Obregón schools, most teachers think that the principal considers them as responsible and dedicated people, while in Aragón and Airport schools, the teachers express an opposite opinion.

To motivate is to encourage someone to take actions directed to the accomplishment of set objectives and to persist until reaching them. So every action towards encouragement must foresee absolutely these three elements: activation, direction and persistence.

Figure 9. Competence: Leadership

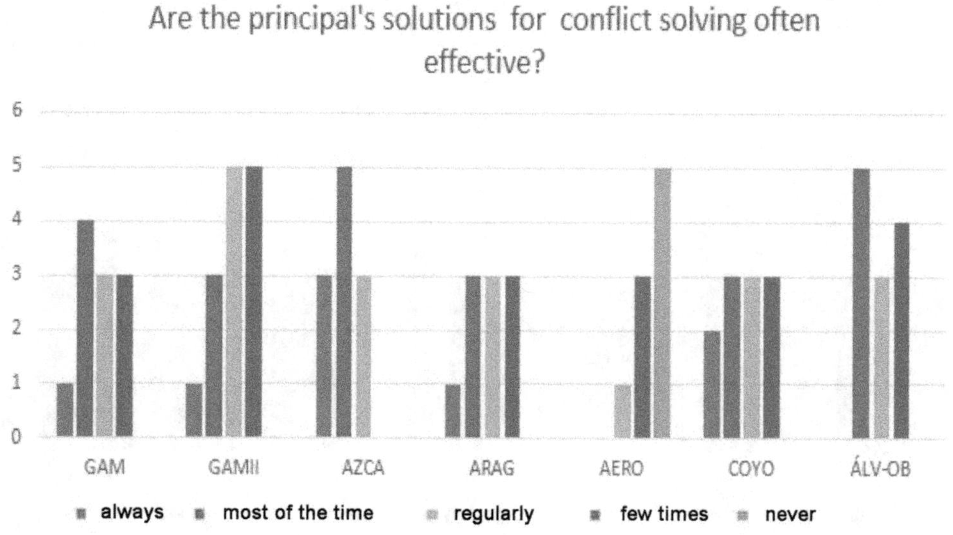

Figure 10. Competence: Leadership

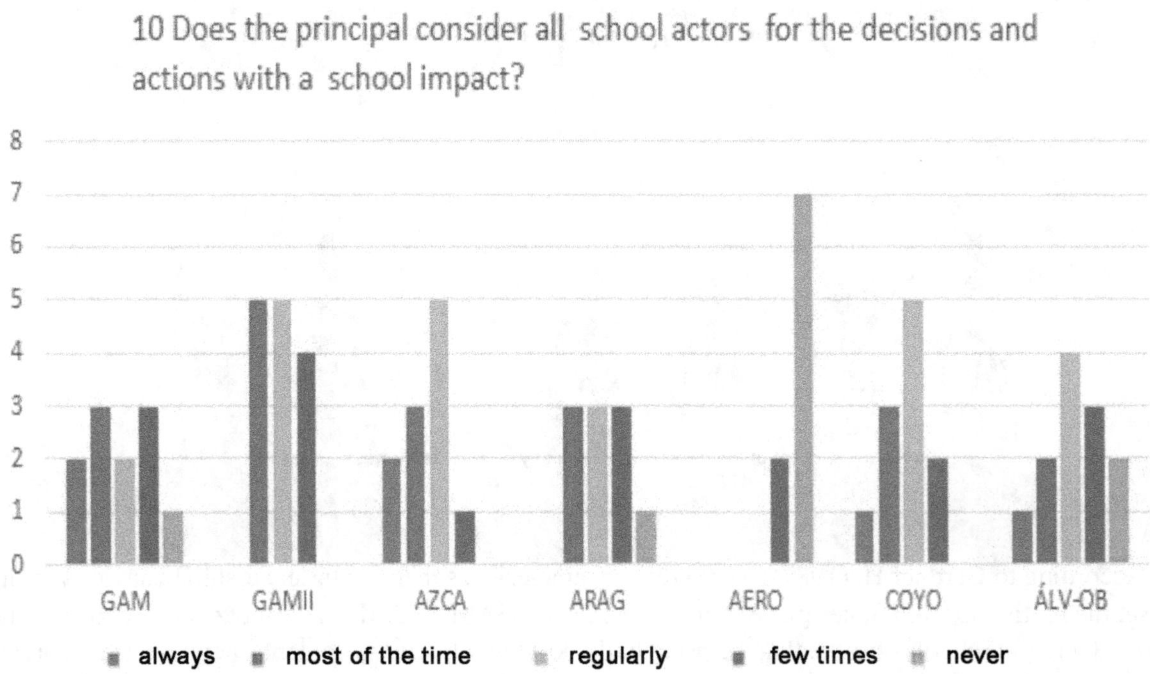

Figure 11. Competence: Leadership

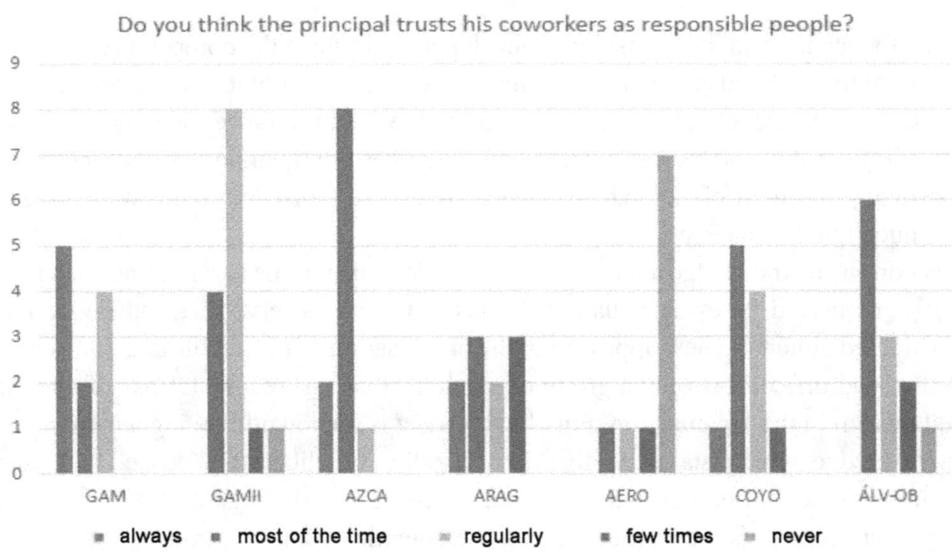

Figure 12. Competence: Leadership

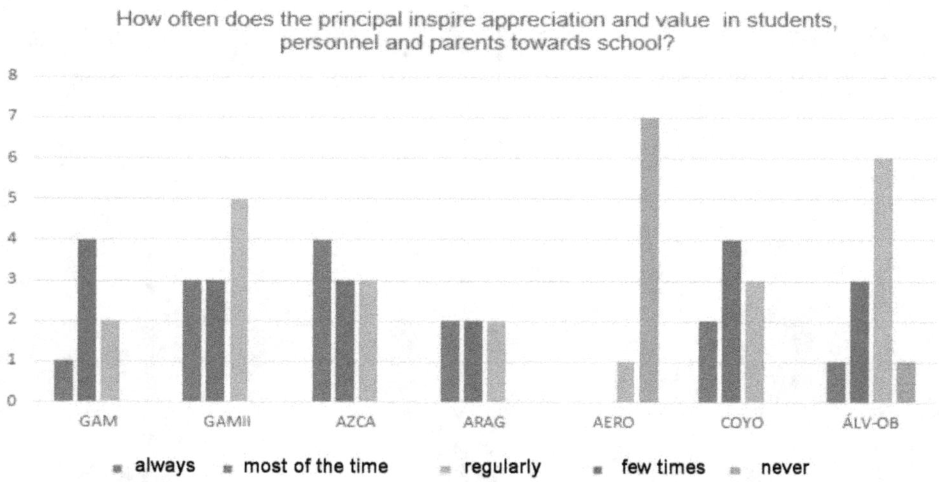

According to Gardner H. (1987), there are 14 characteristics that favour leadership behavior, among these, the motivation skill takes place. The teachers from GAMI, GAMII, Azcapotzalco, Coyoacán and Álvaro Obregón schools observe that the principal's skill to motivate the students, personnel and parents is mid-good whereas the less favourable results are found in Airport and Aragón schools.

3. CONCLUSION

Recapitulating, the leader principal must hold, develop and optimize the competences that will lead his educational school to reach today's required quality. One of the main objectives when carrying out this study in the system of middle school education was to revalue the importance and transcendence that these competences imply for the country's economic and social development, leaving behind backwardness, rejection, inefficacy and inefficiency which, several times, are translated to the students and teachers, and result in educational exclusion.

So forth, according to knowledge management, the leadership must be variable and changing, in regard to the capacities requested for every situation. In this sense, we observe that knowledge management cannot be considered either as a new approach of the organisation of the institution, or a new philosophy assumed by the head office, it is only a group of elements that assure a better use of an asset that has always stayed present in the organisation. Finally, this asset is reknown for being a main resource in the orgnisation: knowledge, which guarantees that this utilization is deliberately focused in the same regard, in the steady improvement of productivity and competitiveness of the organisation (Castrillón, 2006).

Knowledge management is vital for enhancing the potential of the four most important concepts in the top management of the new century. These concepts are as follows:

- Ongoing improvement.
- Quality maximistation.
- Recurrent innovation.
- Organisational learning.

Without knowledge management an organisation can "learn" because no organisation that loses knowledge can keep the necessary basis for learning from its mistakes and take advantage of its successes, and according to Santos Guerra (2006), the school needs to learn.

The conclusions are centered in the principal's managements, over the competences that he holds as a leader, and that he needs to develop and optimize, so that the educational center reaches the desired level of quality; and as a result to avoid any backwardness, inefficacy and inefficiency that, several times, can be translated to the students and teachers, and forms part of the educational exclusion.

It was found that the most significant skills and competences to be developed and/or to be strengthened are: leadership, communication, joint work, empowerment, responsibility sharing, negotiation, conflict solving, anticipation and motivation. According to Pozner (2000), the new labour cultures in the organisations claim for something else to lead; also, a clear vision that encourages and motivates groups, alliances, motivations and acting competences is needed.

In regard to the gathered outcomes, it is considered that: the participating principals present a positive development level of their management competences that, theoretically speaking, must exhibit the efficient leaders, a possible supposition could be attributed to the level of education and experience in leadership positions. As a matter of fact, it must be emphasized that although these participants obtained favourable scores, new qualities must be provided in order to improve management and help reach the desired educational quality, and represent a new standpoint for technological education and that have a positive impact on the student's welfare, their families, the school, the teachers and the own context.

Concerning the main outcomes obtained once the instruments were applied, it was summed up that the leader principal must hold, develop, strengthen and optimize the competencies that will lead his educational center to reach today's required quality and that is necessary to revalue the importance and transcendence that middle education has for the country's economic and social development.

Derived from the outcomes analysis, some suggestions are as follows:

- To consolidate the research outcomes, in a strategy of continuous education for the principals.
- To establish training programmes for the principals, for the development of their management competences.
- To create mechanisms of performance encouragement, that promote motivation, leadership, emotional intelligence for the principals, as an essential tool for an efficient educational management.
- To promote the principal's professionalisation in compliance with the outcomes of the mechanisms of evaluation of their management.
- To carry out research studies, so that the profiles of optimal performance are identified, obtained, and multiplied in the incorporation, designation and appointment of the CONALEP's principals, being certain of addressing the institutional mission.

REFERENCES

Castillo, S. (2002). *Compromisos de la evaluación educativa*. Spain: Prentice.

Castrillón, M. A. (2006). *La gestión del conocimiento*. Available at Rosario University: http://repository.urosario.edu.co/bitstream/handle/10336/1207/BI%2029.pdf?sequence1

Guerra, M. Á. (2006). *La escuela que aprende*. Mexico: Morata.

Minakata, A. (2009). *Gestión del conocimiento en educación y transformación de la escuela*. Notas para un campo en construcción. Available at scielo: http://www.scielo.org.mx/scielo.php?script=sci_arttext&pid=S1665-109X2009000100008&lng=es&nrm=iso

Nirenberg, O., Brawerman, J., & Ruíz, V. (2000). *Evaluar para la transformación; innovaciones en la evaluación de programas y proyectos sociales*. Argentina: Paidós. On line.http://www.ilo.org/public/spanish/region/ampro/cinterfor/publ/papel/13/index.html

Pozner, P. (2000). *Competencias para profesionalización en la Gestión*. UNESCO.

Preciado Sánchez Alma Cecilia. (2006). *Modelo de evaluación por competencias laborales*. S.A. Mexico.

Ramírez, & Medina. (2008). *Educación basada en competencias y el proyecto Tuning en Europa y Latinoamérica. Su impacto en México*. At Ide@s CONCYTEG.

Stufflebeam, D. (1987). *Evaluación sistemática: Guía teórica y práctica*. Spain: Paidós.

Tobón, S. (2006). *Formación basada en competencias*. Bogotá: Ecoe Ediciones.

Vargas, F. (2004). 40 preguntas sobre competencia laboral. Montevideo: CINTERFOR/OIT.

TERMS AND DEFINITIONS

Competencies: They are behaviour *repertoires* that some people handle better than others, which make them more efficient in a particular situation.

Evaluation: A programmed action-based reflection ability, that relies on systemic procedures of recollection, analysis and interpretation of information. Its purpose is to make grounded and communicative value judgments about the activities, and to make recommendations for the decision making process.

Leadership: It is a group of processes that guide the people and the teams, mainly through non-coercive means, towards goal achievement.

Management: It is the group formed by men, machines, technology, information and financial resources, or any others, that meet the objectives set.

Middle School Education: It comprises high-school level, as well as the equivalent levels, and the professional education that does not require high-school or its equivalent.

Chapter 10
Evaluation of Teaching Competency-Based Performance in Middle School Education

María Elena Zepeda Hurtado
Instituto Politécnico Nacional, Mexico

ABSTRACT

The research analyzes the problem of teachers' evaluation of Middle School Education at the Instituto Politécnico Nacional (IPN, for its acronyms in Spanish), which has been practiced using the same instrument since the assessment process started until now. From this approach, the National Education Model of high-schools, and, consequently, of the Instituto Politécnico Nacional is competency-based. There are eight competencies assigned to teachers' development, which are included in the Comprehensive Reform of Middle School Education. The eight teaching competencies are unfolded as attributes that are displayed as performance and/or products, which make up: knowledges, skills and attitudes that are applied in the classroom in order to generate learning environments and to have students develop their own competencies to achieve the high-school degree profile. The general aim of the research is to design an evaluation instrument of middle school education at the IPN, so that students determine the teachers' development according to the model of competencies.

INTRODUCTION: CHARACTERISTIC OF EDUCATIONAL EVALUATION

Not until the problems faced by the Middle School Education were identified in matter of quality, equity and permanence, the Comprehensive Reform of Middle School Education is foreseen (SEP, 2008a), where the identified challenges are addressed, and the levels for landing the reform are sought. In contrast to a traditional practice, there is a special interest in teaching as it promotes the development of generic, disciplinary and professional competencies in students and increases the academic performance in order to meet the degree profile.

DOI: 10.4018/978-1-5225-0457-3.ch010

In the Comprehensive Reform of Middle School Education the teachers' role is strengthened by their own competencies: knowledges, skills and attitudes that are put into practice to generate learning environments, so that the students develop their competencies and meet the degree profile of Middle School Education. Therefore, it is demanding to know which are the limits and possibilities of the teaching professional competencies to establish the aspects that need to be fortified.

Nonetheless, from the implementation of the reform and through the competence-based approach, the instruments to evaluate the teachers' performance of Middle School Education of the (IPN) have not been up-dated: students', academic partners' and authorities' instruments. They do not evaluate the performance of the eight competencies and their related attributes. Furthermore, neither the information drawn by the current instruments on the teachers' performance is up-dated, nor the opportunity areas are certainly identified to improve teaching quality. As a result, the proposal of this work is the design of an instrument for teachers' evaluation.

In any activity, process or procedure, the evaluation is an important stage to establish performances, achievements, deficiencies at a certain period and context. It is focused on decision-making, changes in necessary areas or aspects and the strengthening of those aspects that generate good results.

In the administrative or management process, the evaluation is considered in the stages of: planning, organization, leadership, control and evaluation. In this regard, the evaluation points out the process weaknesses and strengths, and mainly verifies the objectives and goals are met. These administration or management stages are also applied in several education areas: local, national, international; and diverse aspects: students, teachers, curriculum, plans and study programmes, equipments, material, etc.

DEFINITION OF EVALUATION

Evaluation can be defined by the Spanish Royal Academy (2014) as assessment. (From French. *évaluer*). It also means to exhibit the value of an object, to estimate, to appreciate, and to calculate the value of something. As education concerns, under the IPN's educational model, the competency-based evaluation, according to Tobón (2006), is the process by which evidence is gathered and a judgment or trial is made with pre-established criteria in order to offer a feedback that improves suitability.

Institutionally (IPN, 2004:120-121) the evaluation is considered as a process that contributes to quality improvement, offers information to express value judgments and to make decisions. It can be relied on it for an everyday reflection about teaching practices and it will help define the necessary changes and trends for accomplishing the goals and mission of this educational level at the IPN.

Narrowing, the evaluation is perceived as process to assess that a performance or evidence meet the pre-established attributes or parameters, through evidence and instruments that draw information for the decision making process.

EVALUATION FUNCTIONS: TYPES AND PURPOSES

It is considered again Tejeda's proposal (1998) to identify the characteristics of evaluation from questionings, as observed in the Figure 1.

Figure 1. Characteristics of evaluation
Source: Tejeda (1998)

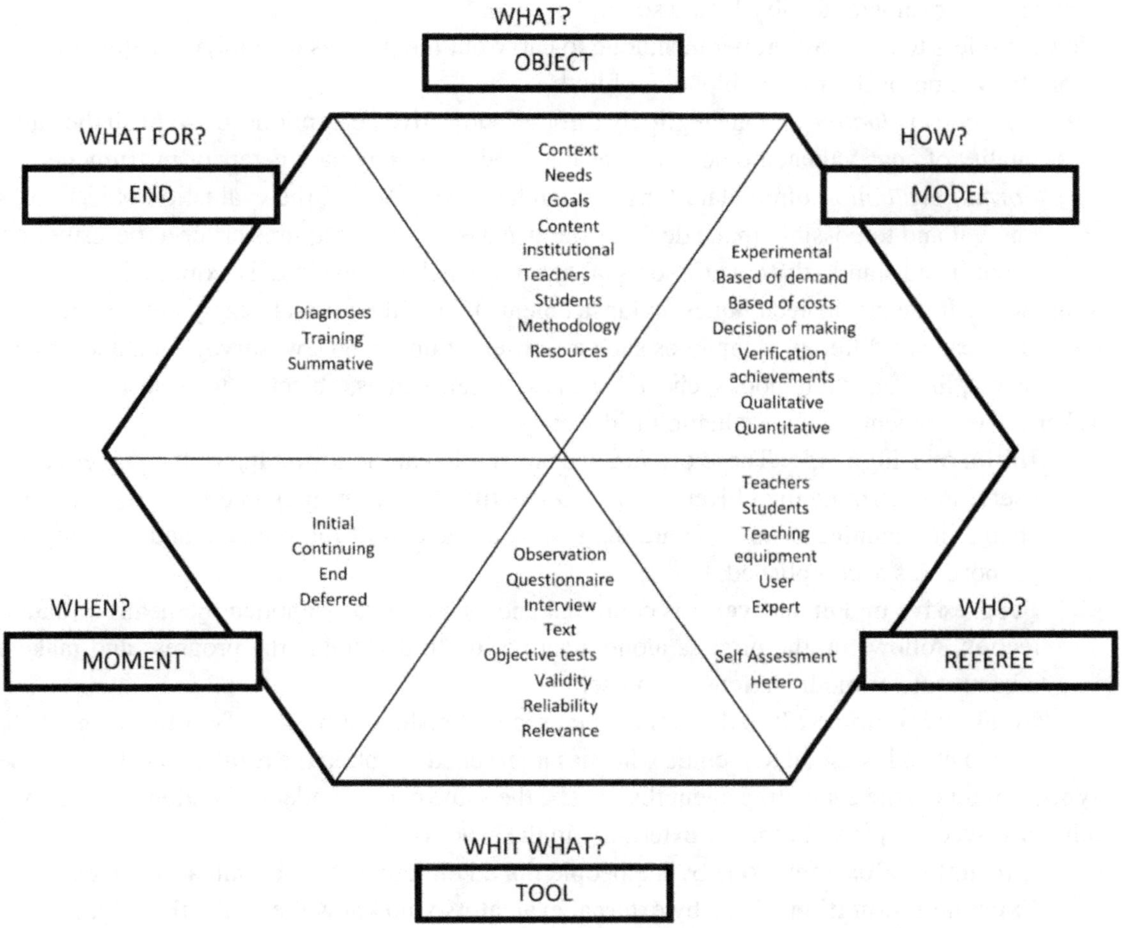

An adaptation is made as the diagnostic evaluation is considered once more in the scheme. The following evaluation classifying questions are considered for the purpose of this work.

- What? Refers to the object of evaluation that means what will be evaluated. It must be considered, on one side, the evidence and criteria which characterize that object and that propose a reference point to establish comparisons.
- In education, the school center, the curriculum, the students, the teachers, the authority, the teaching-learning process, the material, the techniques, the institution and the educational level, among others, can be evaluated. It is also considered:
    - **Partial:** It assesses only an aspect of a process or procedure: students, teachers, material, contents, etc.
    - **Global:** This evaluation seeks to evaluate the process thoroughly.

- What for? It tends to give meaning to the evaluation tasks according to the set goals and the competencies to be developed. It can be done for different reasons: diagnosis, certification, promotion, practice improvement, feedback, and so on.
- How? It refers to the most proper technique to carry out the process by applying a qualitative and quantitative approach or a combination of both.
  - *Informal evaluation* is done regularly through subjective perceptions to establish the value or quality of any evaluated object. It does not need to use any parameters or instruments.
  - *Formal evaluation* offers data for a comprehensive vision of the evaluation object so as to know it and to possibly make decisions. Formal evaluation requires criteria (describer or attribute) and standards (quantity or quality with which the attribute is exhibited).
- What with? It means the techniques and instruments that will be used to carry out the process.
  - By means of different techniques such as: observation, interview, survey, etc., and of instruments, like: anecdote books, check lists, assessment scales, objective tests, test.
- When? The moments when evaluation is done:
  - **Initial or Diagnostic:** These evaluations are applied at the beginning of the process and are useful to determine the objectives and to identify if they are prepared to start, to make any change in planning or to compare the results at the end of the process, and to verify if the purpose was accomplished.
  - **Progressive or Formative:** It is continual and systematically applied by means of data collection, follows up the process along a set period to determine the progress and make any adjustments or modifications in course.
  - **Final or Summary:** It is done once the process finishes, allows verify if the set goals have been met and is useful to include what has intervened to obtain the result in a value judgment.
- Who? It refers to the evaluating agent that can be the same person under evaluation, another or any other involved subjects internal or externally in the process.
  - **Internal Evaluation:** Done by the people linked directly with the evaluation object.
  - **External Evaluation:** Done by external evaluators who know the evaluation object.
  - **Self-Evaluation:** The students evaluate themselves.
  - **Co-Evaluation:** Among peers who develop similar activities.
  - **Hetero-Evaluation:** By people who develop other activities but that linked with the evaluation object.

PRINCIPLES OF EVALUATION

It is convenient to mention in this section the proposal that is made on the scientific characteristics of evaluation (Frade, 2008:16), in which the evaluation is taken as a knowledge and a scientific process because it counts on a methodology, and accepts several facts that must be objective and observable, –so it is a process.

- **Objective:** An attribute that defines to what extent the instruments may identify what is real, what exists, what is, without involving subjective criteria or personal judgments.
- **Valid:** Measures what it has to measure, it refers to the instrument's accuracy.

- **Reliable:** It refers to the consistency of the evaluation when it is applied under different conditions and contexts, and the result gathered is equal, so that does not lead to different interpretations.
- **Complete:** It must consider all the aspects and contents of a programme or curriculum.
- **Comprehensive:** It must include all the involved areas in the assigned task.
- **Significant:** The results and analyses gathered must include contents and be useful for the evaluated teachers, the context in order that the meaning is defined by a reality that needs to be modified by the observed necessities.
- **Predictive:** The aspects, mechanisms, instruments and strategies are defined previously.
- **Conducting the Decision-Making Process:** It must provide information for the decision-making process.
- **Transparent:** An attribute applied to the process as the result; they are auditable, that means, verifiable, controllable or revised.
- **Accountable:** Refers to the work results, achievements or advances for other persons, organizations, authorities, etc.

According to this classification, in this work an evaluation instrument is proposed, by the object of evaluation: teachers' development, by length, it is partial, by the moment, it is progressive or formative, by evaluating agent, it is hetero-evaluation, and internal. By how teaching evaluation is done nowadays, it lacks of some principles due to the fact that the instrument has not been up-dated yet, and the educational model governing the teaching practice does not correspond to the evaluated aspects. As a result, it is not comprehensive, significant and the decision-making process does not rely on valid data.

EVALUATION OF TEACHING PERFORMANCE

The evaluation exercised in the educational field these days has become plainly significant.

The General Law of Education, in Section 4: Evaluation of the System of National Education, Article 29, mentions what corresponds to the National Institute for Education Evaluation, broadly:

The evaluation of the system of national education includes different levels: pre-school education, elementary, secondary and middle school education, and it includes the participation of the federal and local educational authorities, with the aim to set the guidelines, in compliance with the results of the evaluation of the system of national education, that are relevant to contribute to the decisions focused on the improvement of education quality and equity.

The educational authorities are responsible for granting a systematic and lifelong evaluation. Its results will be the basis for the adoption of the proceeding measurements by the educational authorities.

The SEP (2013) conceives performance evaluation as: the action to measure the quality and results of the roles of teachers, principals, supervisors, technical pedagogical advisors or any others.

The SEP (2013) considers that the teaching function must be guided towards quality education and goal accomplishment. The people who cover these tasks must gather personal qualities and professional competences to promote, in social and cultural contexts, the student's learning at maximum. In observance to the profiles, standards and indexes that guarantee the idoneity of knowledges, aptitudes and capacities.

In middle school education, the authorities and the decentralized organisms will be requested to make a proposal of parameters and indexes, together with the authorized profiles, so that the National Institute of Educational Evaluation (INEE, for its acronyms in Spanish) perform the validity tests that assure the idoneity of the parameters and indexes.

Furthermore, this Institute was created by Presidential Decree on August 8th, 2002, as a decentralized public technical organism to support the evaluation endeavor of the National Educational System. As a result, it has offered information and knowledge to the federal and local educational authorities, as well as to the Mexican Society, in order to aid in the decisions made to improve educational quality.

In elementary and highly middle education, evaluates academic achievement, through the periodical application of national tests by ENLACE, in the areas of Spanish, mathematics, natural sciences and social sciences, and through international projects as PISA Programme. Even though these evaluations evaluate the student's achievements, the teacher's role is implicitly present.

The Council for the Evaluation of Middle Higher Type (COPEEMS, for its acronyms in Spanish) is in charge of evaluating the schools that require the entrance and promotion to the National System of Middle Schools (COPEEMS, 2013:134-135). This Council wholly evaluates diverse aspects for the evaluation of the body of teachers, assuming that: The teaching personnel is the element that greatly influences on the quality of the services provides by the school of middle school education. Therefore, it is relevant their preparation, performance, up-date and commitment in their intervention."

The evaluation of the body of teachers takes place considering the accredited or certified teachers by some programme or evaluation instrument reknown by the National System of Middle Schools, that have concluded satisfactorily a preparation teaching programme, as it is the diplomate offered by the ANUIES (2000) and the specialties by the UPN, in the Programme for Teacher's Preparation (PROFORDEMS).

We can observe there have been efforts to evaluate the student's and the teacher's learning, at different educational levels.

COMPETENCE-BASED APPROACH

Performance evaluation can be for the development of a response or a product that demonstrates a competence: knowledge, skills and attitudes are considered as playing techniques evaluate what can be done.

In executing a task or better known as performance can be evaluated:

- **The Method Used:** Set of steps to reach a result.
- **The Product:** An object, a model, an essay, etc.

This type of evaluation requires the integration of specific content knowledge, skills, abilities and attitudes to achieve certain goals.

Under the skills approach, evaluation is the process by which evidence is gathered, so either a judgment or an opinion is made, taking into account predetermined criteria for finally giving a feedback that seeks to improve suitability (Tobon, 2006).

Currently, skills-based education is the foundation of the IPN educational model.

The concept of competition, as it is understood in education, resulting from new theories and basically means knowledge of implementation, "it found" translates into "knowledge": to think, learn to play, how to interpret, how to act in different scenarios from themselves and others in a given context.

It states that "The Institute will establish a programme of evaluation of academic staff. In the programme, it will be used as an element, the information derived from the departmental assessment tests of the students' learning "(IPN, 2004: 145).

The Manual for the redesign of Plans and Programs in the New Model Framework Educational and Academic (IPN, 2004: 167), it returns the evaluation of students and teachers has multiple purposes. For students, it is evaluated:

1. To determine whether an applicant meets the entrance profile to the programme;
2. To demonstrate a subject or learning unit;
3. To leave the program.

As for the teachers, the purpose is to improve teaching practices and identify training needs to improve learning and students' achievement. Among other aspects, the following are considered:

- Results obtained in terms of the program's ability to retain students and the quality of its graduates.
- Adequacy of resources allocated to the program.
- Assignment of resources used and the results obtained.

So that activities designed by teachers must be meaningful and enriching possess characteristics consistent with corporate goals, social needs and consistent with the achievement of the graduate profile.

The purpose of evaluation, as already stated is the teacher, in the case of IPN, at middle school level, the teacher's performance evaluation that is done, is mainly Internal: students, academic peers and authorities, through tools provided by the authority and applied every six-month period.

The assessment made by the students to the teacher's performance is between the second and the third regular session by the end of the semester, through the System of School Administration (SAES, for its acronyms in Spanish). This is a requirement for having access to the student's grades. It consists of 19 questions, with a scale of: never, wrong or rarely, regularly or frequently, and almost always good or very good or well.

The questions are grouped in six areas and contain their respective quality indicators:

1. **Punctuality:** In class attendance, punctuality, in the programmed class-schedule, and in the schedule for extra-class counseling.
2. **Assignment Command:** Command of contents, use of examples, and clarifications of doubts.
3. **Didactic Skills:** Variety of learning activities, organization of themes in a sequence, as well as motivation for student's participation in classroom.
4. **Programme:** Takes into account student's knowledge for the development of the programme, integrates students for the development of themes, and addresses the programme's aims.
5. **Evaluation:** Coincides with the syllabus; the difficulty level matches with what has been taught in class.
6. **Attitude:** Respectful and considers the student's opinions.

The teachers are provided with the results of the evaluation by every group. These results are expressed in a graph that quantifies numerically each of the sis areas, as well as the overall average.

As it could be observed, the criteria and indicators handle terms that do not match with today's Educational Model by competences: organization in sequence of contents, integration of the students for the development of the themes, the accomplishment of the programme's aims, the evaluation must coincide with the thematic content and the degree of difficulty with what has been studied in class.

The teacher's performance evaluation is done in academic pairs, teacher-to-teacher, through an estimate scale on which three levels are identifies: yes, no and partially, in the following areas:

1. Knowledge of the learning unit.
2. Didactic planning.
3. Evaluation of sets of learnings.
4. Participation in events
5. In-class observation (the evaluator needs to be present in the classroom).

Finally, the instrument used by the authorities: Academic presidents and chiefs of department, is accepted on mutual agreement, in the following areas:

1. Academic performance by group.
2. Programme's accomplishment.
3. Institutional academic participation.
4. Righteous hand in of reports and informs.
5. Class attendance and punctuality.

These three instruments broadly mentions are the ones for evaluating the teacher's performance in the middle school system, at the IPN.

On the other hand, under the model by competences aimed at strengthening middle school education, seeking permanence and quality in education (SEP, 2008b), the Ministry's Agreement 447 is published, which states that the teacher's competences in face-to-face schooling modality, allows them to establish the ideal or desirable teacher's profile that aids in the student's integral education.

TEACHING SKILLS

They are the ones that formulate the individual, ethical social, academic, professional and social qualities that middle school teachers must meet, and consequently define the ideal profile that teachers should accomplish. The skills and their main attributes that define the Teacher's Profile at middle school are as set out below.

1. Organizes His Ongoing Training throughout His Career

Attributes:

- Reflects and does research on teaching and relating processes of knowledge construction.
- Incorporates new knowledge and experience to the cultural equipment and translate them into strategies and teaching and learning.

- It is evaluated to improve the process of building knowledge and skills acquisition, and has a favorable disposition for teaching and peer assessment.
- Learns from the experiences of other teachers and participate in shaping and improving their academic community.
- Maintains updated in the use of information technology and communication.
- Updates the use of a second language.

2. Dominates and Structures Knowledges to Facilitate Meaningful Learning Experiences

Attributes:

- Argues nature, methods and logical consistency of imparting knowledge.
- Explains the relationship of different disciplinary knowledge to their teaching and learning processes of students.
- Assesses and explains the links between knowledge previously acquired by students, developed in its course and those who make a study plan.

3. Plans the Teaching and Learning Taking into Account the Competence-Based Approach, and Places Them in Broad Disciplinary, Curricular and Social Contexts

Attributes:

- Identifies prior knowledge and training needs of students, and develop strategies to advance from them.
- Designs work plans based on disciplinary and interdisciplinary research projects oriented towards skills development.
- Designs and use in the classroom classes of materials suitable for the development of skills.
- Contextualizes the contents of a curriculum in the daily lives of the students and the social reality of the community to which they belong.

4. Puts into Practice the Teaching and Learning of Effective, Creative and Innovative Way to Its Institutional Context

Attributes:

- Communicates ideas and concepts clearly in different learning environments and provides examples relevant to students' lives.
- Applies learning strategies and creative solutions to contingencies, taking into account the characteristics of its institutional context, and using the resources and materials available adequately.
- Promotes the development of students through learning, within the framework of their aspirations, needs and possibilities as individuals and in relation to their cultural circumstances.
- Provides relevant literature and guides students in consulting sources for research.

- Uses the information technology and communication with an educational and strategic application in different learning environments.

5. Evaluates Teaching and Learning from a Training Approach

Attributes:

- Establishes criteria and methods of assessment of learning based on the competence approach, and clearly communicated to students.
- Follows up the learning process and academic development of students.
- Communicates observations students constructively and consistently, and suggests ways to overcome them.
- Encourages self-assessment and peer assessment among academicians and among students even to strengthen the teaching and learning.

6. Builds Environments for Autonomous and Collaborative Learning

Attributes:

- Promotes among students self-awareness and self-assessment.
- Promotes among students the desire to learn and provides them opportunities and tools in order to advance their knowledge construction processes.
- Promotes critical, reflective and creative thinking, from the established educational content, current situations and concerns of students.
- Encourages the students individually and in groups, and produces improvement and development expectations.
- Encourages love for reading and oral expression, written or artistic.
- Promotes the use of information technology and communication in the students, so that they acquire, process and interpret information, as well as express ideas.

7. It Contributes to the Creation of an Environment that Facilitates a Healthy and Comprehensive Development for the Students

Attributes:

- Practices and promotes respect for the diversity of beliefs, values, ideas and social practices among his colleagues and among students.
- Promotes dialogue as a mechanism for the resolution of personal and interpersonal conflicts between students and, where appropriate, the channels to receive adequate care.
- Encourages the participation of students in the definition of standards of work and living, and enforces.
- Promotes interest and participation of students with an ecological civic consciousness, ethics and the life of their school, community, region, Mexico and the world.

- Encourages students to express personal opinions, in a framework of respect, and taken into account.
- Helps the school to collect and preserve physical and sanitary condition.
- Promotes healthy lifestyles and choices for human development, such as sports, art and various complementary activities among students.
- Facilitates the harmonious integration of students to the school environment and promotes the development of a sense of belonging.

8. Participates in Continuous School Improvement Projects and Supports Institutional Management

Attributes:

- Assists in building a comprehensive training project aimed at students in collegial manner with other teachers and school managers and teaching staff of technical support.
- Detects and contributes to the solution of school problems through joint efforts with other teachers, administrators and community members.
- Promotes and collaborates with the educational community in projects of social participation.
- Creates and participates in learning communities to improve their educational practice.

In Table 1 a comparative establishes the relationship between the indicators contained in the current evaluation instrument and the skills and attributes listed in RIEMSER.

Table 1. Comparison of instruments

Current Assessment Instrument	Skills and Attributes
1. Punctuality. -In class attendance. -In programmed class-schedule In Schedule for extra-class counseling. **2. Assignment Command.** - Command of contents. -Use of examples. -Clarifications of doubts. **3. Didactic skills.** -Variety of learning activities -Organization of themes in a sequence. -Motivation for student's participation in classroom. **4. Programme.** -Takes into account student's knowledge for the development of the programme. -Integrates students for the development of themes. -Addresses the programme's aims. **5. Evaluation.** -Coincides with the theme content; the difficulty level matches with what has been taught in class. **6. Attitude.** -Respectful -Considers student's opinions.	**2. Has a full command and structures knowledges to facilitate significant learning experiences.** Attributes: Argue the nature, methods and logical consistency of the knowledges taught. **3. Plans teaching and learning processes based on the competence approach, and place them in broadly disciplinary, curricular and social contexts.** Attributes: Identifies the student's prior knowledges and preparation needs, and develops strategies to advance from there. **5. Evaluates the teaching processes through an educational approach.** **úa** Attributes: Communicates his observations to students constructive and consistently, and suggest alternatives for the student's higher preparation. **7. Contributes to the generation of an environment that provides students with a healthy and integral development to students.** Attributes: Practices and promotes respect to a diversity of beliefs, values, ideas and social practices among his colleagues and among students.
Total number of aspects to be evaluated: 6	**Total number of competences: 7**
Total number of indicators: 18	**Total number of attributes: 34**

Source: SEP (2008b).

Table 1 shows that the difference is noticeable between the assessments tools currently employed in contrast to the teaching skills and attributes to be assessed not only in quantity but also in the aspects evaluated. As they have different approaches, and its correspondence is minimal, four attributes are evaluated, but not holistically, in the instrument, when 34 integrated attributes should be included in 7 competences. This research considers as a reference the referred competences for the elaboration of the proposal.

STUDY RESULTS

The research is descriptive because it seeks to specify important properties of individuals, groups, or any other phenomenon-communities to be subjected to analysis. This is a descriptive study a number of issues selected and each is measured independently, so forgive the redundancy-and describe what is investigated "(Hernández, Fernández and Baptista, 2006: 115). In this sense, research is focused on determining the teaching competencies in NMS to design a tool to evaluate them.

The experimental investigation was performed because no deliberately manipulate variables, so that the study phenomena were observed as given in its natural context and then analyse them. As Kerlinger (1979: 116) notes

The research design was trans or cross-sectional because the data were collected at one time. Once, the purpose was to describe the variables, and analyse their impact and interaction at any given moment. Later on, the results obtained by the instrument were organized.

For the methodological process of the study, the variables were teaching skills and their attributes for obtaining the indicators and, thus, to be able to carry out the measurement of teacher's performance.

Competence 1 was not considered for inclusion in the instrument "Organizes his on-going training throughout his career", because this competence requires other types of evidence and tools due to the fact that even if the attributes participate in the process of the teacher's construction of knowledge, the incorporation of new knowledge and experience to its cultural equipment, they are not noticeable in the classroom.

Table 2exhibits the relationship between competence and attributes that give rise to indicators, which in turn form the assessment tool to be proposed.

The instrument was organized from the above table, the operationalization of the variables, skills and attributes, 62 items were posed for choosing an option through the use of Likert scale: Strongly agree, agree, neither in disagreement nor disagree, disagree or strongly disagree.

The pilotage of the instrument was conducted by the judgment criteria of experts, which validated each of the items. The population consisted of students of middle school level. The sample was randomly stratified because the students belonged to second, fourth and sixth semesters.

Table 2. Operationalization of variables

Competence	Attributes	Indicators
2. Has full command and structures knowledges to facilitate meaningful learning experiences.	Argues about nature, methods and logical consistency of imparting knowledge.	Logically explains the origin, methods and the information used in each class.
	Explicit the relationship of different disciplinary knowledge in their teaching and learning processes of students.	Lists the contents of the class with the way students learn.
	Rates and explicit links between knowledge previously acquired by students, developed in its course and those who make a study plan.	Relates knowledges you have, to the course's and the curriculum's contents. Recognizes what you know about a subject and, there from, plans classes.
3. Plans the teaching and learning processes taking into account the competence-based approach, and places them in broadly disciplinary, curricular and social contexts.	Identifies previous knowledge and training needs of students, and develop strategies to advance from them.	Uses the initial assessment to identify the student's prior knowledge.
	Designs work plans based on projects and disciplinary and interdisciplinary research aimed at developing skills.	Works by projects Plans works for students, so that they do unit researches, which can relate to others.
	Designs and uses proper in-class materials for competence development.	Prepares support materials Prepares suitable materials for being used in class.
	Contextualizes the contents of a curriculum in the daily lives of the students and the social reality of the community to which they belong.	Relates contents to everyday life and the community's reality.
4. Puts into practice the teaching and learning processes in an effective, creative and innovative way for the institutional context.	Communicates ideas and concepts clearly in different learning environments and provides relevant examples to students' lives.	Practices and promotes respect for diversity among students
	Applies learning strategies and creative solutions to contingencies, taking into account the characteristics of the institutional context, and uses the available resources and materials properly	Applies learning strategies and creative solutions to problems that arise Faces problems by using available resources and materials. Addresses problems by using resources and material properly.
	Promotes the development of students through learning, within the framework of their aspirations, needs and possibilities as individuals and in relation to their cultural circumstances.	Promotes student's development through learning. For student's development, the teacher considers the aspirations, needs and possibilities the students have as individuals, according to student's cultural circumstances. Considers that the contents worked serve the student's daily life
	Provides relevant literature and guides students in consulting sources for research.	Provides relevant literature. Advises you in consulting research sources.
	Uses information technology and communication with an educational and strategic application in different learning environments.	Uses information and communication technology for teaching Uses information and communication technology to work in other environments outside the classroom.

continued on following page

Table 2. Continued

Competence	Attributes	Indicators
5 Evaluates the teaching and learning processes from the training approach.	Establishes criteria and evaluation methods of learning based on the competence approach, and clearly communicated to students.	Establishes criteria, evidence and assessment tools. Communicates clearly.
	Monitors the learning process and academic development of students.	Monitors the student's learning process. Monitors the student's academic development. Provides support by counseling or tutoring.
	Communicates his observations to students constructively and consistently, and suggests alternatives to overcome them.	Expresses observations of the results constructively. Suggests ways to overcome the evaluation findings.
	Encourages self-assessment and peer assessment among academics and among students even to strengthen the teaching and learning.	Allows self-assessments Encourages peer evaluation. Takes into account the results of self-assessment and peer assessment.
6. Builds environments for an autonomous and collaborative learning.	Favours among students self-awareness and self-assessment.	Favours you know yourself and your values.
	Promotes among students the desire to learn and provides them opportunities and tools to advance their knowledge construction processes.	Motivates you to learn. Provides learning opportunities. Provides tools for learning.
	Promotes critical, reflective and creative thinking, from the established educational content, current situations and concerns of students	Learning situations allow the student's to be critical. Learning situations allow the student's to be reflective. Learning situations allow the student's to be creative. Creates learning situations that analyse information in the student's daily life.
	Motivates students individually and in groups, and produces expectations of improvement and development.	Motivates the student's to improve himself. Motivates the group to overcome problems.
	Promotes the love of reading and oral expression, written or artistic	Fosters a taste for writing and speaking. Fosters a taste for artistic expression.
	Encourages the use of information y and communication technology by students in order to acquire, process and interpret information, and to express ideas as well.	Encourages the use of information and communication technology in order to acquire, process and interpret information. Encourages the use of information and communication technology to express ideas.
7. Contributes to the creation of an environment that facilitates a healthy and comprehensive development for students.	Practises and promotes respect for the diversity of beliefs, values, ideas and social practices among their peers and among students.	Practices and promotes respect for diversity among students.
	Favors dialogue as a mechanism for the resolution of personal and interpersonal conflicts between students and, when appropriate, channels them, so that they receive adequate care.	Favors dialogue to resolve personal and interpersonal conflicts among students. Where appropriate, channels students to receive adequate care.
	Encourages student's participation forr the definition of work and living standards, and enforces them.	Encourages participation from labour and living rules. Enforces rules.

continued on following page

Table 2. Continued

Competence	Attributes	Indicators
	Promotes the interest and participation of students with a civic, ethical and ecological consciousness about their school's life, their community, their region, Mexico and the world.	Learning activities generate a responsibility for the environment through. Learning activities strengthen the student's membership in the community. Learning activities promote the student's sense of identity.
	Encourages students to express personal opinions, in a framework of respect, and takes them into account.	Encourages the student's to express personal opinions in a framework of respect. Takes into account the student's opinions.
	Helps the school collect and preserve physical and sanitary conditions satisfactorily.	School helps collect and preserve physical and sanitary conditions.
	Promotes healthy lifestyles and choices for human development, such as sports, art and various complementary activities among students.	Promotes healthy lifestyles and choices for human development, such as sports, art and various complementary activities.
	Facilitates a harmonious integration of students with the school's environment, and promotes the development of a sense of belonging.	Develops the student's personality comprehensively
8. 8. Participates in continuous improvement school projects and supports institutional management.	Collaborates in building a comprehensive training project aimed at students in collegial manner with other teachers and school managers, as well as with the pedagogically technical teaching staff.	Detects school problems through joint efforts with other teachers, administrators and community members.
	Detects and contributes to the solution of school problems through joint efforts with other teachers, administrators and community members.	Contributes to solving school problems through joint efforts with other teachers, administrators and community members.
	Promotes and collaborates with the educational community in projects of social participation.	Develops activities to encourage the student's participation in the community.
	Creates and participates in learning communities to improve his educational performance.	Developed activities enable peer work.

Source: Self - prepared

STUDY RESULTS

Results of Competence 2

This competence has three attributes: Perception among students in the second, fourth and sixth semesters, which is different; for 2nd and 4th grades, 18.7% strongly agree in the origin, the methods and the information that the teacher uses in every class.

2nd grade students are those who stand out when evaluating the teacher match the class's contents with the way students learn. Among the 6th grade students, only 17.7% strongly agree.

The student's value at a high level that the teacher relates the class's content to the way the students learn with their previous knowledge, with the knowledges contained in the course and the curriculum. The teachers recognize what they know about a subject and, there from, plan the classes and use the initial assessment to identify prior knowledges. The results standing out are mainly those of the 4th grade students, with 19.8% agree, and 6th grade students, 17.7%.

Results of Competence 3

This competence consists of 4 attributes. 6th grade students, 16.6% are those who strongly agree that the teachers shall identify prior knowledges in the first assessment. Working for projects occurs mainly in the 6th semester, at a rate of 20.8%, where the programmes have the projects as an implied way of working, as well as most of the studied units belong to the professional and technological area; at 2nd grade, the students agree on the relationship established between the learning unit with others, with the highest percentage, 17.7%.

In this case the students of 4th (18.7%) are the most noticeable when recognizing the appropriate elaboration and use of materials in the classroom. Moreover, 2nd grade students (17.7%) strongly disagree that the materials used in the classroom are not appropriate.

In this regard, the 6th grade students (17.7%) mainly, identify the teachers relate the content to everyday life and reality, as the programmes have a relationship with the reality where they are applied.

Results of Competence 4

It is divided into five attributes. The 6th semester students in a high percentage of 20.8% are those who more clearly remember the teacher's ideas, concepts and examples; in contrast to the 2nd grade students, who have the least 17.7%.

In the attribute: Applies learning strategies and creative solutions to contingencies, taking into account the characteristics of the institutional context, and using the available resources and materials adequately, the 6th grade students identify that it is achieved, as the teacher applies learning strategies and creative solutions to problems that arise. These students are in complete agreement (18.7%). The 2nd grade students agree that their teachers in face of these problems use materials and resources properly, 17.7%, and once again the 6th grade recognizes full agreement.

The attribute: promotes the development of students through learning, within the framework of their aspirations, needs and possibilities as individuals and in relation to their cultural circumstances arose in three items: Promote your development by learning where the highest evaluation is recorded by the students of 2nd semester identifying totally agree, he highest percentage 25%. Another item, "For your development, consider the aspirations, needs and possibilities you have as an individual and in relation to your cultural circumstances," the highest record was by the 6th semester with 13.5%, and finally, if "You consider that the contents worked are useful for your daily life", the 6th semester students evaluate this attribute more highly, 19.8%.

This attribute: Provides relevant literature and guides students in consultation sources for the research was divided into two statements: provides relevant literature, where the significant fact is that 2nd grade students disagree with a percentage of 20.8% as opposed to the 4th grade students (12.5%) who strongly agree, so it refers to the orientation in consulting research sources, 6th and 4th manifest a universal consent and agreement, respectively, 12.5% and 11.5%.

With regard to the use of information technology and communication for teaching and the use of information technology and communication to work in other environments outside the classroom, assessment highlights the 4th semester to agree on what the teacher makes by 26.7%, whereas the 6th semester (19.8%).

Results of Competence 5

This competence consists of four attributes. The students of 2nd and 4th grade (16.4%) agree and identify that at the beginning of the course they are notified about the evaluation criteria.

A percentage of 19.8%, highlights the students of 4th grade who are in full agreement about that the teacher follows up the student's learning, a minimum difference of 17.7%, the 6th grade pupils are in full agreement.

The results are interpreted as follows: monitors your learning process, 6th grade totally agree by15.6%; monitors your academic development, 4th and 6th grades agree 15.6%; does some counseling or mentoring support 4th and 6th grades are at the same level (17.7%), in complete agreement, which differs from a 2nd grade student (15.6%) who agrees.

In the question about that the teacher mentions the suggestions or alternatives to overcome the observations of the assessment, the 6th grade pupils evaluate fully agree by (17.7%), and it is observed as the highest level, as if the teacher would suggest alternatives to overcome the observations of the assessment. Whereas the students in grades 4 and 6 are at the highest level (13.5%), being strongly agree and disagree.

As for the item: Let you self-evaluate, the 4th grade students agree by 15.6% and, at the same level, in disagreement, the 2nd grade students by 15.6%, 4th at 12.6%. Moreover, for the item he encourages peer assessment, it must be highlighted that the 6th grade totally agreed by 19.8%: the 2nd grade are in agreement by 14.6%, and the teacher takes into account the results of self-assessment and peer assessment, again highlights the valuation of 6th grade students was of 25%.

It is clear that classroom assessment practices are encouraged, in general, however, and in contrast to the other grades, the 6th grade students are only considered.

Results of Competence 6

The competence consists of six attributes. The 4th grade pupils are those who value being totally agree, 19.8%, about that self-knowledge and values are promoted. This obeys to the fact that in the first six months, most of the learning units belong to the humanistic area, and that the skills, content and learning activities have implicit self-awareness and assessment, expressed in the programmes as a generic competence.

Regarding: motivates you to learn emphasizes the 2nd grade group agree by18.7%; provides opportunities to learn, like, the students of 4th grade highlight for agreeing by 18.7%; and provides tools to learn, the 4th grade totally agree by 22.9%.

Learning situations allow you to be critical, students in 4th and 6th grades strongly agree and agree, respectively, representing 17.7%; allow you to be thoughtful, the 4th grade are those who totally agree, 18.7%; the learning situations allow creativity, the 4th grade totally agree, 17.7%; and if they lived situations analyse the data generated in daily life, those of 4th grade who totally agree by 13.5% are highlighted.

Regarding group and individual motivation, the 6th grade pupil's stand out by answering totally agree, 14.6%.

The results about encouraging speaking and writing show that the 2nd grade students agree by 17.7%, and in the promotion of reading at all three levels: 2nd, 4th and 6th grades strongly agree and agree by 15%.

The 6th grade pupils (19.8%) agree on that the teacher encourages the use of technology while the 6th grade students value the use of information and communication technology, process and interpret information by 20.8%.

Results of Competence 7

The competence integrates 7 attributes.

This attribute: Practices and promotes respect for diversity among students, there are two significant facts, those who are in full agreement, 6th grade pupils (22.9%) and 4th grade (20.8%), in contrast to those who disagree, 2nd grade by 14.6%.

The results of students in 6th grade, 18.7%, totally agree to encourage the dialogue to resolve personal and interpersonal conflicts among students, 6th grade value (19.8%) that they are channeled to receive care.

On the contrary, in full agreement, 6th grade (17.7%) stands out for encouraging participation from working and living standards, and for establishing them, 20.8%.

In promoting the interest and participation of students with a civic, ethical and ecological consciousness, in the life of their school, community, region, Mexico and the world, it is noted that in the three items, the 6th grade highlights by 21.9% and 16.7%, respectively. There is a possibility that the programmes of the units of the technological area clearer, more objective and applicable to the civic, ethical and environmental awareness of the projects presented.

In regard to the attribute: Encourages students to express personal opinions, in a framework of respect, which are taken into account, the 2nd degree students highlight, which draws our attention, for the answer in disagreement by 16.7%.

For this attribute: to promote healthy choices for human development, such as sports, art and various complementary activities, the response of students in 6th grade students highlights, representing 14.6%, in complete agreement.

Results of Competence 8

This competition has four attributes. In contributing to the solution of school problems through joint efforts with other teachers, administrators and community members, the response of students in 4th and 6th grades, equivalent to 16.7% stands out.

The 2nd grade students (16.6%) disagree, as they do not perceive a common effort on the detection and the possible solutions or alternative solutions. It is noteworthy that in the first and second levels, the groups are numerous, ranging between 45 and 50 students, so that, by the same amount, the problems are greater and varied.

Attribute: To develop activities that encourage your participation in the community is valued with the highest percentage 14.6% by 6th grade pupils. At this level there are programmes and implicit projects in academic programmes involving more participation with the community by applying knowledge in real contexts in order to contribute to sustainability, resources savings, practices and visits to companies to assess and propose improvements, etc.

As far as if the activities undertaken are related to interact with other classmates, it is observed that the most notably students belong to2nd grade, by fully agreeing on the answer.

Broadly, as the results indicate it, as the students advance in their career, in coursing levels, the teacher's performance is assessed differently, because it seems that the teachers meet more attributes of skills.

You need to pay attention to the responses of students at second grade, that are evaluated as in disagreement, and which are identified in the instrument with the numbers of questions: 6, 17, 29, 40, 54, 55 and 60, dealing with: project work, taking into account the aspirations, the needs and possibilities that students have, the allowed self-assessment, the motivation to excel, to express opinions in a respectful framework, consideration of their opinions, and the detection of problems by a school's joint effort with the school community, which can be areas of opportunity and improvement.

CONCLUSION

Importantly, as a result of this work it was found that the assessment instrument that aims to measure the performance of teachers by the students is valid for assessing seven out of the eight competences that states the Integral Reform of School Education (RIEMSER, for its acronyms in Spanish) of the National Baccalaureate.

The first competition: Organizes his continuing preparation throughout his career and its respective attributes, were not considered in this instrument for validation, as it refers to the teacher's professional development through formal training and experience, which also requires of self-assessment, peer assessment and hetero-evaluation. Thus the students could not verify this competence in the classroom as it does not refer to the teacher's performance in class.

In recent years, the assessment has regained importance, mainly for objective value judgments, that allow to help improve the identified needs of: quality, permanence, relevance, identity, etc. in the Middle School System, so that it complies with the minimum quality standard to be reflected in the students who graduate with a range of skills to cope with functionally in various areas: personal, academic, family, professional, aimed to ensure the permanence of the students and to develop personal and social skills, that as it has been said, several factors intervene for its achievement, such as the teacher's performance.

In the applied instrument, the criteria was used to evaluate the skills and their related attributes in order to compare, or to have a reference about the criteria of the other seven skills that deal with to do, to be, to know and to have the teachers interact with the students..

The evaluation based on competences is a process that involves: to define precisely the skills to be assessed, to build their indicators, by including an academic and professional criteria that defines the type of evidence, strategies and instruments by which the evaluation will be conducted. Also, to analyse the information based on the indicators, to identify the strengths and areas for improvement.

Feedback must be provided to the teachers formally and systematically, so that it is created a space for reflection on the results of the evaluation, with the possibility of changing performance before the group.

The evaluation instrument is proposed to evaluate the performance of the teachers by the students. It consists of 62 items that serve the seven competences that consider the attributes corresponding to each one of them.

This instrument can continue to be applying as far as it has been done through the SAES, the suggestions are made from two perspectives:

- Do not apply to one hundred percent of the students, but a representative sample depending on the number of groups and the number of students that each teacher attends considering the extent and time that can be invested.
- And most importantly, once teachers graph and the results are delivered to the teachers, so that the evaluation accomplishes its feedback and decision making duties. From the results, the analysis processes will be performed, so that the areas of opportunity for reflection and up-date learning processes are identified.
- This same instrument is can be usually modified and adapted taking into account the characteristics of the areas' features: humanities, basic and professional areas and / or technological ones. These latter by major: telecommunications, mechanical and electrical installations, construction and industrial processes.
- For the teacher's evaluation to be comprehensive, other instruments and evidence are integrated, as well as evaluation, like actors: external agencies, authorities, academic peers, etc. Furthermore, the results of failure rates, dropouts, institutional collaboration projects, etc. are analysed

To retake the principles and characteristics of evaluation will be useful at all times: a systematic and comprehensive process that should perform the different characters involved: teachers, students, institution and community. In addition to, it must be considered the process, the results of the student's learning and the teacher's assessment. Furthermore, the results must be taken into account for the purpose of a quantitative and qualitative feedback, and the improvement of the quality of education.

Today we are immersed in a society that requires learning and teaching for a generation of new knowledges, but reality is different. The relationships between students and professor, and the way in which they are teaching have had fewer modifications, as the same patters are repeated, besides adding other conditions: family, school, religion, society. Therefore, it is notorious the unwillingness of students to prepare and hold effort values. Moreover, the generation of fragmented knowledges, information clustering, sounds and images that are no questioned and that obstaculise a reflective and autonomous thinking.

In this way the evaluation of teaching competences open the perception of how complex the profession is, but at the same time, the necessity of creating an evaluation culture, designing and implementing a model of formative evaluation, with methods, instruments and strategies that complete information, as well as the participation of other evaluation actors, that foster a support environment, integrating all the agents implied in knowledge, education and development of teaching competences.

There are still many actions to be done and study in this regard:

- Distinguish between all teaching competences, the most significant of formative processes.
- Concretion of some competences and their evaluative abilities dimension, and on the time, formulation of indicators and performance levels, because some of them are ambivalent.
- Selection of methods, strategies and instruments of complementary teaching evaluation.
- -Establishment of their application in the process of competence performance. During half-year terms, half -year terms, yearly periods...
- Decision making for advancements, competence performance and improvement, in an individual and collegiate way.

How to achieve that each teacher and academies evaluate the teaching competences? It is essential to advance in co-responsible decisions, to define teaching practice in a permanent research, assessment and evaluation process, so that the teachers know which competences must be assumed and performed as the driving force for transforming teaching, learning and generating a teacher-researcher and staying in a process of continuous improvement.

The more every teacher, the academies and the middle school level of the IPN system reach the development of the competences, the great the impact will be in two aspects: pedagogical, it is understood how teachers through their tsk promote the development of competences in students and the degree profiles, and, secondly, professional development, referred to the processes by which the highest competence levels are reached and the vastness of its implications, role and contexts.

Even more, at the higher level, homogeneous education basis for students and decision making are grounded. It is contributed for the elaboration of study plans and programmes, with sequence and continuity, research programmes, *liaison* and extension, as well as norms.

Finally, returning to the purpose of the evaluation of teaching from the institutional point of view, the purpose "is to improve the teaching practices and to identify the training needs in order to improve the student's learning and achievement."

REFERENCES

ANUIES. (2000). *La educación superior en el siglo XXI*. Mexico: ANUIES.

COPEEMES. (2013). *Manual para evaluar planteles que solicitan el ingreso y la promoción en el Sistema Nacional de Bachillerato*. Mexico: COPEEMES. Available at http://www.copeems.mx/normativa/documentos-y-manuales/328-manual-de-operacion

Frade, L. (2008). *La evaluación por competencias*. Mexico: Inteligencia educativa.

Hernández, R., Fernández, C., & Baptista, P. (2006). *Metodología de la investigación*. Mexico: Mc Graw Hill.

IPN. (2004). *Un nuevo modelo educativo para el IPN. Materiales para la Reforma*. Mexico: IPN.

IPN. (2014). *CECyT 11. Wilfrido Massieu*. Available at www.cecyt11.ipn.mx

Kerlinger, F. (1979). *Investigación del comportamiento*. New York: Mc Graw Hill.

Rueda, M., & Díaz-Barriga, F. (2000). *Evaluación de la docencia*. Barcelona: Oikos.

Secretaría de Educación Pública (2008a). *Acuerdo número 442. Reforma Integral de Educación Media Superior (RIEMS)*. Mexico: SEP.

Secretaría de Educación Pública (2008b). *Acuerdo número 447. Competencias docentes para quienes impartan educación media superior en la modalidad escolarizada*. Mexico: SEP.

Secretaría de Educación Pública. (2013). *Ley General del Servicio Profesional Docente*. Mexico: Diario Oficial de la Federación Spanish Royal Academy. Available at www.rae.es/recursos/diccionarios/drae

Tejeda, J. (1998). *Los agentes de la innovación en los centros educativos*. Spain: Aljibe.

Tobón, S. (2006). *Competencias, calidad y educación superior*. Madrid: Magisterio.

ADDITIONAL READING

CENEVAL. (2013). Evaluación de la educación en México. Indicadores EXANI – I. México: Centro Nacional de Evaluación para la Educación Superior (Ceneval).

Comisión técnica de evaluación de la calidad docente (1996). *Evaluación y mejora de la calidad docente la Universidad de la Laguna.* Tenerife: Universidad de La Laguna.

De Miguel Díaz, M. (1998). La evaluación del profesorado universitario. Criterios y propuestas para mejorar la función docente. *Journal of Education, 315*, 67–83.

IPN. (1991). *Reglamento de evaluación.* Mexico: IPN.

IPN (2012). *Gaceta Politécnica.* Mexico: IPN, 43 (4).

IPN. (2012). *Reglamento orgánico del IPN.* Mexico: IPN.

Magaña, M. A. (2001). *Mejoramiento del desempeño docente en la Universidad de Colima a través de la formación de cuerpos académicos.* (Master Thesis). University of Colima, Mexico City, Mexico.

Monereo, C., & Pozo, J. (2007). *Estrategias de enseñanza y aprendizaje. Formación del profesorado y aplicación en la escuela.* Barcelona: Graó.

Noriega, C., & Santos, A. (2004). *Un acercamiento a las telesecundarias con base en los resultados de sus alumnos en el EXANI-I.* México: CENEVAL.

Picardo, O. (2014). *Pedagogía informacional: enseñar a aprender en la sociedad del conocimiento. (2002).* Avalaible at http://www.uoc.edu/web/esp/art/uoc/opicardo0602/opicardo0602.html

Poder Ejecutivo Federal. (2013). *Plan Nacional de Desarrollo 2013-2018.* México: Poder Ejecutivo Federal.

Real Academia de la Lengua Española. (2008). *Diccionario de la lengua española.* Madrid: Espasa.

Secretaría de Educación Pública (SEP,1993). *Ley General de Educación.* Mexico: Diario Oficial de la Federación.

Secretaría de Educación Pública. (SEP, 2012). *Reporte de la encuesta nacional de educación media superior.* Avalaible at http://www.snie.sep.gob.mx/

Stake, R. (1999). *Investigación con estudio de casos.* Madrid: Morata.

Tiana, A. (1998). La evaluación de los sistemas educativos: La situación a finales de los noventa. *Perspectivas, XXVIII*(1), 25–40.

KEY TERMS

Competence: Skills, attitudes, knowledge besides the know-how acquisition.

Evaluation: An indispensable and previous activity conducive to raising the degree; besides being identified with the last stage of the natural process of knowledge which concludes with the issuance of informed judgments; a process leading to decisions and human action.

Middle School Education: It comprises high-school level, as well as the equivalent levels, and the professional education that does not require high-school or its equivalent.

Processes: A series of action or measurements adopted with the purpose or meeting a particular aim.

Results: Objectives achieved through research, study and investigation.

Chapter 11
Impact of Mathematics School Performance at Middle School for Academic Institutional Management Based on the Checkland Methodology

Joel García Mendoza
Instituto Politécnico Nacional, Mexico

Jorge Mejía Bricaire
Instituto Politécnico Nacional, Mexico

Edgar Oliver Cardoso Espinosa
Instituto Politécnico Nacional, Mexico

Fernando Briseño Hurtado
Instituto Politécnico Nacional, Mexico

ABSTRACT

Currently the development of countries has acquired importance as a result of the process of economic globalization, which has established various challenges to the economic activities worldwide. So numerical, mathematical and digital competences, are very important to participating fully in the knowledge society. Thus, the chapter proposal considers Checkland's Methodology as an oriented alternative to analyze the object of study in situations with a high rate of human intervention such as education. The chapter proposal will be organized into three sections: the first one related to the factors involved in school performance, the quality of education and the impact that have the math skills at middle school; the second focused on the characteristics of the methodology of Checkland applied to mathematics, and the third, a key options proposal for designing to the students motivation for a better mathematics learning that allows assessment of the institutional management in performance in such subject and increase educational standards.

DOI: 10.4018/978-1-5225-0457-3.ch011

INTRODUCTION

Currently, the development of the countries has reached a vital importance as a result of the process of economic globalization, numerical, mathematical, competencies are therefore very important to fully participate in the knowledge society and the competitiveness of modern economies.

Which quality education involves providing children and youth the real and effective access to knowledge through a solid formation. This includes the need to prepare students, through processes of learning real.

Therefore in the chapter proposal considered Checkland as an oriented alternative methodology to analyze the object of study, in order to study it with a vision of transformation.

The proposal of the chapter will be organized into three sections: the first related to the factors involved in performance on math and the impact of the Middle High Education (MHE) and Higher Education (HE); the second channeled to the characteristics of Checkland methodology applied to mathematics; the third a proposal of key points for the motivation of adolescents and raise educational standards of the MHE in Mexico.

IMPORTANCE OF DEVELOPING MATHEMATICAL THINKING IN KNOWLEDGE MANAGEMENT

In today's world new ways to obtain indicators seek in various fields of study and disciplines such as the scientific production within the knowledge management as well as the mechanisms that make possible a more efficient learning in various educational systems.

On the other hand the International Institute for higher education in Latin America (IESALC-UNESCO) said clearly in its policies that "it is necessary to consider new forms of knowledge management to upgrade the teaching methods used in higher education" also mentions that it is of vital importance "fostering the development of institutions of higher education based on strategic programs" generate flexible academic and organizational structures, implement new structures, decision making and driving modes, moving toward a responsible of the University management culture and apply a reengineering of management processes".

In this context the importance of developing mathematical thinking in the knowledge management is vital as a fundamental and basic necessary knowledge for the scientific and technological education. On the other hand through various methods and techniques of research inadequacies in the process of training of students as have been detected to obtain, process, evaluate and communicate mathematical knowledge which does not take advantage the potentialities of mathematical thinking for the integral formation of the students.

Thus also mathematics allows students build their thinking and reach capabilities to understand their environment and take part more appropriately. These must also be seen as skills necessary for understanding and the occupational and cognitive interactions of contemporary societies.

On the other hand it is worth mentioning that the development of mathematical thinking is an essential part in management of knowledge for competent social action of the people, in a context marked by a society of knowledge in an economic and cultural globalization. Also the mathematical thought contributes to successful performance of people in situations of social and cultural reality using aware of data, concepts, procedures and provisions, with which people can contribute to describe, interpret, intervene, evaluate and optimize performance in their personal life and their participation in society.

Likewise, mathematical thinking is essential so that people can cope with various changes that are originating in labour world. Mathematical thinking must be linked to expressions of a new structure of expectations, transfers, and emergencies and linked to the world transcendence; with all its challenges and opportunities, related to the interactions to the local and the global one.

Finally, so that a knowledge society could have capacities to generate, appropriating and using the knowledge, to meet the needs of development, and thus build their own future, it must strengthen processes of social learning as a means to ensure the social appropriation of knowledge, and its transformation into useful for personal and collective development results. In this key task, math educators can contribute to this social learning, to strengthen the individual and collective development with quality and equal learning opportunities.

FACTORS INFLUENCING THE ACHIEVEMENT IN MATHEMATICS AND THEIR IMPACT IN THE MHE AND ITS TRANSITION TO HE

In Mexico at the beginning of each presidential term has as background: dissatisfaction with the results of the presidential election; economic crisis; high rates of inflation; stagnation of incomes not only teachers, but of the entire population; disarticulation to the interior of the collaborators of the Ministry of education (SEP) and the absence of a specific plan of work in the education agenda.

This situation has generated a low educational quality that is reflected in the low school performance of students at levels Basic and education average superior to being among the last places in the results of the tests PISA that evaluates the skills in reading comprehension, mathematics and science. So it is important to analyze the factors involved in this low school performance of Mexican children and youth, and take steps so that they can be competitive in this new globalized world and get a quality education standards. One of the points which were dealt with in this paper are the factors involved in poor school performance of mathematics and its impact at the HE.

Mathematics is the instrument that helps the human mind to have an orderly and systematic thinking not only at the time of solving a problem to pen and paper in the classroom, but also in everyday life. On the other hand, school performance is defined as a product of the assimilation of the contents of programmes of study, expressed in scores within a conventional scale (Figueroa, 2004).

Based on this definition can sustain, the performance school, not only are qualifications that students obtained in tests, examinations, or other activities that also affect other important as his development and maturity biological and psychological factors.

Jiménez (2013), asserts that it is checked that everyone when we born with an innate numerical ability so that contact with mathematics among students should not be a torment, scientifically. However, everything depends on the development and the stimulation received. On the other hand also says that while there is a neurological damage caused by lack of oxygen at birth, or any lesion in the frontal lobe of the brain, perhaps the main center of cognitive control involved in higher mental activities, anyone, can develop numerical activities.

On the other hand Prieto (2013), says different scientific studies support that from the first months of life, any baby is able to distinguish between sets of one, two and three items, and numbers play a very important role because it is the first mathematical abstraction that we face.

In this context, we can say that poor performance in mathematics is not a conflict of learning disability, but that involves an infinite number of factors such as: methods of teaching that are mechanical and inflexible, often family and social factors, among others.

Thus, although the exact sciences as mathematics is an essential tool to manage in the world globalized and revolutionized by technology, according to the levels that it considers the Organization for cooperation and economic development (OECD) in Mexico, young people lack the knowledge needed to survive in this modern world.

ORIGINS OF LOW SCHOOL PERFORMANCE

The realities of low school performance in the subjects of mathematics, can be very different, if however there are different factors causing it such as:

Physical factors: specific difficulties, physical absences, which can bring also cognitive difficulties. They can also be very specific impediments to acquire knowledge, auditory, visual, problems of body integration that can decrease the ability of attention

Pupils with poor school performance, carrying with it difficulties very base, e.g. traumatic birth, diseases, admissions to the months of life, etc., can be included among these factors of which many times nobody has realized at the time. In these cases there is a clear cognitive deficit bad integration of information product for early failures in the forms of receive and process it. They are children and youth with hearing or Visual problems among others, but have passed routine medical reviews normally and they look capable and resources because they have been able to compensate very well its shortcomings.

In these situations is essential to early detection, because otherwise they can pass by children or young people distracted or lazy and unjustly receive scolding for not having another attitude towards studies. These cases tend to be studied thoroughly from multidisciplinary teams to carry out relevant curricular adaptation so students can grow at your own pace, in a way different from the standard, but which allows them to develop their potential. Family-school collaboration is required for this.

Psychological factors: children and young people healthy physically but emotionally fragile. Psycho-emotional maturity, for various reasons, has been affected. They have the capabilities, resources, but they may not apply them because they are blocked. This situation can be punctual as a loss of a loved one, major changes in house, separation from parents, wrong room at home, etc.

Among the effects these psychological factors due to we can find us depression, attention disorder with or without hyperactivity, adjustment disorder, autism spectrum disorders, although Asperger's syndromes tend to be spectacularly bright academically, schizophrenia which manifests itself most in adolescents.

Social factors: there are cases of children and young people from families of low purchasing power and low cultural level. Children and young people are at home in an environment that has nothing to do with what live in schools, which may be completely alien to their interests. In these cases, a good intervention from social services can work with the entire family and school, promoting the integration of these two worlds.

IMPACT OF SCHOOL PERFORMANCE ON MHE IN MEXICO

Middle Higher education and higher education have a direct link where the academic achievement of young people is crucial to contribute to the development of Mexico. In these two types of education form youth in skills essential to that they are required for advancement, social and economic of the country, thus also for insertion in this new globalized knowledge-based economy.

Each student must achieve a solid mastery of disciplines and values that must characterize the different professions. It is also important for young people to prepare for to test their abilities in the world of work and study with the expectation to engage in more favourable conditions in the development of the country.

MHE now become part of the mandatory training established in the 3rd article of the Mexican Constitution, aims to deepen in the formation of students, whether at the end of this stage they continue their studies or enter the world of work. For this reason, it is essential to expand opportunities for young people to pursue such education.

Also in MHE, young people, as well as deepen their comprehensive training, start your preparation for various professional and occupational trajectories, however if their academic performance in secondary education was low possibly have a negative impact on the upper level and thus you reach desertion, so to be the prelude to full citizenship is of the utmost importance that to continue his training.

In this context quality learning plays a role of vital importance which should be a constant for the fulfillment of the end of upper secondary education and continue in higher education. So that in this way the preparation of young people in their work performance to be successful and also is an additional requirement. On the other hand the relevance of studies must involve the preparation of men and women to work in more productive and better-paying jobs or as entrepreneurs, in social, labour and technologically changing contexts.

Under this scenario in the institutions of MHE and HE are committed to meet the requirements of education and training throughout the life of the people where the school performance of the students plays an important role for a quality education.

However the problems of low efficiency of secondary education has a negative impact on institutions of higher level, having a high index of reproach and desertion in the sciences mainly in mathematics, emphasizing some important points, so Slisko says (2013) that derived from textbooks approaches, largely mathematics learning, it is situational models that refer to contexts outside the student's life and that any question related to something we don't understand, is a question that is unable to respond.

On the other hand Slisko (2013) believes that "students, mostly devote their best effort to do things right". However, if their learning was not to be expected, not everything is your responsibility, mentioning that in many cases, teachers insist on forcing the facts about mathematical models, to the real world to play on one ideal.

This desire of building mathematical knowledge from situational models invented, context unknown to the student, is evident in the linguistic problems used regularly by teachers. On the other hand mentions that the coherent construction of the situational model, which is nothing more than a mental representation of the situation, allows us to understand what we hear or read. "This translation of the problem is not only influenced by superficial linguistic features, also may be determined by the meanings that evoke those traits, or the shock of everyday knowledge that the student has".

Slisko (2015), points out that this representation can be very different depending on the style of mathematical thinking of the individual, Visual imaginations in connection with previous experiences, including associations and thus any subject seeks to give meaning to what does. If your reading hits what he thinks, distortions, neglect or bad solutions are provoked or you lost interest in mathematics. These processes of representation, the role of reflection is very important, because without this there is no human learning that generates conclusions for the future is not built knowledge

Thus, the first step for the solution of a mathematical problem is to understand the situational problem, which is based on the use of linguistic signs, and then design a plan that allows the student to identify what to do and what result expected. Without this, he said, mathematics become an algorithmic things game, a game of clearances and uses of signs.

In this context raised by Slisko Ignjatov is vitally important debate, where is responsibility of the teacher and the educational system? or Who are responsible for the poor school performance in Mexico? However, not only have to address issues of training and abilities of the teachers, but also requires a modernization in the curricular contents that are adapted to new times and new generations.

Analyzing this situation, some specialists the solution lies in teaching practices, increase the number of programs that deepen in mathematical teaching and review educational policies related to this discipline, which, will give results within two or three decades, says José Antonio de la Peña (2013), President of CRMAT (Centre for Research in Math) also mentions that it is a problem of structural education and old in Mexican society, so any program that runs this year will improve the results next year.

Analyzing this situation, some specialists the solution lies in teaching practices, increase the number of programs that deepen in mathematical teaching and review educational policies related to this discipline, which, will give results within two or three decades, says José Antonio de la Peña (2013), President of CIMAT (Centre for research in math) also mentions that it is a problem of structural education and old in Mexican society, so any program that runs this year will improve the results next year.

He also points out that a good mathematical training is fundamental for the mental development of children and youth, which helps them to be logical, orderly reasoning and develop theories to become independent thinkers.

Näslund, (2012), points out that children and young people who learn to think for themselves can solve the problems of the real world and the world of tomorrow. These children and young people can stand out both in school and in life, and they could be prepared to be productive citizens. Faced with this situation, it is important to note that mathematics and the natural sciences, as well as other disciplines, only can learn is making them in the real world. The skills of critical thinking and problem solving needed to correctly apply a formula cannot be found with a simple search. These skills are necessary for internalizing them and to develop them in the solution of real problems.

Moreover, it is important to note that rather than memorizing formulas and concepts, education in mathematics must show students real experiences and practices so that they can seek relationships, validate theories and communicate within their environment and know the importance of these in the daily life.

Likewise students learn more when they have the opportunity to find their own answers. Moreover rather than transmitters of information, the role of the teacher should guide the students in the resolution of mathematical and scientific problems. Students need to understand the concepts and not just memorize concepts and repeat mechanical procedures that many times is tedious for them and not take them to nothing.

As a summary of all this context can be set both on the upper level and higher, when limited to students the time develop different strategies, cannot develop the confidence and skills they need to acquire the mathematical and scientific thinking. This manifests itself many times in the academic advising are not appropriate to the learner-centered approach to education, and on the other hand used learning strategies are relined by the culture of the image, audiovisual and media fast access to knowledge.

Morín, (1999) mentions that an intelligence unable to perceive the context and the complex world in which we live, makes people blind, unconscious and irresponsible. Thus the role of education and of knowledge in the formation of citizens involves incorporating into educational processes a greater orientation towards personalization of the learning process, towards the construction of the ability to build learning and build values.

THE IMPORTANCE OF LANGUAGE IN THE MATHEMATICS TEACHING

Juarez, and De la Peña, (2013), argue that understand and solve simple word problems has proved to be a complex process, which requires the interaction of at least three types of knowledge: the language, the semantic-situational and the mathematician.

To give validity to his thesis, both researchers performed an exploratory qualitative research with high school students, who were asked to conduct drawings from statements posed simple situational models, some more familiar than others. As a result of this investigation after reading a same statement they found that the students drew different graphics and different situational models, mentioning that each subject is an interpreter other than the world that surrounds him, due to the experiences of life

The same was referred by students, apart from show different interpretations, they expressed difficulties to model even though they already had the language skills necessary for the type of reading proposed. They established that this is due to the understanding, a non-trivial matter that must be treated with utmost care, both in teaching and in the elaboration of textbooks.

They also noted that the results of this research allowed to conclude that students perform better when faced with problems more related, with statements that refer to contexts more familiar, everyday acts of a city. Because despite the fact that there was a difference in situational models, most managed to raise a successful situational model, suitable for the expected mathematical solution. In this sense, teachers must clearly identify the differences between situational model and mathematical model to avoid using contexts unknown to the students.

On the other hand they suggest the situational understanding through the rewriting of Word problems, so that through the productions of the students, encouraging reflection in the face to them. For him, the drawing may be an alternative: we can use drawing as a tool for learning, as a tool for communicating mathematics, a science that is not more than the sensible construction of humans, to understand the patterns of reality.

In this context the Organization for Cooperation and Development of Education (OECD), (2014) mentions that Mexico is one of the few countries where both men and women have improved their performance in math between 2003-2012 (30 men and 26 women). By you can set it to that poor school performance of a pupil can be caused by many factors so the solution or treatment should always be individualized.

On the other hand according to the report of the OECD Mexico is one of the countries where an improvement is observed, however the proportion of students with high yield is very low. Each year

Figure 1. PISA results
Source: OECD, (2014)

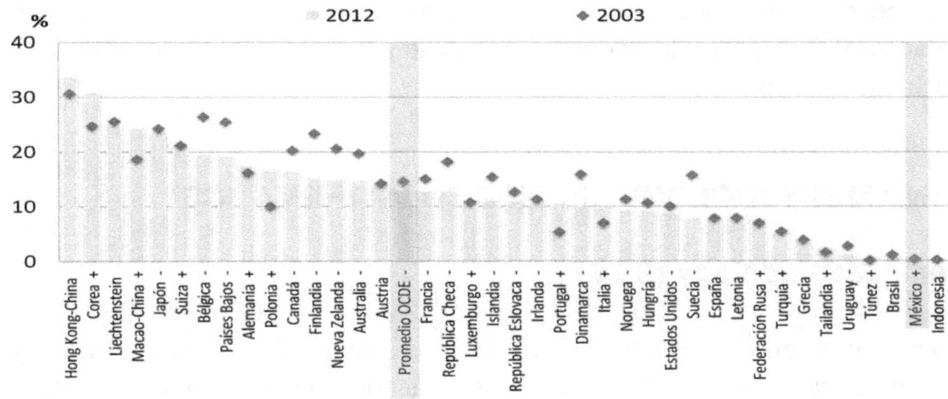

in Mexico, students of 15 years who are those who are studying upper secondary education improved 3-point each year in the PISA test approximately (Figure 1).

It is shown that the education in Mexico is obsolete and that systems of evaluation to qualify teachers and students are not suitable or taken into account to implement measures governing the system of teaching and learning of the students; This originates a low-level academic students, which has been pointed out by experts, organizations and officials. All these situations have triggered in a deterioration of reasoning, verbal and written communication, research and curriculum which preparation which gives high school fails to comply effectively with the needs of the productive sectors.

Another important factor that has to be mentioned is that the new educational model in Mexico points to the incorporation in the learning processes of the technologies of information and communication technology (ICT), just beginning to become a reality in the schools of Basic Education and Middle High Education, public and private media in the country. Today, the technologies allow a rapid appropriation of new knowledge that, for the speed with which it is produced, will hardly be in textbooks or curricula.

On the other hand the evaluation systems lack appropriate methodologies, that have not been assessed to know the level of both sectors and implementing measures, or in the rigor of its application. What recommended some specialists is that the first thing to do is understand and ask ourselves what kind of child and youth want to be in the schools. What should a child know to graduating from elementary school? And to finish the high school or high school? If it does not respond to these questions, you can hardly have a valid model of national education.

In the performance of the students should also be considered other situations as in the conditions under which studies, there has been a neglect for decades of education in Mexico. Where a school does not work, has no books or drinking water, glasses are broken, there are no blackboards or teachers fail to teach class, which often becomes a complete abandonment by federal and State education authorities.

The quality of education in Mexico is particularly troubling. The performance in math and science of Latin American students is also substantially lower (42% versus 73%) in Sciences and math, when compared with the OECD students, implementing the measurement programme standardized PISA. The quality of education in Mexico has important implications for economic growth. So that quality early education is essential both for economic and social success.

Recent research provide convincing evidence that low levels of human capital attributable to the schooling of poor quality in Latin America may account for more than half of the gap in growth between the region and the rest of the world, (inform of the education 2014).

All these factors affecting the education of children and youth in different contexts reveal a clear gap between rich and poor people.

CHECKLAND METHODOLOGY APPLIED TO MATHEMATICS

Soft Systems Methodology (SSM)

Peter Checkland soft systems methodology is a qualitative technique that can be used to apply structured systems to systemic situations. It is a way to deal with situational problems in which there is an activity with a high social, political and human component. Also known as soft systems methodology (SSM) seeks to work with the different perceptions of a situation, defining a systemic learning process, in which different views are discussed and reviewed with the purpose of defining actions aimed at its improvement.

The SSM applies structured systems to today's world of human organizations; It is a useful way of approaching complex situations and corresponding disordered questions, Weeks, (2012). Soft systems methodology originated from the understanding that, structured hard systems are inadequate to investigate issues of large, complex organizations, such as the different education systems, so that this methodology was developed to solve or improve these types of problems

Soft Systems Methodology Stages

Peter Checkland, exposes the SSM is divided into 7 chronological stages, and must be read from 1 to 7, a logical sequence that is most suitable to describe the methodology, but does not have to continue to use it; in principle, a home can be anywhere and phases or stages that are required to achieve the objectives of the research may also be used.

Stages:

1. Non-structured situation.
2. Structured situation.
3. The elaboration of basic definitions.
    - *C*ustomer.
    - *A*ctors.
    - *T*ransformation.
    - *O*wners.
    - *W*eltanschauung.
    - *E*nvironment.
4. Conceptual modelling.
5. Comparison of 4 vs, 2.
6. Feasible and desirable changes.
7. Implementation of changes in the real world.

A study of the education on school performance in the subject of mathematics in Tlalnepantla, Mexico State by applying the soft systems methodology by García (2014). This focused on the averages for students who obtained their secondary education, as well as the points obtained in the test applied by the Metropolitan Commission of Public Institutions of Middle Higher Education (COPIMHE) and the results obtained in the test PISA in Mexico to see at what level this education in Mexico results were very low in the area of mathematics to which the performed research work for a or another way to help improve education, this study focused on the school "official high school No. 118" first thing that was done was to focus on the factors internal and external influencing low school performance in the subject of mathematics, this is made use of survey and interview...

After having done this research within the most relevant work it was found the information shown in the following tables.

In this sample (Table 1) it was found that almost half of the students (48.6%) obtained in junior high school an average end of 8.00 to 8.99, 21.4% obtained an average of 9.00 to 9.999, 20% obtained an average of 7.00 to 7.99 and 10% received an average of 6.00 to 6.99. these averages do not reflect the knowledge, abilities and skills of the students in the MHE.

Table 2 shows that 38.6% of the students of Middle High School No. 118 obtained an overall average in the most recent semester completed to 8.99 8.00, the 22.9% obtained an average of 9.00 to 9.99, 25.7% there were obtained between 7.00 to 7.99 and 12.9% gained 6.00 to 6.99 of general average. Compared to the averages of secondary higher averages are reduced to 10% about high school.

In Table 3 it was found that slightly more than one-third (32.9%) of students from high school No. 118, in the six months from January to July of 2013 obtained an average in mathematics from 8.00 to 8.99, more than one-quarter (28.6%) obtained between 7.00 - 7.99, and only 17.1% obtained from 9.00

Table 1. Final average of students in high school

Averages		Frequency	Percent	Valid Percent	Cumulative Percentage
Valid	6.00-6.99	7	10.0	10.0	10.0
	7.00-7.99	14	20.0	20.0	30.0
	8.00-8.99	34	48.6	48.6	78.6
	9.00-9.99	15	21.4	21.4	100.0
	Total	70	100.0	100.0	

Source: Own preparation based on results in SPSS v. 20

Table 2. Final average of the most recent semester of high school students

Averages		Frequency	Percent	Valid Percent	Cumulative Percentage
Valid	6.00-6.99	9	12.9	12.9	12.9
	7.00-7.99	18	25.7	25.7	38.6
	8.00-8.99	27	38.6	38.6	77.1
	9.00-9.99	16	22.9	22.9	100.0
	Total	70	100.0	100.0	

Source: Own preparation based on results in SPSS v. 20

to 9.99 and the 21.43% obtained from 6.00 to 6.99 average in this subject. This reflected that apparently more than three-quarters (78.6%) of students have averages between 7 and 10 which is not reflected in the external evaluations.

Table 4 shows that the 37.1% of students having difficulty with mathematics for lack of attention, 30% have difficulty due to lack of study, 15.7% is due to the difficulty of math and 14.3% have difficulty because of their personal limitations. This reflects that more than half (67.1%) students your problem lies in the lack of attention and lack of study on this subject.

Noting the previous results, according to Vygotsky (2002) establishes that the student has no difficulty, the difficulty arises when you want him to learn the language from us, for this we must guide and support; rather than impose our interests. The master, not to relate this subject with another, makes the student loses interest, preventing him from finding other alternatives. Thus he also mentions that the teacher must know their students, so you can enhance your skills, where the collective work and play are used as means.

For this research was use the methodology of soft systems of Peter Checkland in the problems on the low performance of students in the course of mathematics in the high school official No. 118.

Stages of the methodology employed:

1. Non-structured situation.
2. Structured situation.
3. The elaboration of basic definitions.
4. The elaboration of conceptual models.
5. Comparison of 4 vs. 2.
6. Feasible and desirable changes.

Table 3. Average in the course of mathematics in the last six months (January-July 2013)

Averages		Frequency	Percent	Valid Percent	Cumulative Percentage
Valid	6.00-6.99	15	21.4	21.4	21.4
	7.00-7.99	20	28.6	28.6	50.0
	8.00-8.99	23	32.9	32.9	82.9
	9.00-9.99	12	17.1	17.1	100.0
	Total	70	100.0	100.0	

Source: Own preparation based on results in SPSS v. 20

Table 4. Difficulties with mathematics are primarily related to

Averages		Frequency	Percent	Valid Percent	Cumulative Percentage
Valid	Lack of attention	26	37.1	37.1	40.0
	Lack of study	21	30.0	30.0	70.0
	In my own limitations	10	14.3	14.3	84.3
	The difficulty of mathematics	11	15.7	15.7	100.0
	Total	70	100.0	100.0	

Source: Own preparation based on results in SPSS v. 20

Table 5. Techniques and instruments used

Techniques	Instruments	Sources	Informants
Poll	Questionnaire	Students	students
Interview	Questionnaire	teachers	Teachers

LEVEL OF THE RESEARCH

Applied: Is made use of tools, methods and techniques that already exist at present to carry out the development of this research applied to the official high school No. 118.

Descriptive: Were they described and analyzed the internal and external factors, processes, and people in the high school official No. 118. In order to know the situation in the course of mathematics problem.

Population and Sample

Population: this research was conducted in the high school official No. 118, which consists of 714 students in total in the morning shift as well as 12 teachers who teach the course of mathematics in different grades.

Sample: Were chosen in a stratified and random way 70 students from a total of 240, only of second degree, since there are evaluations and statistics that reflect the poor performance in the area of mathematics. They chose this grade because that was the performance in the subject of Mathematics problems there are in this was reflected in report the scores of the students, as well as there is a high rate of desertion and reproach.

Data Collection Techniques

Primary: Develop surveys and interviews at the educational institution, using the technique of survey tabulated by the Likert scale; which consists of a series of affirmations or negations, where the respondent select one of five alternative from totally agree to completely at odds.

Secondary: To obtain the amount of approved and disapproved in the course of mathematics students, took the second graders statistics provided by the high school official No. 118 to carry out the research project.

Data Analysis and Processing Techniques

Stage 1: Non-structured situation.

Interviews were conducted with teachers and pupils, to identify where there would be problems, in relation to teaching and performance in the subject of mathematics, these interviews also served to validate the conducted questionnaire.

Stage 2: Structured situation.

The next step after knowing what are the main problems, were drawn up charts of the situation where is contained the mainstays; which helped us to identify internal, external factors and understand how the institution works.

Stage 3: Development of basic definitions.

Based on the interviews with students and teachers, through surveys, the issues have been identified to thus be able to give solution to these situations. These solutions have passed through a process of transformation of social reality that was formulated in the basic definitions. Defined the participants for analysis CADTWE this helped have a good preparation of this analysis.

CATDWE ANALYSIS

- **Customer (C):** The MHS No. 118, parents are indirect beneficiaries, and the direct beneficiaries are the students and the teachers from the institution.
- **Actors (A):** Students and teachers.
- **Transformation (T):** This was the learning-teaching process which includes the training of teachers, study programs.
- **Owner (O):** Middle high school 118 principal.
- **Weltanschauung (W):** To increase the performance of students in mathematics courses.
- **Environment (E):** General Education Law, National Institute for Educational Assessment, Integral Reform of Middle School, Parents.

Stage 4: Development of conceptual models.

From basic definitions that were obtained in the previous stage and once the analysis of these definitions, it enabled to see actions that were performed to carry out the process of the transformation of social reality.

Stage 5: Comparison of 4 vs. 2.

Once the basic definitions were obtained, was the design of the conceptual models and mental processes of the transformation processes that may exist or not in reality, a contrast with the real world, took place between what should be changed in the institution with what already exists on this.

Stage 6: Feasible and desirable changes in this stage were detected possible changes to carry out in the middle high school 118 to see if you can implement in reality; taking care that these changes were culturally systemically desirable and feasible.

To improve the academic performance of students in math, they will generate a positive image of the institution, which will be reflected in the decrease of the desertion in the following years. This work helps to see the importance of making use of a good methodological strategy to improve school performance in the subject of mathematics. As well as also the institution would provide better education and this will be great for the future education of students.

In conclusion this work benefits to students, teachers and parents, strengthening the learning of students by the institution providing the most optimal education for students and this will be better for the future training of students.

There is another study of education by applying the soft systems methodology carried out by Ramon (2004) for this, he focused on the various studies such as what was done in PISA in the city of Mexico also assessments are performed to see at what level this education in Mexico, the results were very low in the course of mathematics for this reason the conducted research work in one way or another to help improve education.

After having done this research paper came to conclusions but more focused on the environment of the student as:

- The support of parents with students.
- The family relationship.
- Changing the image of mathematics course.
- Take care that the schedule of the course of mathematics is not at the last minute.

As conclusion Soft Systems problems, are difficult to define. They have a social component and large policy. When we think about mild problems, lest we think problems but problems situations. It is based on the fact that things are not working in the way that we want it and we want to find out why and if there is anything we can do to alleviate or improve the situation.

KEY ELEMENTS TO THE MOTIVATION OF STUDENTS, ACADEMIC AND ADMINISTRATIVE MANAGEMENT OF THE INSTITUTIONS IN MIDDLE HIGHER EDUCATION IN MEXICO

In this line, already a few years Font (1994) stated that the motivation should be considered in any analysis of the learning of Mathematics: depending on if the student has a motivational pattern positive or negative, their attitude toward math will be different. If the pattern is positive, student, face a difficulty will react to analyzing it, will seek a new strategy, ask the teacher, etc.; If the student presents a negative motivational pattern, face a difficulty, will increase your anxiety and is up to thinking that the cause of the difficulty is their inability and, therefore, will adopt defensiveness, as for example: do nothing, do not ask why ask only fools, will try to copy the answer, etc.

Why Is the Motivation for Learning So Important?

The motivation of students for learning is a very important and vital factor in this new world scenario called globalization where might seem that this new occupational and economic reality should be proportional enough motivation so that young people work hard in school and they continue to be successful students, but many young people are unable or are not willing to make the effort required for innumerable reasons how social economic, family or personal among others, but many simply lack motivation and which takes them to school failure.

What Can You Do to Motivate Teens and Raise Educational Standards?

In international studies carried out by various authorities have established that no factor associated only to educational success there is. Green Andy (n.d.) academic, who has analyzed the evolution of the systems of education in East and West, has established that "none of the traditional indicators, whether class, the selection size. Educational expenditure, teaching styles, time invested in learning, are systematically correlated with results in several countries.

Results of the educational process in different countries are the result of a group of factors, ones about features on internal systems of education, and other social contexts ". He also mentions that in several countries such as France, Germany, Japan Korea in the South and Sweden, tend to promote a culture of learning in which parents and teachers have high expectations of the educational achievements of children, where education systems are designed to provide all students with opportunities and motivation, they reward those who is going well in education.

Both in the East and in the West increasingly accepted that schools provide learning environments where students like to be, where you experience a sense of self-worth, enthusiasm or challenge in learning, important factor that does not exist in many Mexican educational institutions.

Traditionally, the psychology of education has analyzed the motivation of students to learn Mathematics. These investigations have been made mostly from the perspective of academic motivation, to focus on the context of the classroom (Alonso, 1991, 1997; Alonso & Montero, 2001; Escaño & Gil de la Serna, 2001, 2006; Gonzales, 1997; Garrido, 1996; among others). Most of these authors agree in saying that academic motivation is the opposite of indifference, i.e. a student is motivated academically when does not remain indifferent to any new learning or task that intends it, or put another way, when more indifferent displays a student, less motivated is. There are several subtypes of academic motivation as described below:

- Competence motivation, based on increasing competition itself.
- Control motivation, which seeks maximum autonomy to act without being forced.
- intrinsic motivation, based on experience absorbed by the nature of the tasks.
- Achievement motivation, based on experience the pride that follows success.
- Motivation for fear of failure, to avoid the experience of shame or humiliation that accompanies failure.
- Motivation for the prize, to win prizes or rewards.

Under this situation of motivation in its different subtypes as a relevant factor, it is important to mention that a quality education is the best guarantee for the development of all countries. Education is the basis of peaceful and respectful coexistence, and a fairer society.

Mexico currently requires major transformations in the educational system where taken into account the factor motivation, taking into account the philosophical bases, humanist and social to give impetus to public education to have a quality education.

Education is a fundamental human right that should be available to all Mexicans. It is not enough to provide a space for students in schools of all levels; It is necessary that education form for coexistence, human rights and social responsibility, people care, understanding of the environment, the protection of the environment, the implementation of productive skills, and, in general, for the comprehensive development of human beings. A good educational system must be inclusive, promoting equity and never a means to maintain or play privileges only some few.

Today's world said urgent progress of knowledge resulting in technological and social changes that in the past would have been unexpected. Development that each country can achieve in the coming decades will largely depend on the capacity of students to meet the challenges posed by the knowledge society in this new era of technological change.

Access to timely and up-to-date information is necessary to participate in the knowledge society. But this is not enough. It requires a culture of appreciation and use of knowledge which allow to discern and assess, train for citizenship and solidarity. This culture is gestated from basic education, deepens in upper secondary education and should be encouraged in higher education. It requires to strengthen capacities for analytical and critical reasoning, reading comprehension, written and verbal expression, creativity and, prominently, the ability to learn to learn.

A quality education will improve the ability of the population to communicate, work in groups, solve problems and effectively use information technologies, as well as a better understanding of the environment in which we live and the innovation. The educational task is the responsibility of authorities, teachers, students, parents and of society as a whole. The sectoral programme of education in Mexico raises the conjunction of efforts, because only with the sum of well-organized wills it will be possible to comply with the aims of education.

Another important point is to mention that in order to develop programs for the conditions of poverty that continue to affect a significant part of the national population also have hindered the educational task.

Another additional aspect that strongly influences education is the relationship of the school with its surroundings. Communication with parents is source of understanding and mutual collaboration in the educational task. It should be avoided that such participation consist of payment of mandatory contributions that today, by law, are forbidden in public schools. The collaboration of the families and schools should serve the purpose of building a peaceful coexistence based on respect for human rights and the gender perspective. It will also be necessary to strengthen the schools links with health authorities and which provide priority assistance to students with serious personal and family problems.

The educational transformations require time and perseverance to ensure the quality of learning. Therefore, it will be necessary to devote efforts to the consolidation of the National System of Middle High School (NSMHS) and the strengthening of the professionalization of teachers and directors. Improving indicators to support decision-making, promote universalization of the common curriculum framework at the Federal, State and private campuses of education upper middle and develop programs of training and updating of Directors for the school management.

Overcome the problems that limit healthy coexistence in schools, promote the certification of relevant skills and reduce the number of schools that have a high concentration of students from low-performing school. The increase of the population enrolled in the EMS has been the basis for the growth of the coverage of higher education, so the abandonment of studies in upper secondary education is, without a doubt, one of the most severe challenges of the educational system.

This phenomenon not only have high economic and social costs, but it perpetuates the conditions of exclusion and poverty. The causes of the problem include economic, educational and family factors. Its reduction becomes a relevant objective of education policy and involves, among others, the momentum of action articulated, aimed to support young people in situation of handicap, a growing professionalisation of teaching and school management, greater relevance of curricula and study programmes and the prevention of risks that affect young people. Your attention should respond to a holistic approach and to merge education authorities, school directors, teachers, parents and students.

Despite the profound effects of initial education in the physical, intellectual and emotional development of people, the country does not have a national policy on the subject. This policy shall provide for the review of policy instruments and new schemes of pedagogical support and work with parents, basically.

Actions for quality education has been uneven and inequitable. Schools small and remote, with populations with higher incidence of poverty and marginalization, as in the case of indigenous communities, remain systematically lower results. Certainly one of the challenges to overcome for a quality education in Mexico is to strengthen the capabilities of management of the schools, in the context of its environment, for the achievement of learning, mainly in institutions located in contexts of poverty and marginalization.

In relation to social factors, the question is how to work with these children and young people?

In relation to social factors, the question is how to work with these children and young people?

- The education of emotion and expression.
- Cultivation of a taste for learning from learning significant and adjusted to the level of the student.
- The development of social skills.

The educational crisis that affects in these times, displayed particularly high levels of repetition and dropping out of school due primarily to poor motivation - stimulus of the student. In this problem is the result of a design of a unequal curriculum according to (UNAM) magazine.

Without a doubt, the teacher is a very important figure in the teaching-learning process. Which means that a large percentage of the majority of teachers who chose that profession is because they want to convey and share their knowledge, and although their professional preparation is the best and they have Bachelor's degree, master's and/or doctorate, most of the time can not engage as they would like in their teaching that the environment in which they operate is not the suitable due to many factors both internal and external.

In the current educational process, teachers already do not can be perceived as a simple transmitter of knowledge, has to be a companion and guide students in their path of learning in which both have to go farming and generating new knowledge, often teachers fail or ignore this fundamental lack of stimulus initiative, tangible and intangible.

Currently, the professional preparation of teachers in what refers to the mathematical knowledge should be excellent and specialized, so do not think that just by longer mathematical classes, can be given when in fact they should prepare to be teachers and achieve a specialization and be good teachers.

On the other hand is very unquestionable that the trigger so that a student wishes to obtain a meaningful learning part of a good motivation, a very important factor in the human part of the students and teachers. Bueno and Castañedo (1998), claim that academic achievement motivation manifests itself in the classroom in two behaviors or fundamental elements:

The level of difficulty of the chosen tasks and the choice of a group to work. Subjects with low academic achievement motivation tend to choose very easy tasks where they have secured success or very difficult tasks in which no procurement does not affect them since the difficulty is high for all. You could say that many students have the motivation that is limited by the difficulty of the work, being the least likely motivated to find groups of people as discouraged as they to not feel then discriminated against. Those who have high motivation will be able to go beyond risking to perform slightly more complex tasks.

On the other hand the model posed by Wigfield and Eccles (1992), expectative-valor is based on the theory of achievement motivation. This model provides four sources of value that may be a task to the executor. The knowledge of these sources by the teacher can help students foster the motivation to perform a task.

The value of procurement, refers to the importance that has for the subject well to do this activity. The intrinsic value is the intrinsic motivation that the subject has to deal with that activity. The value of utility, is the future use which believed to have that activity to their interests and needs. The cost or labour demand, is the sacrifice that the individual must do to comply with the requirements of the task.

Students who fail constantly to a subject in the school are made difficult to sustain the motivation to succeed, to attribute their failures to external factors that do not depend on it, the student didn't find reason to improve and that's because I attribute their failure to something that cannot be controlled. But if the student attributed its failure to a lack of any skill it is likely that it efforts to overcome it. This is just one example of how students can attribute their successes or failures, and how this influences their motivation.

On the other hand academic achievement motivation may be influenced by a social impact. According to Escartí (1994), motivational climate is called and can be made up of parents, teachers and peers influencing externally. Youth are oriented to the goals that most predominate in the environment and it is in adolescence where influence this environment more forcefully since you want to avoid embarrassment or failure.

Garcia (2005), establishes that from a school or academic approach, currently the latest motivational models consider the motivation as a hypothetical construct that explains the start, perseverance of a behaviour towards a certain goal academic focused on learning, performance, self, social valuation or the avoidance of work. In addition, in this process are involved four components: the value given to the goals, the perception of their competence, the causal attributions and emotional reactions (Pintrich & De Groot, 1990).

On the other hand Wolters (1998) shows how goals regulate the achievement motivation as the force that holds the individual persistent to achieve its goal. In this case students learning-oriented use intrinsic motivation while students with performance goals used more extrinsic motivations.

Some other authors define the need for achievement as a success in a competition with a criterion of excellence, and mentioned that academic achievement motivation is based on this need in which the subject maintains constant acting to achieve success. But the excellence criteria are not the same for all people, while for some it can be a task successfully and, for others it might be better pay than they never surrendered or perhaps pay better than others or pay enough to get rid of a task regardless of whether this academic achievement motivation you may feel well if you manage success or embarrassment if you get the failure.

According to (Barbera & Molero, 1996), mentioned that many studies show that the student who meets an academic achievement motivation high, tends to higher academic performance that fellow who meets an academic achievement motivation low. Raised it the reasons why academic achievement motivation is higher in short:

There are realistic goals long-term

- Perceive their goals as instrumental to its future success.
- Are innovative and persevering.
- Analyze your results in a positive way.

- They are responsible for their actions.
- They have an activation to work with standards of excellence.

In many investigations it is concluded that a motivated student will almost certainly get a good academic performance, we can also say that a high academic achievement motivation affects the academic performance and at the same time a good academic performance will serve as a stimulus to make students feel motivated to keep looking for good results.

Alsina (2000), points out that educating, in mathematics, is not transmitted only formulas and recipes, a large part of the professors of mathematics has worked from the confusion of believing that they must be simply explained algorithms and also considering that the ultimate challenge of mathematics would be the emotions that people feel happy doing math do you hope go to class, which is known to transmit the illusion by the discovery, for sharing what you're doing.

The youth of today, young people of the 21st century, are more familiar with the computer and the Internet since they have acquired the culture of the image that offer media, where to easily find any information. Their learning should no longer be merely receptive, but interactive and audiovisual through mediators that motivate the approach to knowledge in a meaningful way.

Counseling improve the performance of students; Therefore, they are necessary for students and an effective means of rapprochement between the student and the knowledge to raise achievement, so you should update its methods and strategies for greater understanding and learning.

PROPOSED IMPROVEMENT PLAN

To create appropriate learning environments, proposes this improvement project, whose implementation, will allow to strengthen the system of campus.

- Generate a system of academic advising to address low student achievement, that motivates the approach to knowledge in a meaningful way, through innovation in the field of learning with amplifiers of knowledge, technological, interactive and audiovisual, chords to their times.

With the implementation of this proposal, students will strengthen their knowledge and skills, giving them greater security and confidence in the process of development of competencies. It will also reflect on exploitation and adoption rates increasing, as well as the decrease of reproach and dropout rates.

- Design, develop or acquire, interactive and educational software and multimedia programs updated with the constructivist approach focused on learning.
- Design, develop or acquire, tutorials, for different educational objectives, with the aim that the student can "learn how to learn", as society evolves.
- Implement a system of academic advising online, assisted by computer, taking advantage of the Internet portal, with academic advisors within hours most requested by students, for those who can not attend personally to consultants or for those who will present exam regularization, special consideration or internship. Online counseling, may be quite useful to encourage students to enhance their communication, work and study skills, fostering their academic performance.

- Conditioned spaces suitable and equipped with technology for the delivery of counseling including: academic advising for math, physics, chemistry and English room, equipped with media and teaching materials with three areas: to) an area for individual consultants, binas or trinas; b) an area for consulting group and c) an area for computer and remote consultants.

Finally it is worth mentioning that educational institutions recover and transform their ability to transmit a significant culture and contributes to recreate or inherent capacities for economic efficiency and political democratization, it requires a profound transformation of its structures and dynamics of management. The pedagogical management of campuses is a fundamental key to the transformation process.

REFERENCES

Alsina, C. (2000). L'entrevista. *Biec*, *31*, 8–9.

Barbera, E., & Molero, C. (1996), Motivación social. In Psicología de la motivación. Madrid: síntesis.

Bueno, J. A., & Castañedo, C. (1998). *Psicología de la educación aplicada*. Madrid: CCS.

De la Peña, J. A. (2013). *Matemáticas, Boletín informativo de la Academia Mexicana de Ciencias No. 11*. Recuperado de: http://issuu.com/amcboletin/docs/amc-boletin11

Escartí, A., & Cervelló, E. (1994). La motivación en el deporte. In *Entrenamiento psicológico en el deporte* (pp. 61–90). Valencia: Albatros Educación.

Figueroa, C. (2004). *Sistemas de Evaluación Académica (Primera Edición)*. El Salvador: Editorial Universitaria.

Font, V. (1994). Motivación y dificultades de aprendizaje en matemáticas. *SUMA*, *17*, 10–16.

García, J. (2014). Rendimiento escolar en la preparatoria oficial no 118 del estado de México en la asignatura de Matemáticas, ciclo escolar 2011-2012.

García & Gonzales. (2005). La motivación en secundaria un estudio empírico. *Revista complutense, 16*(1), 339-352.

Jiménez, F. (2013). *Matemáticas: México no atina a dominarlas*. Recuperado de: http://www.sinembargo.mx/29-05-2013/631646

Morín, E. (1999). *Los siete saberes necesarios a la educación del futuro*. UNESCO.

Näslund, E. (2012). *El camino hacia el éxito en matemáticas y ciencias: Desafíos y triunfos en Paraguay*. Recuperado de: http://idbdocs.iadb.org/wsdocs/getdocument.aspx?docnum=37283442

OCDE. (2014). *Panorama de la educación 2014*. Recuperado de: http://www.oecd.org/edu/Mexico-EAG2014-Country-Note-spanish.pdf

Pintrich, P., & De Groot, A. (1990). Motivational and self-regulated learning components of classroom academic performance. *Journal of Educational Psychology*, *82*, 33–40.

Prieto, C. (2013). *Matemáticas: México no atina a dominarlas*. Recuperado de: http://www.sinembargo.mx/29-05-2013/631646

Ramón, J. (2004). *Aplicación de metodologías de sistemas suaves de Checkland para el diseño de un programa de formación docente en matemáticas: caso de estudio: Colegio Agustín de Hipona*. Instituto Politécnico Nacional, Escuela Superior de Ingeniería Mecánica y Eléctrica.

Slisko, J. (2015). *Bajo rendimiento en matemáticas, asociado a la enseñanza*. Recuperado de: http://angulo7.com.mx/index.php/educacion/12379-bajo-rendimiento-en-matematicas-asociado-a-la-ensenanza

Weeks, P. (2012). *Descripción de la metodología de sistemas blandos de Checkland*. Disponible en http://www.12manage.com/methods_checkland_soft_systems_methodology_es.html

Wigfield, A., & Eccles, J. (1992). The development of achievement task values: A theoretical analysis. *Developmental Review*, *12*(3), 265–310. doi:10.1016/0273-2297(92)90011-P

Wolters, C. (1998). Self-regulated learning and college students' regulation of motivation. *Journal of Educational Psychology*, *90*(2), 224–235. doi:10.1037/0022-0663.90.2.224

Section 3

Elementary Education as Early Factor of Knowledge Management

Chapter 12
Assessment of Academic Management as a Success Factor for Knowledge Management

Limin-tzen Esmeralda Bueno Gasca
Instituto Politécnico Nacional, Mexico

ABSTRACT

In this research several elements are exposed through a network of processes which build a quality academic system in a sequence "diagnosis-planning-management". To get the information which would generate these criteria, a Likert questionnaire for 30 students and 8 teachers was designed; also an interview for a manager based on standardized indicators by the Ministry of Education to get the self-evaluation. The gathered information generated the value judgment that when it was applied to the evaluation of the academic management, some results were highlighted. Finally, this research establishs as objective the design of a relevant proposal to ensure that the academic management achieve quality processes based on the application of knowledge management and also get the improvement of its services based on self-assessment.

PREAMBLE

Educational institutions currently stand at an axis of analysis, both academic-scientific and professional level. Alvarez (2014) states that the transformation of school organization has the purpose of finding the right answer to the demands and criticisms from the public opinion according to the education given.

Alvarez (2014) also states that a great deal of the problem lies on the idea that the school organization usually remains widely apart from the teaching-learning process, and it tends to pay insufficient attention to the sociocultural context of students.

For this reason, it is necessary that the centers provide incentives to the students which help them grow physically, socially and intellectually as well as build the bases for their professional training.

DOI: 10.4018/978-1-5225-0457-3.ch012

Due to the fact that Quintana (2007) reckons schools as multifunctional institutions whose primary mission is to educate and instruct the students, without forgetting the objectives which have been assigned by the legal framework that defines them and by the educational framework.

Meanwhile, Münch (2010) promotes the transformation process in schools, from the perspective of the organizational theory and educational sciences; because it is undeniable that there is a strong relationship between organizational structures of schools and the teaching models which are being developed in them.

However, Alvarez (2014) points out that the organizational structure which exists in the institutions causes the limiting teaching practice as well as the development of new teaching models of education, to encourage the skills training of the student.

Therefore, within an educational organization there are several articulated elements through a network of processes, which altogether build an academic system, the one that needs to keep developing and with quality.

It means, organizations need to manage the academic processes to achieve the quality education based on quality criteria; from the perspective of Alvarez (2014) it is proposed the sequence "diagnosis-planning-management" to achieve it.

As for the diagnosis and planning, they are presenting features to drive the goals of education in establishments, however, to achieve the objectives with quality, Cardoso, et. al. (2011) suggests to lean on the evaluation of academic management, itself consists on an activity for appreciating the value and maturity (or level of excellence) of the processes from the organization in order to determine their effectiveness and efficiency, and to know the extent in which the needs and expectations from different stakeholders are being achieved.

Thus, to conduct an evaluation is necessary to establish standards as: 1) effectiveness and efficiency, the ones which measure the accomplishment of the objectives achieved and the resources used; 2) relevance and importance, whose relationship is closely marked by the satisfaction of the social needs and the use of the acquired skills; 3) equity, which indicates the variety of educational offerings for different socio-cultural needs. Based on these criterial indicators, standards and benchmarks are built which let compare and qualify the characteristics and attributes from the school.

Academic Processes, Information, and Management

The concept of management comes from the etymological basis, which comes from Latin *gestio*, *gestionis*, composed of gestus (fact, concluded), participle of the verb *gerere* (do, carry out) and the suffix -tio- (-tion = action and effect). Highlighting, in this way, the origin of the word manage or manager. (WordReference.com, 2015).

Huergo (2009) refers to the concept of management as the art of making possible a course and achieve a goal in the middle of difficulties and the unpredictability of some events.

Meanwhile, Alvarez (2007) highlights that management is a dynamic process that succeeds in linking the fields of the conventional management with those from the organization, under the guidance and animation of an effective leadership from a director, exercised in the context of multiple leaderships and it is oriented towards the fulfillment of the institutional mission.

Thus, relating the last concepts to the activities of an academic system, the definition of academic management is built, which Lopez (2010) interprets as a series of curricular processes that involve not only the activities of teaching, but the administrative-type ones which are performed by the school in order to achieve the goals of education.

Specifically, an academic system has activities such as the registration process, selection of students, student admissions, curricula, pedagogical models, program offerings, academic-administrative information and student tracking.

This is why, Münch (2010) states that inside the academic management exist the following functions, such as: human resources devoted to teaching, infrastructure and equipment, socio-cultural context and control of students, curricula and programs, organizing of the professorship and teaching-learning processes.

Based on the above, the tangible part of the academic administration can be understood, but there is an intangible part inside the same organization, which is located on the knowledge of best practices, the experience of the administrative and academic staff and in the vision which is in the socio-economic and cultural context that surround the educational body.

In fact, it is noteworthy what Zamboni (2003) assumes about the Academic Management as idea (conceptual) and as action (operational). It means that the set of ideas and principles inside an educational organization, their development, their conflicts, their actions, their way of learning and communicating ideas or information would be the intangible part of the educational body and processes within the organization as: instructional design, teaching, educational technology and administration are the tangible part.

Then, it is understood that the synergy of the operational processes from the educational organizations requires a huge investment in training resources for their various members; in order to maintain the minimum range of errors in the negotiations. However, the learning levels of each person are not homogeneous and this training or knowledge transmission is very often slow or ineffective, keeping the organization in a state of intermittent crisis.

In this sense, it is confirmed the one established by Inciarte (2006) stating that teaching and learning are correlated processes. So, they both cannot be confused, since learning is subjective and it happens inside each subject; although its dominance may eventually externalize it in specific words and actions, but this concept is restricted to human beings. While it is undeniable the individual and endogenous nature of school learning, which consists not only of personal representations, but lies on the plane of social activity and shared experience.

Based on the above, the academic management requires a review of its processes and especially the social interaction between teachers, students and other members from the educational community, and in relation to the contents, which lead the student learning (Inciarte, 2006).

Therefore, to consider a school as successful, knowledge can be integrated in the activities that are part of the objectives defined in its mission; since, the importance given to the organizational knowledge allows the creation of knowledge as well as the distribution and intelligent inclusion in the organization and in the products and services (Nonaka and Takeuchi, 1995).

In the same way, Basáñez, et. al, (2012) suggest that by strengthening the existing knowledge and creating new one, it provides the necessary conditions for this to flow through the organization; resulting in advanced organizations with agile knowledge and with the ability to innovate besides the changes of the environment.

It means that when we see the above suggestions as a management process, they would involve: 1) knowledge creation, 2) continuous innovation; 3) competitive advantage. Obtaining, by this way, knowledge management. Senge (2007).

The issues that arise around knowledge management are: 1) the needs for organizations to preserve the knowledge of good practices to give continuity to their most critical processes; 2) the benefits and competitive advantages that allow knowledge; 3) provide the necessary conditions for good practice to flow through the organization; 4) obtain an advanced organization in agile knowledge and capable of innovating through the market fluctuations.

Obviously, knowledge management involves developing of the necessary competences inside the organizations to be shared and used among its members as well as to be valued and assimilated if it is outside of itself.

For this reason, Basáñez, et. al, (2012) suggests the need to plan, coordinate and control the flows produced in the educational organization in relation to the activities and their environment; to create specific skills.

On the other hand, people, procedures, knowledge cycle, the spiral of knowledge, technologies and organization are integrated components in knowledge management; variables considered in the model for quality management, can facilitate strategies for the decision making, obtaining the continuous quality to provide an added value to the educational organization, know and organize the intangible assets for a better management, stimulate the human communication and build culture with shared horizons; projecting the business leadership to the social context that it is served, and learn best practices, disseminate them and encourage changes to innovate and reduce costs.

Thus, the above emphasizes the following dimensions within the academic management: 1) instructional design which involves teaching models, strategies, areas, instructional leadership and dialogue in the context; 2) management and administration academic whose emphasis is related to planning, organizing, monitoring and evaluation of the academic processes; 3) teaching skills or pedagogical practices for the teaching-learning process; 4) application of time-motion in the classroom and 5) academic monitoring.

The proposal comes from the staff who form teams and organizations, both at the operational level, and tactical and management; since it involves a commitment to report in order to acquire and structure the organizational knowledge, and using projects for diagnostic processes, designing, implementation and evaluation.

Hence, people along with technology, communication, learning, teamwork, leadership, training, innovation and culture, are the identifying variables in knowledge management to justify, develop and implement strategies in the assessing of the academic management in order to obtain the highest quality of the service with criteria of effectiveness, efficiency, relevance, significance and equity, as shown in Figure 1.

Assessment of Academic Management

The knowledge from the assessment depends on the needs, aims and objectives of the evaluated and the evaluator.

So the assessment is understood as the process of identifying, obtaining and providing the useful and descriptive information about the value and worth of the targets, planning, implementation and the impact of a particular object, in order to serve as a guide for the decision making, solve the problems of accountability and promote the understanding of the phenomena involved (Stufflebeam, et. al, 2011).

The focus of the evaluation of the academic management is in order to appreciate the value and maturity (or level of excellence) of the processes of the organization so their effectiveness and efficiency can be determined, and to know to what extent the needs and expectations of different stakeholders are being fulfilled (Cardoso, 2006).

In this regard, it is worth noting the statement by Alvarez (2014) about contextual assessments, which are presented from two perspectives. On the one hand, the ones called basic, that are performed before

Figure 1. Dynamics of the tangible and intangible activities of the academic management in an educational organization
Source: Own elaboration

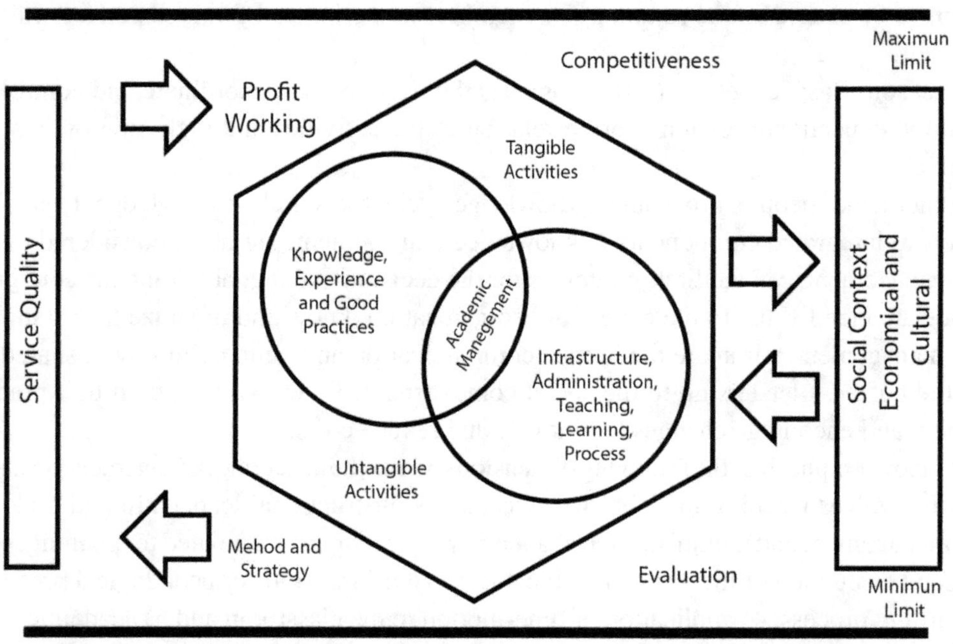

starting production and even before setting up the system, in order to collect information which justify or not the need of the school or the establishment of certain support services.

Among the main evaluation models there is a variety of classifications, which are determined by: 1) objectives, 2) judgments, 3) decisions, 4) criteria 5) goals, 6) context and 7) certification.

In fact, the assessment model of the Context, Information, Processes and Products (CIPP) was devised by Stufflebeam et. al (2011) in order to generate a convenient, continuous and cyclical tool for getting the improvement of the system, as it is shown in Figure 2.

Figure 2. Phases CIPP model by Stufflebeam and Guba
Source: Stufflebeam, et. al, 2011

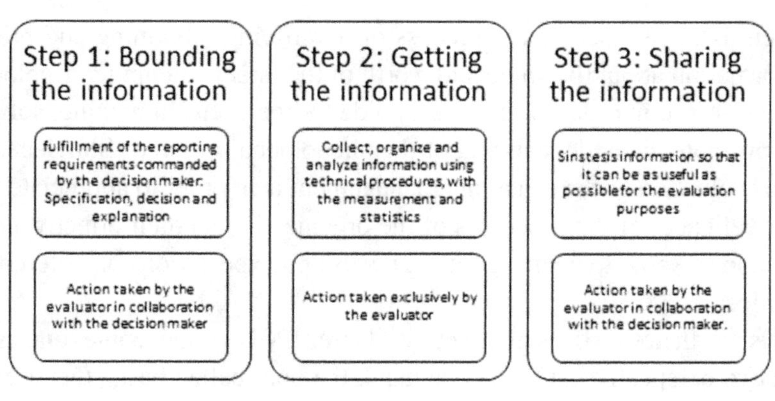

The CIPP model is more focused on education systems and human services; as the basic ideology is especially the concept that the evaluation is not to demonstrate, but to improve a system.

One advantage of the CIPP model is that the context may be covered by the identification and assessment of the preconditions as indicated Stufflebeam et. al (2011). That is, the information exists before the project starts and this takes importance, according to Alvarez (2014), to give an overview of the requirements which a school faces up.

Thus, allowing in an assessment inputs (of information) before and during the project and the possibility of carrying out only the assessment of the context, input, process, product or some combinations from these, it will depend on the needs of the center. So, the CIPP model is considered effective for an evaluation for a continuous improvement or betterment.

The applications of the academic evaluation in an educational center, it is considered important that the evaluation includes actions for the decision-making and accountability; relevant approach mentioned by Alvarez (2014) and Cardoso, et. al (2011).

Under the same line, the evaluation for Stufflebeam (2011) is exposed as part of the context, input, process and product; since, it suggests using this information as guidance for decision making, training function, to provide knowledge and for the summative function, as it is shown in Table 1.

Evaluators can plan and determine the level of value in order to help the staff in a career development and process control in the program. Moreover, fulfilling the needs of the context and achieve the School objectives meritorious to its service.

So, a CIPP evaluation can examine customer needs of the school; exposing opportunities as an improvement program, including educational technologies and important school training to help in the educational quality of the Educational Center.

Collecting and examining intuitions about the problems of the school as well, which need to change; and to assess the effectiveness of the goals and institutional priorities in the system. As it is shown in Figure 3.

Based on the above, an evaluation can be motivated from the organization of the institution as a regular measure of the state of the school or as a response to certain sectors of satisfaction with the work of the personnel. Therefore, the CIPP assessment presents four areas of evaluation which are: 1) context assessment which is motivated from outside of the school, if an accredited agency requests a study and it can lead to a decision itself about the introduction of any change in the system.

2) The results of the evaluation input which can be used to decide whether a solution strategy has been found promising enough to move forward with the development; 3) evaluation of the process and 4) evaluation of the product or service. As it is shown in Table 2.

Table 1. Importance of evaluation for the decision-making and responsibility

	Context	Data Input	Process	Product
Decision making (formative orientation)	Guide to choice selection and Prioritization	Guide to the selection of the program strategies. Data input for the process-plan assignation	Guide to application	Guide to completion, continuation, modification or delivery.
Accountability (summative orientation)	Relationship of objectives and bases for its selection along with a list of needs, opportunities and problems	List of planning and strategy chosen and the reasons for that choice between alternatives.	Ratio of the actual process	List of achievements and making recycled

Source: Stufflebeam et. al (2011) development.

Figure 3. Descriptive diagram of the CIPP evaluation in the improvement of a system
Source: Stufflebeam et. al (2011) design

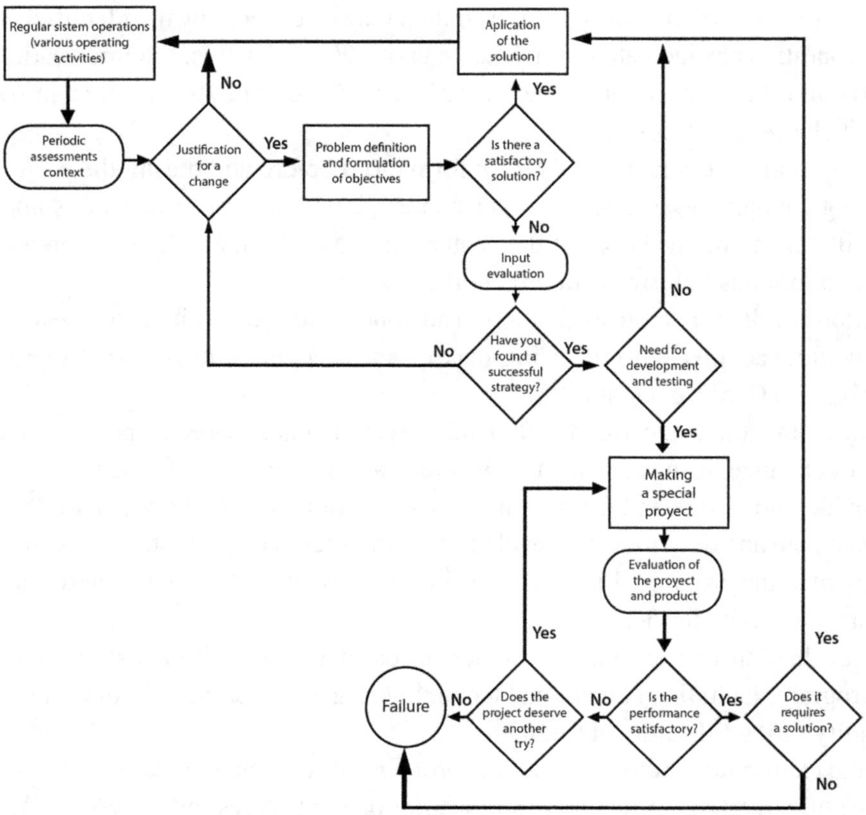

Table 2. Overview of the CIPP evaluation by type of evaluation

	Context Evaluation	Evaluation Input	Process Evaluation	Product Evaluation
Objective	Define the institutional context, identify the population objective and assess their needs.	Identify and assess the ability of the system.	Provide information for rescheduled decisions and judge the activities and aspects of the procedure	Collect descriptions and judgments about the results.
Method	Such as systems analysis, inspection, review of documents, auditions, interviews, diagnostic tests and the Delphi technique	Inventory and analyse the available human and material resources.	Control potential limitations of the procedure and remain alert to the unexpected actions.	Define operationally and assess the criterial results, by collecting customer judgements
Relative to decision making in the process of change	Decide the framework that needs to be applied, the targets related to fulfil the needs or the use of the opportunities and the goals related to solving problems	Select the support resources, the solution strategies and the planning procedures in order to structure the activities of change; as well as providing a basis for making value judgments.	Carry out and improve the planning and program procedures, to exercise control in the process.	Decide the continuation, completion, modification or adaptation of activity of change. And present a clear statement of desired and undesired effects; positive and negative.

Source: Stufflebeam et. al (2011)

An important point to highlight is that the evaluation of the process has as its main mission to obtain continuous information that can help the personnel to carry out the program as it is planned, and they also help evaluators to know the monitoring of the programs.

Another evaluation model that is closely linked to the academic management; it is the model of accreditation. The one that it is carried out within the processes for granting a credit to a school by the authorities in the assessment, as it is shown in Figure 4.

The Accreditation Model establishes standards and indicators to guide schools and they can provide an educational service of quality and equity. Since the challenges of implementing standards of learning in a school where the context is multicultural present different levels of challenge in the academic management. The ones which can be overcome by implementing a systemic evaluation and quality objectives.

An accreditation model promotes inside the educational organization self-evaluations of diagnostic type; to determine levels of efficiency and effectiveness within the institution and thus help people who are part of the education system continue with a line of improvement based on the training and introduction to educational innovation.

Actually, with this evaluation model accreditation and quality achievements are obtained; through the assessment of the administrative personnel who control the academic management in the school and thus understand whether the resources are shared out effectively and efficiently. Therefore, the main pinnacle to achieve quality in the educational services is inside the knowledge management and human resources.

Alvarez (2014) has said, that one of the causes that generate some of the problems in the administrative and academic management, is presented in the level of leadership that the organization presents; the same which is considered as criterion in this accreditation model. However, these leaders trained for teaching areas of knowledge; are often focused on more academically administrative environments

Figure 4. Accreditation model
Source: Stufflebeam et. al (2011)

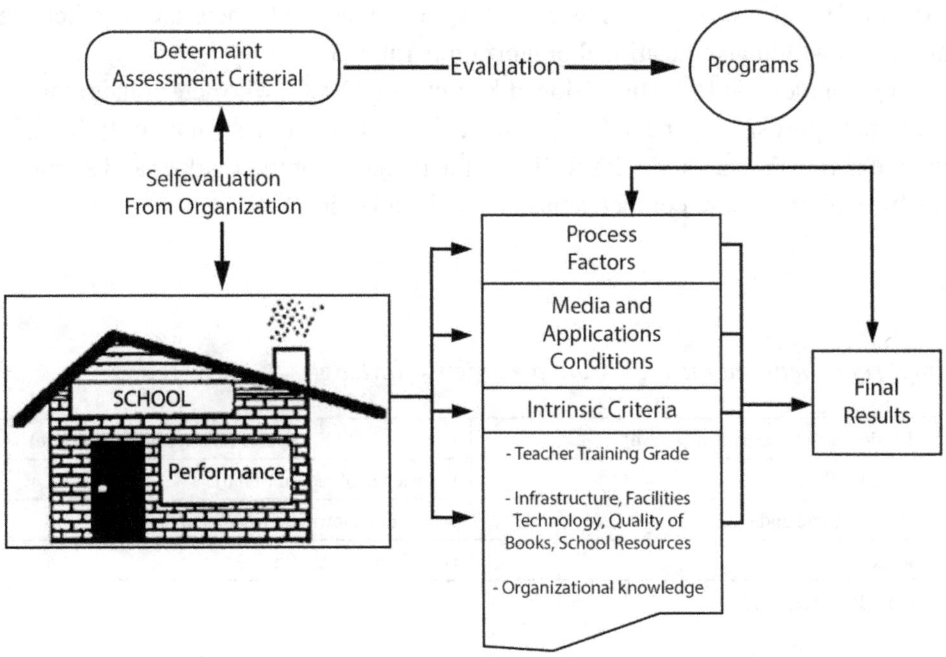

instead of promoting good practices within the organization. So in this way, low profile synergies are generated in the labor-collaborative environment.

Therefore, it is necessary to include in the accreditation assessment model the vision of intelligent organizations and knowledge management. And so generating effectively the necessary strategies to promote effective leadership and relevant processes within the school.

Sergen (2007) emphasizes in his theory is the systems thinking, who exposes organizations as links of people with collaborative activities and as a result mutual effects are generated. Effect that produces knowledge in a system or team discipline of learning, whose framework part from a body of knowledge and tools that have been developed for a long time to allow total and clear patterns of the organization; and at the same time, they help to modify actions that generate the problems in an organization. That is, generating the capacity in the organization members to suspend assumptions and integrate a genuine thinking together.

Meanwhile Nanoka et. al (1995) defines knowledge as a dynamic human process, created by a major flow of information that is fed by expectations and organizational culture of people. Therefore, the active behavior intends to establish cycles of knowledge creation, and the organization requires to put special emphasis on the generation, conversion, transfer and diffusion processes of it in order to maximize the production of products which are consequences of these cycles.

The importance given to the organizational knowledge that enables the creation and distribution of knowledge and its intelligent inclusion as in the organization as in the products and service are the basis for the creation of institutions considered successful. (Nonaka, 1995)

So, the intrinsic criteria within the evaluation model for accreditation involves nine aspects to generate advanced educational enterprises with intelligent organizations which are: a) People, b) communication c) learning, d) teamwork, e) leadership, f) training, g) innovation, h) organizational culture and i) technology (Basañez, 2012).

Maintaining the relationship between the organizational knowledge and the model of accreditation, they are considered as factors of the process to the nature of knowledge; which is divided in personal knowledge (tactical) and the public knowledge (explicit) whose characteristics affect the control of academic processes within an educational organization Table 3.

The foregoing is understood with the vision of Kerschberg (2000), who determines that the knowledge with organizational approach can be defined as the information that has value to it; that is, information that can generate actions associated with fulfilling the demands of the market, and supporting the new opportunities by exploiting core competencies of the organization.

Table 3. Comparison between the tactical and explicit knowledge

Tactical Knowledge (Subjective)	Explicit Knowledge (Objective)
Knowledge of experience (body)	Knowledge of reason (mind)
Simultaneous knowledge (here and now)	Sequential knowledge (there and then)
Analogical knowledge (practice)	Digital knowledge (theory)

Source: Prepared by (Basañez, 2012)

Meanwhile, Nanoka et. al (1995) defines it as active to make a difference; due to the fact that organizational knowledge is composed of people who are holders of knowledge, the ones who build and drive the bases to generate the organizational memory.

But Berrio (2013) emphasizes that this knowledge requires an input and active support from the company to be exploited, that is why it requires the study of this for its management and proper use as it is done with other commodities.

Therefore, Nanoka et. al (1995) provides four key factors around the development of the organizational knowledge, as it is shown in Table 4.

Thus, it is appropriate to include a thread within the accreditation model that is proposed by Basañez (2012), which stands in the center of the process to people and motivation as the key to knowledge management, as it is shown in Figure 5.

In the evaluation of academic management models are included which can generate strategic enhancement tools oriented to the customers, the process improvement based on intelligent organizations

Table 4. Key factors around the creation of organizational knowledge

Factor	Description
Intention	The organization must have the explicit intention of creating optimal conditions for the growth of the spiral of organizational knowledge.
Autonomy	Allowing some level of autonomy in its personnel, which encourages instances of generating new ideas and display new opportunities, thus motivating participants to generate new knowledge
Fluctuation and creative chaos	Encouraging interaction between its members and the external environment, where teams face the routines, habits and self-imposed limitations in order to stimulate new perspectives on how to do things.
Redundancy	Allowing levels of redundancy within their operations. This causes that the different points of view established by the people who are part of the teams allow it to share and combine.

Source: Compiled by (Basañez, 2012) based on Nonaka et. al (1995) and (Sergen, 2007)

Figure 5. Knowledge management
Source: Prepared by (Basañez, 2012)

to accredit the educational service in the center and the quality assessment based on the self-assessment of the educational organization.

In regard to the last point and under the same line of management, evaluation and quality the European Quality Management Model EFQM (2003) is taken up; model used to promote the improvement of the quality in the service based on nine criteria contextualized for the school and the self-assessment of the organization. Since, this model promotes the foundations of the situational diagnosis and starting point to intervene into the permanent improvement.

This model can be used as: a) a tool for self-assessment, b) a way to compare best practice between organizations, c) guide to identify areas for improvement, d) basis for a common vocabulary and way of thinking and e) Framework for management systems in an Educational Center (Brull, 2010).

The principles of this model are: a) results orientation, b) customer orientation, c) leadership and consistency, e) management by processes and facts, f) development and involvement of people, g) continuous learning process, innovation and improvement, h) development of partnerships j) social responsibility in the organization.

In consequence of the above, this model EFQM (2003) has been applied by Martinez (2005) to measure the excellence of schools, with the intention of demonstrating the level of achievements fulfilled by the education authorities; thinking that these organizations are like systems whose movements are around the quality of its services.

So the involvement of the organization is required in the process of self-assessment and decision making, as well as the account all the factors involved in improving the quality of services from the school demanded by the society. Because of this, Brull (2010) defines the EFQM (2003) with the following critical to the proper functioning of the organization and moreover Martinez et. al (2005) refers to them as the basis for the concepts of excellence and assessment of a school (shown in Table 5).

As stated in Table 5, now the nine contextualized criteria are exposed to evaluate the academic administration in a school of languages, but with an educational context; which were proposed by Martínez et. al (2005) for an educational center. To illustrate better these criteria in Table 6 are divided into two types (facilitators and results).

At this point, it is understood that the research use more than one evaluation model to achieve the purpose of generating the plan of improvement in academic management; but this requires involving people, processes, information, context and school policies.

Research Methodology

The research has no hypotheses; since this was not experimental and descriptive; that is, only the current situation was characterized concretely, indicating the most unique or distinguishing features existing in the organization (Hernandez, et. al, 2010).

This characterization of the School of Languages was created with the information obtained by applying the instruments to the specific sample within the organization or universe based on a method of cross section. In the application of the instruments provided by the SEP (2007) and data collection were performed in a single moment of time.

The instruments for this research were a Likert questionnaire applied to 30 students; an open questionnaire administered to 8 teachers and an interview with a manager. It is important to emphasize that the design of the instruments and the implementation thereof were made based on the regulations stipulated

Table 5. Concepts of excellence for the design of criteria from the EFQM model with emphasis on education

Concept	Description
Customer orientation	Excellence depends on the balance and fulfilled of the needs of all the relevant customers, including those who work in the organization, the ones who request its services, suppliers and society in general, and all those with an interest in the organization.
Leadership and constancy of purpose	Leadership helps achieve excellence if the vision and purpose are aligned in the organization.
Results orientation	Excellence is achieved when the results satisfy the groups involved in the organization. The improvements proposed need to be based on reliable information, including facts and perceptions of school members and customers.
Development, implementation and recognition of people	Excellence is maximized by contributing to the development and involvement of people who work in an organization in the improving processes through teamwork. The potential of each person who work in an organization needs to be developed, and this is enhanced when the values are shared, and there is mutual trust, which encourages partnership achievements and goals in the organization.
Management by processes and facts	Excellence is achieved through management with a focus on processes and facts in a systemic way. All activities need to be linked and be managed as a system, with the understanding and involvement of all members of the school. In this way, the school gets better returns when its processes are based on actions in response to identified needs. In fact, in this case the process is defined as a set of interrelated or interacting activities which transforms inputs into results.
Partnership Development	Excellence is achieved by developing and maintaining value adding partnerships in people, institutions and organizations that provide products, services or knowledge to the school. Providers, in an organization that pursues excellence, need to become partners, whose base is the relationship of trust and adding value. In this way the organization works more effectively when sharing with partner knowledge to support its policies and strategies for effective operation of its processes and its staff.
Continuous learning, innovation and improvement	Excellence is achieved by challenging the status quo, making change happen and using learning to create innovation and improvement opportunities. The decisions to take on the resulting projects need to arise them from the knowledge of the operation of the organization; and in turn, this is based on a review of results, in line with the previous criteria used in the definition of projects and programs, such as the mission, policy and strategy. Therefore, the elements that determine it are: 1) the training of personnel, 2) collaboration, 3) resource efficiency, 4) planning processes 5) evaluation and 6) feedback; so they allow changes, innovation and opportunity for improvement.
Social responsibility of the organization	Excellence is achieved exceeding the minimum regulatory framework in which the organization operates and trying to understand and respond to the expectations of the stakeholders and society. At this point, members of the school require behave based on ethics that gives meaning to individual actions beyond that may arise from the standards or legal requirements and thus get the answers to the needs of the group and especially with a particular social context.

Source: Based on information from Martinez et. al (2005)

in the manual for self-evaluation of schools for quality management, providing them by the Secretary of Public Education SEP (2007) in Mexico.

Subsequently, the evaluation parameters were established based on the similarities of the data within the information collected and with this, the frequency to make value judgments and benchmarks of quality for each process comprising the Academic Management of the School Language were calculated.

Obtained Results

To start the percentages of items that are related to knowledge management in the organization are exposed, which are: 1) knowledge information, 2) analyzing information and 3) organizational knowledge. The same which were included in the self-assessment test at the school (Figure 6).

Table 6. Criteria EFQM (2003) proposed by Martinez et. al (2005) to assess the level of excellence of a school with an emphasis on academic management

Agents Criteria	Description
Leadership	Leaders develop and facilitate the achievement based on the mission and vision. The five elements in it are: development of mission, vision and ethical principles; staff involvement to ensure the development, implementation and continuous improvement. They interact with customers and partners, reinforcing the culture of excellence in people, define and drive change in the organization.
Politics y strategies	Organizations implement strategies focused on stakeholders. The four elements in it are: the needs and current and future expectations, the information on the performance indicators, research, learning, outdoor activities, it is developed, reviewed and updated, communicated and deployed through a framework of key processes.
People	Excellent organizations manage, develop and bring out the full potential of people who are part of them. Promote justice and equality and involve people. The five elements in it are: planning, management, resource efficiency, identification and development of knowledge; empowering people and responsibility.
Alliances and Resources	Organizations plan and manage external partnerships also suppliers and internal resources in support of its policy, strategy and process efficiency. Integrates the management of economic and financial resources and management of buildings, equipment and materials.
Processes	It is composed of elements such as design and systematic management of processes, research on the needs of customers and staff; developing a plan for education and training center. Plan teaching, student assessment and teaching-learning processes. It also generate the development of extracurricular and complementary activities. It also includes all the processes of management, and customer relationship; verification of continuous improvement based on the results and the design of indicators to set targets for improvement.
Result Criteria	**Description**
Customer Results	The measure results to determine the extent of the students on the basis of which are defined in the vision and mission of the school. The analysis of the results can generate the performance indicators as well.
Personal results	These results show the achievement of objectives of every person who integrates the organization based on the school plan and satisfaction of methodological and teaching training.
Result in society	Excellent organizations comprehensively measure the results obtained and compared them with the expected results; to generate performance indicators and returns which cover social needs.
Key findings in the organization	The results based on the policies and strategies are measured; but it is required to include indicators of educational outcomes and other services provided by the center.

Source: Based on information from Martinez et. al (2005) and Brull (2010)

Based on the percentages and retaking the accreditation model with emphasis on intelligent organizations; It shows that there is a continuous collection of information in the organization, but this information is only in the administrative areas of the organization and therefore the rest of the organization still remains problematic processes to achieve the objectives of educational quality.

So, it can be confirmed what was said by Sergen (2007), Kerschberg (2000) and Nanoka (1995) that the importance given to organizational knowledge, enables the creation and distribution of knowledge and intelligent inclusion in the organization and products and service are the basis for the creation of institutions considered as successful

Hence, the organization can achieve accreditation and excellence if it promotes knowledge throughout the organization. However, with the percentages obtained in the knowledge information items and in the organizational knowledge; it can be integrated the result of the action due to the administration.

Since these rates are in the most basic of the achievements and require greater interest from leaders to promote such relevant information and thus achieving in the organization the systemic thinking which let achieve the educational objectives.

Figure 6. Percentage of items related to knowledge
Source: Prepared

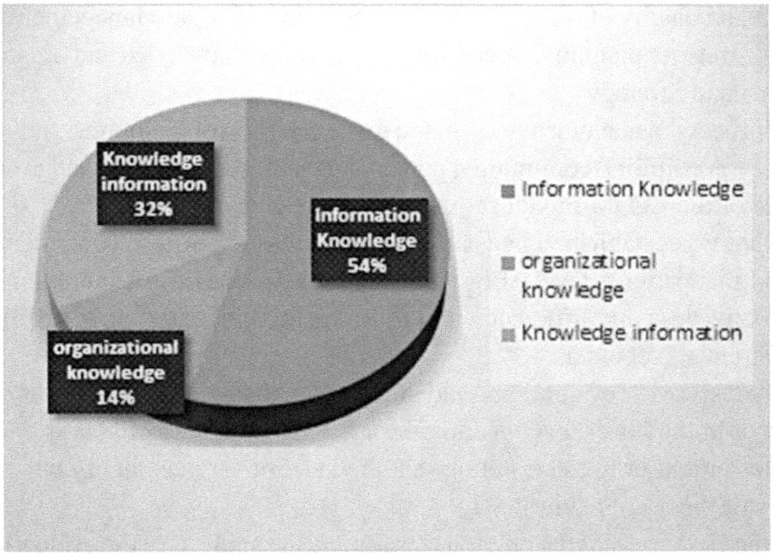

Otherwise, the accreditation of the organization will be done in a longer time than it was expected by the educational and loan authorities. It was clearly confirmed what Basanez, et. al, (2012) told; that the knowledge management involves the development of the necessary competences within organizations to share and use them among its members and to value it and assimilate it if it is outside of this. For this reason, he suggests the need to plan, coordinate and control the flows produced in the educational organization in relation to the activities and their environment; to create specific skills.

Moreover, applying the management model to evaluating the Academic Management of the School, it was required to use the percentages obtained in the self-assessment, whose evaluation indicators were linked to the criteria of the European Foundation for Quality Management, EFQM (2003); shown in Table 7and whose sum of the percentages of value judgments keeps 100%.

Table 7. Criteria agents and results to European Foundation for Quality Management (EFQM) Education Center

Model European Foundation for Quality Management (EFQM)			
Criteria Agents	**Value Judgments [%]**	**Criteria for Results**	**Value Judgments [%]**
Leadership and management style	14	Client Result	11
Policy and Strategy	10	Resulted in the development of People	9
People Management and Development	14	Results in Company	9
Resources and Partners	10	Global result or key	11
Processes	12		
TOTAL	60	TOTAL	40

Source: EFQM (2003) Model, Brull (2010) and Martínez (2005)

Now, the results and linkages of each indicator of school self-evaluation criteria of the EFQM (2003) model are defined as follows: the indicators of user knowledge, relationship with users, systems of work, human development and quality of life, integrated the criteria of People Management and Development.

The indicators of strategic planning, operability of planning, knowledge and organization, integrated the criterial of Policy and Strategy.

The indicator of process management was joined to the criterion of Resources and Associates. Finally, indicators of social responsibility, community, personal development, people and group of interest were joined to the criteria of the EFQM model results as they are shown in Table 8.

Thus confirm what was established by Cardoso (2006) whose purpose of academic evaluation is to assess the value and maturity (or level of excellence) of the processes of the organization in order to determine their effectiveness and efficiency and to know to what extent it is fulfilling the needs and expectations of different stakeholders

Therefore, the analysis of the evaluation Academic Management Education Center is indicated at half of the development or in the lower level of satisfactory. That is, the effectiveness and efficiency of the organization are intermittent or regular; noting that the level of service quality has some improvement processes, but many of these are made slowly.

Hence, for a detailed overview of the previous results and the analysis of the evaluation of the academic management of the school. The percentages obtained in each indicator as a result of the organization (Table 9) are exposed; in which the result of knowledge of users with a positive and favorable trends were seen, but the spread of the goal and values in the organization are intermittent. Also, the actions implemented to improve the relationship with the user, requires more action.

Furthermore, the indicator of information and analysis presents a regular quality achievement; since communication within the organization is biased and one-way. Causing that good practices or improvements are not recognized in different areas.

Finally, the knowledge and organization indicator is in the achieving regular inferior limit; that is, that the organization fulfils the basic minimum knowledge of good practice and teacher training.

In this sense, it is confirmed what Basáñez, et. al, (2012) said, that by strengthening existing knowledge, create new knowledge, provides the necessary conditions for this to flow by the organization; resulting in advanced organizations with agile knowledge and ability to innovate besides the changes of the environment.

Table 8. Results of self-assessment indicators integrated to European Foundation for Quality Management (EFQM) criteria

Criteria Agents	Value Judgments [%]	Criteria for Results	Value Judgments [%]
Leadership and management style	10.5	Client Result	6.1
Policy and Strategy	5.4	Resulted in the development of People	6.9
People Management and Development	6.7	Results in Company	3.4
Resources and Partners	5.7	Global result or key	4.8
Processes	8.1		
OVERALL RATING		**57.64%**	

Source: Authors

Table 9. Results of self-assessment items from the Education Center in percentages; whose analysis parameters are: 1 = Excellent (80% - 100%); 2 = Satisfactory (79% - 60%); 3 = Regular (59% - 30%); 4 = Poor (29% - 0%)

Indicator	Percentage [%]	Indicator	Percentage [%]
User knowledge	60%	Quality of life	37.5%
Relationship users	54.2%	Design of products, services and processes	57.14%
Leadership	75%	Administrative Process	57.14%
Strategic Planning	54.16%	social responsibility	37.5%
Operability of planning	55%	Community	55.35%
Information and analysis	55%	Staff Development	77.77%
Knowledge and organization	37.5%	People	42.85%
Working systems	45.83%	Interest Groups	43.75%
Human Development	45%		

Source: Authors

However, in this school people, procedures, knowledge cycle, the spiral of knowledge, technologies and organization are not yet integrated in the knowledge management and therefore they do not have easy strategies for decisions making and get continuous improvement to provide added value to the educational organization, know and organize intangible assets for better management, promote human communication and build culture with shared horizons.

And so the projection of business leadership has no impact on the social context that he serves; because learning good practice is not widespread, and encouraged throughout the organization and thereby the reduction in innovation in the organization.

Finally the percentage of processes, products, information and context to determine the evaluation based on CIPP model with emphasis on the customer and thus to generate a continuous and cyclical strategic tool for improving the educational system organizational approach to client. As it is shown in Figure 7.

Figure 7. Percentages generated by the CIPP evaluation
Source: Prepared

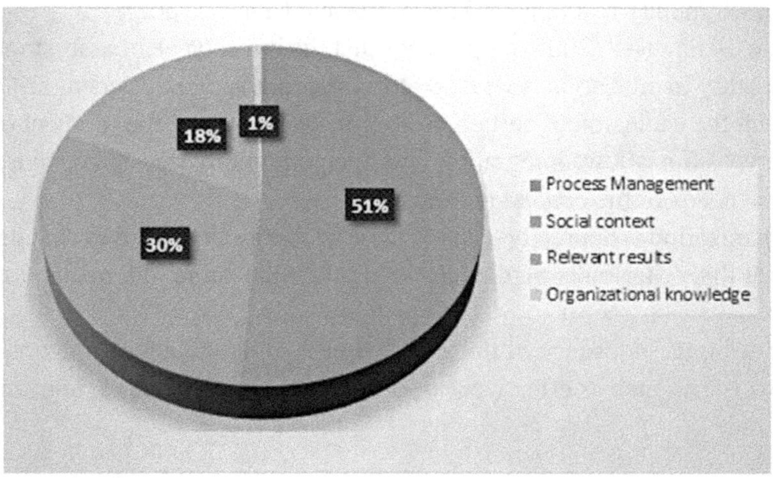

As a result of this chart emphasizes the point made by Álvarez (2014) who states that much of the problem is that the school organization usually remains largely outside the teaching-learning process, and that tends to pay insufficient attention to context sociocultural student

It means that the organization is only immersed in performing successfully the processes to achieve the quality of their services, but ironically they neglect knowledge management and the main needs of the context; avoiding achieve effective and efficient results as it was planned by the organization.

With such a condition, it should be noted what Álvarez (2014) said about the vision of the management of academic quality processes, which summarized in the following sequence "diagnosis-planning-management." Thus distractions are avoided in people who form the educational organization and so they can reach the fulfillment of the vision and mission of the center, based on the effective leadership and training of intelligent systems thinking organizations.

CONCLUSION

The main conclusions are: I) The Academic Management of an educational center of languages affects the curriculum, organizational and pedagogical purposes for quality service; II) Knowledge management is linked to the development of innovative processes to adapt the accomplishments to the challenges which involve the needs of the context and articulate organizational goals with management; III) The professionalization creates favorable conditions for achieving certification of teaching and generate relevant services; IV) Promoting transformational leadership among teachers and principals will empower the interest in the objectives of education and thus the right conditions for a learning organization will be generated whose synergy is good practices.

The goals of education are growing in parallel with the needs to become competent in the workplace; so knowledge management in teaching will include synergies in the effective leadership to transform teaching.

Considering the situation in the evaluation determines that a quality school requires to have relevance and significance criteria in their services; so the organization can satisfy the demands of the context and thus promote the quality of life in their environment.

Understanding the quality of a school requires to establish the factors and criteria on which it develops and interacts itself. In other words, it means that for the evaluation of an educational organization that provides a service to the community, it is necessary to understand and consider the phenomena which pertain to the same community and thus to the Educational Centre itself.

In the same sense, Schmelkes (2005) emphasizes that the importance of assessing education schools parts from the inequality in education; that is, that in the process of assessment criteria exist as equity which help to prevent the exclusion of certain socioeconomic levels at the moment of establishing that a school is of quality, as this allows integration with the community through design multiple curricula that fulfil the diverse needs of the context around them

So; when the organization is not ready to solve these problems they need to change some operational factors to ensure that this criterion is marked as good under the value judgments that generate evaluation in the school.

Under the same vein, the relevance of the assessment falls on the educational organization when it gives importance to criteria such as effectiveness, efficiency, equity, demand, relevance, social context, development of knowledge and innovation. And especially when it seeks the continuous improvement of the organization.

In this way, the school may reach the goals, objectives and achievements stablished by the organization when it offers its services.

Also, obtaining the quality certification externally, where such an educational organization can fulfil the educational objectives properly managing the existing resources in an organization such as: knowledge, investment, time, human resources and conventions; so that one or several social identities with diverse interests success benefit.

Summing up, it is stated that to speak of quality in an educational center requires to considerate that its services provide basic skills to the client or learner and promote high expectations of knowledge in the organization through transformational leadership and participatory within the administration.

Another point that must be promoted within the educational organization, by the management, is constantly monitoring their academic students, all staff promote an orderly and pleasant climate for learning.

The school also must communicate its mission, vision, goals and values throughout its organization; it means, including its staff, students and their context. So that it can get a collaborative activity to reach the educational goals and beyond in service.

From that perspective, getting comprehensive communication within an educational organization, it is marked as coming through effective leadership and also promote it in every one of its members that make up the educational structure.

This action falls on the issues raised by Schmelkes (2005) about leadership within the Schools; which requires a pedagogical exercise and depending on the learning of students.

So, leadership lies on the management exercise, teaching and community because leadership is not unilateral, nor pointed. For this reason, to promote it within the organization and cultivate it in each of the members makes the Educational Center be able to create a sense of commitment and collegiality among members that make up the educational service and also sharing decisions, achievements, commitments, goals and successes with all its external and internal system.

With this vision, it is established that leadership, communication and knowledge are the main providers of effective quality within an organization. As these will only be exercised by the human factor. However, this means that if the human factor is at a lower limit of knowledge and skills; then the organization will be in a lower limit of the quality of its services

Therefore, training teachers and systems thinking within the organization are the key to generate successful educational intelligent organizations.

Returning to the last point Sergen (2007) displays the solution to promote the synergy of learning organizations and in the same order Berrio (2013) proposes the knowledge management within organizations that provide excellent customer service.

Meanwhile Alvarez (2014) communes with the existence of participative and transformational leadership by managers; but Münch (2010) includes in this idea the educational leadership.

Perhaps the most compelling reason for building learning organizations is that only now we start understanding the skills that organizations need to possess. Because, for many decades the efforts to build learning organizations were like blind men forward, until they came to know the skills, knowledge and ways for the development of such organizations

Therefore, it is important to distinguish learning organizations from traditional authoritarian ones, it is that in the first ones exist a mastery of certain basic disciplines such as management, evaluation, innovation and planning.

Within the evaluation of the Academic Administration, affects leadership and knowledge management as inspiring to promote systemic thinking; it is difficult to conceive that an organization reach greatness without goals, values and missions.

Therefore, when there is a genuine vision, people excel and learn not because they were ordered, but because they wish. Often the shared vision of an educational center goes around the charisma of the leader or around a crisis that curtails all members of the organization.

So, the practice of shared vision involves skills to configure sharing "future visions" which provide a genuine commitment rather than merit. But getting that, it requires understanding the common needs and perspectives of education members.

To start the Evaluation of Academic Management is important to collect the information in an educational organization throughout tools (questionnaires and interviews) to give base to the measurement process.

So that such instruments are based on facts and contextualized organizational data and thus allow reviewers to determine the quality of the processes and services. Thus, the satisfaction of customers is ensured and the level of commitment of the specifications for a particular activity or process is measured.

Under this view an instrument can be repeatable and extrapolated so that they become an indicator of an evaluation process that seeks to improve quality. Likewise, it requires instruments to integrate criteria and indicators for the Assessment of Academic Management to obtain the relevant value judgments that will help the design of the strategic plan for improving the quality measurement unit.

In fact, Schmelkes (2005) explains that the evaluation begins to diagnose and identify the most important problems in an educational center. So, you should first identify those issues that prevent coverage, enabling the absence of children, the irresponsibility of teachers, the descent of the studies, and low achievement.

As illustrative action, it is explained that to obtain such information is necessary to consult parents, teachers, students and staff that integrates the organization; through surveys or interviews. But these instruments need to have specific indicators established by the evaluator; in this case the Ministry of Public Education (SEP 2007).

Indicators such as the user's knowledge perceive the value provided by the center and involves the development community to strengthen the relationship and thus obtain a satisfactory evaluation and preferential. In fact knowing relevant aspects and opinions that users have about the Education Centre, giving the basis for decision-making and school improvement.

So explaining the criteria Student or User require of some indicators such as: 1) Detection of needs and expectations of the user, 2) user participation in identifying needs, 3) Addressing the needs and expectations by management, 4) detection and user satisfaction, 5) Attention of conflict management, 6) Attention of users per address, 7) integration of parents in user activities.

And these are applied in an integrated survey items for students, but this design can be in various forms. But to clarifying, for this investigation the design was Likert kind; whose value judgments as: 1) totally disagree, 2) agree 3) disagree and 4) strongly disagree

Briefly, some questions are incorporated in the survey, in which the required indicators are highlight for the diagnosis of the School.

Student Questionnaire (Users)

1. Take into account my opinion to improve my teaching.
2. The manager intervenes to solve the issues between students.
3. The teachers encourage us throughout the course.
4. What I learn in the Education Centre is useful to me in my daily life.
5. I am happy with the way my teachers teach.
6. The school grounds are good for my learning.
7. The Education Centre informs my parents about my school achievement.

Moreover, to collect information from teachers and principals, leadership criteria were established; whose indicators are: 1) Resources Organization, 2) Organization of complementary activities and 3) Knowledge of mission, vision and values.

Other criteria included is planning, with indicators of 1) organizing academic meetings, 2) Attention to educational demands, 3) Development of school plans, 4) Distribution of human resources 5) Promotion and 6) accreditation.

An approach which is important to integrate in the development of instruments is the information and knowledge; whose indicators are: 1) attendance of teachers versus group 2) successful practices, 3) innovative actions, 4) participation in organizational structure in the best academies.

Inside the information and knowledge component a criterial called Human Development is taken apart, the one that presents indicators as: 1) Evaluation of teachers and staff, 2) Incentives for merits, 3) promotion of resources, 4) Assistance to the faculty to improve teaching.

So, based on these indicators, some questions for a directive interview are given and a teacher questionnaire which some examples of the items used in such instruments are arising.

It is understood that the questionnaire and interview use open questions and thus to get more information about the organization.

Teacher Questionnaire

1. What are the socioeconomic characteristics of my students?
2. What is the purpose of the academic meetings in the school?
3. What is the teaching style I use to achieve the expected learning?
4. What kind of training is promoted in the school?
5. What are the policy actions that facilitate me as a teacher to get my academic goals?
6. What are the criteria used by the Educational Center for the design of evaluations?
7. What are the obligations, rights and responsibilities that you have as a teacher in the school?

Interview Directive

1. What kind of researches are done to know the demand of current and potential users (students, parents)?
2. What investigations has it been done to structure educational services which are in your organization?
3. What are the mechanisms of assessment used to determine the degree of satisfaction, preferences and commitment of the user regarding the services the school?

4. What strategies do you develop to receive and provide solutions to the complaints from users? (Knowledge, information, advice)?
5. What are the main skills required for leaders?
6. How does it involve in the improvement activities?
7. How do you incorporate in its scholar planning the social, environmental and legal aspects?

Thus, with the instrument it is intended to gather the relevant information which is relevant to the Education Centre and its Academic Management and thus assessing the quality of service.

But every time that a change is intended to be introduced in the organizational culture, there are a number of factors that can become an obstacle, and this becomes real when we try to combine the knowledge management with the academic management.

Since knowledge management is the intangible part of the organization, and when we try to cover this management it may be helpful to try to understand factors, criteria and common indicators which have been detected at the time of implementing management initiatives and which are overcome as the level of maturity of the organizations is increasing.

Understanding the meaning and implications of capturing and sharing knowledge requires time. Increasingly management guidelines related to the roles and evaluation of the jobs include knowledge sharing.

A knowledge-oriented culture will last if it is properly supported. A decisive factor is the real and sustained support from the senior management to communicate and highlight the importance of Academic Management based on Knowledge Management.

Many times the competitive internal environment of educational organizations encourages the knowledge hoarding; and the only possession of knowledge is seen as power and security, accounting for many, it represent the continuity in their job, feeling indispensable.

The values and behaviors of managers can have a big effect on the action of employees to share. Since a good leader needs to lead by example; so if the manager needs the organization to be communicated, he needs to be the first to contact the organization.

Another important point to note about the academic management through knowledge management, is the satisfaction of innovation. People often get more satisfaction to invent something, than to build on the idea of another. The existence of certain functional elements represents a major obstacle to share knowledge.

Some incentives and evaluation systems encourage knowledge retention. Even when they are established with the objective to encourage sharing, they can restrict cultural changes with the possible chilling effect of the recognition system.

There are considerable differences among national, regional, local and social cultures that can take deferential interpretations and behaviors. Trust and communication can be adversely affected if those differences are not well managed.

Knowledge is transmitted through the common language, but a common organizational language is not used to describe experiences and it does not help foster good experiences and practices. So it is not feasible to communicate what someone knows.

On the other hand, educational organizations usually compare them with operating machine and it is thought that changing the process is sufficient to obtain the desired results. But they forget that within the organization there is a structure made up of people, and if they base their knowledge on learning and reflection, the changes are more effective and radical.

In addition, organizations often fail to retain the knowledge gained and lessons learned in the past. People who possessed knowledge leave and don´t let anything documented for further treatment and consultation.

Therefore, growing up in a virtual work environment can help or hinder the Academic Management. Because, while there are technological collaboration tools that can be hugely beneficial for a knowledge management initiative, it is clear that people still learn face to face.

So, some managers seem to believe that the act of giving workers information will ensure the value of your organization. But the value of knowledge is not only in the media access, but in human interactions than the environment provides.

Finally, it is important to understand that knowledge does not grow forever; that is, to grow and evolve the organizational knowledge, the Academic Management and knowledge, it is necessary to forget the traditions formed in an initial thought in the organization, but doing things providing creativity and innovation.

Thus the Academic Management and Knowledge Management influence in managers to plan and continue in the improving processes, designing activities to enhance awareness and increase competitiveness among the faculty and students and finally promoting innovation through the better use of resources and the creation of individual and collective knowledge

REFERENCES

Álvarez, G. I. (2014). *Cultura de evaluación y desafíos para el desarrollo de las instituciones educativas.* México, D. F.: LIMUSA. *S.A. DE, C*, V.

Basañez, A. J. (2012). *Metodología de Evaluación y Gestión del Conocimiento dinámico por procesos utilizando como soporte TIC en el entorno colaborativo de trabajo basado en el modelo de creación de conocimiento de Nonaka-Takeuchi. Tesis Doctoral.* Available January 2015 in www.uco.es/publicaciones

Berrío, H. J. (2013). Knowledge Management as a Basis for Managements of Research Centers in Public Universities.Dimension Business Magazine, 11(1), 116-125.

Brull, A. E. (2010). *El Modelo EFQM de excelencia, Tarragona.* Available at www.Brullalabart.com: http://www.dipta.cat/sites/dipta/files/media/efqm-tema.pdf

Cardoso, E. E. (2006). *Evaluación de la Organización Académico Administrativa de tres programas de Maestría en el campo de la educación con Relación a Parámetros del CONACyT.* Phd Thesis. México: Instituto Politécnico Nacional.

Cardoso, E. R. (2011). *Evaluación de la organización académico administrativa con base en la metodologías de los sistemas suaves: El caso de la licenciatura de turismo.* Retrieved on September 28, 2013, Educare Electronic Journal, ISSN 1409-4258: http://www.redalyc.org/pdf/1941/194118804005.pdf

EFQM. (2003). *E. F. Modelo de excelencia EFQM.* Obtenido de Fundación Europea para la Gestión de la Calidad: http://www.efqm.org: https://www.ucv.es/documentos/calidad/EFQM.pdf

Hernandéz, S. F. (2010). *Metodología de la Investigación, Quinta edición.* México: Mc Graw Hill.

Huergo, J. (2009). *Región 11.educar.ar.* Retrieved on February 21, 2014, Management Process: http://www.region11.edu.ar/publico/portal/doc/biblioteca/los%20procesos%20de%20gestion.pdf

Inciarte, A. M. (2006). *Gestión Académico-Administrativo en la educación básica.* Available at Revista Venezolana de Management ISSN: 1315-9984: http://www.scielo.org.ve/scielo.php?pid=S1315-99842006000200005&script=sci_arttext

Kerschberg, L. (2000). *Knowledge Management: Managing Knowledge Resources for the Intelligent Enterprise*. Chile: XXIII Taller de Ingeniería de Sistemas.

López, A. A. (2010). *Evaluación Formativa.* Retrieved on March 2, 2014, of Teaching English: file:///C:/Users/HP/Downloads/50-255-3-PB.pdf

Martínez, C. y. (2005). *El modelo de excelencia en la EFQM y su aplicación para la mejora de la calidad de los centros educativos.* Available at UNED Faculty of Education, ISSN: 1139-613X: http://revistas.uned.es/index.php/educacionXX1/article

Münch, L. (2013). *Liderazgo y dirección. El liderazgo en el siglo XXI.* México: Trillas.

Münch, L. G. (2010). *Administración y planeación de Instituciones Educativas*. México: Trillas.

Nonaka, I. (1995). *The Knowledge Creating Company*. New York: Oxford University Press.

Quintana, M. C. (2007). Organización y dirección de centros educativos innovadores. El centro educativo versátil. Aravacas, Madrid, Spain: McGraw Hill.

Schmelkes, S. (2005). *La evaluación de los Centros Escolares*. México: Departamento de Inevstigaciones Educativas CINVESTAV - IPN.

SEP. S. d. (2007). *Manual de Autoevaluación de centros escolares para la gestión con calidad, Segunda Edición.* Recovered from: http://www.dgep.sep.gob.mx:8080/autoevaluacion/Autoevaluacion/Descargas/Modelo_Nacional_Doctos/2GUIA_AUTOEVALUACION.pdf: http://www.dgep.sep.gob.mx:8080/autoevaluacion/Autoevaluacion/Descargas/Modelo_Nacional_Doctos/HERRAMIENTAAPOYOAUTOEVALUACION.pdf

Sergen, P. (2007). *La quinta disciplina.* Recuperado el 9 de Febrero de 2014, de Libros de Peter Senge: http://www.alumnos.inf.utfsm.cl/~vpena/ramos/ili260/textos/La_Quinta_Disciplina.pdf

Stufflebeam, D. Y. (2011). *Evaluación Sistemática. Guía Teórica y práctica.* Centro de Publicaciones del M. E. C. y Espasa Libros, S. L. U. .

WordReference. (2015). Retrieved from http://www.wordreference.com/definicion/enciclopedia

Zamboni, H. Y. (2003). *Propuestas innovadoras en la gestión académica.* Argentina: III Coloquio Internacional sobre Gestión Universitaria en América del Sur.

Chapter 13
Evaluation of the Management of Second Language Study Development Program at Secondary School in Mexico

Jorge Mejía Bricaire
Instituto Politécnico Nacional, Mexico

Fernando Briseño Hurtado
Instituto Politécnico Nacional, Mexico

Edgar Oliver Cardoso Espinosa
Instituto Politécnico Nacional, Mexico

Joel García Mendoza
Instituto Politécnico Nacional, Mexico

ABSTRACT

It is currently determining programmes of teaching of foreign language especially in Latin American countries, to go in line with quality policies demanded by international agencies. In Mexico the Second Language Study Development Program (English), represents a new model for the teaching of English as a second language. The present paper aims to propose indicators that allow to evaluate the academic governance of this program at the secondary level, based on the general theory of systems and above all in the pursuit of a quality education; the criteria are: teachers; Teaching-learning processes; Infrastructure support and training materials; certification; Accreditation of the subject index; Learning products; Planning; Students and address. The above demonstrates the need to develop indicators that can serve as a guide for the constant improvement of the management of the programme, and to ensure the students English learning.

INTRODUCTION

Currently, the development of Nations is of utmost importance, especially for the globalized world in which we live, which requires that countries have, every day, different ways of facing the challenges of global economic activities emanating from these. (Cardoso, Ramos and Cerecedo, 2011:58), also within this scenario requires a sense of immediacy and international membership, which should be guaranteed by the education system through the effective learning of English. (Ballestero and Batista, 2007:106)

DOI: 10.4018/978-1-5225-0457-3.ch013

In this regard Ramirez (2011) notes that in this international context, trends and prospective international policy give place to the teaching of foreign languages at an early age, including those issued or endorsed by various agencies, such as UNESCO (2003) and the OECD (2008), has led to a lot of countries are promoting the incorporation of the teaching of English with properly articulated programs to assist in the continuous learning of the language. Specifically, in Latin America this momentum gained greater momentum at the end of the 90's in countries like Argentina, Chile and Colombia, (Tocalli-Beller, 2007; Vera, 2008) cited by Ramirez, (2011).

Mexico of course is not the exception, for this reason, the SEP recognized the need to incorporate the subject of English and in order to implement the various actions that enable the articulation of that module launched national program in basic education (PNIEB) or NEPBE (National English Program in Basic Education); which arise curricula for the three levels of basic education, which were designed based on the alignment and the approval of national and international standards (September, 2009). Then the program changed its name to Second Language Study Development Program (SLSDP) without significant changes.

BACKGROUND OF THE PROGRAMS OF ENGLISH TEACHING IN MEXICO

This brief analysis begins with the study of the 1982 English teaching program, as it is considered that before the implementation of this plan there a program defined with objectives, approach and methodology. Its main objective was the formal language knowledge, in addition to the student should be able to read literature in the studied language (target language), as the literary language was considered superior to the spoken. Order to achieve this objective, students should learn and memorize grammar rules and vocabulary in the target language, in order to translate literary texts.

Then then emerged the programme of study of English within the framework of the National Agreement for the Modernization of Basic Education (NAMBE) in 1993, which was found on the bases of the communicative approach (Communicative Language Teaching), had intended to develop the communicative competence, understood as the capacity of knowing "what to say, who and how to say it in a way appropriate in any given situation" moved the attention of formal knowledge of the language to participation in communicative situations, that is, the communication was its primary purpose (SEP, 2006).

In this sense, the communicative-functional focus on the teaching of second languages and foreign languages starts to be implemented in 1971 in the Council of Europe in order to promote the mobility of University students in those countries. In a first stage, Wilkins (1976), cited in SEP (2009), distinguished synthetic approaches (in which students re-summarize linguistic aspects listed in programs or textbooks) and analytical approaches (in which students discuss presented input functionality).

The synthetic approach involves teaching segmented and separate the elements of a foreign language (grammar, phonology and functions) and considered that the acquisition of the same is a process of gradual accumulation of those parts that are integrated at the time of use to communicate. The analytical approach organizes the aspects of the language teaching taking into account the purposes for which students are learning that language and communicative situations in which to use it.

Thus, communicative-functional approach aimed at teaching language as communication and not to the communication apart from learning of formal aspects of language as system and focusing only on their functional usage examples. The synthetic approach both in the analytical, the emphasis is on knowledge and skills that students should acquire as a result of the processes of teaching and learning.

Then, at the beginning of the eighties, in the world and especially Europe emerge programmes oriented to the process (process-oriented-syllabus) as better as the production-oriented programs.

According to Nunan (1988), this type of program emphasizes learning experiences that facilitate the acquisition of a language. Task-based approach is an option that allows the teacher to implement a process-oriented program.

The approach based on tasks within the framework of the communicative approach uses a program oriented to the process to overcome the problems that the product-oriented programs elicited the teaching of second languages and foreign languages, especially in outside contexts (where students do not have the possibility of being in direct contact with the language learning).

In this task-based approach, edited by N. Prabhu (1984), the focus continues to be the meaning, but are taught the necessary linguistic material through tasks. These tasks are activities in which the students articulate and used different aspects of language (phonological, lexical, grammatical and contextual), the different English (listening, oral, reading comprehension and writing) and different strategies of learning, production and communication.

Taking into account the above, the approach taken by this curriculum design, is the communicative approach based on tasks ("Communicative Task-based Approach") that is implemented through projects ("Project-Work"). These projects will be made from a problematic situation ("Problem-solving situation") to be solved by the students guided by the teacher and taking into account the particular characteristics of each group.

In this approach in which as a result of the comprehensive reform of secondary education RIES was launched the program of study of foreign language, English 2006, which had intended that students participate in social practices of the language and develop the communication in any field.

Then, in the framework of regulations that establishes the third constitutional article, the National Development Plan 2007-2012 and the objectives set out in the Sectoral Programme of Education, The SEP recognized the need to incorporate the subject of English to that Plan, for this purpose and in order to implement the various actions that enable the articulation of English teaching, launched the national English program in basic education (PNIEB, or NEPBE: National English Program in Basic Education), from which are derived the programs of study for the three levels of basic education, which have been produced from the alignment and the approval of national and international standards (September, 2009). Therefore, the program is instituted as the new paradigm in the teaching of the English language from 2009 and 2014 changes name to Second Language Study Development Program (SLSDP).

Thus for the SLSDP, the purpose of the teaching of English for basic education is that students obtain the knowledge required to participate in social practices of language and written with native and non-native speakers of English by means of specific competences (SEP, 2009).

In particular the purpose of the teaching of English in cycle 4 of basic education (1st, 2nd and 3rd) of high school is that students consolidate their dominance of English in basic communicative situations and develop competences specific, characteristic of social practices of the language, communicative situations varied in which understand and produced, in general, oral and written texts on various topics, this within the framework of the implementation of the programme (SEP, 2009).

In this respect is the Table 1, showing the main features of the curriculum for the learning of English in Mexico.

In this way to extent that English programmes have changed and therefore the needs of teacher training this, from the perspective of Ramirez (2011), the problems associated with these changes to programs, also, include those related to knowledge of the program, attitudes and levels of acceptance, the levels

Table 1. Main features of the curriculum for English learning in Mexico

Study Programme	Methodological Approach	Specific Proposal
Program of study of English teaching, 1982, SEP.	(Grammar-translation Method)	The student is able to read literature in the studied language (target language), because the literary language is considered superior to the spoken. To achieve this goal, students must know and memorize grammar rules and vocabulary in the target language, in order to translate literary texts.
English study Program in 1993 NAMBE	(Communicative Language Teaching)	It aims to develop the communicative competence, understood as the capacity of knowing "what, who and how to say it in an appropriate manner, in any given situation," shifts the attention of formal knowledge of the language to participation in communicative situations i.e., communication is its primary purpose.
Integral Reform to Secondary Education (RIES) 2006; Programs of study	(Content-based, Task-based Approaches)	Students participate in social practices of the language and develop communication in any field.
NEPBE; Study programmes 2011	(Content-based, Task-based Approaches)	The purpose of the of English teaching in cycle 4 of basic education (1 St, 2nd, and 3rd high school) is that students consolidate their dominance of English in basic communicative situations and develop competences specific, characteristic of social practices of the language, communicative situations varied in which understand and produced, in general, oral and written texts on various topics

Source: Own preparation from SEP, (2006)

of consistency between discourse and practice coverage, financing, infrastructure, bonding with school principals, as well as the follow-up programs; situations that lead to the revision of the needs created for teachers from these challenges.

IMPORTANCE OF KNOWLEDGE MANAGEMENT AND INTELLECTUAL CAPITAL IN ENGLISH AS A SECOND LANGUAGE ACQUISITION

The knowledge management is an emerging discipline that it will be affirming with the emergence of new paradigms in national and international economic systems. Changing technological paradigms that characterize it, changes in the way to manage organizations and systems, specifically the so-called intangible assets that form the intellectual capital; thus, focusing on the ability to innovate and create faster value based on knowledge and its quick update in various fields through learning. (Peluffo and Catalán, 2002:7-8)

So, these distinctive features of the management of the knowledge, can generate emerging actions for the systematization of the actions to be able to direct to the fulfillment of the targets intellectuals, the dissemination of knowledge, research and the design of new programs at educational institutions.

In this way, one of the most important aspects to explain the processes of creative value of the organizations, which constitute today's society and knowledge economy, has been, without a doubt, the proposal of the concept of Intellectual Capital, as expression of the wealth possessed by that which is not visible or tangible but that, however, there is as Although the financial States have not it evaluated and presented under the conventional principles of accounting information, its impact on the creation of value for the Organization of reference and for the economic system as a whole is evident. (Bueno, 2002:9)

These intellectual resources, make it necessary to take into account the components of the system (human capital, material capital and relational capital) intellectual to lead educational and programs to the institution towards the achievement of the objectives. In the case of second language acquisition programs, these components are priority for the proper management of knowledge and therefore academic.

The reason is justified in pertinent reasons such as social, financial and educational; on one hand, a) proper management of human capital, allows better, certified teachers that guarantee an adequate methodology in language teaching; (b) the proper management of material capital allows to obtain resources for obtaining infrastructure and ICT that are ideal for learning; (c) the management of relational capital allows the program to have a social impact and obey the same target which is the learning of the English.

For Bueno, in 2012, these aspects which, in addition, will help the organizations themselves and system comprising them can design and deploy science policy and research with higher doses of efficiency plans, seeking a balance and systemic fairness that will facilitate the good attainment of possible strategies related to development and excellence of the capacity of the educational programs of the above-mentioned institutions.

UNDERSTANDING THE CHALLENGES: A CASE

Teaching English in Mexico for many years has had more points of divergence than convergence; This in turn characterized by Government enthusiasm against the policies of international banks, multinational corporations and governing bodies of the phenomenon of globalization causing an abrupt change and constant programs of study, lack of certified language professionals, the weak knowledge of official study programmes by the teachers, lacking material resources institutions as well as a crowded public education; they constitute the framework of a little encouraging picture in the teaching and learning of English as a second language in our country.

In order to investigate the problems in the teaching of English before the change of program of study, was conducted an investigation with the aim of evaluating the perceptions of teachers with regard to the SLSDP, the theoretical foundation, evaluation and its challenges in the fulfilment of the objectives of the pilot program in a school zone in the State of Mexico with the purpose of generating proposals for improvements in the strategic operation of the plan.

The methodology of the study was evaluation because it focused to assess the perceptions of teachers in the secondary level; also tried a non-experimental research because the variables are not manipulated since they had already happened, by what inferences about relationships were performed without intervention or direct influence in order to describe its behavior in its natural context for further analysis (Hernández, *et al.* 2005).

Then, a cross-sectional design was carried out since the data were collected in a single moment of time; in December 2012. The instrument that was applied was a questionnaire, which was composed of the following dimensions based on the composition of the PNIEB: 1) General data; 2) regulatory framework; 3) purposes; 4) basis and teaching approach; 5) curriculum standards; 6) the learning organization; 7) assessment; 8) teaching materials; 9) teaching guidelines; 10) characteristics of English teaching.

This questionnaire was designed on a measure of scale frequently Likert-type of five degrees which allowed to measure the opinions of teachers; This then, because it is a procedure that is focused to determine differences in degree or intensity with respect to the object of study which in this case is the subject of English within the framework of the implementation of the SLSDP. The main conclusions were reached with the research described, were as follows:

The teaching staff has significant profile of specialization in the field of language, however in the formation of the Faculty in the graduate is still low, so it is necessary for teachers to adopt a vertical professional language teaching-oriented.

Meanwhile teachers should be familiar with the Organization of the contents of teaching and learning outcomes expected develop understanding, specifically the oral and written expression, in addition that, teachers should be aware of the Organization of the teaching contents and expected learning outcomes which are oriented to develop relevant attitudes towards the language and communication within the framework of the implementation of the programme in the classroom, directly with the students.

In relation to the assessment, teachers should know the regulations, as well as the establishment of criteria and indicators to carry out rigorous ongoing evaluation as contemplates it the curricula of English. The results described above lead to assert that the issue of the functioning of the programme and the teaching of English in basic education is based on the infrastructure and the design of schools, the lack of sufficient material to carry out the process of teaching-learning in the classroom, as well as the needs of teacher training which must be oriented to the domain of the contents of the language, towards the certification of language teachers, in the domain of pedagogy and forms of education.

These results coincide with the findings of research reports carried out by Ramírez Pamplón and Cota, (2011); Mejía, Cardoso & Briseño (2013); Fierro, Martinez and Cordero, (2014); Mejía, et al., (2014) where the identification of several problems in the teaching of English, are focused on two basic dimensions: the training of teachers and updating needs; and the conditions of infrastructure and conditions of the medium for the educational practice and learning of the students at the basic level.

The problems associated with these basic components, include those related to the knowledge of the program, the attitudes and levels of acceptance, the levels of consistency between discourse and practices of teachers, coverage, financing, infrastructure, bonding with school principals, as well as the follow-up programs; situations that lead to the revision of the needs created for teachers from these challenges.

GENERAL SYSTEMS THEORY APPLIED TO EDUCATION FIELD

Nowadays the systemic approach is so common that it is even part of the activities and everyday processes of human beings. Today's world is a society composed of organizations, which are made by individuals, as well as several subsystems that work in a coordinated manner, so that we can say that man himself is a system which is immersed in other systems, in which is variously interrelated.

So it is said that systems are a set of elements interrelated each other allowing to obtain a result or achieve several objectives. So these systems have as features, objectivity and all, goals or purposes in which you want to get.

General systems theory or theory of systems (TGS) is an effort to study intertransdisciplinario that tries to find the common properties to entities which arise in all levels of reality, but are traditionally object from different academic disciplines. Its origin is attributed to the Austrian biologist Ludwig von Bertalanffy, who coined the name in the middle of the 20th century.

The GST seeks to discover isomorphisms[1] at different levels of reality that allow:

- Use the same terms and concepts to describe essential features of very different real systems; and find general laws applicable to the understanding of their dynamics.
- First, encourage the formalization of the descriptions of reality; then, allow modelling of the interpretations that are made from it.
- Facilitate theoretical development in fields in which it is difficult to abstraction of the object; or by its complexity, its historicity, i.e. by its unique character. Historical systems are equipped with memory, and no one can understand them without knowing and take into account your particular trajectory in time (Johansen, 1982).
- Overcome the opposition between the two approaches to knowledge of the reality: the analytical, based on reduction and the systemic operations, based on the composition.

The systems approach considers the Organization as an entity that is in constant interaction with their environment. He also points out the existence of diverse relationships between internal components called subsystems. Its main representatives are Chester Barnard, Herbert Simon and George Homans.

Thus, this theory conceptualizes the Organization as a system or a whole unit compound two or more interdependent subsystems with certain limits associated with a supra-system which is the environment. Based on the above, presents a substantial difference with the traditional organization theory since it uses a highly structured closed system approach; While systems, conceptualizes it as an entity open to the requirements of the environment.

Based on Figure 1, is that the Organization as open system requires inputs that it uses for the production of a good or generation of a service, which are the first outings, is also needed to meet the needs of its members.

Figure 1. Inputs and outputs of an organization
Source: Rodríguez, J. (2003). Introducción a la administración con enfoque de sistemas, p. 447.

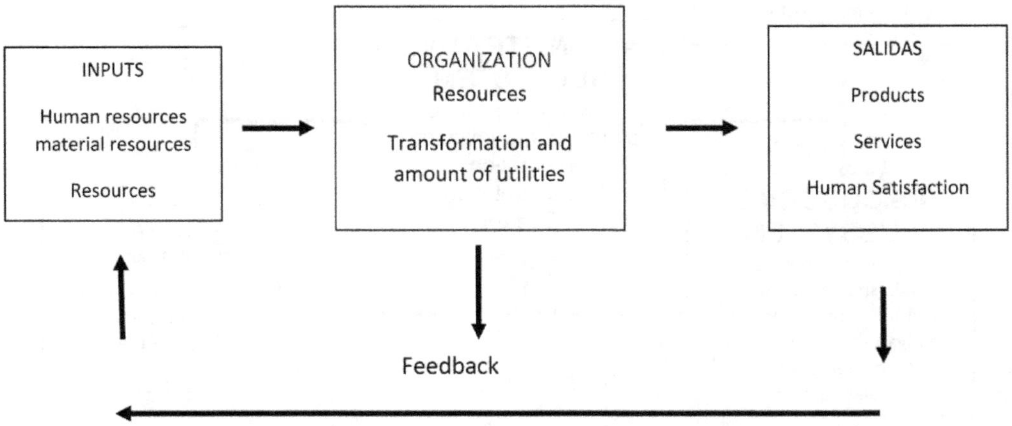

Specifically, an organization is a system integrated open socio-technical of several major subsystems: objectives and values, technical, psycho-social, structural and administrative as shown in Figure No. 2 (Kast and Rosenzweig, 2002)

From Figure 2, is that the subsystem's objectives and values makes reference to the purposes which should reach an organization. The technical subsystem focuses on the knowledge, techniques and infrastructure required for the performance of tasks.

For his part, psychosocial subsystem is made up of individuals and groups in interaction, so it covers the individual behavior, motivation, the relationship of function and position, groups and cooperation dynamics. It also examines the feelings, values, attitudes, expectations and aspirations of the people.

Meanwhile, the structural subsystem is responsible for the ways in which tasks or activities of the Organization are split (differentiation) and are coordinated (integration). That is why it considers statutes and manuals of the Organization to designate the descriptions of position and position, as well as the rules and procedures that can be applied.

Finally, the administrative subsystem covers the Organization to relate to their environment, set objectives, develop strategic and operational plans, design the structure and establish control processes. In this way, this component is the development of phases of the administrative process: planning, organization, implementation, monitoring and evaluation.

Therefore, for the systems approach an organization is made up of these five components, which are mutually interrelated and, if working properly, it is said that the organization is in equilibrium, i.e. achieved its objectives and goals both for members and for the specific environment in which it operates. On the other hand, if one or more of these components do not perform their tasks or activities in

Figure 2. The subsystems of an organization
Source: Kast, Fremont and Rosenzwig, James (2002). Administración en las organizaciones, p. 120.

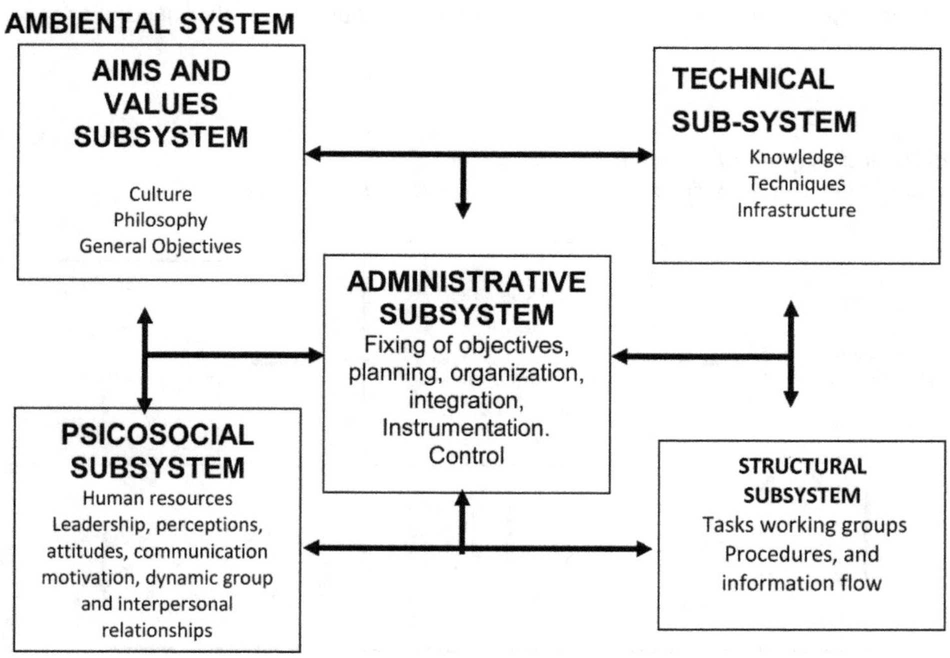

an appropriate manner, the Organization enters an imbalance, by which arise problems which hinder the achievement of the goals and objectives.

In relation to the environment, the systems approach considers the existence of two forms of organization: the lineal-mechanic and the organic - adaptable is shown in Table 2.

In this sense, a mechanic-lineal organization has an extremely rigid behavior, based on a routinization of activities and under the features of theories of science, classical, and bureaucratic management. Conversely, an organic – adaptable organization possesses a dynamic performance based on the skills and attitudes of its members, its tasks and activities are based on innovation and decisions are conducted by consensus, so it takes up the contributions of the behavioral sciences.

The educational environment exerts a great influence on the organization, to provide you with the basic element: the human resource, which presents a specific profile in terms of abilities and skills that were learned during the years of schooling. The legal aspect set of laws and rules that define the field of action of the same, in terms of what it can plan and develop. The economic component designates the conditions of the market or markets in which is located the organism from certain basic indicators such as inflation, exchange rate, interest rate, among others. As well as the behavior of the Government authorities in terms of economic policy.

EVALUATION OF THE INSTITUTIONAL ACADEMIC MANAGEMENT OF THE PFESL PROPOSAL

Educational research reports referred to the problems of the teaching of English in Mexico, countries of Latin America, Spain and other parts of the world, as well as the described research experience and which is considered particularly relevant for the creation of this work, they can pose a set of criteria and indicators to assess the academic governance of the PNIEB and thus verify if actually the latter can guarantee satisfactory levels of quality in the teaching of English.

Precisely, the implementation of an evaluation that contributes to the constant improvement of the institutional academic administration of such a program, allow the continuation of the quality policy adopted by Mexico and countries in the region of Latin America and the Caribbean, in respect of this concept Alvarez and Topete (2004:17) mentioned to Muñoz Izquierda (1988) and the latter argues that the quality of education term is associated with the capacity of educational institutions how individuals

Table 2. Characteristics of a mechanic-lineal organization and one organic - adaptable

Mechanic-Lineal	Organic – Adaptable
1. The environment is relatively stable and secure.	1. The environment is relatively uncertain and unstable.
2. The objectives are well defined and maintained.	2. The objectives are not well defined and they are not maintained.
3. Technology is relatively stable and uniform.	3. Technology is relatively dynamic.
4. There are routine activities and productivity is the primary objective.	4. - -There are various non-routine activities in which innovation and creativity are important.
5. - Decision-making is programmable and the coordination and control processes tend to allow a structured strictly hierarchical system.	5. - Using heuristic processes of decision-making, control and coordination are produced by reciprocal adjustments. The system is more flexible and less hierarchical.

Source: Kast, Fremont and Rosenzweig, (2002). *Administración en las organizaciones*, p. 122-123.

formed in her womb; to fulfill the requirements of the economic, political and social development of the community to which they are integrated.

The search for improvement in the management institutional academic, in this case, part of the identification of the factors that lead to the achievement of the effective learning of English in the level, in terms of institutional conditions and context, as well as the inputs and processes that favour the achievement of the expected results. Currently the quality of study programmes revolves around how to carry out this process of evaluation of a more consistent and effective way with the learning needs of the students and based on the economic, political and cultural demands of the society, as well as of the productive sector and services (Cardoso and Cerecedo, 2011: 76). In this regard, the recommendations proposed are the following:

1. The program must have a basic outline of planning, however with a more flexible option; This so that in each school zone is determined the scope of the purpose itself, according to the needs of each school zone and in particular with the infrastructure that each school has, in order to ensure access and inclusion with equity and social responsibility of students of primary and secondary
2. It is necessary to provide follow-up on the progress of each student, so not only should give an account of the work with the program only with evidence as so far have been carried out, but rather should focus evaluation in learning the four skills, using tests that have a basic scheme, 100% editable and adjustable to the needs of each school zone adapted to each Center's material infrastructure, and, finally, carried concentrated out of these evaluations, carry out the analysis, observe the areas showing weakness and feedback these. So each generation increase their skills and properly develop the social practice of the language required.
3. The training needs of teachers and recruitment of those new entrants; This according to the application of the PNIEB, must be oriented to the domain of the contents of the language, towards the international certification of language teachers (TOEFEL, FIRST CERTIFICATE) in the domain of pedagogy and of forms of Education Teaching Knowledge Test (TKT), as well as also the knowledge of adolescents or with subjects who work with.
4. Currently the organization of each State coordination appears to be efficient, however, coordinators, as well as the managers of the programme in each regional department or school zone of the country, must have a certain degree of specialization and organizational knowledge, course of English language also. Create an incentive program, as well as provide budget and freedom to exercise with reference to the needs of each school is preponderant.

In this way in Table 3 and Table 4, the general criteria for this assessment is taken from the models proposed by Alvarez and Topete (2004); Cardoso and Cerecedo (2011), in turn based on the general theory of systems which can be seen in Figure 3, it should be noted that the order in which these are presented does not imply any ranking, because it is considered that they are both relevant and necessary. The indicators are related to the following criterio: 1) teachers; 2) teaching-learning processes; (3) infrastructure support and training materials; (4) certification; (5) accreditation of the subject index; 6) 7 learning products) planning; 8) students and 9) management.

Table 3. Indicators to assess the institutional academic management of the SLSDP

Teachers	Teaching-Learning Process	Infrastructure Support and Training Materials	Certification	Accreditation of the Subject Index
• Proportion of teachers with postgraduate studies: master and doctorate. • Proportion of teachers with permanent appointment. • Years of service in the system. • Number of academic products made by individual teachers. •Number of certifications. •Number of professors with the profile that teaches English.	• Proportion of students per course achieved the satisfactory level of learning. • Percentage of the course objectives achieved percentage of the learning goals of the curriculum by students. • Number of students per teacher in each course • Proportion of groups served by teacher. • Number of different subjects that each teacher teaches. • Number of hours for tutoring. • Existence of graduate's studies.	• Number of classrooms for the teaching of the subject of English. • Number of computers in the computer center. • Proportion of computers with internet access. • Proportion of computers with proper maintenance. • Number of audiovisual resources • Proportion of the resources of audiovisual support in optimal conditions. • Number of titles in English available to the library in the field of education. • Percentage of the acquis which is updated. • Percentage of authentic materials. • Percentage of the acquis which is updated to the nature of the program.	• Number of teachers who obtain certification PET. • Number of teachers who obtain certification TOEFEL. • Number of teachers who get the FIRST CERTIFICATE OF ENGLISH. • Time for obtaining the certification • Secondary students who obtain certification KET at the end of the level.	• Number of students who pass the course • General average obtained by the students in the subject of English • Number of students who do not certify the subject.

Source: Own preparation

Table 4. Indicators to assess the institutional academic management of the SLSDP

Learning Products	Planning	Students	Management
•Number of products obtained by students. • Number of students getting the basic skills • Number of presentations of the work carried out during the implementation of the different units.	• Number of annual planning delivered by teachers. • Number of weekly planning delivered by teachers. • Percentage of effectiveness of compliance activities in this plan	• Number of students. •Number of students during the session. •Number of students reaching a certification • Age of adolescents	• Existence of a management team that develops a system of strategic leadership. • Existence of a management team that spreads and applies the values of the institution and the program. • Existence of a management team that fulfills its social responsibility. • Existence of short and medium-term action plans that allow the achievement of the objectives of the programme. • Proportion of options of training, updating and training for teachers in the field of the teaching of a second language.

Source: Own preparation

Figure 3. Input, process and output of Second Language Study Development Program
Source: Own preparation from Cardoso, E. and Cerecedo, M. (2011:78)

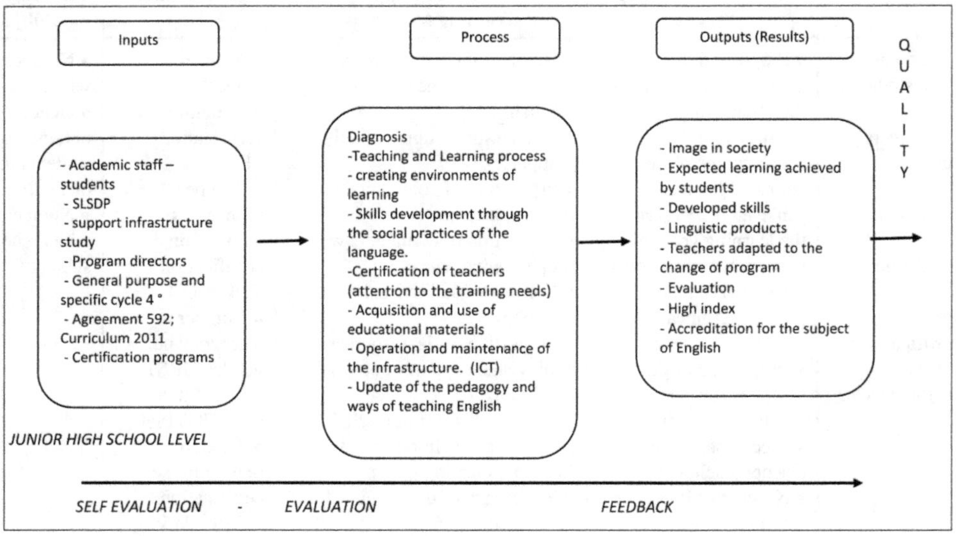

CONCLUSION

In the international context, trends and prospective international policy give place to the teaching of foreign languages at an early age, this endorsed by international organizations, by this SEP recognized need to incorporate various actions that enable the articulation of this subject, by such reason is put into operation the national program of English in basic education.

In addition an investigation carried out in 2012, made it clear that the issue of the functioning of the programme and the teaching of English in secondary education is depending on the infrastructure and the design of schools, the lack of sufficient material to carry out the process of teaching-learning in the classroom, as well as the needs of teacher training which must be oriented to the domain of the contents of the language towards certification of language teachers, in the domain of pedagogy and forms of education, and also in the knowledge of adolescents or with the subjects with whom they work, so necessary that teachers have a pedagogical update suitable to create conducive learning environments for teaching this language.

Must be the good institutional academic management grants legitimacy and gives compliance objectives of achieving a quality education and to achieve it is essential an assessment tool that will allow continuous improvement of the program. Hence the need that each evaluation is promoted by the principals in each institution, but with the participation of the different, supervisors and teachers involving different regional coordination of the programme.

REFERENCES

Álvarez, I., & Topete, C. (2004). Búsqueda de la calidad en la educación básica. Conceptos básicos, criterios de evaluación y estrategia de gestión. *Latin American Journal of Educational Studies, 34*(3), 11-36. Available at http://www.redalyc.org/articulo.oa?id=27034302

Ballestero, C., & Batista, J. (2007). Evaluación de la enseñanza del inglés con fines específicos en educación superior. *Omnia, 13*(1), 105-129. Available at http://www.redalyc.org/articulo.oa?id=73713106

Bueno, E. (Ed.). (2002). *Gestión del Conocimiento en Universidades y Organismos Públicos de Investigación*. Spain: Universidad Autónoma de Madrid.

Cardoso, E., & Cerecedo, M. (2011). Propuesta de indicadores para evaluar la calidad de un programa de posgrado en Educación. *Electronic Journal of Educational Research, 13*(2), 68-82. Available at http://redie.uabc.mx/vol13no2/contenido-cardosocerecedo.html

Cardoso, E., Ramos, J., & Cerecedo, M. (2011). Evaluación de la organización académico administrativa con base en la metodología de los sistemas suaves: El caso de la licenciatura en turismo. *Electronic Journal Educare, 15*(1), 57-78. Available at http://www.redalyc.org/articulo.oa?id=194118804005

Fierro, L., Martínez, L., & Hernández, G. (2014). La formación del profesor de inglés en las escuelas primarias públicas. *Electronic Journal educ@upn.mx*, 16.

Hernández, R., Fernández, C., & Baptista, P. (2006). *Metodología de la investigación*. México: Mc Graw Hill, Interamericana.

Johansen, O. (1982). *Introducción a la teoría general de sistemas*. México: Limusa.

Kast, E., Fremont, E., & James, E. (2003). *Administración de las organizaciones enfoque de sistemas y contingencias*. México: Mc Graw Hill.

Mejía, J., Briseño, F., & Cardoso, E. (2013). *Evaluación de las Percepciones de los docentes con respecto al Programa Nacional de Inglés en la Educación Básica.* Ponencia publicada en la memoria electrónica del XII Congreso Nacional de Investigación Educativa, p. 7.

Mejía, J., Cardoso, E., Briseño, F., & García, J. (2014). Propuesta de criterios e indicadores para la evaluación de la gestión académica institucional del Programa Nacional de Inglés en la Educación Básica (PNIEB) en el nivel secundaria. Ponencia publicada en la memoria electrónica del II Congreso Internacional de Educación Evaluación. México: Universidad Autónoma de Tlaxcala-UNAM.

Nunan, D. (1988). *Syllabus Design*. Oxford, UK: OUP.

Organización para la Cooperación y el Desarrollo Económico. (2008). *Globalization and Linguistic Competencies. Responding to Diversity in Language Environments*. Available at http://www.oecd.org/dataoecd/55/15/41363216.pdf

Peluffo, M. & Catalán, E. (2002). *Introducción a la gestión del conocimiento y su aplicación al sector público*. Santiago de Chile: CEPAL-CECLAC.

Prabhu, N. (1984). Procedural Syllabuses. In T.E. Reed (Ed.), Trends in Language Syllabus Design. Singapore University Press/RELC.

Ramírez, J., Pamplón, E., & Cota, S. (2012). Problemática de la enseñanza del inglés en las primarias públicas de México. *Iberoamerican Journal of Education*, *2*(60). Available at http://www.rieoei.org/deloslectores/5020Ramirez.pdf

Rodríguez, J. (2003). *Introducción a la administración con enfoque de sistemas*. México: ECAFSA.

SEP. (2006). *Plan de estudios México*. SEP.

SEP. (2007). *Programa Sectorial de Educación*. SEP.

SEP. (2009). *Programa Nacional de inglés en la Educación Básica*. SEP.

SEP. (2011). *Plan de estudios*. SEP.

United Nations Educational, Scientific And Cultural Organization. (2003). Education in a Multilingual World. París: UNESCO.

KEY TERMS AND DEFINITIONS

Educational Competence: Complex development processes which are suitable in set contexts, by integrating different knowledge (knowing how to be, knowing how to do, knowing to know, knowing to live with), in order to do activities and/or solve problems with a sense of challenge, motivation, flexibility, creativity, understanding and undertaking, within an approach of meta-cognitive thinking, ongoing improvement and ethical commitment, which are aimed at contributing to personal development, the construction and strengthening of the social networking, the continuous search of a sustainable economic and business development, and the care and protection of the environment and the living organisms.

Effectiveness: Criteria focuses on determining the scope of objectives and goals of a program.

Efficiency: Criteria focused on determining the distribution of resources to operate a program.

Knowledge: Is an intangible possession of every human being, it is acquired through experience or education.

Program: Instrument curriculum where teaching and learning activities, allowing scholars to guide their practice with regard to the objectives to be achieved, are organized to develop skills in students based on a set of content, resources and facilities.

ENDNOTE

1 Isomorphism: (from the Greek iso-morphs: Similarly) is intended to capture the idea of having the same structure.

Compilation of References

Aboites, H. (2012). *La medida de una nación. Los primeros años de la evaluación en México.* México: UAM, CLACSO, ITACA.

Acevedo, A., Linares, C., & Cachay, O. (2009). La economía y la sociedad del conocimiento. Hacia la tercera revolución: *La información*. Available at http://www.redalyc.org/articulo.oa?id=81620150002

Aguerrondo, I. (2009). La escuela inteligente en el marco de la gestión del conocimiento. *Innovación Educativa*. Available at http://www.redalyc.org/articulo.oa?id=179414895004

Alavi, M., & Leidner, D. (2001). Knowledge Management and Knowledge Management Systems: Conceptual Foundations and Research Issues. *Management Information Systems Quarterly*, *25*(1), 107–136. doi:10.2307/3250961

Alcantara, A., & Zorrilla, J. (2010). Globalización y educación media superior en México. En busca de la pertinencia curricular. *Perfiles educativos*. Available at http://www.redalyc.org/pdf/132/13211845003.pdf

Al-Fahim, M. (2006). *From rags to riches: A story of Abu Dhabi*. London: London Centre of Arab Studies.

Alsina, C. (2000). L'entrevista. *Biec*, *31*, 8–9.

Álvarez, I., & Topete, C. (2004). Búsqueda de la calidad en la educación básica. Conceptos básicos, criterios de evaluación y estrategia de gestión. *Latin American Journal of Educational Studies, 34*(3), 11-36. Available at http://www.redalyc.org/articulo.oa?id=27034302

Alvarez, R., & Sandoval, J. (2005). La cooperación inter-universitaria entre México y Venezuela para el estudio de la globalización, la integración y las relaciones fronterizas: un balance de 10 años. *Aldea Mundo*. Available at http://www.redalyc.org/articulo.oa?id=54301808

Álvarez, G. I. (2014). *Cultura de evaluación y desafíos para el desarrollo de las instituciones educativas.* México, D. F.: LIMUSA. *S.A. DE, C,* V.

Álvarez, I., & Romay, M. (2015). *Cultura de evaluación y desafíos para el desarrollo de las instituciones educativas.* México: Limusa.

Alvavi, M. (2001). Review: Knowledge management and knowledge management systems: conceptual foundations and research issues. *MIS Journal Quarterly, 38*(3).

Amaya, K., Iriarte, M., & Perozo, D. (2006). Gestión del conocimiento como capacidad interna. *Telos*. Available at http://www.redalyc.org/articulo.oa?id=99318557007

Andersen, A. (1999). *Knowledge Management Assessment*. KMAT.

Anderson, D., & Gallini, N. (1998). *Competition policy and intellectual property rights in the know-ledge based economy.* Calgary: University of Calgary Press.

Antonacopoulou, E. P., & Gabriel, Y. (2001). Emotion, learning and organizational change: Towards an integration of psychoanalytic and other perspectives. *Journal of Organizational Change, 14*(5), 435–451. doi:10.1108/EUM0000000005874

ANUIES. (2000). *La educación superior en el siglo XXI.* Mexico: ANUIES.

Aparicio, P. (2009). Educación y jóvenes en contextos de desigualdad socioeconómica. *Tendencias y perspectivas en América.* Available at http://www.redalyc.org/articulo.oa?id=275019727012

Archibald, R. B., & Feldman, D. H. (2011, June 14). What bubble? *Inside Higher Ed.* Retrieved from www.insidehighered.com

Argyris, C., & SchÖn, D. A. (1978). *Organizational learning: A theory of action perspective.* Reading, MA: Addison-Wesley.

Armenta, N. G., Pacheco, C. C., & Pineda, E. D. (2008). Factores económicos que intervienen en el desempeño académico de los estudiantes universitarios de la Facultad de Ciencias Humanas de la Universidad autónoma de Baja California. *Revista IIPSI, 11*(1), 153-165. Recuperado de http://sisbib.unmsm.edu.pe/bvrevistas/investigacion_psicologia/v11_ n1/pdf/a10.pdf

Arnold, N. W., & Crawford, E. R. (2014). Metaphors of leadership and spatialized practice. *International Journal of Leadership in Education: Theory and Practice, 17*(3), 257–285. doi:10.1080/13603124.2013.835449

Arras, A., Hernández, O., & López, J. (2012). *Redes y confianza: dimensiones del capital social en las microempresas rurales en Chihuahua, México.* Available at http://www.scielo.org.mx/scielo.php?script=sci_arttext&pid=S018506362012000200003&lng=es&nrm=iso

Ashton, E. (1997). Extending the scope of metaphor: An examination of definitions of old and new and their significance for education. *Educational Studies, 23*(2), 195–208. doi:10.1080/0305569970230204

Badri, M., & Al Khaili, M. (2014). Migration of P–12 education from its current state to one of high quality: The aspirations of Abu Dhabi. *Policy Futures in Education, 12*(2), 200–220. doi:10.2304/pfie.2014.12.2.200

Ballestero, C., & Batista, J. (2007). Evaluación de la enseñanza del inglés con fines específicos en educación superior. *Omnia, 13*(1), 105-129. Available at http://www.redalyc.org/articulo.oa?id=73713106

Barbera, E., & Molero, C. (1996), Motivación social. In Psicología de la motivación. Madrid: síntesis.

Barrera, J. Y. (2011). Teorías del Desarrollo Económico. In Contribuciones a la Economía, Noviembre 2011. Universidad de Pinar del Río. Cuba.

Basañez, A. J. (2012). *Metodología de Evaluación y Gestión del Conocimiento dinámico por procesos utilizando como soporte TIC en el entorno colaborativo de trabajo basado en el modelo de creación de conocimiento de Nonaka-Takeuchi. Tesis Doctoral.* Available January 2015 in www.uco.es/publicaciones

Berger, P., & Luckmann, T. (1966). *The social construction of reality.* Penguin.

Berrío, H. J. (2013). Knowledge Management as a Basis for Managements of Research Centers in Public Universities. Dimension Business Magazine, 11(1), 116-125.

Berverley, C. (agosto, 2002). Educación y mercado del trabajo en América Latina, frente a la globalización. *Revista de la CEPAL,* 77, 123-141. Recuperado de http://www.eclac.org/ publicaciones/xml/9/19289/lcg2180e_Carlson.pdf

Biografias. (n.d.). Available at www.biografiasyvida.com/biografia/n/nyerere.htm

Blunt, P. (1991). Organization, culture and development. *International Journal of Human Resource Management*, *2*(1), 55–71. doi:10.1080/09585199100000051

Bolman, L. G., & Deal, T. E. (2003). *Reframing organizations – artistry, choice, and leadership* (3rd ed.). San Francisco, CA: Jossey Bass.

Borroto, J. (2007). La gestión del conocimiento en la nueva economía. Algunos apuntes. *Ciencia en su PC*. Available at http://www.redalyc.org/articulo.oa?id=181315033004

Boyce, M. (1995). Collective centering and collective sense-making in the stories and storytelling of one organization. *Organization Studies*, *16*(1), 107–137. doi:10.1177/017084069501600106

Briceño, G. (2012). Ser estudiante en la sociedad de la información y el conocimiento: la escuela y sus actores ante el cambio cultural. *Sinéctica*. Avalilable at http://www.scielo.org.mx/scielo.php?script=sci_arttext&pid=S1665-109X2012000100004&lng=es&nrm=iso&tlng=es

Briseño, F., Cardoso, E. O. & Mejía, J. (2014). Diagnóstico de oportunidades escolares de egresados y egresadas del nivel medio superior del municipio de Tlalnepantla del estado de México. *Revista Electrónica Educare, 18*(2), 141-157. Recuperado de10.15359/ree.18-2.7

Brull, A. E. (2010). *El Modelo EFQM de excelencia, Tarragona*. Available at www.Brullalabart.com: http://www.dipta.cat/sites/dipta/files/media/efqm-tema.pdf

Bueno, E. (Ed.). (2002). *Gestión del Conocimiento en Universidades y Organismos Públicos de Investigación*. Spain: Universidad Autónoma de Madrid.

Bueno, J. A., & Castañedo, C. (1998). *Psicología de la educación aplicada*. Madrid: CCS.

Buitrago, D. Y. (2006). *Repository. UdeRosario*. Obtenido de La gestión del conocimiento. Documento No. 29. Available at http://repository.urosario.edu.co/bitstream/handle/10336/1207/BI%2029.pdf?sequence=1

Bunc, M. (1992). Global economy in the age of science-based knowledge. New York: UNITAR.

Burden-Leahy, S. (2009). Globalization and education in the postcolonial world: The conundrum of the higher education system of the United Arab Emirates. *Comparative Education*, *45*(4), 525–544. doi:10.1080/03050060903391578

Burkle, M., & Robles, H. (2004). *Hacia la construcción de indicadores del conocimiento: Una perspectiva desde el desarrollo*. Retrieved from www.cibersociedad.net

Burnes, B. (2014). *Managing change* (6th ed.). Harlow: Pearson.

Burns, J. M. (1978). *Leadership*. New York, NY: Harper & Row.

Burrell, W. G., & Morgan, G. (1979). *Sociological paradigms and organizational analysis*. London: Heinemann.

Butcher, D., & Atkinson, S. (2001). Stealth, secrecy and subversion: The language of change management. *Journal of Organizational Change Management*, *14*(6), 554–569. doi:10.1108/EUM0000000006142

Cabrera, A. (2009). América Latina y la globalización. *Opinión Jurídica*. Available at http://www.redalyc.org/articulo.oa?id=94512330003

Cameron, E., & Green, M. (2009). *Making sense of change management* (2nd ed.). Philadelphia, PA: Kogan Page.

Camisón, C., Fabra, M., & Monfort, V. (2011). *La fidelidad del turista al destino en el caso español.* Spain: Estudios turísticos.

Cañedo, T., & Figueroa, A. (2013). La práctica docente en educación superior: una mirada hacia su complejidad. *Sinéctica.* Available at http://www.scielo.org.mx/scielo.php?script=sci_arttext&pid=S1665-109X2013000200004&lng=es&nrm=iso

Cañedo, R. (2008). *Educación superior y mercado de trabajo: El caso de los egresados de la Universidad Autónoma de Guerrero. (Tesis doctoral inédita).* San José, Costa Rica: Universidad de Costa Rica.

Cardoso, E. E. (2006). *Evaluación de la Organización Académico Administrativa de tres programas de Maestría en el campo de la educación con Relación a Parámetros del CONACyT.* Phd Thesis. México: Instituto Politécnico Nacional.

Cardoso, E. R. (2011). *Evaluación de la organización académico administrativa con base en la metodologías de los sistemas suaves: El caso de la licenciatura de turismo.* Retrieved on September 28, 2013, Educare Electronic Journal, ISSN 1409-4258: http://www.redalyc.org/pdf/1941/194118804005.pdf

Cardoso, E., & Cerecedo, M. (2011). Propuesta de indicadores para evaluar la calidad de un programa de posgrado en Educación. *Electronic Journal of Educational Research, 13*(2), 68-82. Available at http://redie.uabc.mx/vol13no2/contenido-cardosocerecedo.html

Cardoso, E., Ramos, J., & Cerecedo, M. (2011). Evaluación de la organización académico administrativa con base en la metodología de los sistemas suaves: El caso de la licenciatura en turismo. *Electronic Journal Educare, 15*(1), 57-78. Available at http://www.redalyc.org/articulo.oa?id=194118804005

Cardoso, E., & Cerecedo, M. (2011). Propuesta de Indicadores para Evaluar la Calidad de un Programa de Posgrado en Educación. *Revista Electrónica de Investigación Educativa, 13*(2), 68–82.

Carrillo, J. (2004). Desarrollo basado en el Conocimiento. In *Transferencia. Año. 17. Núm. 65. Enero 2004.* Mexico: Instituto Tecnológico de Monterrey.

Castells, M. (2006). The Network Society: from Knowledge to Policy. Center for Transatlantic Relations. Center for Transatlantic Relations.

Castillo-Alemán, G. (2011). Las políticas educativas en México desde una perspectiva de política pública: gobernabilidad y gobernanza. *Magis*, (9), 639-652. Available at http://cippec.org/mapeal/wp-content/uploads/2014/05/CASTILLO-ALEMAN-Las-pol-ed-en-M%C3%A9xico-dde-una-persp-de-pol-p%C3%BAb.pdf

Castillo, S. (2002). *Compromisos de la evaluación educativa.* Spain: Prentice.

Castrillón, M. A. (2006). *La gestión del conocimiento.* Available at Rosario University: http://repository.urosario.edu.co/bitstream/handle/10336/1207/BI%2029.pdf?sequence1

CEPAL. (2000). *Universidad y desarrollo. Proyecto latinoamericano.* México: Autor.

Chahuán, K. (2009). Evaluación cualitativa y gestión del conocimiento. *Educación y Educadores.* Available at http://www.redalyc.org/articulo.oa?id=83412235010

Chaparro, F. (2006). *Una estrategia de Desarrollo basado en el Conocimiento para el Eje Cafetero. Reflexiones sobre su potencialidad y cómo medirlo.* Pereira: Universidad del Rosario.

Chapman, D., Austin, A., Farah, S., Wilson, E., & Ridge, N. (2014). Academic staff in the UAE: Unsettled journey. *Higher Education Policy, 27*(1), 131–151. doi:10.1057/hep.2013.19

Checkland, P. (1999). *Systems thinking, systems practice: Includes a 30-year retrospective*. New York, NY: John Wiley & Sons.

Cherkowski, S., & Walker, K. (2014). Flourishing communities: Re-storying educational leadership using a positive research lens. *International Journal of Leadership in Education: Theory and Practice*, *17*(2), 200–216. doi:10.1080/13603124.2013.827240

Cibulskas, G. (2006). *Švietimo subjektų pasipriešinimui edukaciniams pokyčiams įtaką darantys veiksniai: Lietuvos švietimo reformos atvejis* [Educational entities resistance to changes in factors affecting the Lithuanian education reform case] (Unpublished doctoral dissertation). Kaunas Technologijos Universitetas, Kaunas, Lithuania.

Comisión Europea. (2004). Competencias clave para un aprendizaje a lo largo de la vida. Un marco de referencia europeo. Puesta en práctica del programa de trabajo Educación y Formación 2010. Grupo de trabajo B. Competencias clave. *Comisión Europea. Dirección General de Educación y Cultura.* Available at http://www.educastur.princast.es/info/calidad/indicadores/doc/comision_europea.pdf

CONACyT. (2014). *Programa Nacional de Posgrados de Calidad. Programas vigentes.* Retrieved 2014, from www.conacyt.mx/index.php/becas-y-posgrados/programa-nacional-de-posgrados-de-calidad/convocatorias-avisos-y-resultados/4165-listado-pnpc-2014/file

CONOCER. (1997). *La normalización y certificación de Competencia Profesional: Medio para incrementar la productividad de las empresas*. Mexico: CONOCER.

COPEEMES. (2013). *Manual para evaluar planteles que solicitan el ingreso y la promoción en el Sistema Nacional de Bachillerato*. Mexico: COPEEMES. Available at http://www.copeems.mx/normativa/documentos-y-manuales/328-manual-de-operacion

Cordero, G., Luna, E., & Patiño, N. (2011). La profesionalización de los maestros de educación básica. Retos para las instituciones de educación superior. *Perfiles Educativos*. Available at http://www.redalyc.org/articulo.oa?id=13221258020

Cornejo, J. (2012). Retos impuestos por la globalización a los sistemas educativos latinoamericanos. *Revista Mexicana de Incestigación educativa*. Available at http://www.scielo.org.mx/scielo.php?script=sci_arttext&pid=S1405-66662012000100002&lng=es&nrm=iso

Cortes C. & Pineda J. (2006). Aproximación a la gestión del conocimiento. *Revista ventana informática, 15,* 170.

Darceles, M. (2007). Gestión del conocimiento y creatividad. Revista *Escuela de Administración de Negocios*. Available at http://www.redalyc.org/articulo.oa?id=20611495010

Davidson, C. R. (2009). *Abu Dhabi: Oil and beyond.* New York, NY: Columbia University Press.

De Ibarrola, M. (2009). El incremento de la escolaridad de la PEA en México y los efectos sobre su situación laboral y sus ingresos, 1992-2004 *REDIE. Revista Electrónica de Investigación Educativa, 11*(2), 1-19. Recuperado de http://www.redalyc.org/articulo.oa?id=15512151002

De la Peña, J. A. (2013). *Matemáticas, Boletín informativo de la Academia Mexicana de Ciencias No. 11.* Recuperado de: http://issuu.com/amcboletin/docs/amc-boletin11

Deal, T. E., & Kennedy, A. (1982). *Corporate cultures: The rites and rituals of corporate life*. Reading, MA: Addison-Wesley.

DEL MORAL. (2007). *Anselmo, PAZOS, Juan, RODRIGUEZ, Esteban, RODRÍGUEZ-PATÓN, Alfonso y SUÁREZ, Sonia; Gestión del conocimiento.* Madrid: International Thomson Editores.

Denning, S. (2002). The narrative lens: Storytelling in 21st century organizations. *Knowledge Directions*, *3*(2), 92–101.

Díaz, C. (2012). Tendencias y requerimientos del mercado de trabajo en la economía del conocimiento. Estudio sobre los egresados del CUCEA. *Revista de la Educación Superior*. Available at http://www.scielo.org.mx/scielo.php?script=sci_arttext&pid=S0185-27602012000100001&lng=es&nrm=iso

Díaz, J. (2004). *Modelo de gestión del conocimiento (GC) aplicado a la universidad pública en el Perú*. Available at http://sisbib.unmsm.edu.pe/Bibvirtual/monografias/Principal.asp

Domínguez, D., Sandoval, M., Cruz, F., & Pulido, A. (2013). Problemas relacionados con la eficiencia terminal desde la perspectiva de estudiantes universitarios. *Revista Iberoamericana sobre Calidad, Eficacia y Cambio en Educación*. Available at http://www.rinace.net/reice/numeros/arts/vol12num1/art2.htm

EFQM. (2003). *E. F. Modelo de excelencia EFQM*. Obtenido de Fundación Europea para la Gestión de la Calidad: http://www.efqm.org: https://www.ucv.es/documentos/calidad/EFQM.pdf

EGREES, European Group of Research on Equity of the Educational Systems. (2003). *Equity of the European Educational System. A set of indicators*. Department of Theoretical and Experimental education University of Liège: European Commsissión, Directorate General of Education and Culture Project Socrates SO2-61OBGE. Bruselas, Recuperado de: http://ec.europa.eu/education/programmes/socrates/observation/equality_en.pdf

Escartí, A., & Cervelló, E. (1994). La motivación en el deporte. In *Entrenamiento psicológico en el deporte* (pp. 61–90). Valencia: Albatros Educación.

Escribano, G. (2005). Teorías del Desarrollo Económico. Universidad Nacional de Educación a Distancia. Madrid.

Eumed. (1991). Available at www.eumed.net/cursecon/dic/l.htm#interdependencia

Fajnzylber, F. (1991). *Boletín del Proyecto Principal de Educación, UNESCO/OREALC, No. 26*. Santiago de Chile.

Fernández, J. (2013). *Formación y práctica docente Facultad de ciencias de la educación*. Ediciones D.D.S. México.

Fierro, L., Martínez, L., & Hernández, G. (2014). La formación del profesor de inglés en las escuelas primarias públicas. *Electronic Journal educ@upn.mx*, 16.

Figueroa, C. (2004). *Sistemas de Evaluación Académica (Primera Edición)*. El Salvador: Editorial Universitaria.

Findlow, S. (2006). Higher education and linguistic dualism in the Arab Gulf. *British Journal of Sociology of Education*, *27*(1), 19–36. doi:10.1080/01425690500376754

Font, V. (1994). Motivación y dificultades de aprendizaje en matemáticas. *SUMA*, *17*, 10–16.

Frade, L. (2008). *La evaluación por competencias*. Mexico: Inteligencia educativa.

Fullan, M. (1993). *Change forces: Probing the depths of educational reform*. London: Falmer.

Fullan, M. (2001). *The new meaning of educational change* (3rd ed.). Toronto: Teachers College Press & Irwin Publishing.

Fundación Este País. (2005). México ante el reto de la economía del conocimiento. *Este país Tendencias y Opiniones*. Available at http://archivo.estepais.com/site/category/ep/?n=174

Gaad, E., Arif, M., & Fentey, S. (2004). Systems analysis of the UAE education system. *International Journal of Educational Management*, *20*(4), 291–303. doi:10.1108/09513540610665405

Gagliardi, P. (1986). The creation and change of organizational cultures: A conceptual framework. *Organization Studies*, *7*(2), 117–134. doi:10.1177/017084068600700203

Garbanzo, V., & Guiselle, M. (2012). Educación superior pública en américa latina: Características y desafíos. *Revista Gestão Universitária na América Latina*. Available at Obtenido de http://www.redalyc.org/articulo.oa?id=319327514012

García & Gonzales. (2005). La motivación en secundaria un estudio empírico. *Revista complutense, 16*(1), 339-352.

García, J. (2014). Rendimiento escolar en la preparatoria oficial no 118 del estado de México en la asignatura de Matemáticas, ciclo escolar 2011-2012.

Giovanni, R. (2001). *E. Principales Teorías sobre el Desarrollo Económico y social. Nómadas No. 4. Revista crítica de Ciencias Sociales y Jurídicas*. Universidad Complutense de Madrid. España.

Giroux, H. (2005). *Border crossings: Cultural workers and the politics of education* (2nd ed.). New York, NY: Routledge.

Gonzalez & Saxe-Fernandez. (2002). Globalidad, neoliberalismo y democracia. In *El mundo actual: situación y alternativas*. Mexico: Siglo XXI editores.

González, P. (2014). Innovación y economía del conocimiento. ¿Qué hay que aprender para México y cuál es el papel de las élites? *Revista Enfoques: Ciencia Política y Administración Pública*. Available at http://www.redalyc.org/articulo.oa?id=96031437008

González, J., & Wagenaar, R. (2003). *Tuning Educational Structures in Europe*. Spain: Universidad de Deusto.

Guerra, M. Á. (2006). *La escuela que aprende*. Mexico: Morata.

Gutiérrez, B., & Martínez, M. (2009). Dimensiones de sustentabilidad en las instituciones de educación superior. Propuesta para un centro de investigación. *Revista de la educación superior*. Available at http://www.scielo.org.mx/scielo.php?script=sci_arttext&pid=S0185-27602009000400007&lng=es&nrm=iso

Gutierrez, L. (2009). El devenir de la educación media superior. El caso del estado de México. *Tiempo de Educar*. Available at http://www.redalyc.org/articulo.oa?id=31113164007

Gutiérrez, L. (enero-junio, 2009). El devenir de la educación media superior. El caso del estado de México. *Tiempo de Educar, 10*(19), 171-204. Recuperado de http://www.redalyc.org/articulo.oa?id=31113164007

Guzmán, R., & Adriano, A. (2013). Conocimiento, economía, desarrollo y sociedad: trazos desde la complejidad. *Enclaves del pensamiento*. Available at http://www.scielo.org.mx/scielo.php?script=sci_arttext&pid=S1870-879X2013000200006&lng=es&nrm=iso

Hager, P., Holland, S., & Becket, D. (2002). *Enhancing the learning and employability of graduates: The role of generic skills*. Australia: Business/Higher Education Round Table.

Hall, G. E. (2013). Evaluating change processes: Assessing extent of implementation (constructs, methods and implications). *Journal of Educational Administration, 51*(3), 264–289. doi:10.1108/09578231311311474

Hannan, M. T., & Freeman, J. (1989). *Organizational ecology*. Cambridge, MA: Harvard University Press.

Hannan, M. T., Polos, L., & Carroll, G. R. (2007). *Logics of organization theory: Audiences, code, and ecologies*. Princeton, NJ: Princeton University Press.

Hargreaves, A. (1996). *Profesorado, cultura y posmodernidad. Cambian los tiempos, cambia el profesorado*. Madrid, España: Morata.

Hargreaves, A. (1994). *Changing teachers, changing times: Teachers' work and culture in the postmodern age*. New York, NY: Teachers College Press.

Hargreaves, A. (2003). *Teaching in the knowledge society: Education in the age of security*. New York, NY: Teachers College Press.

Hargreaves, A. (2006). Educational change over time? The sustainability and nonsustainability of three decades of secondary school change and continuity. *Educational Administration Quarterly*, *42*(3), 3–41. doi:10.1177/0013161X05277975

Hatch, M. J. (1997). *Organisational theory*. Oxford, UK: Oxford University Press.

Hatherley-Greene, P. J. (2012). *Cultural border crossings in the UAE*. Retrieved from the Sheikh Saud Bin Saqr Al Qasimi Foundation for Policy Research website: www.alqasimifoundation.com/

Hernández, A. (2009). Gestión de la calidad y gestión del conocimiento. *Boletín Científico Técnico INIMET*. Available at http://www.redalyc.org/articulo.oa?id=223018305004

Hernández, G., & Díaz, F. (2013). Una mirada psicoeducativa al aprendizaje: qué sabemos y hacia dónde vamos. *Sinéctica*. Available at http://www.scielo.org.mx/scielo.php?script=sci_arttext&pid=S1665-109X2013000100003&lng=es&nrm=iso

Hernández, R., Fernández, C., & Baptista, P. (2006). *Metodología de la investigación*. D.F., México: Mac Graw Hill.

Hernandéz, S. F. (2010). *Metodología de la Investigación, Quinta edición*. México: Mc Graw Hill.

Hofstede, G., & Hofstede, G. J. (2005). *Cultures and organizations: Software for the mind*. New York, NY: McGraw-Hill.

Hofstede, G., Hofstede, G. J., & Minkov, M. (2010). *Cultures and organizations: Software of the mind* (3rd ed.). New York, NY: McGraw-Hill.

Huergo, J. (2009). *Región 11.educar.ar.* Retrieved on February 21, 2014, Management Process: http://www.region11.edu.ar/publico/portal/doc/biblioteca/los%20procesos%20de%20gestion.pdf

Hunziker, W., & Krapf, K. (1942). *Outline of the general theory of tourism*. Zurich: Polygraphischer Verlag AG.

Inciarte, A. M. (2006). *Gestión Académico-Administrativo en la educación básica*. Available at Revista Venezolana de Management ISSN: 1315-9984: http://www.scielo.org.ve/scielo.php?pid=S1315-99842006000200005&script=sci_arttext

Instituto Nacional de Estadística Geografía e Investigación INEGI. (2014). *Matrícula escolar en educación superior por entidad federativa según sexo, ciclo escolar 2013/2014*. Available at http://www3.inegi.org.mx/sistemas/sisept/default.aspx?t=medu42&s=est&c=21791

IPN. (2004). *Un nuevo modelo educativo para el IPN. Materiales para la Reforma*. Mexico: IPN.

IPN. (2014). *CECyT 11. Wilfrido Massieu*. Available at www.cecyt11.ipn.mx

Izquierdo, C. M. (2003). *Origen y consecuencias de las desigualdades educativas. Investigaciones realizadas en América Latina sobre el problema*. México: Fondo de Cultura Económica.

Jelinek, M., Smircich, L., & Hirsch, P. (1983). Introduction: A code of many colors. *Administrative Science Quarterly*, *28*(3), 331–338. doi:10.2307/2392245

Jiménez, F. (2013). *Matemáticas: México no atina a dominarlas*. Recuperado de: http://www.sinembargo.mx/29-05-2013/631646

Jiménez, R., & Diana, M. (2012). La informalidad laboral en américa latina: ¿Explicación estructuralista o institucionalista? *Cuadernos de Economía*. Available at http://www.redalyc.org/articulo.oa?id=282125048006

Johansen, O. (1982). *Introducción a la teoría general de sistemas*. México: Limusa.

Kabasakal, H., Dastmalchian, A., Karacay, G., & Bayraktar, S. (2012). Leadership and culture in the MENA region: An analysis of the GLOBE project. *Journal of World Business*, *47*(4), 519–529. doi:10.1016/j.jwb.2012.01.005

Kane, M. (1992). The assessment of professional competence. *Education and the Health Professions*, *15*(2), 163–182. doi:10.1177/016327879201500203 PMID:10119160

Kast, E., Fremont, E., & James, E. (2003). *Administración de las organizaciones enfoque de sistemas y contingencias*. México: Mc Graw Hill.

Katz, D., & Kahn, R. L. (1978). *The social psychology of organizations* (2nd ed.). New York, NY: John Wiley & Sons.

Keeley, M. (1980). Organizational analogy: A comparison of organismic and social contract model. *Administrative Science Quarterly*, *25*(2), 337–362. doi:10.2307/2392458

Kerlinger, F. (1979). *Investigación del comportamiento*. New York: Mc Graw Hill.

Kerschberg, L. (2000). *Knowledge Management: Managing Knowledge Resources for the Intelligent Enterprise*. Chile: XXIII Taller de Ingeniería de Sistemas.

Kirk, D. (2010). The development of higher education in the United Arab Emirates. *The Emirates Occasional Papers, 74*, 1-57.

Knight, J. (2014). *Professional development for faculty and staff in Ras Al Khaimah's higher education institutions*. Ras Al Khaimah: Sheikh Saud Bin Saqr Al Qasimi Foundation for Policy Research.

Knight, J. (2011). Education hubs: A fad, a brand, an innovation. *Journal of Studies in International Education*, *15*(3), 221–240. doi:10.1177/1028315311398046

Knight, J. (2013). The changing landscape of higher education internationalization – for better or worse? *Perspectives: Policy and Practice in Higher Education*, *17*(3), 84–90.

Krüger, K. (2006). El concepto de sociedad de conocimiento. Universidad de Barcelona.

Lakoff, G., & Johnson, M. (1980). *Metaphors we live by*. Chicago, IL: University of Chicago Press.

Lara, P. (2005, Noviembre). Gestión de contenidos en el e-learning: acceso y uso de objetos de información como recurso estratégico. *Revista de Universidad y Sociedad del Conocimiento, 2*(2).

Littlemore, J. (2001). Metaphoric competence: A language learning strength of students with a holistic cognitive style. *TESOL Quarterly*, *35*(3), 459–491. doi:10.2307/3588031

Litz, D. (2014). *Perceptions of school leadership in the United Arab Emirates* (Unpublished doctoral dissertation). University of Calgary, Calgary, AB.

López, A. A. (2010). *Evaluación Formativa*. Retrieved on March 2, 2014, of Teaching English: file:///C:/Users/HP/Downloads/50-255-3-PB.pdf

López, N. (2005). Equidad educativa y desigualdad social. Desafíos de la educación en el nuevo escenario latinoamericano. Buenos Aires: Instituto Internacional de Planteamiento de la Educación, UNESCO.

Low, E. L., & Lee, S. K. (2012). Bringing Singapore's teacher education beyond its shores. *Educational Research for Policy and Practice*, *11*(1), 43–51. doi:10.1007/s10671-011-9116-7

Macpherson, R., Kachelhoffer, P., & El Nemr, M. (2007). The radical modernization of school and education system leadership in the United Arab Emirates: Towards indigenized and educative leadership. *International Studies in Educational Administration*, *35*(1), 60–77.

Mansell, J. (2009, June 9). How children became customers. *The Guardian*. Retrieved from www.theguardian.com

Marginson, S. (2013). La Educación Superior como autoformación: el caso de estudiantes transfronterizos. *Revista de la educación superior*. Available at http://www.scielo.org.mx/pdf/resu/v43n169/v43n169a2.pdf

Martin, A. (2003). An experience of teaching in the United Arab Emirates. *English Today*, *19*(2), 49–54. doi:10.1017/S0266078403002098

Martínez, C. y. (2005). *El modelo de excelencia en la EFQM y su aplicación para la mejora de la calidad de los centros educativos*. Available at UNED Faculty of Education, ISSN: 1139-613X: http://revistas.uned.es/index.php/educacionXX1/article

Mata, Y., & Pesca, C. (2011). La gestión del conocimiento en las universidades como baluarte organizacional. *InterSedes: Revista de las Sedes Regionales*. Available at http://www.redalyc.org/articulo.oa?id=66622603005

Matus, G., & Molina, F. (2006). *Metodología cualitativa: un aporte de la Sociología para investigar Bibliotecología*. Valparaíso: Universidad de Playa Ancha.

Mcardale, M. (2012, February 13). Envisioning a post-campus America. *The Atlantic*. Retrieved from www.theatlantic.com

Meadows, D. H. (2008). *Thinking in systems: A primer*. White River Junction, VT: Chelsea Green.

Mejía, J., Briseño, F., & Cardoso, E. (2013). *Evaluación de las Percepciones de los docentes con respecto al Programa Nacional de Inglés en la Educación Básica*. Ponencia publicada en la memoria electrónica del XII Congreso Nacional de Investigación Educativa, p. 7.

Mejía, J., Cardoso, E., Briseño, F., & García, J. (2014). Propuesta de criterios e indicadores para la evaluación de la gestión académica institucional del Programa Nacional de Inglés en la Educación Básica (PNIEB) en el nivel secundaria. Ponencia publicada en la memoria electrónica del II Congreso Internacional de Educación Evaluación. México: Universidad Autónoma de Tlaxcala-UNAM.

Mejía, L., Osorio, M. d., & Navarro, J. A. (2008). Impacto de la práctica docente sobre la calidad de la enseñanza en el nivel medio superior. *Espacios Públicos*. Available at http://www.redalyc.org/pdf/676/67602119.pdf

Méndez, M., & Zenteno, N. (2009). *La educación de posgrado con un enfoque humanista en un mundo globalizante: el caso del Colpos*. Available at http://www.scielo.org.mx/pdf/sine/n32/n32a5.pdf

Mendoza, J. (2014). *Cobertura de la educación superior en México. Tendencias, retos y perspectivas*. México: ANUIES.

Mercado, A., Miyamoto, K., & O'connor, D. (2008). *Inversión extranjera directa: tecnología y recursos humanos en los países en Desarrollo*. El colegio de México. Available at https://books.google.com.mx/books?id=Qmj21zYfSm0C&pg=PA8&lpg=PA8&dq=Teoria+del+Capital+humano+O%C2%B4connor&source=bl&ots=tI7sbPCjE4&sig=YQeXgnkoo7wx_4QdrGCrjxNuZzc&hl=es&sa=X&ei=vW5WVe6CN4SLsAWKwICwBg&ved=0CDUQ6AEwAw#v=onepage&q=Teoria%20del%20Capital%20humano%20O%C2%B4connor&f=false

Mercer, J. (2005). Challenging appraisal orthodoxies: Teacher evaluation and professional development in the United Arab Emirates. *Journal of Personnel Evaluation in Education*, *18*(3), 273–287.

Mertens, L. (1997). *Competencia laboral: sistemas, surgimiento y modelos*. Mexico: OIT.

Minakata Arceo, A. (2009). Gestión del conocimiento en educación y transformación de la escuela: Notas para un campo en construcción. *Sinéctica*, (32), 17-19.

Minakata, A. (2000). El maestro que aprende: educación para una nueva época. *Sinéctica*, (17), 14-23.

Minakata, A. (2009). *Gestión del conocimiento en educación y transformación de la escuela*. Notas para un campo en construcción. Available at scielo: http://www.scielo.org.mx/scielo.php?script=sci_arttext&pid=S1665-109X2009000100008&lng=es&nrm=iso

Minakata, A. (2009). Gestión del conocimiento en educación y transformación de la escuela. Notas para un campo en construcción. *Sinéctica*. Available at http://www.scielo.org.mx/scielo.php?script=sci_arttext&pid=S1665-109X2009000100008&lng=es&nrm=iso

Ministerio del Poder Popular para la Educación. (2008). La evaluación en el sistema educativo bolivariano. *Educere*. Available at http://www.redalyc.org/pdf/356/35604024.pdf

Miranda, F. I. (2014). Educación media superior en méxico. Hacía una política de reescolarización. *Revista iberoamericana de educación*. Available at http://www.rieoei.org/deloslectores/6223Miranda.pdf

Mitriff, I., & Kilmann, R. H. (1975). Stories managers tell: A new tool for organizational problem-solving. *Management Review*, (July): 18–28.

Morecroft, J. D. W., Asay, D., & Sterman, J. D. (Eds.). (1994). *Modeling learning organizations*. Portland, OR: Productivity Press.

Morey, A. I. (2004). Globalization and the emergence of for-profit education. *Higher Education*, *48*(1), 131–150. doi:10.1023/B:HIGH.0000033768.76084.a0

Morgan, G. (1998). *Images of organization – the executive edition*. Thousand Oaks, CA: Sage.

Morín, E. (1999). *Los siete saberes necesarios a la educación del futuro*. UNESCO.

Münch, L. (2013). *Liderazgo y dirección. El liderazgo en el siglo XXI*. México: Trillas.

Münch, L. G. (2010). *Administración y planeación de Instituciones Educativas*. México: Trillas.

Muñoz, C. (2003). *Desarrollo de una propuesta para la construcción de indicadores de impacto social de la educación en América Latina y el Caribe*. Recuperado de: http://www.prie.oas.org/espanol/documentos/Indicadores_impacto_social_sp.PDF

Muñoz, D., Aguado, D., & Lucía, B. (2003). El largo camino hacia la Gestión del Conocimiento. *Revista de Psicología del Trabajo y de las Organizaciones*. Available at http://www.redalyc.org/articulo.oa?id=231318052005

Muñoz, C. (2001). *Implicaciones de la escolaridad en la calidad del empleo. In Los jóvenes y el trabajo: La educación frente a la exclusión social* (pp. 155–200). D.F., México: Universidad Iberoamericana. Recuperado de; http://www.oei.es/etp/jovenes_trabajo.pdf

Nagles, D. (2007). La gestión del conocimiento como fuente de innovación. *Revista Escuela de Administración de Negocios*. Available at http://www.redalyc.org/articulo.oa?id=20611495008

Näslund, E. (2012). *El camino hacia el éxito en matemáticas y ciencias: Desafíos y triunfos en Paraguay*. Recuperado de: http://idbdocs.iadb.org/wsdocs/getdocument.aspx?docnum=37283442

Navickaite, J., & Janiunaite, B. (2010). Barriers of school principals' transformational leadership in implementing change: Theoretical insights. *Socialiniai Mokslai*, *4*(70), 69–81.

Nicks-McCaleb, L. (2005). The impact of state funded higher education on neighborhood and community in the United Arab Emirates. *International Education Journal*, *6*(3), 322–334.

Nirenberg, O., Brawerman, J., & Ruíz, V. (2000). *Evaluar para la transformación; innovaciones en la evaluación de programas y proyectos sociales*. Argentina: Paidós. On line.http://www.ilo.org/public/spanish/region/ampro/cinterfor/publ/papel/13/index.html

Nonaka & Takeuchi. (1995). *The Knowledge-Creating Company*. Oxford, UK: Oxford University Press.

Nonaka, I. (1995). *The Knowledge Creating Company*. New York: Oxford University Press.

Nonaka, I., & Takeuchi, H. (1995). *The knowledge-creating company: How Japanese Companies Create the Dynamics of Innovation*. New York: Oxford University Press.

Norma Internacional ISO 9000. (2005). *Sistemas de gestión de la calidad - Fundamentos y vocabulario*. Switzerland.: ISO 2005.

Nunan, D. (1988). *Syllabus Design*. Oxford, UK: OUP.

OCDE. (2002). *Working Party on Indicators for the Information Society*. Estocolmo.

OCDE. (2014). *Panorama de la educación 2014*. Recuperado de: http://www.oecd.org/edu/Mexico-EAG2014-Country-Note-spanish.pdf

OCDE/GD. (1996). The knowledge based-economy. *OCDE, 102*(96), 11.

OECD. (2013). *Panorama de la educación 2013 Indicadores de la OCDE*. Spain: Santillana.

OMT. (2015). *¿Porque el turismo?* Available at http://www2.unwto.org/es/content/por-que-el-turismo

Ordorika, I. (2006). Educación superior y globalización: las universidades públicas frente a una nueva hegemonía. *Revista Electrónica Scielo, 3*(5), 31-47. Recuperado de http://www.scielo.org.mx/pdf/anda/v3n5/v3n5a3.pdf

Organización para la Cooperación y el Desarrollo Económico. (2008). *Globalization and Linguistic Competencies. Responding to Diversity in Language Environments*. Available at http://www.oecd.org/dataoecd/55/15/41363216.pdf

Ortiz Pabón. (2007). *Efraín, NAGLES GARCÍA, Nofal; Gestión de tecnología e innovación. Teoría, proceso y práctica*. Bogotá: Universidad EAN.

Peluffo, M. & Catalán, E. (2002). *Introducción a la gestión del conocimiento y su aplicación al sector público*. Santiago de Chile: CEPAL-CECLAC.

Perez, D., & Dressler, M. (2007). Tecnologías de la información para la gestión del conocimiento. *Intangible Capital*. Available at http://www.redalyc.org/pdf/549/54930103.pdf

Pilar, R. (2008). Reseña de "Claves del desarrollo científico y tecnológico de América Latina" de Sebastián, J. (ed.). *Andamios. Revista de Investigación Social*. Available at http://www.redalyc.org/articulo.oa?id=62811466016

Pimienta, J. (2012). *Las competencias en la docencia universitaria*. Pearson Educación de México.

Piña, A. D. (2009). *Las políticas públicas en materia educativa*. México: SEP.

Pineda, L. (2013). Colombia frente a la economía de conocimiento, ¿un callejón sin salida? *Estudios Gerenciales*. Available at http://www.redalyc.org/articulo.oa?id=21229786006

Pintrich, P., & De Groot, A. (1990). Motivational and self-regulated learning components of classroom academic performance. *Journal of Educational Psychology, 82*, 33–40.

Plasencia, S. R., Vizconde, L. E., Ruiz, I. R., Araujo, M. E., & Salazar, P. (2008). Estudio: Factores socio-económicos y su relación con el rendimiento académico en estudiantes de la Universidad Nacional de Cajamarca. Recuperado de http://nuevo.unc.edu.pe/paginas/educacion/IIEDUCA/Archivos/Articulo%20Cientifico%20-%20PLASENCIA%20 CARRERA.pdf

PND. (2013-2018). *Plan Nacional de Desarrollo.* Retrieved from http://pnd.gob.mx/

Poovey, M. (2001). The twenty-first century university and the market: What price economic viability? *Differences: A Journal of Feminist Cultural Studies, 12*(1), 1–16. doi:10.1215/10407391-12-1-1

Pozner, P. (2000). *Competencias para profesionalización en la Gestión.* UNESCO.

Prabhu, N. (1984). Procedural Syllabuses. In T.E. Reed (Ed.), Trends in Language Syllabus Design. Singapore University Press/RELC.

Preciado Sánchez Alma Cecilia. (2006). *Modelo de evaluación por competencias laborales.* S.A. Mexico.

Preston, W. (1982). Poetry ideas in teaching literature and writing to foreign students. *TESOL Quarterly, 16*(4), 489–502. doi:10.2307/3586467

Prieto, C. (2013). *Matemáticas: México no atina a dominarlas.* Recuperado de: http://www.sinembargo.mx/29-05-2013/631646

Programa Nacional de Desarrollo 2012-2018. (n.d.). Retrieved from pnd.gob.mx/wpcontent/uploads/2013/05/PND. pdfhttp://pnd.gob.mx/

Quintana, M. C. (2007). Organización y dirección de centros educativos innovadores. El centro educativo versátil. Aravacas, Madrid, Spain: McGraw Hill.

Ramírez, & Medina. (2008). *Educación basada en competencias y el proyecto Tuning en Europa y Latinoamérica. Su impacto en México.* At Ide@s CONCYTEG.

Ramírez, J., Pamplón, E., & Cota, S. (2012). Problemática de la enseñanza del inglés en las primarias públicas de México. *Iberoamerican Journal of Education, 2*(60). Available at http://www.rieoei.org/deloslectores/5020Ramirez.pdf

Ramón, J. (2004). *Aplicación de metodologías de sistemas suaves de Checkland para el diseño de un programa de formación docente en matemáticas: caso de estudio: Colegio Agustín de Hipona.* Instituto Politécnico Nacional, Escuela Superior de Ingeniería Mecánica y Eléctrica.

Ramos, V. (2000). *La educación y la circularidad de la pobreza: Resultados de la encueta nacional de hogares 1997-1998.* Perú: Instituto Nacional de Estadística e Informática.

Reyes, G. E. (2009). Teorías de Desarrollo Económico y Social: Articulación con el planteamiento de Desarrollo Humano. Revista Tendencias. Revista de la Facultad de Ciencias Económicas y Administrativas, 10(1).

Reyes, G. (2002). *E. Comercio y Desarrollo: Bases conceptuales y enfoque para América Latina y el Caribe.* Zona Económica.

Rivera, M. (2014). Desarrollo económico y trayectorias históricas. Una aproximación al caso de Brasil y México. *Problemas del desarrollo.* Available at http://www.scielo.org.mx/scielo.php?script=sci_arttext&pid=S0301-70362014000400002&lng=es&nrm=iso

Rivera, M. A. (2005). Cambio histórico mundial, capitalismo informático y economía del conocimiento Problemas del Desarrollo. *Revista Latinoamericana de Economía.* Available at http://www.redalyc.org/articulo.oa?id=11820075003

Rodriguez, K., & Salgado, L. (2009). Puntos críticos sobre la reforma en Educación básica y media superior en México. *Revista del Centro de Investigación*. Available at http://www.redalyc.org/articulo.oa?id=34213107009

Rodríguez, J. (2003). *Introducción a la administración con enfoque de sistemas*. México: ECAFSA.

Rodríguez-Ponce, E., Cohen-Hornickel, W., Pedraja-Rejas, L., Araneda-Guirriman, C., & Rodríguez-Ponce, J. (2014). La gestión del conocimiento y la calidad de la docencia de postgrado en las universidades: un estudio exploratorio. INNOVAR. *Revista de Ciencias Administrativas y Sociales, 24*(52), 59-66. Available at http://www.redalyc.org/articulo.oa?id=81830435015

Rogers, E. M. (1962). *Diffusion of innovations*. Glencoe, NY: Free Press.

Romo, A., Villalobos, M., & Guadalupe, L. (2012). *Gestión del conocimiento: estrategia para la formación de investigadores*. Available at http://www.scielo.org.mx/scielo.php?script=sci_arttext&pid=S1665-109X2012000100007&lng=es&nrm=iso

Romo, A., Villalobos, M., & Guadalupe, L. (2012). Gestión del conocimiento: estrategia para la formación de investigadores. *Sinéctica*. Available at http://www.scielo.org.mx/scielo.php?script=sci_arttext&pid=S1665-109X2012000100007&lng=es&nrm=iso

Rosental, M., & Iudin, P. (1973). *Diccionario Filosófico*. La Habana: Editora Política.

Royero, J. (2006). Las redes de I+D como estrategia de uso de las TIC en las universidades de América Latina. *Universities and Knowledge Society Journal*. Available at http://www.redalyc.org/articulo.oa?id=78030205

Ruatta, A. B. (2000). *Filosofía de la Otredad.* Recuperado el 12 de enero de 2015, de "La enseñanza de los derechos humanos en la universidad": Available at https://www.unrc.edu.ar/publicar/cde/Barra%20Ruatta.htm

Rueda, M. (2013). *La evaluación educativa: un análisis de sus prácticas*. Mexico: UNAM.

Rueda, M., & Díaz-Barriga, F. (2000). *Evaluación de la docencia*. Barcelona: Oikos.

Ruiz, J. (2004). *Como hacer una evaluación de centros educativos 3ª*. Madrid: Narcea Ediciones.

Sabino, C. (1992). *El Proceso de Investigación*. Caracas, Venezuela: Panamericana.

Sackmann, S. A. (1991). *Cultural knowledge in organizations: Exploring the collective mind.* Newbury Park, CA: Sage.

Saíz, J. (2012). Ética, capital intelectual y gestión del conocimiento. *Revista Escuela de Administración de Negocios*. Available at http://www.redalyc.org/articulo.oa?id=20625032004

Salama, P. (2011). Luchas contra la pobreza en América Latina. El caso de la pobreza rural en Brasil. *Revista Latinoamericana de Economía*. Available at http://www.redalyc.org/articulo.oa?id=11819780002

Sánchez, C., & Ríos, H. (2011). La economía del conocimiento como base del crecimiento económico en México. *Revista Venezolana de Información, Tecnología y conocimiento*. Available at http://www.redalyc.org/articulo.oa?id=82319126004

Sánchez, M., & Vega, J. (2006). La gestión del conocimiento y su relación con otras gestiones. *Ciencias de la información*. Available at http://www.redalyc.org/articulo.oa?id=181418190003

Sanoja, P. (2007). ¿Globalización sin convergencia? *Revista Venezolana de Economía y Ciencias Sociales*. Available at http://www.redalyc.org/articulo.oa?id=17721562003

Santa, S., & Herrero, V. (2010). Producción científica de América Latina y el Caribe: una aproximación a través de los datos de Scopus (1996-2007). *Revista Interamericana de Bibliotecología*. Available at http://www.redalyc.org/articulo.oa?id=179015630005

Santos, B. D. (2009). *Una epistemología del Sur*. México: FLACSO.

Sashkin, M. J., & Walberg, H. J. (Eds.). (1993). *Educational leadership and school culture*. Berkeley, CA: McCutchan.

Sauntson, H., & Morrish, L. (2011). Vision, values and international excellence: The 'products' that university mission statements sell to students. In M. Molesworth, R. Scullion, & E. Nixon (Eds.), *The marketization of higher education and the student as consumer* (pp. 73–85). New York, NY: Routledge.

Schein, E. H. (1992). *Organizational culture and leadership* (2nd ed.). San Francisco, CA: Jossey-Bass.

Schmelkes, S. (2005). *La evaluación de los Centros Escolares*. México: Departamento de Inevstigaciones Educativas CINVESTAV - IPN.

Schoepp, K. W. (2011). The path to development: Expatriate faculty retention in the UAE. *International Education*, *40*(2), 58–75.

Schumpeter, J. (1963). *Teoría del Desenvolvimiento Económico*. Mexico: Fondo de Cultura Económica.

Schwahn, C., & McGarvey, B. (2011). *Inevitable: Mass customized learning: Learning in the age of empowerment*. Lexington, KY: CreateSpace.

Schwartz, D. (2006). *Encyclopedia of Knowledge Management*. Idea Group Reference. doi:10.4018/978-1-59140-573-3

Secretaría de Educación Pública (2008a). *Acuerdo número 442. Reforma Integral de Educación Media Superior (RIEMS)*. Mexico: SEP.

Secretaría de Educación Pública (2008b). *Acuerdo número 447. Competencias docentes para quienes impartan educación media superior en la modalidad escolarizada*. Mexico: SEP.

Secretaría de Educación Pública (SEP). (2013). *Bachillerato general*. Recuperado de http://www. dgb.sep.gob.mx/02-m1/01-dgb/bachillerato_general.php

Secretaria de Educación Pública, (2012). *El enfoque formativo de la evaluación*. Mexico: SEP

Secretaria de Educación Pública, S. E. P. (2015). *Comunicado 014*. Available at http://www.comunicacion.sep.gob.mx/index.php/comunicados/enero-2015/876-comunicado-014-destaca-chuayffet-chemor-logros-visibles-en-educacion-superior-en-el-marco-de-la-reforma-educativa

Secretaría de Educación Pública. (2013). *Ley General del Servicio Profesional Docente*. Mexico: Diario Oficial de la Federación Spanish Royal Academy. Available at www.rae.es/recursos/diccionarios/drae

Secretaría de Educación Pública. SEP. (2014). *Programa Sectorial de Educación 2013-2018*. Available at http://www.sep.gob.mx/es/sep1/programa_sectorial_de_educacion_13_18

SECTUR. CESTUR, CONACYT. (2012). *Alineación de los programas de estudio de educación turística a las necesidades del campo laboral*. Mexico: Universidad La Salle Cancún. Available at http://ictur.sectur.gob.mx/pdf/estudioseinvestigacion/sintesisprincipalesestudios/PROYECTO_FINAL_ALINEACION_Final_10L.pdf

Sen, A. (1987). Equality of What? In *En: liberty, equality and law. Selected Tanner lectures on moral philosophy*. Salt Lake City, UT: University of Utah Press.

Senge, P. M. (1990). *The fifth discipline: The art and practice of the learning organization*. London: Century Business.

Senge, P. M. (2006). *Presence: An exploration of profound change in people, organizations, and society*. New York, NY: Currency.

SEP. (2006). *Plan de estudios México*. SEP.

SEP. (2007). *Programa Sectorial de Educación*. SEP.

SEP. (2009). *Programa Nacional de inglés en la Educación Básica*. SEP.

SEP. (2011). *Plan de estudios*. SEP.

SEP. (2013-2014). *DGPyEE, Formatos 911*. Retrieved 2013, from http://www.sep.gob.mx/es/sep1/programa_sectorial_de_educacion_13_18#.UzU7sPmSyz4

SEP. S. d. (2007). *Manual de Autoevaluación de centros escolares para la gestión con calidad, Segunda Edición.* Recovered from: http://www.dgep.sep.gob.mx:8080/autoevaluacion/Autoevaluacion/Descargas/Modelo_Nacional_Doctos/2GUIA_AUTOEVALUACION.pdf: http://www.dgep.sep.gob.mx:8080/autoevaluacion/Autoevaluacion/Descargas/Modelo_Nacional_Doctos/HERRAMIENTAAPOYOAUTOEVALUACION.pdf

Sergen, P. (2007). *La quinta disciplina.* Recuperado el 9 de Febrero de 2014, de Libros de Peter Senge: http://www.alumnos.inf.utfsm.cl/~vpena/ramos/ili260/textos/La_Quinta_Disciplina.pdf

Sergiovanni, T. J. (1994). Organizations or communities? Changing the metaphor changes the theory. *Educational Administration Quarterly*, *30*(2), 214–226. doi:10.1177/0013161X94030002007

Shaw, D., & Mahlios, M. (2013). Adult literacy students' metaphors of reading and writing. *International Journal of Research Studies in Education*, *3*(1), 21–34.

Shaw, K. E., Badri, A., & Hukul, A. (1995). Management concerns in the United Arab Emirates state schools. *International Journal of Educational Management*, *9*(4), 8–13. doi:10.1108/09513549510088381

Silva, L. C. (1997). *Cultura Estadística e Investigación Científica en el Campo de la Salud: Una Mirada Crítica*. La Habana, Cuba: Díaz de Santos.

Slisko, J. (2015). *Bajo rendimiento en matemáticas, asociado a la enseñanza*. Recuperado de: http://angulo7.com.mx/index.php/educacion/12379-bajo-rendimiento-en-matematicas-asociado-a-la-ensenanza

Smircich, L. (1983). Concepts of culture and organizational analysis. *Administrative Science Quarterly*, *28*(3), 339–358. doi:10.2307/2392246

Smith, L. (2009). Sinking in the sand? Academic work in an offshore campus of an Australian university. *Higher Education Research & Development*, *28*(5), 467–479. doi:10.1080/07294360903154118

Solow, R. (1963). *Capital Theory and Rate of Return*. Amsterdam: North-Holland Publishing Company.

Staton, M. (2011, September 15). The disruption is here. *Inside Higher Ed*. Retrieved from www.insidehered.com

Stiles, D. R. (2004). Pictorial representation. In C. Cassell & G. Symon (Eds.), *Essential guide to qualitative methods in organizational research* (pp. 127–139). London: Sage. doi:10.4135/9781446280119.n11

Stufflebeam, D. Y. (2011). *Evaluación Sistemática. Guía Teórica y práctica.* Centro de Publicaciones del M. E. C. y Espasa Libros, S. L. U. .

Stufflebeam, D. (1987). *Evaluación sistemática: Guía teórica y práctica*. Spain: Paidós.

Tedesco, J. C. (2000). *Educar en la sociedad del conocimiento*. Buenos Aires, Argentina: FCE.

Tejeda, J. (1998). *Los agentes de la innovación en los centros educativos*. Spain: Aljibe.

The World Bank Group. (2014). *World Development Indicators: Science and technology*. Available at http://wdi.worldbank.org/table/5.13

Tobón, S. (2006). *Competencias, calidad y educación superior*. Madrid: Magisterio.

Tobón, S. (2006). *Formación basada en competencias*. Bogotá: Ecoe Ediciones.

Tobón, S. (2007). *Gestión curricular y ciclos propedéuticos*. Bogotá: ECOE.

Torres, S., Barona, C., & Omar, G. (2010). Infraestructura tecnológica y apropiación de las TIC en la Universidad Autónoma del Estado de Morelos. Estudio de caso. *Perfiles Educativos*. Available at http://www.scielo.org.mx/scielo.php?script=sci_arttext&pid=S0185-26982010000100006&lng=es&nrm=iso

Tovar, C., & Díaz, E. (2010). Dispersión del ingreso y demanda de educación media superior y superior en México. *Análisis Económico*. Available at http://www.redalyc.org/articulo.oa?id=41313083006

UNESCO. (2008). *Estándares de competencias en TIC para docentes*. Available at http://www.oei.es/tic/UNESCOEstandaresDocentes.pdf

United Nations Educational, Scientific And Cultural Organization. (2003). Education in a Multilingual World. París: UNESCO.

United Nations Organization. (1945). *Charter of the Unite Nations*. San Francisco: Author.

Valencia Rodríguez, M. (2005). El capital humano, otro activo de su empresa. *Entramado, 1*(2), 20-33. Available at http://www.redalyc.org/articulo.oa?id=265420471004

Vargas, F. (2004). 40 preguntas sobre competencia laboral. Montevideo: CINTERFOR/OIT.

Villa, L. (2007). La educación media superior ¿igualdad de oportunidades? *Revista de la Educación Superior*. Available at http://www.redalyc.org/pdf/604/60414105.pdf

Villa, L. (enero-marzo, 2007). La educación media superior: ¿Igualdad de oportunidades? *Revista de la Educación Superior, 36*(1), 93-110. Recuperado de http://www.redalyc.org/articulo.oa?id=60414105

Villalobos Monroy, G., & Pedroza Flores, R. (2009). Perspectiva de la teoría del capital humano acerca de la relación entre educación y desarrollo económico. *Tiempo de Educar, 10*(20), 273-306. Available at http://www.redalyc.org/articulo.oa?id=31112987002

Wallin, D. L. (2010). Looking to the future: Change leaders for tomorrow's community colleges. *New Directions for Community Colleges*, *2010*(149), 5–12. doi:10.1002/cc.390

Weeks, P. (2012). *Descripción de la metodología de sistemas blandos de Checkland*. Disponible en http://www.12manage.com/methods_checkland_soft_systems_methodology_es.html

Wenger, E., McDermott, R., & Synder, W. M. (2002). Cultivating Communities of Practice: a Guide to Managing Knowledge. Harvard Business School Press.

Wenger, E. (1999). *Communities of practice: Learning, meaning, and identity*. Cambridge, UK: Cambridge University Press.

Wigfield, A., & Eccles, J. (1992). The development of achievement task values: A theoretical analysis. *Developmental Review*, *12*(3), 265–310. doi:10.1016/0273-2297(92)90011-P

Williams, J. (1998). *Don't they know it's Friday: Cross cultural considerations for business and life in the Gulf*. Dubai, UAE: Motivate Books.

Wolters, C. (1998). Self-regulated learning and college students' regulation of motivation. *Journal of Educational Psychology*, *90*(2), 224–235. doi:10.1037/0022-0663.90.2.224

WordReference. (2015). Retrieved from http://www.wordreference.com/definicion/enciclopedia

Worthen, Sanders, & Fitzpatrick. (1996). *Program evaluation. Alternative approaches and practical guidelines*. New York: Adison – Wiley Longman.

WTO. (2003). Introducción a TedQual. Una Metodología para la Calidad en Educación y Formación Turística. Spain: World Tourism Organization (WTO-UNWTO).

WTO. (2014). Panorama OMT del turismo internacional. Spain: World Tourism Organization (WTO-UNWTO).

Young, R. & Harmony, S. (1998). *Working with faculty to design undergraduate information literacy programs: a how–to–do–it manual for librarians*. London: Neal-Achuman Publishers.

Zabala, A. y Arnau, L. (2007). La enseñanza de las competencias. *Aula de Innovación Educativa, 161*.

Zamboni, H. Y. (2003). *Propuestas innovadoras en la gestión académica*. Argentina: III Coloquio Internacional sobre Gestión Universitaria en América del Sur.

About the Contributors

Edgar Oliver Cardoso Espinosa holds a PhD in Sciences and has a specialty in Administrative Sciences. He is a Research of the Instituto Politécnico Nacional of the Escuela Superior de Comercio y Administración (ESCA), Unidad Santo Tomás, México. He is a Member of the National Researchers System (SNI), Level I. He has published articles nationally and internationally and has participated in national and international congresses. He is coordinator of the PhD Program in Management and Innovation Policy conducted by the IPN at the headquarters of the ESCA.

* * *

Jorge Mejía Bricaire is colaborator of Researching on Division of Postgraduate Studies and Research of the Superior School of Commerce and Administration (ESCA) of the Instituto Politécnico Nacional, México. In his position conducts research projects focused on the management and development of education in educational programs at basic level. He has participated in national and international congresses.

Leticia Refugio Chavarria is a Professor and Investigator of IPN.

Jésica Alhelí Cortés is a Master of Science in Systems Engineering, graduated from the National Polytechnic Institute.

Juan de Luna Flores is Doctor in Education from Escuela Normal Superior de México. Professor and associate researcher in the post- graduate programme, "Management, leadership and institutional development in the knowledge society," that supports the Masters programme on Management and Development and Education (MAGDE), at the Instituto Politécnico Nacional, México. Professor at Instituto Tecnológico of Tlalnepantla during 32 years. Professor in the PhD Programme on Pedagogy at the Escuela Superior de México.

Isaías Álvarez García is Doctor in Education. Harvard University. Professor and Researcher at Post-graduate programmes at the Instituto Politécnico Nacional, México. He coordinates the research programme called, "Management, leadership and institutional development in the knowledge society," that supports the Masters programme on Management and Development and Education (MAGDE), at the IPN. He also works as a professor and researcher at the Post-graduate programme (MAGDE). He has also been professor and coordinator of the post-graduate programmes, such as the International Program sponsored by the Organization of American States (OAS), Masters in Management of Programmes for the Development of Human Resources (MADRH) 1980-1981; Masters programme on Management of Higher Education Institutions (MAIES) (1984-1988); Masters in Management and Development of Education (MAGDE) 2007-2014. As a researcher, he belongs to the National System of Researchers of the National Council for Science and Technology (CONACYT). Level II. (2006-2024). Over more than 30 years, he has published several books and articles on preparation of teachers, principals and educational leaders, design and development of new educational models and professional curriculum, prospective and participative planning, design, development and evaluation in educational and social programmes, in Mexico and in other countries.

Rosa María Rivas García is graduate of Master of Science in Business Administration. Bachelor of Tourism. She is currently a doctoral student in Management Science at the Higher Education School of Commerce and Administration (ESCA), Campus Sto. Tomás, at the Instituto Politécnico Nacional, México. She is a professor of higher education at the School of Tourism at the IPN.

Limin-tzen Esmeralda Bueno Gasca is graduate of the School of Chemical and Extractive Industries (ESQIE) Engineering in 2003 as Materials and Metallurgical Engineer from the Instituto Politécnico Nacional, México. Ten years later decides to join the Masters program in Business Administration in Management and Development of Education (MAGDE) as a graduate student in the School of Commerce and Administration (ESCA) Unit Sto. Tomas belonging to I PN. Action motivated by the desire to make a small improvement to the Mexican education through research and development. She has participated in national and international congresses.

Maribel del Carmen Casas Haro, Doctorate Candidate in Languages, Texts and Contexts, at the University of Granada, Spain. Research stay at the University of Granada (2013). Bearer of DEA (Diplome on Higher Studies in Interpretation and Translation at the same University, (2012). Master Of Sciences in Administration and Education Development (2009). Teaching experience in the areas of English language and methdology at the Instittuto Superior de Intérpretes y Traductores (2006 - 2015). Professor and associate researcher in the graduate programme, "Management, leadership and institutional development in the knowledge society," that supports the Masters programme on Management and Development and Education (MAGDE), at the Institute of National Polytechnique (IPN). (2013 -2015). Professor in the major of Internationat Business, at the Higher Education School of Commerce and Administration (ESCA), Campus Sto. Tomás, at the IPN. (2014-2015). Particiption in different national and international Seminaries and Congressess on Education, Management and Languages over the last 15 years. Joint participation with members of the ISPP (International Study of Principals Preparation), held by several universities of several countries. Publication of different articles in the areas of Education and Management.

Melanie Van den Hoven is a lecturer in the Language and Culture Division at Emirates College for Advanced Education, Abu Dhabi. She has also previously taught in South Korea and Canada. She is is an EdD candidate at the University of Durham, England. Her research interests include intercultural education, intercultural communication and English language education.

Fernando Briseño Hurtado is graduate of Master in Business Administration in Management and Development of Education in the School of Commerce and Administration (ESCA) Santo Tomas in the

Instituto Politécnico Nacional, México. Engineer in Industrial Chemistry at the ESIQIE the National Polytechnic Institute, specializing in teaching skills by the National Pedagogic University (UPN), Mexico. In his position conducts research projects focused on the management and development of education in educational programs at senior level. He has participated in national and international congresses.

María Elena Zepeda Hurtado is graduate of M.Sc. in Management and Development of Education at the Higher Education School of Commerce and Administration (ESCA), Campus Sto. Tomás, at the Instituto Politécnico Nacional, México. Professor at the Center of Science and Technology Studies (CECyT) No. 11 "Wilfrido Massieu" the National Polytechnic Institute. She has participated in national and international congresses.

David Litz is an assistant professor in the Language and Culture and Educational Leadership Divisions at Emirates College for Advanced Education and he has also previously taught in South Korea and Canada. He holds an EdD from the University of Calgary and his professional interests include comparative education, educational management, and educational policy and development in the MENA region.

Leticia Refugio Chavarría López is graduate of Master of Science in Business Administration. Degree in Accounting from the ESCA. Coordinator of the MBA in Sustainable Business at the Higher Education School of Commerce and Administration (ESCA), Campus Sto. Tomás, at the Instituto Politécnico Nacional, México. She has participated in national and international congresses.

Eduardo Antonio Vanegas López is Doctor of Administrative Sciences, graduated from Higher Education School of Commerce and Administration (ESCA), Campus Sto. Tomás, at the Instituto Politécnico Nacional, México. Doctor in Law, graduated from the IIDE. He is professor of the Doctorate in Management and Innovation Policy conducted by the IPN. He has participated in national and international congresses.

Ricardo Morán Martínez is graduate of Master in Management, Graduated from the National Polytechnic Institute Student of Management PhD in the Instituto Politécnico Nacional, México. Teacher of Secondary School was born in México City. He is currently a doctoral student in Management Science at the Higher Education School of Commerce and Administration (ESCA), Campus Sto. Tomás, at the Instituto Politécnico Nacional, México. He has participated in national and international congresses. He is professor of higher education in Mexico City in the Universidad del Valle de Mexico and secondary school teacher is the subject of technology.

Joel García Mendoza: Researcher since 2012 on Division of Postgraduate Studies and Research of the Superior School of Commerce and Administration (ESCA).Master in Business Administration in Management and Development of Education in the School of Commerce and Administration (ESCA) Santo Tomas, the National Polytechnic Institute (IPN). Degree in Architecture from the Autonomous Metropolitan University (UAM-A), specializing in teaching skills by the National Pedagogic University (UPN), Mexico. In his position conducts research projects focused on the management and development of education in educational programs at senior level.

Diana Patricia Skewes Muñoz is Bachelor of Education degree from the Ecole Normale Superieure in Mexico, with seven years of teaching experience, specializing in the teaching of language and literature and a MBA in Management and Development of education provided by the Instituto Politécnico Nacional, México. She has participated in national and international congresses.

Jesús Gerardo Alfaro Patiño is Public Accountant graduated from Instituto Politécnico Nacional, now to get the master's degree in administration management and development of education in the IPN, interested in research issues on the development of management skills in education. He has participated in national and international congresses.

Jésica Alhelí Cortés Ruíz is graduate of Master of Science in Systems Engineering, graduated from the National Polytechnic Institute. She is currently a doctoral student in Management Science at the Higher Education School of Commerce and Administration (ESCA), Campus Sto. Tomás, at the Instituto Politécnico Nacional, México. She has participated in national and international congresses.

Eduardo Antonio Vanegas: Doctor of Administrative Sciences, graduated from the National Polytechnic Institute. Doctor in Law, graduated from the IIDE.

Index

www.ingramcontent.com/pod-product-compliance
Lightning Source LLC
LaVergne TN
LVHW080528300926
849162LV00007B/1561

* 9 7 8 1 5 2 2 5 0 4 5 7 3 *